D0451736

Canary
Islands

Sarah Andrews
Josephine Quintero

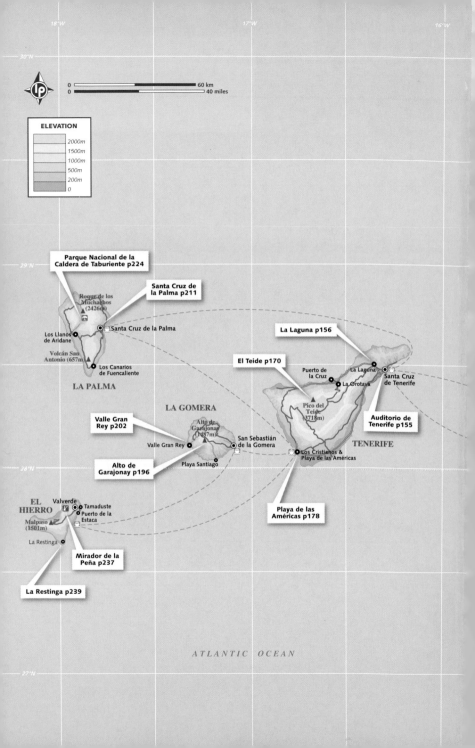

ELEVATION

2000m
1500m
1000m
500m
200m
0

0 —— 60 km
0 —— 40 miles

Parque Nacional de la
Caldera de Taburiente p224

Santa Cruz de
la Palma p211

Roque de los
Muchachos
(2426m)

Los Llanos
de Aridane

Santa Cruz de la Palma

Volcán San
Antonio (657m)

Los Canarios
de Fuencaliente

LA PALMA

La Laguna p156

El Teide p170

Puerto de
la Cruz

La Laguna

Santa Cruz
de Tenerife

La Orotava

LA GOMERA

Valle Gran
Rey p202

Alto de
Garajonay
(1487m)

Pico del
Teide
(3718m)

Auditorio de
Tenerife p155

Valle Gran Rey

San Sebastián
de la Gomera

TENERIFE

Alto de
Garajonay p196

Playa Santiago

Los Cristianos &
Playa de las Américas

EL
HIERRO

Valverde

Tamaduste

Puerto de la
Estaca

Malpaso
(1501m)

La Restinga

Playa de las
Américas p178

Mirador de la
Peña p237

La Restinga p239

ATLANTIC OCEAN

30°N

29°N

28°N

27°N

18°W

17°W

16°W

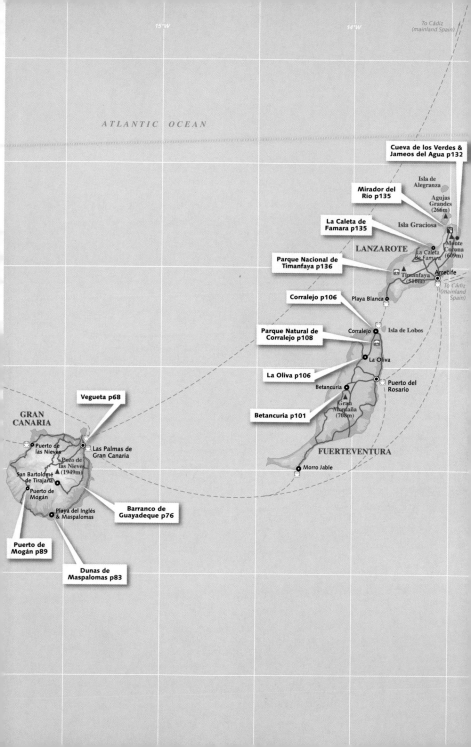

ATLANTIC OCEAN

To Cádiz (mainland Spain)

15°W

14°W

Cueva de los Verdes & Jameos del Agua p132

Isla de Alegranza

Mirador del Río p135

Agujas Grandes (266m)

La Caleta de Famara p135

Isla Graciosa

LANZAROTE

La Caleta de Famara

Monte Corona (609m)

Parque Nacional de Timanfaya p136

Timanfaya (510m)

Arrecife

To Cádiz (mainland Spain)

Corralejo p106

Playa Blanca

Parque Natural de Corralejo p108

Corralejo

Isla de Lobos

La Oliva p106

La Oliva

Vegueta p68

Betancuria

Puerto del Rosario

GRAN CANARIA

Betancuria p101

Gran Montaña (708m)

Puerto de las Nieves

Las Palmas de Gran Canaria

Pozo de las Nieves (1949m)

FUERTEVENTURA

San Bartolomé de Tirajana

Puerto de Mogán

Morro Jable

Playa del Inglés & Maspalomas

Barranco de Guayadeque p76

Puerto de Mogán p89

Dunas de Maspalomas p83

On the Road

SARAH ANDREWS Coordinating Author

El Hierro's rough, rugged coastline is captivating, and I spent a lot of time exploring the coves and swimming holes here. The day this photo was taken, I'd headed to one of the most beautiful places on the whole island – **Charco Manso** (p236) – where the ceaseless waves have battered the volcanic rocks into caves, tunnels and arcs that were so gorgeous they gave me goose bumps. There at the Charco, I met a few local Herreños, who led me to all the prettiest spots, like a nearly hidden cave where sunlight makes the water look orange and green, and a delicate arch that soars more than 10m above the water. It was unforgettable.

JOSEPHINE QUINTERO This photo was taken on the first day I drove to **El Teide** (p170). The volcano is visible from places all over the island, but nothing prepares you for actually getting up close and personal with Tenerife's emblematic pyramid. As you drive closer, the scenery is constantly shifting and changing, with colours, rock shapes and terrain that are simultaneously stark and extraordinarily beautiful. I walked several trails around the base, but the cable car was temporarily out of order so my planned trip to the peak was thwarted. I *will* be back!

See full author bios page 274

CANARY ISLANDS HIGHLIGHTS

No matter what kind of holiday you have in mind – an active one spent hiking and windsurfing, a culture-packed one visiting museums and seeing pre-Hispanic artefacts, or an utterly relaxing one where your biggest worry is how much sunscreen to use – the Canary Islands have something in store for you. Each island is a world of its own, ranging from the vast beaches of Fuerteventura, to Tenerife's towering El Teide peak, to the dense and verdant forests of La Palma.

Gran Canaria

This island lives up to its continent-in-miniature cliché, with pine-clad mountains, charming villages, a sophisticated city and pack-'em-in coastal resorts. The climate is similarly diverse, as are the activities on offer, varying from dusk-to-dawn partying to trekking in the hinterland.

❶ Vegueta

Seek out this historical gem, which is more like a Spanish village than a capital-city barrio. Vegueta (p68) is a delight, with cobbled streets, great buildings and an imposing cathedral. It's also home to the island's most enticing mix of bars and restaurants.

❷ Puerto de Mogán

Relax with an early morning coffee, along with the fishermen after they have returned with their catch (and before the coach tours start rolling in). Puerto de Mogán (p89) has unspoilt charm with its waterways, bridges and seriously cute harbour.

❸ Dunas de Maspalomas

Pretend you're taking a trip to the Sahara and follow one of the walking trails, or take a camel ride in these dunes (p83). These shimmering sands cover a mammoth 400 hectares and are thankfully protected from the possibility of bulldozers moving in.

❹ Barranco de Guayadeque

The best time to visit this lush, green ravine (p76) is spring, when the almond blossom is in brilliant pink-and-white bloom. Year-round, however, it is lush and dramatic, flanked by steep mountains where caves have been dug out for restaurants, bars and a chapel.

Fuerteventura

Fuerteventura is best known for its
beaches. And quite rightly so. This is the
island of world-class water sports and
golden sands that stretch for miles. Mean-
while the interior is a beguiling combo
of simple villages against a patchwork of
ancient volcanoes, lofty palm trees and lots
(and lots) of goats.

1 Parque Natural de Corralejo

About as far removed from leafy trees and kiddies' swings as you can get, this park (p108) has natural sand dunes with vast expanses of soft powdery sand. It's the kind of desert scene that will have you kicking off your shoes and doing cartwheels.

2 Betancuria

If rolling hills are a dim and distant memory, visit verdant Betancuria (p101), which enjoys an evocative valley location flanked by rare green slopes. The town is a handsome place that oozes history and prosperity (it was once the island's capital).

3 La Oliva

This blink-and-you-miss-it town (p106) has a low-key vibe and is worth a wander. Seek out the Casa de los Coroneles, which looks like something constructed from a sophisticated Lego set, but contains one of the Canaries' best collections of cutting-edge modern art.

4 Corralejo

You can still imagine Corralejo (p106) as a simple fishing village, especially when you're gazing over the waves and dining on the catch-of-the-day, while the narrow, cobbled streets of the old town exude a small-is-beautiful charm, with low-rise buildings, cheery terraces and a pretty cove.

Lanzarote

This island has a stark beauty. The volcanic moonscape is most vivid in the island's centre, while to the north there's a gentle greenness. The south is home to the best beaches, while throughout the island César Manrique demonstrates how man can work with nature with extraordinary results.

❶ Cueva de los Verdes & Jameos del Agua

No point arguing about which Manrique sight is tops; there are several. But the Cueva de los Verdes and Jameos del Agua (p132) are right up there. They both combine magical natural phenomena with Manrique's flair for architectural (and PR!) wizardry.

❷ La Caleta de Famara

This windswept beach (p135) is the complete antithesis of the tourist-driven resorts in the island's south. A mecca for windsurfers and kite boarders, its vibe is young and low-key with suitably unstuffy bars and restaurants fronting the surf.

❸ Mirador del Río

There are plenty of eye-catching views on Lanzarote, but the Mirador del Río (p135) caps the lot. Yet another memorable Manrique creation, this is the best place to view the Chinijo Archipelago, with spectacular sweeping views from a mountain-top vantage point.

❹ Parque Nacional de Timanfaya

Another example of the power and unpredictability of nature, this national park (p136) is the result of one of the most catastrophic eruptions of all time. The park's heart is extraordinary, with volcanoes, craters and a landscape etched and coloured by nature over centuries.

Tenerife

This island is full of colour, life and diversity. The north is cultured and verdant, with historical charm; the west is quieter, with an alluring sense of space; the east has volcanic terrain and great surf spots and the south is a big and brash holiday playground with superb white sandy beaches.

① El Teide

Hike around the base of El Teide (p170), where the trails take you deep into an alien landscape; the red, yellow and brown craters are like giant prehistoric molehills. Top it off by taking the cable car to the summit for the ultimate heady experience.

② La Laguna

Visit this town (p156) for one of the best-preserved historical quarters on the island – all cobbled alleys, spruced-up merchants' houses and pine-balconied mansions. This unique vernacular architecture is a world away from the anonymous concrete blocks of the southern beach resorts.

③ Playa de las Américas

Be a party animal for a night, donning the blinkers and checking out the neon-framed hot spots at this gloriously over-the-top resort (p178). The nightlife here has to be the flashiest, loudest, brightest and most varied on the Canary Islands.

④ Auditorio de Tenerife

Check out the great wave of this Sydney Opera House–lookalike concert hall (p153) in Santa Cruz de Tenerife. Designed by Spanish architect Santiago Calatrava (commissioned to design New York City's new World Trade Center), orchestral performances take place here weekly.

La Gomera

Scored with plunging ravines and surrounded by seemingly impenetrable rock cliffs, La Gomera's endless dips and rises were forged by volcanoes and sculpted by erosion. A verdant pre–Ice Age laurel forest dominates the centre, while green banana plantations fill the valleys. Beautiful, unspoilt La Gomera offers excellent hiking opportunities and plenty of good beaches.

① Alto de Garajonay

Hiking in Parque Nacional de Garajonay is a must, but with so many trails it can be hard to choose one. You can't go wrong with the trek up to the Alto de Garajonay (p196), heading through a fern-filled rainforest up to sun-baked peaks.

② Valle Gran Rey

A stunning gorge runs down to meet the island's longest beach in Valle Gran Rey (p202), where you'll find terraced hillsides dotted with white farmhouses and studded with palm trees.

1

La Palma

Nicknamed 'the pretty island', lush La Palma is the archipelago's greenest island, making it one big outdoor playground for walkers and cyclists. Wind and curve your way along the north's lonely highways to glimpse the wild beauty of the island's forests, or head south for the dry, lunar-like volcanic landscapes.

1
2

2

1 Santa Cruz de la Palma

Although La Palma's biggest claim to fame is its natural beauty, its capital city (p211) also tempts with its uniquely Canarian colonial-style architecture, such as the colourful houses along the waterfront, with balconies dating to the 16th century.

2 Parque Nacional de la Caldera de Taburiente

Unplug from the real world by strolling through this constantly changing national park (p224), where you'll wander through whisper-soft pine forests, across splashing springs, beside weird rock formations and up to stunning lookouts.

El Hierro

The archipelago's smallest island, wind-blasted El Hierro is also the least known. A jagged coastline, rough volcanic interior and quiet agricultural villages make it a true escape. Days are spent diving into the Atlantic swells rolling into coastal hamlets, feasting on simple grilled-fish dinners and strolling along the interior's lonely-yet-lovely trails.

① Mirador de la Peña

Miradores (lookout points) are dotted throughout the island, providing great picnic spots and Kodak moments. The best is Mirador de la Peña (p237), where a restaurant and rock garden (the handiwork of Lanzarote architect César Manrique) overlook El Golfo.

② La Restinga

Scuba divers descend in droves (by El Hierro's standards anyway) to this formerly sleepy fishing village (p239). Warm, calm water and a vibrant marine life make this one of the best diving spots anywhere in Europe.

Contents

Regional Map Contents

La Palma p208

Lanzarote p122

Tenerife p146

La Gomera p187

Fuerteventura p96

El Hierro p230

Gran Canaria p61

Getting Started

Independent travel or package tour? One island or several? Plane or ferry? Set itinerary or spontaneous serendipity? There are many ways to organise a trip to the Canaries, and the one you choose depends entirely on your tastes and your plans for the trip.

If relaxing is your goal, it's best to choose a home base where you can chill out for a few days or a week, taking day trips or even hopping over to a nearby island. If you do this, arranging a flight-and-hotel (or flight-and-apartment) package deal will give you the best value; if you can get the rental car thrown in too, all the better. But if money isn't your main concern, consider basing yourself in a *casa rural* (rural farmhouse), which rarely partner with big tour operators. It will be a bit more expensive, but also more special. Either way, you'll need to book in advance.

If you plan to move around a lot, you're probably better off looking for a cheap flight, then booking lodging separately. Once you're on the island it's easy to find spare rooms, especially out of peak season. If you're picky, plan your itinerary in advance and book hotels or apartments before you leave home.

Island hoppers can fly or ferry to their chosen destinations within the archipelago. Flights are €60 per leg, no matter where you go. Ferries cost €20 to €50, depending on the length of the trip and the type of ferry. For more information, see the Transport chapter on p258.

If you're planning to go scuba diving, sailing, hiking or biking and need a guide or rental, it would be a good idea to reserve in advance, especially if your plans aren't flexible. That said, it's usually possible to call up the day before and arrange an excursion.

See Climate Charts (p248) for more information.

WHEN TO GO

When it comes to sunshine, the Canary Islands are caught in a kind of weather warp, with an eternal spring-summer climate. They're a year-round destination; you can pretty much take your pick of when to go.

The winter months – December to March – *are* a tad cooler but still paradise compared to mainland Europe, the UK and most of North America. This makes winter the islands' busiest period. The summer months – July to September – are a rival high season, mainly because that's when mainland Spaniards elect to go on their annual holiday. The Carnaval

---

DON'T LEAVE HOME WITHOUT...

- Getting waxed
- Your local and international driving licence (p262)
- Sunscreen and a hat – remember, you're closer to Africa than Europe
- Adapter plug for electrical appliances (p245)
- A good book – hard to find on the islands
- Your iPod and island playlist
- An oversize beach towel – most hotels and apartments won't let you use theirs
- Hiking boots (and poles if you're really intrepid)
- A backpack for day trips

TOP PICKS

CANARY ISLANDS
Santa Cruz
Algeria

RURAL RETREATS
Escape from it all at these out of-the-way spots.

- El Nísparo (p219), La Palma – for a true break from the world, head to this *casa rural* near Fuencaliente

- El Sitio (p243), El Hierro – a cluster of restored farm huts where activities include yoga classes and massage

- Ibo Alfaro (p197), La Gomera – to retreat with style, there's no better spot than this hotel

- Hotel Rural Mahoh (p112), Fuerteventura – perfect for romance, this intimate hotel is surrounded by a lovely cacti garden

- Hacienda del Buen Suceso (p80), Gran Canaria – the oldest estates on the archipelago pairs old-world style with modern comfort for the ultimate pampered retreat

BEACHES
So much sand, so little time.

- Playa Carpinteras (p88), Gran Canaria – beyond the bustle, this hidden strip is a locals' secret

- El Médano (p176), Tenerife – at 2km in length it's the island's longest beach and has the best breezes for windsurfers

- Playa de Sotavento de Jandía (p113), Fuerteventura – a series of drop-dead-

- gorgeous beaches popular with swimmers and windsurfers

- La Caleta de Famara (p135), Lanzarote – this hidden little island paradise is definitely no built-up beach resort

- Playa de Alojera (p200), La Gomera – at the end of a twisted highway, this little cove is home to a calm, inviting beach

WALKS
Get off the beach and out of the car, and discover the wild, natural beauty of the islands.

- Ruta de los Volcanes (p221), La Palma – see the archipelago's most active volcanic area up close and personal

- Up to the Alto de Garajonay (p196), La Gomera – the highest point on the island; from here you can see across to Gran Canaria

- Roques de García (p171), Tenerife – if chugging up to the summit of El Teide is

- too much, hike in its shadow among these strange rock formations

- Camino de Jinama (p238), El Hierro – constant, soul-satisfying views unfold before you on this downhill hike overlooking El Golfo

- Isla de Lobos (p108), Fuerteventura – bird-watching and pristine beaches make the loop around this tiny island a real treat

CANARY CULTURE CONNECTIONS

- Las Palmas de Gran Canaria (p65), Gran Canaria – opera, dance, theatre and film festivals make it a hot spot for refined culture

- Auditorio de Tenerife (p155), Tenerife – designed by the famed Santiago Calatrava, this iconic auditorium invokes a crashing wave and has become Santa Cruz's cultural icon

- Parque Ecológico de Belmaco (p218), La Palma – the first ancient rock carvings on

- the archipelago were found at this spot in the island's south

- Ecomuseo de Guinea (p242), El Hierro – this fascinating outdoor museum depicts islanders' lifestyles through the centuries

- César Manrique (p119), Lanzarote – Lanzarote's favourite son, César Manrique left wonderfully designed *miradores* (lookout points) all over his homeland

season (February/March) is an intensely popular period, when anyone and everyone decides to partake in the fun.

For maximum value on airfares and accommodation, the best periods are from November to mid-December and, better still, April to June (with the notable exception of the Easter rush). The latter especially is a great time to be around.

COSTS & MONEY

Daily living expenses on the Canary Islands are lower than those in most countries of Western Europe. Accommodation, which is plentiful, can be a bargain compared to other popular European holiday destinations. Food, too, is inexpensive for both self-caterers and avid restaurant-goers. Car hire is cheap, taxi transport good value over short distances and public buses are generally economical. Flying between the islands can be a bit more expensive but time-saving. Theme and amusement parks are all pricey, especially for large family groups.

The daily budget you'll need depends largely on the kind of trip you have planned; whether or not you're self-catering, if you plan to eat in restaurants or pack picnics, and whether your hotel includes meals. To stay in a comfortable midrange hotel, eat one formal and one simple meal out each day, and hire a car, expect to pay at least about €100 per person per day.

TRAVEL LITERATURE

Diving in Canaries (Sergio Hanquet) If you plan to explore the archipelago's underwater wonderlands, this is a great source of information and inspiration.

Lanzarote (Michel Houellebecq) By turns savage and clinical, hilarious and disturbing, Houellebecq takes a package tour and gets to know some of his fellow travellers.

More Ketchup Than Salsa: Confessions of a Tenerife Barman (Joe Cawley) This humorous memoir takes a look at the Brits-abroad culture on Tenerife, as seen from behind the bar run by the author and his girlfriend.

The Guanches – Survivors and their Descendants (José Luis Concepción) This book is helpful for those interested in knowing about the islands' history and in honouring the legacy of its indigenous peoples.

Todos los Mojos de Canarias (Flora Lilia Barrera Álamo and Dolores Hernández Barrera) Get hooked on *mojo* (spicy salsa sauce) before you even taste it, with this book devoted to the ubiquitous and delicious Canary Islands sauce.

INTERNET RESOURCES

Additional online resources and island-specific tourist offices are listed in the individual island chapters.

Canary Island Flora (www.canaryislandflora.com) A fascinating site covering the varied plant life on the islands.

Canary Travel (www.canary-travel.com) A great travel resource to the islands.

Dive Canary Islands (http://canaryislands.dive-international.net) All about diving in the Canaries.

EcoTurismo Canarias (www.ecoturismocanarias.com) An interesting site covering wildlife, rural accommodation and related services.

Lonely Planet (www.lonelyplanet.com) Great travel information, online booking and internet-only features and blogs about the islands.

Vive Canarias (www.vivecanarias.com) An informative site with plenty of information on the local arts scene, a good festival directory and plenty of entertainment listings.

HOW MUCH?

Sun lounge with big umbrella €5

Cocktail with little umbrella €8

Local bus ticket €1

Apartment for two €60

Bottle of local wine €11

LONELY PLANET INDEX

Litre of petrol (unleaded) €0.60

Bottle of water from €0.80

Bottle of beer €2.50

Serving of *papas arrugadas* (wrinkly potatoes) €1.50

Souvenir T-shirt €20

Snapshot

It's all too easy to land in the Canary Islands and, feeling the sun on your face and the breeze in your hair, scurry straight to an idyllic beach resort or quiet rural retreat, not to be heard from again until the morning of your flight out. Yet while we're sunbathing, swimming, sailing, snorkelling and strolling, the 'real' Canaries are chugging along in the background.

Construction is strong in the archipelago; proof of that is the 2.5 million tons of concrete that's poured annually into hotels, homes and businesses. Agriculture is still alive and well; thousands of Canarios work as farmers, and their growing number of crops (planted across around 520 sq km) are responsible for tasty fruits and veggies and for the often-photographed, well-tended landscapes. New crops such as grapes, avocados, tropical fruits and flowers are contributing to a modern farming miniboom. The fishing industry is also still strong.

Still, there's no doubt that the prosperity we see in many parts of the islands was brought in large part by tourism. When Spanish dictator Francisco Franco opened Spain to the sun-starved masses in the 1960s, he paved the way for development (and overdevelopment) on the islands. Naturally, this large-scale construction brings its own problems.

With few rivers or sources of fresh water on the islands, getting clean drinking water has always been a problem. Added to that are issues related to erosion, with the depletion of nearby marine life and the general degradation of coasts and tourist areas. Thanks in large part to vocal environmental groups, leaders are beginning to take note. One particularly encouraging step was taken in 2007 by El Hierro, which set in motion a plan to make the island energy self-sufficient, using only renewable energy sources like water, wind and solar power. Less encouraging is what's happening on Tenerife and La Palma, where projects for new ports, golf courses and hotels are being pushed through over the screaming voices of environmentalists.

These seven islands were long some of the poorest regions of Spain, and only decades ago this territory was practically an afterthought to mainland Spain. Although prosperity has brought the Canaries closer to the mainland, the perceived separation still strikes a real nerve with islanders. Whatever you do, don't refer to the Iberian Peninsula as Spain – you are in Spain! A minority of islanders, however, argue just the opposite, insisting that the Canaries would be better off as an independent country. This sentiment, although often visible in the form of scrawled 'Spanish Go Home!' graffiti, is not a real threat to unity.

Ironically, the islands that have traditionally been sources of poverty-driven emigration are now the recipients of mass immigration. The presence of African immigrants, who arrive almost daily by boat to the islands, is one of the most polarising issues facing the Canaries today. The human drama played out on the beaches here, where sunbathing tourists are at times the first to greet the often infirm and dehydrated immigrants, is heart-wrenching. Aside from constantly calling on the Spanish government and the European Union for help, the Canaries so far have no solution to this situation.

FAST FACTS

Population: 1.99 million

Number of hotel beds: 176,000

Coastline length: about 1500km

Unemployment: 115,000 people (11.5%)

History

MYTHOLOGICAL BEGINNINGS

We can't pinpoint the date of the discovery of the islands now known as the Canaries, but we can say with certainty that they were known, or at least postulated about, in ancient times. In his dialogues *Timaeus* and *Critias,* Plato (428–348 BC) spoke of Atlantis, a continent sunk deep into the ocean floor in a great cataclysm that left only the peaks of its highest mountains above the water. Whether Plato believed in the lost continent's existence or had more allegorical intentions remains a matter of conjecture. In the centuries since Plato's death, those convinced of the existence of Atlantis have maintained that Macronesia (the Canary Islands, the Azores, Cape Verde and Madeira) constitutes the visible remains of the lost continent.

Legend also has it that one of the 12 labours of Hercules was to go to the end of the world and bring back golden apples guarded by the Hesperides (daughters of evening), offspring of Hesperis and Atlas, the latter a Titan in Greek and Roman mythology who gave his name to the Atlantic Ocean and the Atlas mountain ranges in Morocco. Hercules supposedly had to go beyond the Pillars of Hercules (the modern Strait of Gibraltar) to reach the paradisiacal home of these maidens. Hercules carried out his task and returned from what many later thought could only have been the Canary Islands – about the only place to fit the ancients' description.

Classical writer Homer identified the islands as Elysium, a place where the righteous spent their afterlife. For all their storytelling, there is no concrete evidence that either the Phoenicians or Greeks ever landed on the Canaries. It is entirely possible, however, that early reconnaissance of the North African Atlantic coast by the Phoenicians and their successors, the Carthaginians, took at least a peek at the easternmost islands of the archipelago. Some historians believe a Phoenician expedition landed on the islands in the 12th century BC, and that the Carthaginian Hanno turned up there in 470 BC.

The expanding Roman Empire defeated Carthage in the Third Punic War in 146 BC, but the Romans appear not to have been overly keen to investigate the fabled islands, which they knew as the Insulae Fortunatae (Fortunate Isles). A century-and-a-half later, shortly after the birth of Christ, the Romans received vaguely reliable reports on them, penned by Pliny the Elder (AD 23–79) and based upon accounts of an expedition carried out around 40 BC by Juba II, a client king in Roman North Africa. In AD 150, Ptolemy fairly accurately located the islands' position with a little dead reckoning, tracing an imaginary meridian line marking the end of the known world through El Hierro.

History of the Canary Islands by José M Castellano Gil and Francisco J Macios Martín is a fairly straightforward summary of the islands' past. This book is published in various languages by the Centro de la Cultura Popular Canaria.

THE ISLANDS' ORIGINAL INHABITANTS

The origin of the islands' first inhabitants has long been a source of mystery, with theories being volleyed about for decades but none accepted as definitive. Everyone agrees that the Canary Islands had no indigenous population and that they've been inhabited since before the birth of Christ. So the people living here had to come from somewhere. But the question was, where?

The Spanish conquistadors' tales of Tinerfeños being tall, blonde and blue-eyed fostered many convoluted theories about how Celtic immigrants from mainland Iberia, possibly even related to the Basques, somehow made their way to the island. More fancifully, some saw a drop of Nordic blood in them – did Norse raiding parties land here in the 8th or 9th centuries?

Recently, however, historians using archaeological, cultural and linguistic studies have thrown out these theories in favour of a simpler, if more boring, one. Spotting similarities between the dwellings, burial practices and rock carvings of the various ancient tribes living in the Canaries and the Libyan-Berber peoples of North Africa, they've concluded that the original inhabitants of the islands came from the Maghrib, the area spanning from present-day Tunisia to Morocco. Place names and the handful of words from the Canary Islands' languages (or dialects) that have come down to us bear a striking resemblance to Berber tribal languages. Also, the occasional case of blue eyes and blondish hair occurs among the Berbers too.

Studies from the University of La Laguna in Tenerife have proposed that as the Romans conquered northern Africa from the 1st century BC to the 1st century AD they exiled some people groups to the Canaries. This would explain why the tribes had no knowledge of seafaring; they were inland peoples. If the Romans exiled them soon after arriving in the territory, the people would have had no opportunity to learn Latin script or Roman building techniques. And if the Romans never visited the islands again it was perhaps because they saw no reward worthy of such a long, difficult journey.

Carbon dating of the sparse archaeological finds has pushed back the known date of the earliest settlement to around 200 BC, although earlier occupation is conceivable. For a long time, learned observers maintained that the islands were first inhabited by Cro-Magnon man, the Neolithic predecessor of modern *Homo sapiens*. Such conclusions have emerged from the comparison of ancient skulls of indigenous inhabitants with Cro-Magnon remains discovered around the Mediterranean. Historians wrinkle their noses at the idea now, but if the theory were proved true (which seems unlikely) it would throw the doors of speculation wide open, since Cro-Magnon man came onto the scene as long as 40,000 years ago.

Exactly when, and in what number, people occupied the islands remains a mystery. What seems clear, however, is that they came from several north African tribes. One of them may have been the Canarii tribe, which could explain the islands' present name. Certainly, by the time European swashbucklers started nosing around the islands in the Middle Ages, they were peopled by a variety of tribes.

FIRST ENCOUNTERS

Virtually no written record remains of visits to the Fortunate Isles until the 14th century. The first vaguely tenable account of a European landing comes in the late 13th or early 14th century when the Genoese captain Lanzarotto (or Lancelotto) Malocello bumped into the island that would later bear his name: Lanzarote. From then on, slavers, dreamers searching for the Río de Oro (the River of Gold route for the legendary African gold trade, which many thought spilled into the Atlantic at about the same latitude as the islands) and missionaries bent on spreading the Word all made excursions to the islands.

Of these missions, the most important and influential was the Italian-led and Portuguese-backed expedition of 1341. Three caravels (two- or three-masted sailing ships) charted a course around all seven islands and took note of even the tiniest islets: the Canary Islands were finally, and more or less accurately, on the map.

THE CONQUEST BEGINS

On 1 May 1402, Jean de Béthencourt, lord of Granville in Normandy (France) and something of an adventurer, set out from La Rochelle with a small and ill-equipped party bound for the Canary Islands. The avowed aim, as the

The average height of a Guanche (the original island inhabitants) man was 1.7m. The average height of a Guanche woman was 1.57m.

priests brought along for the ride would testify, was to convert the heathen islanders. Uppermost in de Béthencourt's mind was more likely the hope of glory and a fast franc. With his partner, Gadifer de la Salle, he may have hoped to use the Canaries as a launch pad for exploration of the African coast in search of the Río de Oro. That project never got off the ground, and the buccaneers decided to take over the islands instead. So commenced a lengthy and inglorious chapter of invasion, treachery and bungling. Many Guanches would lose their lives or be sold into slavery in the coming century, with the remainder destined to be swallowed up by the invading society.

De Béthencourt's motley crew landed first in Lanzarote, at that stage governed by Mencey Guardafía. There was no resistance and de Béthencourt went on to establish a fort on Fuerteventura.

That was as far as he got. Having run out of supplies, and with too few men for the enterprise, he headed for Spain, where he aimed to obtain the backing of the Castilian crown. What had started as a private French enterprise now became a Spanish imperialist adventure.

All the myths and outer-edge theories about Guanche history can be found at http://istina .rin.ru/eng/ufo/text/243 .html.

GUANCHE SOCIETY

Guanches, a name originally used to describe only the inhabitants of Tenerife, came from the words *guan*, meaning 'man,' and *che*, meaning 'white mountain', in reference to the snowcapped El Teide. But, with time, the name came to be used for all the tribes of the archipelago – the Canarios, Bimbaches, Majos, Benahoritas and Gomeros.

For all their differences, these pre-Hispanic tribes had much in common. Their Stone Age economies relied on farming, herding, hunting and gathering, and their diets were based on meat (goat and fish) and *gofio*, made of toasted and ground barley. These staples are still eaten today.

Women made pottery. Implements and weapons were fashioned roughly of wood, stone and bone. Goat-skin leather was the basis of most garments, while jewellery and ornaments were largely restricted to earthenware bead-and-shell necklaces. The majority of islanders lived in caves, although on the eastern islands some built simple low houses with rough stone walls and wood-beam roofs.

Oddly enough, the Guanches seem to have known nothing of sailing, at best using simple dugouts for coastal fishing or to move occasionally between the islands. Among the Guanches' primitive weapons were the *banot* (lance), rocks and the *tenique* (a stone wrapped up in animal hide and used as a mace).

The Guanches worshipped a god, known as Alcorac in Gran Canaria, Achaman in Tenerife, and Abora in La Palma. It appears the god was identified strongly with Magec (the sun). Tenerife islanders commonly held that Hades (hell) was in the Teide volcano and was directed by the god of evil, Guayota.

The head of a tribe or region enjoyed almost absolute rule, although justice was administered through a council of nobles, which gathered under the branches of a dragon tree. Between them, the chief and aristocrats owned all property, flocks and fields, leaving the plebs to get along as best they could.

Although living in an essentially patriarchal society, women did have some power. On Gran Canaria, in particular, succession rights were passed through the mother rather than the father. But when times got tough, they got tougher still for women. Infanticide was practised throughout the islands in periods of famine, and it was girls who were sacrificed, never boys.

The island clans were not averse to squabbling, and by the time the European conquest of the islands got under way in the 15th century, Tenerife was divided into no less than nine tiny fiefdoms. Gran Canaria had also been a patchwork of minor principalities, but by the 15th century these had merged to form two kingdoms, one based around the town of Gáldar, the other around Telde. Fuerteventura was another island divided in two, and tiny La Palma boasted an astonishing 12 cantons (small territorial divisions). The other islands were each ruled by one *mencey* (Guanche king).

De Béthencourt returned in 1404 with ships, men and money. Fuerteventura, El Hierro and La Gomera quickly fell under his control. Appointed lord of the four islands by the Spanish king, Enrique III, de Béthencourt encouraged the settlement of farmers from his Norman homeland and began to pull in the profits. In 1406 he returned for good to Normandy, leaving his nephew Maciot in charge of his Atlantic possessions.

SQUABBLES & STAGNATION

What followed was scarcely one of the world's grandest colonial undertakings. Characterised by continued squabbling and occasional revolt among the colonists, the European presence did nothing for the increasingly oppressed islanders in the years following de Béthencourt's departure.

The islanders were heavily taxed and many were sold into slavery; Maciot also recruited them for abortive raids on the remaining three independent islands. He then capped it all off by selling to Portugal his rights – inherited from his uncle – to the four islands. This move prompted a tiff with Spain, which was eventually awarded rights to the islands by Pope Eugene V. Lowkey rivalry continued for years, with Portugal only recognising Spanish control of the Canaries in 1479 under the Treaty of Alcáçovas. In return, Spain agreed that Portugal could have the Azores, Cape Verde and Madeira.

Maciot died in self-imposed exile in Madeira in 1452. A string of minor Spanish nobles proceeded to run the show, all eager to sell their rights to the islands almost as soon as they had acquired them.

Numerous commanders undertook the business of attacking the other islands with extraordinarily little success. Guillén Peraza died in an attempt to assault La Palma in 1443. In 1464 Peraza's brother-in-law Diego de Herrera, the appointed lord of La Gomera, attempted a landing on Gran Canaria and another landing near present-day Santa Cruz de Tenerife. By 1466 he had managed to sign a trade treaty with the Canarios, and won permission to build a defensive turret in Gando Bay.

THE FALL OF GRAN CANARIA

In 1478 a new commander arrived with fresh forces (including, for the first time, a small cavalry unit) and orders from the Catholic Monarchs of Spain, Fernando and Isabel, to finish the Canaries campaign once and for all. Juan Rejón landed and dug in at the site of modern Las Palmas de Gran Canaria. He was immediately attacked by a force of 2000 men under Doramas, *guanarteme* (island chief) of the island's Telde kingdom. Rejón carried the day but fell victim to internal intrigue by making an enemy of the spiritual head of the conquered territories, Canon Juan Bermúdez, accusing him of incompetence.

The investigator sent from Spain, Pedro de Algaba, sided with Bermúdez and had Rejón transported to the mainland in chains. But, once there, Rejón convinced the Spanish authorities that he'd been unjustly treated and was

Might you be related to the ancient Guanches? Probably not, but islanders are being encouraged to join up with Family Tree DNA (www .familytreedna .com/public/Guanches -CanaryIslandsDNA) to map out the Guanche's DNA and discover where descendants are today.

The Canary Islands Through History by Salvador López Herrera attempts to trace the story of the Guanches and the Spanish conquest of the archipelago. This is a quirky volume of at times dubious academic worth.

IN TOUCH WITH THE GUANCHES

Ancient Guanche cave paintings and petroglyphs (rock carvings), the oldest dating to AD 150, are found throughout the archipelago. No one knows what these whorling, squiggling designs expressed – spiritual sentiments, perhaps? But they're one of the most tangible connections with Guanche culture still evident on the island. Small museums and tourist offices like the ones in **Parque Ecológico de Belmaco** (p218), **Los Letreros** (p240) and **Cueva Pintada** (p81) let you see them up close and personal. For a full overview of all the 'rock art' in the Canaries, visit the fabulous online **Rock Art Gallery** (www.almogaren.org/gallery/canarias.htm).

given carte blanche to return to the Canaries to re-establish his control. One of his first acts was to have Algaba, his erstwhile accuser, arrested and executed. However, this act of vengeance proved his final undoing, as Queen Isabel believed the punishment unwarranted and had Rejón replaced by Pedro de Vera.

De Vera continued the campaign and had the good fortune to capture the island's other *guanarteme*, Tenesor Semidan (known as Don Fernando Guanarteme after his baptism), in an attack on Gáldar by sea. Tenesor Semidan was sent to Spain, converted to Christianity and returned in 1483 to convince his countrymen to give up the fight. This they did and de Vera subsequently suggested that some might like to sign up for an assault on Tenerife. Duly embarked, de Vera committed the umpteenth act of treachery that had marked the long years of conquest: he packed them off to be sold as slaves in Spain. But the Canarios learnt of this and forced the ships transporting them to dock at Lanzarote.

After the frightful suppression of a revolt on La Gomera in 1488 (see p193), de Vera was relieved of his post as captain-general of the conquest.

A fabulous online library of digitised primary source documents from the 18th and 19th centuries, the Humboldt Project (http://humboldt.mpiwg-berlin.mpg.de) is a must for Canary history buffs.

THE FINAL CAMPAIGNS

De Vera's successor was Galician Alonso Fernández de Lugo, who in 1491 received a royal commission to conquer La Palma and Tenerife. He began in La Palma in November and by May of the following year had the island under control. This he achieved partly by negotiation, though the last *mencey* (Guanche king) of La Palma, Tanausú, and his men maintained resistance in the virtually impregnable crater of the Caldera de Taburiente. Only by enticing him out for talks on 3 May and then ambushing him could de Lugo defeat his last adversary on the island. For La Palma, the war was over.

Tenerife provided the toughest resistance to the Spaniards. In May 1493 de Lugo landed on Tenerife, together with 1000 infantry soldiers and a cavalry of 150, among them Guanches from Gran Canaria and La Gomera.

In the ensuing months the Spaniards fortified their positions and attempted talks with several of the nine *menceys*, managing to win over those of Güímar and Anaga. Bencomo, *mencey* of Tahoro and sworn enemy of the invaders, was sure of the support of at least three other *menceys*, while the remaining three wavered.

In the spring of the following year, de Lugo sent a column westwards. This proved a disaster. Bencomo was waiting in ambush in the Barranco de Acentejo ravine. The Spanish force was decimated at a place now called La Matanza de Acentejo (Slaughter of Acentejo). De Lugo then thought better of the whole operation and left Tenerife.

By the end of the year he was back to engage in the second major battle of the campaign – at La Laguna on 14 November 1494. Here he had greater success, but the Guanches were far from defeated and de Lugo fell back to Santa Cruz. At the beginning of the New Year a plague known as the *modorra* began to ravage the island. It hardly seemed to affect the Spaniards but soon took a serious toll on the Guanches.

For background on a few far-fetched but entertaining theories on the origins of the Gaunches, check out http://istina.rin.ru /eng/ufo/text/243.html.

On 25 December 1494, 5000 Guanches under Bencomo were routed in the second battle of the Acentejo. The spot, only a few kilometres south of La Matanza, is still called La Victoria (Victory) today. By the following July, when de Lugo marched into the Valle de la Orotava to confront Bencomo's successor, Bentor, the diseased and demoralised Guanches were in no state to resist. Bentor surrendered and the conquest was complete. Pockets of resistance took two years to mop up, and Bentor eventually committed suicide.

Four years after the fall of Granada and the reunification of Christian Spain, the Catholic monarchs could now celebrate one of the country's first imperial exploits – the subjugation in only 94 years of a small Atlantic archipelago defended by Neolithic tribes. Even so, the Spaniards had some difficulty in fully controlling the Guanches. Many refused to settle in the towns established by the colonists, preferring to live their traditional lives out of reach of the authorities.

Nevertheless, the Guanches were destined to disappear. Although open hostilities had ceased, the conquistadors continued shipping them as slaves to Spain. Remaining Guanches were converted en masse to Christianity, taking on Christian names and the surnames of their new Spanish godfathers.

Some of the slaves would be freed and permitted to return to the islands. Although the bulk of them were dispossessed of their land, they soon began to assimilate with the colonisers. Within a century, their language had all but disappeared: except for a handful of words, all that comes down to us today are the islands' many Guanche place names.

The Guanches – Survivors and their Descendants by José Luis Concepción is a fine tome that looks at the fate of the islands' first inhabitants. The author also wrote a volume on traditional island customs, called Costumbres, Tradiciones Canarias (published in English and German).

ECONOMIC & FOREIGN CHALLENGES

From the early 16th century, Gran Canaria and Tenerife in particular attracted a steady stream of settlers from Spain, Portugal, France, Italy and even Britain. Each island had its own local authority, or *cabildo insular,* although increasingly they were overshadowed by the Royal Court of Appeal, established in Las Palmas in 1526. Sugar cane had been introduced from the Portuguese island of Madeira, and soon sugar became the Canaries' main export.

The 'discovery' of the New World in 1492 by Christopher Columbus, who called in to the archipelago several times en route to the Americas, proved a mixed blessing. It brought much passing transatlantic trade but also led to sugar production being diverted to the Americas, where the cane could be grown and processed more cheaply. The local economy was rescued only by the growing export demand for wine, produced mainly in Tenerife. *Vino seco* (dry wine), which Shakespeare called Canary Sack, was much appreciated in Britain.

The website www .abouttenerife.com /tenerife/history.asp gives an easy-to-read summary of Tenerife's history.

Poorer islands, especially Lanzarote and Fuerteventura, remained backwaters, their impoverished inhabitants making a living from smuggling and piracy off the Moroccan coast – the latter activity part of a tit-for-tat game played out with the Moroccans for centuries.

Spain's control of the islands did not go completely unchallenged. The most spectacular success went to Admiral Robert Blake, one of Oliver Cromwell's three 'generals at sea'. In 1657, a year after war had broken out between England and Spain, Blake annihilated a Spanish treasure fleet (at the cost of only one ship) at Santa Cruz de Tenerife.

British harassment culminated in 1797 with Admiral Horatio Nelson's attack on Santa Cruz. Sent there to intercept yet another treasure shipment, he not only failed to storm the town but lost his right arm in the fighting.

ISLAND RIVALRIES

Within the Canary Islands, a bitter feud developed between Gran Canaria and Tenerife over supremacy of the archipelago. The fortunes of the two rested largely with their economic fate.

When the Canaries were declared a province of Spain in 1821, Santa Cruz de Tenerife was made the capital. Bickering between the two main islands remained heated and Las Palmas frequently demanded that the province be split in two. The idea was briefly but unsuccessfully put into practice in the 1840s.

La Gomera was the last place Christopher Columbus touched dry land before setting sail to the New World.

In 1927 Madrid finally decided to split the Canaries into two provinces: Tenerife, La Gomera, La Palma and El Hierro in the west; Fuerteventura, Gran Canaria and Lanzarote in the east.

FRANCO'S SPAIN

In the 1930s, as the left and the right in mainland Spain became increasingly militant, fears of a coup grew. In March 1936 the government decided to 'transfer' General Franco, a veteran of Spain's wars in Morocco and beloved of the tough Spanish Foreign Legion, to the Canary Islands.

The Canary Islands after the Conquest by Felipe Fernández-Armesto, a leading authority on the islands' history, is a fairly specialised work concentrating on 16th-century life in the Canaries.

Suspicions that he was involved in a plot to overthrow the government were well-founded; when the pro-coup garrisons of Melilla (Spanish North Africa) rose prematurely on 17 July, Franco was ready. Having seized control of the islands virtually without a struggle (the pro-Republican commander of the Las Palmas garrison died in mysterious circumstances on 14 July), Franco flew to Morocco on 19 July. Although there was virtually no fighting on the islands, the Nationalists wasted no time in rounding up anyone vaguely suspected of harbouring Republican sympathies.

The postwar economic misery of mainland Spain was shared by the islands, and again many Canarios opted to emigrate. In the 1950s the situation was so desperate that 16,000 migrated clandestinely, mainly to Venezuela, even though by then that country had closed its doors to further immigration. One-third of those who attempted to flee perished in the ocean crossings.

TOURISM, 'NATIONALISM' & CURRENT EVENTS

When Franco decided to open up Spain's doors to northern European tourists the Canaries benefited as much as the mainland. Millions of holidaymakers now pour into the islands year-round.

General Franco stayed in the Hostal Madrid in Las Palmas de Gran Canaria the night before launching his coup.

Always a fringe phenomenon, Canaries nationalism started to resurface in opposition to Franco. MPAIC (Movimiento para la Autodeterminación e Independencia del Archipiélago Canario), founded in 1963 by Antonio Cubillo to promote secession from Spain, embarked on a terrorist campaign in the late 1970s. Dodging Spanish authorities, Cubillo fled to Algeria in the 1960s, but in 1985 he was allowed to return to Spain.

In 1978 a new constitution was passed in Madrid with devolution as one of its central pillars. Thus the Canary Islands became a *comunidad autónoma* (autonomous region) in August 1982, yet they remained divided into two provinces.

The main force in Canary Islands politics since its first regional election victory in 1995 has been the Coalición Canaria (CC). Although not bent on independence from Spain (which would be unlikely), the CC nevertheless puts the interests of the islands before national considerations. Fringe groups, however, do push for independence, and while those supporting independence are in the minority, they are gaining strength.

Immigration from Africa and other parts of the world has changed the Canaries' population landscape drastically over the past decade and has forced the islands to reassess their relationship with the continent. Over the past 10 years the islands have made cooperation with Africa a major priority, investing around €17 million in education, health and infrastructure in Africa, especially in transport and communication links with the continent.

The past few years have also seen a struggle between intense development and concerted efforts to preserve the islands' natural resources and beauty. Political groups, islanders and ecologists are in constant discussions about the best way to combine the archipelago's dependence on tourism, and the perceived need for more hotels, ports and golf courses, with the pressing need to conserve water resources, combat marine pollution and prevent development from infringing on the flora and fauna that have made the islands a nature lover's paradise.

The Culture

REGIONAL IDENTITY

It's hard to sum up the peoples and traditions of seven islands into one neat description. Mannerisms, expressions, food, architecture and music vary significantly from island to island and rivalries (especially between heavyweights Tenerife and Gran Canaria) are strong. Yet among all seven islands is a fierce pride in being Canarian, and the belief that their unique history and culture sets them apart from the rest of Spain. While most of the Canary Island locals have the classic Mediterranean looks of the Spaniards – dark hair, flashing eyes and olive complexion – you might find that they don't think of themselves as all that Spanish.

Soon after the 1982 electoral victory of the socialists at national level, the Canary Islands were declared a *comunidad autónoma*, one of 17 autonomous regions across Spain. And a few vocal Canarios would like to see their islands become completely autonomous – keep an eye peeled for splashes of graffiti declaring 'Spaniards Go Home'.

The region's flag is a yellow, blue and white tricolour, to which the few militant *independentistas* add seven stars to represent the islands. The archipelago's division into two provinces, Tenerife and Gran Canaria, remains intact, as does the rivalry between the two provinces – so much so that the regional government has offices in both provincial capitals, which alternate as lead city of the region every four years!

LIFESTYLE

The greatest lifestyle change that has come to the Canary Islands has been the tourism industry. In a matter of decades a primarily agricultural society became a society largely dependent on the service industry. Traditional lifestyles on small *fincas* (farms) or in fishing villages have been supplanted by employment in the tourism sector. This may go some way to explaining a certain reticence in the local population – after all, work is work – so don't take offence when it seems there's a distance between you and the locals a lot of the time.

As the islands close the gap between their traditional, rural lifestyles and the fast-paced, modern lifestyle of the rest of Spain, some problems are inevitable. The cost of living has skyrocketed, forcing those who have kept traditional agriculture jobs to supplement their income with positions in the tourism industry. As the economy becomes more like mainland Europe's, the bureaucracy does too; evidence of this are the half-built houses dotting the rural landscape. Years ago, no one paid much attention to who built houses where. But modern urbanisation laws require permits for nearly any construction, something that islanders accustomed to the old ways are reluctant to get, forcing some towns to halt construction midproject while the slow wheels of bureaucracy turn. Education is yet another issue; since the

---

NAMING NAMES

Although the term Canario has come to designate all of the islanders, it once referred more strictly to the people of Gran Canaria alone (now more often as not referred to as Grancanarios or Canariones). The people of Tenerife are Tinerfeños; those of Lanzarote are not Lanzaroteños but Conejeros; Fuerteventura, Majoreros (from the Guanche name for much of the island, Maxorata); La Gomera, Gomeros; La Palma, Palmeros; and El Hierro, Herreños.

SHOE BIZ

The most famous shoe designer in the world, Manolo Blahnik was born in 1943 in Santa Cruz de Tenerife. The son of a Czech father and Spanish mother, he spent his childhood among banana plants – an unlikely beginning for a world-famous fashion designer if there ever was one. He was always fascinated by feet and shoes, and as a child he made shoes for monkeys and iguanas out of tiny pieces of foil.

He left the banana plantation to study in Geneva, but he soon moved to Paris and finally settled in London, where he worked as a fashion photographer and became friends with the city's jet set. In the 1970s Blahnik was dreaming of getting into theatre set design, but when a friend of a friend (who just happened to be the editor of US *Vogue*) saw his shoe-design sketches she insisted he keep at it.

The rest is history, and today 'Manolo's' costing €500 to €2500 grace the feet of fashionable women across the globe. Superfan Sarah Jessica Parker claimed her Manolo's last longer than most marriages, Madonna has claimed his shoes are 'better than sex', and Linda Evangelista and China Chow both have shoes named after them. Although the designer does get back to Tenerife every now and again to visit his mother, who still lives on the family farm, you'll be hard-pressed to find any of his shoes here; his only two signature shops are in London and New York.

small islands have no universities, young people have to study in Tenerife or Gran Canaria and this can deplete a family's already over-stretched budget. After school, many college-educated islanders end up leaving the island of their birth to look for better jobs on Tenerife, Gran Canaria or the mainland. By necessity, many Canary families are separated.

Still, family is still at the heart of Canary culture. Big island celebrations, like El Hierro's *Bajada de la Virgen de los Reyes* (Descent of the Virgin), held every four years, are always celebrated with family, and islanders come from as far away as the Americas to reunite with family and friends. Most religious and cultural celebrations are also family-focused. Although families now are smaller than they used to be – one or two children is the norm – they're still an important social unit. As elsewhere in Europe, couples are waiting longer to get married (the average age is 31 for women and 34 for men) although not necessarily later to have kids (the average age is 30), proving that Canary society is not as traditional as it once was.

In any case, kids are treated as *los reyes de casa* (kings of the house) and have a freedom to run and play rarely seen outside southern Europe. On a sadder note, some wives do not enjoy such freedom; while the macho image is not as prevalent as it once was, domestic violence is still a very big concern here, and each year women lose their lives at the hands of their husbands or partners.

ECONOMY

The Canary economy, fuelled by tourism and agriculture, has made great strides over the past few decades, but the region is still far from being an economic powerhouse. The average hourly wage is just over €9 (less than €1 higher than the 2001 average) and the average family income hovers around €23,600. Unemployment is high at 11.5%.

While incomes are relatively low, the cost of living is almost as high here as it is on the mainland. The price of housing has doubled since 1999, making independence virtually impossible for many young people. So far, the government has done a poor job of providing enough fixed-price housing for those unable to afford the steep prices.

The Canary Islands receive a lot (some Spaniards say more than their fair share) of money from the European Union (EU). The vast improvements in roads and infrastructure here is in large part thanks to the investments made by the EU over the past few years.

More than any other region of Spain, there is inequality between males and females in the workforce. Women's average annual earnings are about €4000 less than men's. Also, the region leads Spain in the number of part-time contracts for women, with 53% of all women working in possibly unstable, part-time jobs.

POPULATION

The archipelago's total population is scraping two million, with 83% of inhabitants living on the two main islands, Tenerife and Gran Canaria. Immigration from the EU, Africa and South America is responsible for the population boom the islands are experiencing; Tenerife gained more than 14,000 inhabitants between 2005 and 2006 alone, nearly all of them non-Spaniards. All the other islands experienced at least some population growth as well, though on a smaller scale. In 2006, populations of the smaller islands ranged from 89,700 in Fuerteventura to 10,670 in El Hierro.

SPORT

The Canary Islands are a sport-friendly destination, as they have a balmy, sunny climate, plenty of coastline and a laid-back, outdoor lifestyle that rewards activity. As part of Spain, there are no prizes for guessing the top sport here: football (soccer).

Lucha Canaria

The Guanches of Tenerife were a particularly robust and warlike crowd who loved a trial of strength. Any island party was an excuse for indulging in tests of manhood. Apart from jumping over steep ravines and diving into the ocean from dizzying heights, one favourite pastime was wrestling. Rooted in this ancient diversion lies the essence of the modern *lucha canaria* (Canarian wrestling).

One member of each team faces off his adversary in the ring and, after a formal greeting and other signs of goodwill, they set about trying to dump each other into the dust. No part of the body except the soles of the feet may touch the ground, and whoever fails first in this department loses. Size and weight are not the determining factors (although these boys tend to be as beefy as rugby front-row forwards), but rather the skill with which the combatants grapple and manoeuvre their opponents into a position from which they can be toppled.

If you want to find out if any matches are due to be held locally, ask at the nearest tourist office.

EMIGRATION

The Canarios have long looked across the Atlantic to further shores, and a high proportion of Cubans and continental Americans can claim a Canarian gene or two.

Following in the wake of Christopher Columbus, Canarios were among the earliest colonisers. In the early days, the most popular destinations were Cuba, La Hispañola (today's Dominican Republic and Haiti) and Puerto Rico in the Caribbean. On the mainland, pioneers settled around Buenos Aires in Argentina, Montevideo in Uruguay and Caracas in Venezuela. Further north, Canarios were well represented in Florida, Louisiana, Yucatán and Nueva España (Texas) – it was a group of Canaries emigrants who, on 9 March 1731, founded San Fernando (today's San Antonio, Texas).

The Roque Cinchado, one of the rock formations at the Roques de García, used to be featured on Spain's 1000 peseta banknote.

The average age of Canary residents is 37. The average age of Herreños (El Hierro residents) is 42, making it the 'oldest' island. More than 12% of the Spanish population on the islands is older than 65.

There were two later surges in emigration, both spurred as much by poverty on the islands and the need to escape as by hope of a new life and new deal over the waters. In the Canaries, the 1880s are called the decade of *la crisis de la cochinilla* (the cochineal crisis), when synthetic dyes swamped the international market and killed off the local cochineal cottage industries. Later, the hard times that Spain endured following the Spanish Civil War and WWII were even harder on the archipelago, and lasted right through until the 1960s.

Find out about the latest lucha canaria matches at www.federaciondelucha canaria.com.

In the Franco era, many Canarios left without a passport or papers and arrived illegally in the new land (the Americas). Here, they were interned in camps and then set to work, cutting cane in the sugar plantations in order to earn their keep – arduous labour from which they escaped to better-paid work at the first opportunity.

MULTICULTURALISM

Nowadays the Canary Islands, for so long a region of net emigration, admit more people than they export. Workers in the hotel, restaurant and construction industries, and migrants from northern Europe seeking a place in the near-perpetual sun, all bolster the islands' population figures.

With nearly 400,000 tourist beds in hotels, apartments and houses across the islands, there is a steady influx of people from across the world, mainly Europe. Some of those tourists decide to stay and make a life here; nearly two-thirds of the archipelago's 9.3 million tourists are German or British, so it should be no surprise that these are also the largest expat communities.

A newer phenomenon are the immigrants from the Americas, many of them family members of Canarios who emigrated to Venezuela or other South American countries who are now returning to the islands of their ancestors. The number of African immigrants is also significant. Overall, about 12% of the population is non-Spanish.

Recent Immigration

Since the Canary Islands are so close to the coast of Africa, thousands of people searching for a better life and livelihood make dangerous journeys across the Atlantic each year. While tourists picnic and sunbathe on Canary beaches, simple fishing boats (packed with up to 150 sub-Saharan Africans) arrive on those same beaches almost daily, more often than not accompanied by authorities who immediately begin the long process of returning them to their home countries; a process that is often left unfinished. These immigrants have faced 10-day trips across the ocean, and they often arrive weak and dehydrated.

The islanders, while sensitive to the immigrants' plight, insist that there is simply not space for so many people – unemployment is already high and there aren't enough jobs to go around, they say. In 2005 the permanent African population on the islands was only about 26,000, but that number does not reflect the hundreds who arrive almost daily in hopes of making a new life in Europe. The issue is constantly debated in the press and among politicians.

RELIGION

One of the primary concerns of the conquistadors from Spain was to convert what they perceived to be the heathen of these far-flung islands to the one true faith. As the conquest proceeded, the indigenous inhabitants were swiftly converted to Christianity, usually as part of the terms of surrender.

Catholicism has left a deep-rooted impression on the Canaries. Although the depth of the average Canario's religiosity may be a subject of speculation, the Church still plays an important role in people's lives. Most Canarios are baptised and confirmed, have church weddings and funerals and attend church for important feast days – although fewer than half regularly turn up for Sunday Mass. Many of the colourful and often wild fiestas that take place throughout the year have some religious context or origin.

ARTS
Architecture
Any pre-Hispanic architecture you can spot on the islands is either a reconstruction or heavily restored; the Guanches lived more often than not in caves, and virtually nothing of the rudimentary houses they built remains today outside museums like El Hierro's Ecomuseo de Guinea (p242).

The colonial period architecture reflects the influences of the Spaniards, Portuguese, French, Flemish, Italian and English. By the time the conquest of the islands was completed at the end of the 15th century, the Gothic and *mudéjar* (a type of Islamic architecture) styles already belonged more to the past than the present. The interior of the Catedral de Santa Ana (p69) in Las Palmas is nevertheless a fine example of what some art historians have denominated Atlantic Gothic. The bell tower of the Basílica de la Virgen del Pino (p79) in Teror, Gran Canaria, retains its Portuguese Gothic identity.

Only a few scraps of *mudéjar* influence made it to the islands. Probably the best examples are the fine wooden ceilings (known as *artesonado*) in the Iglesia de Nuestra Señora la Concepción (p157) in La Laguna, Tenerife. Not far behind are those of the Iglesia de Santa Catalina (p160) in Tacoronte, Tenerife, and those of the Iglesia del Salvador (p213) in Santa Cruz de la Palma.

You can get the merest whiff of *plateresque* (meaning silversmith-like, so called because it was reminiscent of intricate metalwork) energy at the Catedral de Santa Ana in Las Palmas and the Iglesia de Nuestra Señora la Concepción – the latter a veritable reference work of styles from Gothic through *mudéjar* to *plateresque*. Baroque, the trademark of the 17th century, left several traces across the archipelago and is best preserved in the parish church of Betancuria (p101), Fuerteventura.

Neoclassical, neogothic and other styles demonstrating a perhaps less creative, more derivative era are represented from the late 18th century onwards in imposing public buildings in the bigger cities. The Iglesia de San Juan (p80) in Arucas is an impressive piece of neogothic architecture – a shame it's not the genuine article.

Modernism makes an appearance along the Calle Mayor de Triana and in the private houses of the Triana district of Las Palmas de Gran Canaria.

Modern Canary architecture's greatest genius is, without doubt, Lanzarote native César Manrique. His ecologically sensitive creations, often using volcanic stones and other Canary materials, are found throughout the islands, but especially on Lanzarote. His designs are so compelling that some people base an entire trip around visiting them all. For details, see p119.

The icon of contemporary Canary architecture is Santiago Calatrava's 'wave', the multifunction Auditorio de Tenerife (p155) dominating the waterfront of Santa Cruz de Tenerife with its unmistakable profile of a wave crashing onto shore. Las Palmas de Gran Canaria is another architectural hot spot; interesting architectural spaces include the interior of the Atlantic Modern Art Centre by Sáenz de Oiza, the Auditorio Alfredo Kraus (p74) by Óscar Tusquets, and the Woermann Tower by Iñaki Ábalos and Juan Herreros.

Although architect César Manrique is no longer living, his cultural foundation (www.fcmanrique.org) is still active on the islands.

Literature
Until the arrival of the conquering Spaniards in the 15th century, the Guanches appear not to have known writing. Very much a frontier world

even after the conquest, the Canaries were not an immediate source of world-renowned writers, and little local literature made it into English translation.

The first writer whose work became known beyond the islands was the Tinerfeño writer José de Viera y Clavijo (1731–1813), an accomplished poet known above all for his painstaking history of the islands, *Noticias de la Historia General de Canarias*. His contemporary Tomás de Iriarte (1750–91), born in Puerto de la Cruz, was for years something of a dandy in Madrid court circles. He wrote several plays but his *Fábulas Literarias,* poetry and tales charged with a mordant wit, constituted his lasting work.

Nicolás Estévanez (1838–1914) spent much of his life outside the Canaries, first as a soldier and politician in Madrid and then in exile for 40 years in France. His poems, in particular 'Canarias', marked him as the motor behind the so-called Escuela Regionalista, a school of poets devoted to themes less universal and more identifiable with the archipelago.

Another of the islands' great historians emerged about the same time. Agustín Millares Torres (1826–96) is remembered for his monumental *Historia General de las Islas Canarias*.

Benito Pérez Galdós (1843–1920) grew up in Las Palmas de Gran Canaria, moving to Madrid in 1862. A prolific chronicler of his times, he produced 46 novels and numerous other books and plays.

The poet Josefina de la Torre (1907–2002) first achieved fame in the late 1920s. As the 20th century wore on, the poets of the Vanguardia took centre stage. Among the Canaries' exponents were Pedro Perdomo Acedo (1897–1977) and Felix Delgado (1904–36).

Carmen Laforet Díaz's (1921–) *Nada,* written in the wake of the civil war, is the partly autobiographical account of a young girl's move from her home in the Canary Islands to study in post-civil war Barcelona, where she is obliged to live in squalor with her grandmother. She has followed this up with other novels of lesser impact and, in 1961, *Gran Canaria,* a guide to her home island.

One of the most creative talents to emerge among the postmodern poets of the 1980s was Yolanda Soler Onís (1964–). *Sobre el Ámbar,* written from 1982 to 1986, is a collection of pieces with images sourced largely from an exploration of the islands' poetic traditions.

Other contemporary novelists to look out for are Roberto Cabrera and E Díaz Marrero.

Isaac de Vega was one of the 20th century's outstanding Canaries novelists. His *Fetasa* (1957) is a disturbing study of alienation and solitude and is without doubt the book that kick-started other typically 'Canarian' works of the period.

Music

The symbol of the Canarios' musical heritage is the *timple,* a ukulele-style instrument of obscure origin. Although many thought it was a variation of the Italian mandolin or the Spanish and Portuguese *guitarillo,* it now appears that Berber slaves, shipped in for farm work by the early Norman invaders under Jean de Béthencourt, might have introduced it to the islands.

It's a small, wooden, five-stringed instrument with a rounded back (it is said the original Berber version was made of a turtle shell) and a sharp tone. There is also a four-string version known as the *contra* or *requinto,* prevalent in Lanzarote.

The *timple* has travelled widely, as emigrants from the islands took it with them to Latin America, where it was incorporated into their instrumental repertoire.

Whenever you see local traditional fiestas, the *timple* will be there accompanying such dances as the *isa* and *folía* or, if you're lucky, the *tajaraste* – about the only dance said to have been passed down from the ancient Guanches.

The Canaries' best-loved folk group, Los Sabandeños, has been singing and strumming since 1966, when these Tinerfeños banded together in an effort to recover and popularise Canary culture across the islands. It's impossible to quantify the effect this group of nearly 25 men (including a few new recruits) has had on the islands. Its CDs of light, melodic music are widely available.

Over the centuries there has been no shortage of immigration from Andalucía in the south of Spain, and with it came another musical tradition. Popular Andalucían dances such as the *malagueñu* have become part of the local island folk tradition.

Rosana Arbelo, born in Lanzarote in 1962, is a fine *cantautor* (singer-songwriter) whose lyrics tend to the melancholy, accompanied by an appealing mix of Cuban, Spanish and African rhythms. However, the islands' most established *cantautor,* and one appreciated across all Spain, is Tenerife's Pedro Guerra.

> Download songs from the Canaries' best-loved folk group, Los Sabandeños, at www.sabanda.org.

Visual Arts

In the 17th century, Gaspar de Quevedo from Tenerife was the first major painter to emerge from the Canary Islands. Quevedo was succeeded in the 18th century by Cristóbal Hernández de Quintana (1659–1725), whose paintings still decorate the Catedral in La Laguna (p157) in Tenerife. More important was Juan de Miranda (1723–1805), among whose outstanding works is *La Adoración de los Pastores* (The Adoration of the Shepherds) in the Iglesia de Nuestra Señora de la Concepción (p152) in Santa Cruz de Tenerife. His best known acolyte was Luis de la Cruz y Ríos (1776–1853), born in La Orotava and above all a portraitist.

In the 19th century, Valentín Sanz Carta (1849–98) was among the first Canarios to produce landscapes. Others of his ilk included Lorenzo Pastor and Lillier y Thruillé, whose work can be seen in the Museo de Bellas Artes (p151) in Santa Cruz de Tenerife.

The Canaries' main exponent of impressionism was Manuel González Méndez (1843–1909), whose *La Verdad Venciendo el Error* (Truth Overcoming Error) hangs in the *ayuntamiento* (town hall) of Santa Cruz de Tenerife.

Néstor Martín Fernández de la Torre (1887–1938), whose speciality was murals, is best represented by his *Poema del Mar y Poema de la Tierra* (Poem of the Sea and Poem of the Earth).

The Cuban-Canario José Aguiar García (1895–1976), born of Gomero parents, grew up in Cuba. A prolific painter, he too reached the apogee of his craft in his murals. His works are spread across the islands; the *Friso Isleño* (Island Frieze) hangs in the casino in Santa Cruz de Tenerife.

All the great currents of European art filtered through to the Canary Islands. Of the so-called Coloristas, names worth mentioning include Francesco Miranda Bonnin (1911–63) and Jesús Arencibia (1991–93), who created the big mural in the Iglesia de San Antonio Abad (p69) in Las Palmas de Gran Canaria.

The first surrealist exhibition in Spain was held on 11 May 1935 in Santa Cruz de Tenerife. The greatest local exponent of surrealism, Tinerfeño Óscar Domínguez (1906–57), ended up in Paris in 1927 and was much influenced by Picasso. Others of the period include Cubist Antonio Padrón (1920–68), Felo Monzón (1910–89) and Jorge Oramas (1911–35).

Leading the field of abstract artists was Manuel Millares (1921–72), native of Las Palmas de Gran Canaria. Lanzarote's César Manrique (1919–92) also enjoyed a considerable degree of international recognition.

Canarios currently working hard at the canvas include Cristino de Vera (1931–), who lives in Madrid and displays elements of a primitive expressionism in his paintings, María Castro (1930–) and José Luis Fajardo (1941–), who uses just about any materials that come to hand in his often-bizarre works.

Environment

THE LAND

The seven islands and six islets that make up the Canary Islands archipelago are little more than the tallest tips of a vast volcanic mountain range that lies below the Atlantic Ocean. Just babies in geological terms, the islands were thrown up 30 million years ago when great slabs of the earth's crust (called tectonic plates) collided, crumpling the land into mammoth mountains both on land, as in the case of Morocco's Atlas range, and on the ocean floor, as in the case of the Cape Verde islands, the Azores and the Canaries. These Atlantic islands are collectively referred to as Macronesia. After the initial creation, a series of volcanic eruptions put the final touches on the islands' forms.

There is still plenty of activity across the floor of the Atlantic Ocean, and many peaks lie out of sight below the surface. Occasionally, new volcanic islands are puffed up into the light of day, but they are generally little more than feeble mounds of loose ash and are quickly washed away.

These days in the Canary Islands, you can best get a feel for the rumblings below the surface on Lanzarote, where the Montañas del Fuego (p136) still bubble with vigour, although the last eruptions took place way back in 1824. Of the remaining islands, not an eruptive burp has been heard from Fuerteventura, Gran Canaria, La Gomera or El Hierro for centuries; Tenerife's most recent display was a fairly innocuous affair in 1909; and it was La Palma that hosted the most recent spectacle – a fiery outburst by Volcán Teneguía in 1971.

La Palma is the steepest island in the world, relative to its height and overall area.

The seven main islands have a total area of 7447 sq km. Their size may not be great, but packed into them is just about every imaginable kind of landscape, from the long, sandy beaches of Fuerteventura and dunes of Gran Canaria to the majestic Atlantic cliffs of Tenerife and mist-enveloped woods of La Gomera. The easternmost islands have an almost Saharan desertscape, while corners of La Palma and La Gomera are downright lush. The highest mountain in Spain is 3718m Pico del Teide (El Teide; p170), which dominates the entire island of Tenerife.

None of the islands has rivers, and lack of water remains a serious problem. Instead of rivers, webs of *barrancos* (ravines) cut their way from the mountainous interiors of most of the islands to the coast. Water flows along some, but others remain dry nearly year-round.

Lanzarote and Fuerteventura, the two most easterly islands, would be quite at home if attached to the nearby coast of continental Africa (which is just 115km away). Lanzarote takes its present appearance from a series of massive blasts in 1730. The lava flow was devastating in many ways, but it created fertile ground where before there was nothing. Today, Lanzarote produces a wide range of crops grown mostly on volcanic hillsides. Another by-product of that eruption are the Montañas del Fuego (Mountains of Fire) in the Parque Nacional de Timanfaya, where volcanic rocks still give off enough heat to sizzle a steak (literally – see it being done at the Restaurant del Diablo, p136). North of the island are clustered five of the archipelago's six little islets (the other is Isla de Lobos, p108, just off the northern tip of Fuerteventura).

Gran Canaria is roughly a circular-based volcanic pyramid. Its northern half is surprisingly green and fertile, while south of the 1949m peak of Pozo de las Nieves (p79) the territory is more arid and reminiscent of Gran Canaria's eastern neighbours. For the variety of its geography, flora and climate, the island is often dubbed a 'continent in miniature'.

Gran Canaria's big brother, at least in terms of size, is Tenerife – every bit as much a mini-continent. Almost two-thirds of the island is taken up by the rugged slopes of the volcanic peak and crater El Teide, which is not only Spain's highest peak but also the third-largest volcano in the world, after Hawaii's Mauna Loa and Mauna Kea. A further string of mountains, the Anaga range, spreads along the northeastern panhandle. The only real lowlands are around La Laguna and alongside parts of the coast. The staggering cliffs of the north coast are occasionally lashed by Atlantic rain squalls, which are arrested by the mountains, giving the southwest and southeast coasts a more serene weather picture.

The remaining western islands share much in common. Better supplied with spring and/or rainwater, they are green and ringed by rocky, ocean-battered coastlines. La Palma's dominant feature is the yawning funnel known as the Caldera de Taburiente (p224), where the highest peak is the Roque de los Muchachos (2426m). The centre of La Gomera's high *meseta* (plateau) is covered by a Unesco World Heritage–listed laurel forest, the Parque Nacional de Garajonay (p195). El Hierro, the smallest of the Canary Islands and a Unesco-listed biosphere reserve (see the boxed text, p231), is mountainous – the highest peak is Malpaso at 1501m – with a coastline that seems designed to be a fortress.

El Teide is the highest peak in all of Spain.

El Teide & Other Volcanoes

El Teide is what's known as a shield volcano – huge and rising in a broad, gently angled cone to a summit that holds a steep-walled, flat-based crater. Although seemingly quieter than Italy's Vesuvius, Etna and Stromboli, all of which still have it in them to cause quite a fright, Teide is by no means finished.

Wisps of hot air can sometimes be seen around Teide's peak. Where the lava is fairly fluid, steam pressure can build up to the point of ejecting lava and ash or both in an eruption through the narrow vent. The vent can simply be blown off if there is sufficient pressure.

Stratovolcanoes, similar to the shield volcanoes, are also found on the islands, and sometimes they literally blow their top. Massive explosions can cause the whole summit to cave in, blasting away an enormous crater. The result is known as a caldera, within which it is not unusual for new cones to emerge, creating volcanoes within volcanoes. There are several impressive calderas on Gran Canaria, most notably Caldera de Bandama (p79). Oddly enough, massive Caldera de Taburiente (p224) on La Palma does not belong to this group of geological phenomena, although it was long thought to.

The Volcanoes of the Canary Islands by Vivente Araña and Juan Carracedo is a series of three volumes about – what else? – Canary Island volcanoes. Lovely photos and informative text.

When volcanoes do erupt, they belch out all sorts of things: ash, cinders, lapilli (small, round bombs of lava) and great streams of molten rock. Volcanic eruptions, however, don't just come through one central crater. Often subsidiary craters form around the main cone as lava and other materials force fissures into the mountain and escape that way.

WILDLIFE
Animals

Perhaps 'wildlife' is a little misleading. Sure, there are wild lives out there in the natural areas of even the most populated islands, but they tend to be small and shy and largely undetected by the untrained eye. Bugs abound, and lizards and birds are the biggest things you'll see – in some cases they are quite big indeed, like the giant lizard of El Hierro (p242). There are around 200 species of birds on the islands, though many are imports from Africa and Europe. Among the indigenous birds are the canary (those in

VOLCANIC ORIGINS

You don't have to be long in the Canary Islands to notice the astonishing variety of volcanic rock. Towering cones, tiny lightweight pebbles, rough untameable badlands (deeply eroded barren areas), smooth and shiny rock, red rock, black rock…they're all scattered about, blasted out of the earth's surface by the countless eruptions that have rocked the archipelago over its history.

The way a volcano erupts is largely determined by its gas content. If the material seething beneath the surface has a high gas content, the effect is like shaking a bottle of fizzy drink; once the cap's off, the contents spurt out with force. In the case of volcanoes, what are called pyroclasts – cinders, ash and lightweight fragments of pumice – are hurled high into the air and scattered over a wide area.

If the mix is more viscous, the magma wells up, overflows a vent, then slows as it slithers down the mountain as lava, cooling all the while until its progress is stopped. You'll see several such congealed rivers, composed of spiky and irregular clinker (volcanic slag), in the Parque Nacional de Timanfaya on Lanzarote and around the slopes of Teide. Look also for obsidian (fragments or layers of smooth, shiny material, like black glass) and scoria (high in iron and magnesium and reddish-brown in colour since it's – quite literally – rusting).

the wild are a muck-brown colour, not the sunny yellow colour of their domesticated cousins) and a few large pigeons.

The ocean is home to more thrilling wildlife (no offence to the birds). The stretch of water between Tenerife and La Gomera is a traditional feeding ground for as many as 26 species of whales, and others pass through during migration. The most common are pilot whales, sperm whales and bottlenose dolphins.

Whale watching is big business around here, and 800,000 people a year head out on boats to get a look. A law regulates observation of sea mammals, prohibiting boats from getting closer than 60m to an animal and limiting the number of boats following pods at any one time. The law also tries to curb practices such as using sonar and other devices to attract whales' attention. Four small patrol boats attempt to keep a watchful eye on these activities.

Still, many environmentalists argue that boats disrupt whales feeding patterns and can be harmful. If you decide to take a whale-watching tour, join up with a reputable company, like Katrin (p174) on Tenerife or the Club de Mar (p204) on La Gomera.

> The pamphlet-style *Whales and Dolphins of the Canary Islands* by Volker Boehlke is a great introduction to common species and likely behaviours.

Aside from the majestic marine mammals, there are many other life forms busy under the ocean. The waters around the Canary Islands host 350 species of fish and about 600 species of algae. You can see them up close by going scuba diving or snorkelling. See the activities sections of individual island chapters for more information.

ENDANGERED SPECIES

The giant lizard of El Hierro (p242) was once common on the island, though its numbers began seriously dwindling in the early 1900s. By the 1940s nary a trace was to be found, and the species was given up for lost. Miraculously, a tiny population of the lizards managed to survive on a precipice, and a pair was discovered and captured by a local herdsman. Now there is a recovery program working to breed the lizards in captivity and slowly introduce them into the wild.

> The giant lizard of El Hierro grows as long as 45cm.

Plants

The islands' rich volcanic soil, varied rainfall and dramatic changes in altitude support a surprising diversity of plant life, both indigenous and introduced. The Canary Islands are home to about 2000 species, about half of them endemic to the islands. The only brake on what might otherwise be a still-more-florid display in this largely subtropical environment is the shortage of water. Even so, botanists will have a field day here, and there are numerous botanical gardens scattered about where you can observe a whole range of local flora.

Up to an elevation of about 400m, the land is home to plants that thrive in hot and arid conditions. Where farmland has been irrigated, you'll find bananas, oranges, coffee, sugar cane, dates and tobacco. In the towns, bougainvillea, hibiscus, acacia, geraniums, marigolds and carnations all contribute to the bright array. Of the more exotic specimens, the strelitzia, with its blue, white and orange blossoms, stands out. These exotics have all been introduced to the islands. The dry, uncultivated scrublands near the coast, known as *tabaibales,* host various indigenous plants such as *cardón (Euphorbia).*

At elevations of around 700m, the Canaries' climate is more typical of the Mediterranean, encouraging crops such as cereals, potatoes and grapes. Where the crops give way, stands of eucalyptus and cork take over. Mimosa, broom, honeysuckle and laburnums are also common.

Higher still, where the air is cooler, common plants and trees include holly, myrtle and laurel. The best place to explore forest land is in La Gomera's Parque Nacional de Garajonay (p195), host to one of the world's last remaining Tertiary-era forests and declared a Unesco World Heritage site. Known as *laurisilva,* it is made up of laurels, holly, linden and giant heather, clad in lichen and moss and often swathed in swirling mist.

Up to 2000m in altitude, the most common tree you're likely to encounter is the Canary pine, which manages to set down roots on impossibly steep slopes that would defeat most other species. It is a particularly hardy tree, with fire-resistant timber that makes fine construction material.

Up in the great volcanic basin of the Parque Nacional del Teide (p170) on Tenerife are some outstanding flowers. Apart from the feisty high-altitude Teide violet (the highest-altitude flower in Spain), with its seemingly delicate blossom thriving in the volcanic soil at the peak of El Teide, one of the floral symbols of the Canaries is the flamboyant *tajinaste rojo,* or Teide viper's bugloss *(Echium wildpretii),* which can grow to more than 3m high. Every other spring, it sprouts an extraordinary conical spike of striking red blooms

If you're interested in getting involved with marine conservation, in particular the protection of whales, get in touch with the Atlantic Whale Foundation (www .whalenation.org), a group that organises educational trips, volunteer opportunities and conservation campaigns on Tenerife. The website is a mine of information.

More than half of Spain's endemic plant species are found in the Canary Islands.

NOT-SO-FRIENDLY FIDO

If you come across a solid-looking dog with a big head and a stern gaze, you are probably getting to know the Canary dog, known in Spanish as the *presa canario.* This beast is right up there with the pit bull as a tenacious guard dog, loyal and chummy with its owners but rarely well disposed to outsiders.

The breed is also known as the *verdino* (from a slightly greenish tint in its colouring) and opinion is divided regarding its origins. Probably introduced to the islands in the wake of the Spanish conquest in the 15th century, and subsequently mixed with other breeds, the Canary dog has been used for centuries to guard farms and cattle. When it comes to stopping human intruders, no other dog is so full of fight. It is prized by owners for its fearlessness and loyalty.

One can only speculate about the dogs mentioned in Pliny's description of ancient King Juba's expedition to the islands in 40 BC. These dogs were said to be exceptionally robust and there are those who are convinced that the *verdino*'s ancestors were indeed present on the islands 2000 years ago. But as usual, the accounts are conflicting.

Some academics maintain that the conquistadors were none too taken with these animals, considering them wild and dangerous, and eventually set about having the majority of them destroyed.

Other accounts suggest that the Spaniards found no such animals on their arrival and, hence, later introduced their own. Whatever the truth, the Canary dog is now prized as a local island breed.

like a great red poker. After its brief, spectacular moment of glory, all that remains is a thin, desiccated, spear-shaped skeleton, like a well-picked-over fish. Leave well alone; each fishbone has thousands of tiny strands that are as itchy as horsehair.

Although much of the vegetation is common across the islands, there are some marked differences. Fuerteventura, Lanzarote and the south of Gran Canaria distinguish themselves from the rest of the islands with their semidesert flora, where saltbush, Canary palm and other small shrubs dominate. Concentrated in a couple of spots – the cliffs of La Caleta de Famara on Lanzarote, and Jandía on Fuerteventura – you will find more abundant flora. This includes the rare, cactuslike *cardón de Jandía*, several species of daisy and all sorts of odd cliff plants unique to these islands.

NATIONAL PARKS

With more than 40% of its territory falling under one of eight categories of parkland, the Canary Islands are one of the most extensively protected territories in Europe.

At the top of the park pyramid are the four *parques nacionales* (national parks), administered at state level from Madrid. The regional government handles the other seven varieties of protected spaces, which range from rural parks to the more symbolic 'site of scientific interest'.

Only since the late 1980s have real steps been taken to protect the islands' natural diversity. A series of laws establishing and then enforcing protected spaces pushed the effort from merely good intention to a solid structure of parks and protected spaces.

The islands' four national parks, for instance, are largely protected from human interference by rules banning visitors from free camping or straying from defined walking paths. You can contribute by obeying the rules on where you are permitted to hike and keeping all your rubbish with you – what you take in you should also take out.

There are also several World Heritage sites, declared and protected by Unesco.

ENVIRONMENTAL ISSUES

As in mainland Spain, the 1960s saw the first waves of mass sea-and-sun tourism crash over the tranquil shores of the Canary Islands. The government of the day anticipated filling up the state coffers with easy tourist dollars,

www.canarias.org has extensive information on the archipelago's flora, fauna and volcanic origins.

National Parks and Flora of the Canary Islands, published by Otermin Ediciones, is an easy-to-read overview of the Canaries' four national parks and the plants found in them.

The Parque Nacional del Teide is Spain's most-visited national park, receiving around 3.3 million visitors a year. Most of them, however, barely wander beyond the highway snaking through the park.

THE TREE WITH A LONG, SHADY PAST

Among the more curious trees you will see in the Canary Islands is the *drago* (dragon tree; *Dracaena draco*), which can reach 18m in height and live for centuries.

Having survived the last ice age, it looks different – even a touch prehistoric. Its shape resembles a giant posy of flowers, its trunk and branches being the stems, which break into bunches of long, narrow, silvery-green leaves higher up. As the plant (technically it is not a tree, though it's always referred to as one) grows, it becomes more and more top-heavy. To stabilise itself, the *drago* ingeniously grows roots on the outside of its trunk, eventually creating a second, wider trunk.

What makes the *drago* stranger still is its red sap or resin – known, of course, as 'dragon's blood' – which was traditionally used in medicine.

The plant once played an important role in Canary Island life, for it was beneath the ancient branches of a *drago* that the Guanche Council of Nobles would gather to administer justice.

The *drago* is one of a family of up to 80 species (*Dracaena*) that survived the ice age in tropical and subtropical zones of the Old World, and is one of the last representatives of Tertiary-era flora.

CANARY NATIONAL PARKS & UNESCO RESERVES

Park Name	Features	Activities	For Kids	Page
Parque Nacional del Teide, Tenerife	Spain's highest mountain, the volcanic peak of Teide, volcanic landscapes	Riding the cable car to the peak, hiking around Roques de García	The little ones will love the cable car	170
Parque Nacional de Garajonay, La Gomera	A prehistoric laurel forest, horizontal rain, pines	Hiking to the top of the Alto de Garajonay, cycling down from the summit	The La Laguna Grande has a playground and recreational area	195
Parque Nacional de Timanfaya, Lanzarote	Volcanic activity, warm volcanic rocks due to molten lava beneath the surface	Eating at the Restaurant del Diablo, touching and walking on hot volcanic lava	A camel ride at the Museo de las Rocas	136
Parque Nacional de la Caldera de Taburiente, La Palma	Towering rock walls, slopes of pines	Hiking into the cauldron-like Caldera in the park's centre	The walks around La Cumbrecita are ideal for short legs	224
Gran Canaria Biosphere Reserve (In 2005 Unesco declared one-third of the island a biosphere reserve)	Water basins, beaches and marine areas where unique vegetation (around 100 species are unique to the island) thrives	Scuba dive or snorkel off the coast	Hunt for crabs at the beach	58
Lanzarote Biosphere Reserve (Unesco has declared the entire island a biosphere reserve)	Unique plants, marine reserve, volcanic landscape	Walking among some of the archipelago's most dramatic volcanic landscapes, relaxing on volcanic beaches	Older kids will gawk at César Manrique's weird architecture	118
La Palma Biosphere Reserve (In 2002 Unesco declared the entire island a biosphere reserve)	The laurel forest of Los Tiles, ancient rock carvings, pine forests, endemic flora and fauna	Hiking in Los Tiles or along the Ruta de los Volcanes	Easy-access lookouts let the little ones enjoy the view too	206
El Hierro Biosphere Reserve (Unesco has declared the entire island a biosphere reserve)	Bimbache etchings, pine forests, twisted juniper trees	Driving through El Pinar, walking among the junipers in El Sabinar	Stop in the Hoya del Morcillo recreation area	229

and local entrepreneurs enthusiastically leapt aboard the gravy train. Few, however, gave a thought to what impact the tourists and the mushrooming coastal resorts might have on the environment.

The near-unregulated building and expansion of resorts well into the 1980s has created some monumental eyesores, particularly on the southern side of Tenerife and Gran Canaria. Great scabs of holiday villas, hotels and condominiums have spread across much of the two islands' southern coasts. And the problem is not restricted to the resorts – hasty cement extensions to towns and villages mean that parts of the islands' interiors are being increasingly spoiled by property developers and speculators.

The massive influx of visitors to the islands over recent decades has brought or exacerbated other problems. Littering of beaches, dunes and other areas of natural beauty, both by outsiders and locals, remains a burning issue. Occasionally, ecological societies organise massive rubbish cleanups along beaches and the like – worthy gestures but also damning evidence of the extent to which the problem persists.

Spot the Canaries' otherworldly volcanic landscapes in films like *Star Wars*, *The Ten Commandments* and the original *Planet of the Apes*, all shot (in part) on the islands. Parque Nacional del Teide is an especially popular film location.

RESPONSIBLE TOURISM – WATER CONSERVATION

Though the use of desalinated sea water is on the rise, all visitors should do their part to conserve water, starting with some common-sense strategies, such as limiting shower time, turning off the tap when not using water and requesting that hotel towels not be laundered every day – instead, hang them up to dry and reuse.

For the islands' administrators, it's a conundrum. Tourism has come to represent an essential pillar of the Canaries' economy, which quite simply it cannot do without. They argue that profits from the tourist trade are ploughed back into the community. However, this is still fairly haphazard and there have long been calls for more regional planning – and, every year more insistently, for a total moratorium on yet more tourism development. Short-term moratoriums are at times established on an island-by-island basis. Some of the damage done over the years, especially to the coastline, is irreversible.

One of the hottest issues of recent years is the proposed port of Gandilla, a huge commercial port slated to be built in southeastern Tenerife. While politicians argue that the port is necessary for the island economy, there's no denying its severe impact on the land. Environmentalists say 5km of coastline would be destroyed by the port.

The basic issue is prosperity (or perceived prosperity) versus preservation, and it's repeated across the islands. In La Palma, politicians have proposed building five new golf courses, some on protected land, while ecologists say the golf courses would unnecessarily destroy natural resources. On Gran Canaria, a new shopping centre in Gáldar is causing concern, while around Lanzarote and Fuerteventura the buzz about possible offshore petroleum deposits is stirring the environmentalists.

For the latest on what's riling ecologists on the islands, check into www .atan.org, containing a treasure trove of passionate articles denouncing poor ecological practices on Tenerife.

One island that's taken steps toward conservation is El Hierro, where, in 2007, the government unveiled a plan to become the world's first island able to meet all its energy needs with renewable sources (wind, water and solar) alone.

Water

One of the islands' greatest and most persistent problems is water, or rather the lack of. Limited rainfall and the lack of natural springs have always restricted agriculture, and water is a commodity still in short supply.

Desalination appears the only solution for the Canaries; pretty much all potable water on Lanzarote and Fuerteventura is desalinated sea water.

In summer, the corollary of the perennial water problem is the forest fire. With almost clockwork regularity, hundreds of hectares of forest are ravaged every summer on all the islands except the already-bare Lanzarote and Fuerteventura.

Environmental Organisations

The islands are swarming with environmental action groups, some more active than others. Most are members of **Ben Magec – Ecologistas en Acción** (Ben Magec – Ecologists in Action; ☎ 928 36 22 33; www.benmagec.org). A few of the myriad individual groups you'll find on the islands are listed below.

Aire Libre (☎ 922 49 33 06; www.airelibrelapalma.org; La Palma)

Asociación Canaria Para Defensa de la Naturaleza (☎ 928 26 24 66; www.ascanasociacion .com; Gran Canaria)

Asociación Tinerfeña de Amigos de la Naturaleza (☎ 922 27 93 92; www.atan.org; Tenerife)

El Guincho (☎ 928 81 54 32; www.benmagec.org/elguincho; Lanzarote)

Guanil (☎ 928 87 07 43; www.ecologistasenaccion.org; Fuerteventura)

Tagaragunche (☎ 679 60 01 10; www.tagaragunche.com; La Gomera)

Outdoors

Being outdoors is what the Canary Islands are all about. With temperatures ranging from about 18°C in winter to 24°C in summer, and an average rainfall hovering around 250mm, you're almost guaranteed the perfect weather for whatever activity suits your fancy. And the astonishing variety of landscapes here – from La Gomera's humid and verdant Parque Nacional de Garajonay to the vast lunarscapes of Lanzarote – means that the same pursuit will be different on each island.

Most trekkers and adventure seekers gravitate toward the smaller islands, especially La Gomera, La Palma and, for water sports, Lanzarote, but it's possible to get away from the crowds and test your adventuresome spirit on any of the seven islands. All boast excellent hiking and biking trails and the abundance of water sports is obvious. Countless outfitters offer guidance (details are provided in the individual island chapters), but if you decide to set out on your own it's essential to be well-informed about possible dangers, route length and difficulty, and to have the appropriate gear and clothing.

WALKING & HIKING

Hundreds of trails, many of them historic paths used before the days of cars and highways, crisscross the islands. A good place to start is the national parks – the Parque Nacional del Teide (p170) on Tenerife, the Parque Nacional de Garajonay (p195) on La Gomera and the Parque Nacional de la Caldera de Taburiente (p224) on La Palma all have excellent hiking. Each of these parks offers a variety of walks and hikes, ranging from easy strolls ending at lookout points to multi-day treks across mountains and gorges.

To get a feel for the destruction and power of volcanoes, head to El Teide. Here you can walk across the barren *cañadas* (flatlands) that surround the base of the volcanic peak, or you can hike up to the mouth of El Teide itself, where on clear days you'll gasp at the views of the valley below, the ocean and the islands in the distance. For something in between, take the 1½-hour walk

Discovery Walking Guides, which publishes guidebooks and accompanying maps to El Hierro, La Palma, La Gomera and Tenerife; and Sunflower Books, which has books about all the islands, are both great resources for hikers.

RESPONSIBLE WALKING

- Carry out *all* your rubbish. Don't overlook easily forgotten items such as silver paper, orange peel, cigarette butts and plastic wrappers. Empty packaging should be stored in a dedicated rubbish bag. Make an effort to carry out rubbish left by others.

- Never bury your rubbish: digging disturbs soil and ground cover and encourages erosion. Buried rubbish will likely be dug up by animals, which may be injured or poisoned by it. It may also take years to decompose.

- Cut down on waste by taking minimal packaging and no more food than you will need. Take reusable containers or stuff sacks.

- Sanitary napkins, tampons, condoms and toilet paper should be carried out despite the inconvenience. They burn and decompose poorly.

- Contamination of water sources by human faeces can lead to the transmission of all sorts of nasties. Where there is a toilet, please use it. Where there is none, bury your waste. Dig a small hole 15cm (6in) deep and at least 100m (330ft) from any watercourse. Cover the waste with soil and a rock. In snow, dig down to the soil.

- Ensure that these guidelines are applied to a portable toilet tent if one is being used by a large trekking party. Encourage all party members to use the site.

around the Roques de García, just south of the peak, where the landscape is varied and not too challenging.

If you like some shade every now and again, try Garajonay, home to one of the last vestiges of the ancient *laurisilva* forest that once covered southern Europe. Thanks to a near-permanent mist (called horizontal rain), this green forest is dripping with life and moss. It's beautiful, but the dampness makes walking downright cold, so be sure to bring a jacket. From the park's highest point, the Alto de Garajonay, you can see Tenerife and El Teide – if the clouds don't interrupt the view.

The Caldera de Taburiente offers a landscape somewhere between the verdant Garajonay and the stark Teide. You can hike along the rock walls of the park's interior or meander among the pine forests on the outer slopes of the park. Visiting the caldera's interior is a bit more complicated than accessing other parks, simply because no road runs through it. Be prepared to commit at least a half-day if you want to do anything more than drive up to a *mirador* (lookout point) and walk around.

National parks aren't the only spots with good hiking trails. Among our other favourites are the Ruta de los Volcanes (p221) and the walk to the Marcos and Cordero Springs in the Unesco-protected Los Tiles biosphere reserve (p227), both on La Palma. Also highly recommended are the Camino de Jinama (p238) on El Hierro, and the dunes of Maspalomas (p83) on Gran Canaria. For a truly spectacular walk, sign up for the 'Tremesana' guided hike (p137) in the Parque Nacional de Timanfaya; you'll have to plan in advance, but the effort will be well rewarded.

You can walk in the Canary Islands any time of year, but some trails become dangerous or impossible in rainy weather, and others (like the trek up to the peak of El Teide) are harder to do in winter, when parts of the trail are covered in snow. Be aware that while along the coast and in the lowlands it's normally warm and sunny, as you head into higher altitudes, the wind, fog and air temperature can change drastically, so always carry warm and waterproof clothing. Don't forget to take water along with you, as there are few water sources or vendors out along the trails.

SCUBA DIVING & SNORKELLING

The variety of marine life and the warm, relatively calm waters of the Canary Islands make them a great place for scuba diving or snorkelling. You won't experience the wild colours of Caribbean coral, but the volcanic coast is made up of beautiful rock formations and caves. As far as life underwater goes, you can spot around 350 species of fish and 600 different kinds of algae.

Scuba schools and outfitters are scattered across the islands, so you won't have trouble finding someone willing to take you out. A standard dive, with equipment rental included, costs around €30, but a 'try dive' (a first-timer diving with an instructor) can be double that. Certification classes start at €220 and generally last between three days and a week, though they can be much more expensive depending on the certification level. Many scuba outfitters also offer snorkelling excursions for nondivers, and prices tend to be about half the cost of a regular dive.

The southern coast of El Hierro is considered one of the top spots for scuba diving. There is a wealth of marine life there, thanks in part to the lack of development on the island. Also, the waters in the Mar de las Calmas (p239) are among the warmest and calmest of the archipelago, which increases visibility and makes the whole experience more enjoyable.

Lanzarote offers enviable diving conditions as well, with visibility up to 20m and especially warm waters. One word of warning – all divers here must be registered, though the permit price is usually included with

---

The islands' hiking trails are divided into three categories: GR (long-distance, multiday trails), PR (shorter, one-day routes) and SL (local paths under 10km). All are signposted.

For many people, La Palma is considered the best island for walking. The website www.tour lapalma.com details many of the island's best routes, with detailed hiking maps available to download.

Diving in Canaries by Sergio Hanquet is a big hardback book with luscious photographs of the underwater life you'll find around the Canaries.

your equipment rental. One of the best areas for diving is along Puerto Calero (p140), where you will find marlin, barracuda and a host of other fish. There are spots of orange coral and interesting underwater caves nearby too.

On Tenerife, most diving outfitters are congregated around the southern resorts, though the area around Los Gigantes (p174) has the reputation of having the best diving conditions of the lot. It's possible to do wreck dives (where you explore sunken boats and the like), cave dives and old-fashioned boat dives. Marine life in these waters ranges from eels to angel sharks and stingrays.

On Gran Canaria, Puerto de Mogán (p89) is the main dive centre, and there are plenty of boats heading out to dive in and around the caves and wrecks that lie not far offshore.

Get a rundown on dive sites around Tenerife and Lanzarote at www .divesitedirectory.co.uk /canary_islands.html.

BOATING

Ah, so much ocean, so little time! There's no reason to stay landlocked when it's so easy to hire a sailing boat, take a day cruise or paddle a sea kayak. The water conditions around the islands vary greatly, and some places may be too rough for a novice navigator, but there are areas where you'll have no problem.

In Tenerife, rent a boat or sign up for an excursion with companies in Puerto Colón (p180) and navigate the waters between Tenerife and La Gomera with the shadow of El Teide behind you.

In La Gomera, daily cruises setting off from the Las Vueltas port in Valle Gran Rey (p202) float past kilometre after kilometre of impenetrable rock cliffs before arriving at one of the island's most unique sites, Los Órganos (The Organs), a rock formation seen only from the water that indeed looks just like an enormous pipe organ carved into the rock.

RESPONSIBLE DIVING

Please consider the following tips when diving and help preserve the ecology and beauty of the reefs.

- Never use anchors on a reef, and take care not to ground boats on coral.
- Avoid touching or standing on living marine organisms or dragging equipment across the reef. Polyps can be damaged by even the gentlest contact. If you must hold on to the reef, only touch exposed rock or dead coral.
- Be conscious of your fins. Even without contact, the surge from fin strokes near the reef can damage delicate organisms. Take care not to kick up clouds of sand, which can smother organisms.
- Practise and maintain proper buoyancy control. Major damage can be done by divers descending too fast and colliding with the reef.
- Take great care in underwater caves. Spend as little time within them as possible, as your air bubbles may catch within the roof and thereby leave organisms high and dry. Take turns to inspect the interior of a small cave.
- Resist the temptation to collect or buy corals or shells or to loot marine archaeological sites (mainly shipwrecks).
- Ensure that you take home all your rubbish and any litter you may find as well. Plastics in particular are a serious threat to marine life.
- Do not feed fish.
- Minimise your disturbance of marine animals. *Never* ride on the backs of turtles.

Deep-sea-fishing buffs will enjoy the trips out of Puerto Calero (p140), Lanzarote, where daily cruises combine fishing with shark spotting.

SURFING, WINDSURFING & KITE BOARDING

Plan a surfing holiday on the eastern islands at www.surfcanarias.com.

Surfing, windsurfing and kite boarding are popular water sports on most of the islands. Schools offering classes and equipment rental are scattered around the windier coasts and there are a variety of spots to choose from, ranging from the beginner-friendly sandy beaches of Fuerteventura to the wilder waves of eastern Tenerife. Classes and equipment rental for all three sports are widely available in popular resort areas.

La Caleta de Famara (p135) and Isla Graciosa (p134) on Lanzarote offer world-class surf breaks. There's great windsurfing around the Bahía de Pozo Izquierdo (p85) on Gran Canaria, and the Las Palmas area offers decent waves for surfers too. On Fuerteventura, head to the area around El Cotillo (p111), Corralejo (p106) and the Isla de Lobos (p108), where waves really start pumping around late September and continue throughout the winter. The southern coast of Fuerteventura, in particular Playa de Sotavento de Jandía (p113) and Playa de Barlovento de Jandía (p116), are also great windsurfing spots.

On Tenerife, Las Galletas (p184) is a popular windsurfing spot, and nearby El Médano (p176) is considered one of the best places in the world for windsurfing. International competitions are held here every year, and enthusiasts from all over the globe converge on the long, sandy beaches to test the waters. Beginners beware – it's harder than it looks, and before renting equipment invest in one of the classes offered by numerous local companies. Courses last between two days and a week and prices vary widely according to how much you're aiming to learn.

True thrill seekers can try the latest surfing trend, kite boarding, which involves being connected to a huge, parachutelike kite, standing on a short board and letting the wind take you where it will. Watching the boarders with know-how leap and flip is amazing, but you have to be a real dare-

---

SWIMMING

Year-round sun and warm water (18°C to 26°C) makes swimming an obvious activity in the Canary Islands. From the golden beaches of the eastern islands to the volcanic pools of the western islands, there are plenty of splashing opportunities.

Beaches come in every shape and size – long and golden, intimate and calm, windy and wavy, rocky and picturesque, solitary and lonely, action-packed and family-friendly. Our list of favourite beaches is on p21.

You do need to be cautious, especially when swimming in the ocean. The first rule is never, ever swim alone. There can be very strong currents and undertows in the Atlantic, and rip currents can be so strong that they can carry you far from shore before you can react. If you're caught in a current, swim parallel to the shore (don't try to get to the beach) until you're released. Then make your way to shore.

The water quality around the Canary Islands is generally excellent. The only place you may find pollution is near ports (the occasional small oil spill is not unheard of) and on overcrowded tourist beaches. Smokers seem to think of some beaches as a huge ashtray, so you may need to watch out for butts, especially if you have kids.

There are two jellyfish species you should watch out for: the Portuguese man-of-war and the luminescent purple stinger. Both can sting. If you're stung, first remove any tentacles stuck to the skin (using gloves) then apply vinegar to the skin. If you're stung on the face or genitalia, or have difficulty swallowing or breathing, contact a doctor.

ACTIVITIES FOR THE LITTLE ONES

If the kids are all beached out, there are plenty of island attractions to capture their attention, not least the islands' natural spaces. Canarios love to picnic, and rural parks and road-side picnic spots, more often than not with a kids' play area, are dotted throughout the islands. On the western islands, national parks are a good place to look for easy hikes, while the flatter eastern islands are ideal for bike rides with older kids.

The ideas below are just to get you started. See individual island chapters for more information on kid-friendly activities.

Water & Theme Parks

On the big islands especially, water parks abound. On Lanzarote, Costa Teguise's **Aquapark** (p123) keeps kids happy with rides and slides, and Fuerteventura's sprawling **Baku Water Park** (p96) has all the usual rides plus dry activities like crazy golf.

Zoos

Wildlife parks are a resort staple, and there are plenty of them here. Southern Tenerife boasts **Camel Park** (p184) and **Jungle Park** (p181), while **Loro Parque** (p163) in Puerto de la Cruz is a favourite in the north of the island. You'll find similar parks near Maspalomas, on Gran Canaria.

Boats

Whale- and dolphin-watching cruises, available on Tenerife and La Gomera, are good options for older kids with decent attention spans (bear in mind that you might not spot something immediately). For something a bit different, hop on Lanzarote's Submarine Safaris (p140) to explore the depths of the Atlantic.

---

devil to try it. Areas with several windsurfing outfitters are also likely to be home to a kite-boarding school or two.

GOLF

In the past decade, southern Tenerife has become the Canary Islands' golf hot spot. Golfers who love the balmy temperatures that let them play year-round have spawned the creation of a half-dozen courses in and around the Playa de las Américas (p178) alone. The courses are aimed at holiday golfers and are not known for being particularly challenging.

For an overview of golfing on Tenerife, see www.tenerifegolf.es.

You'll also find a few courses around Las Palmas de Gran Canaria, and a course or two dotted around Lanzarote and Fuerteventura.

The lack of water on the islands makes golf a rather environmentally unfriendly and difficult sport to sustain. Golf course owners say the water for those lush greens comes from runoff and local water purification plants, but environmental groups say the golf courses take water from agriculture. The truth is in there somewhere, and local politicians, golfers, environmentalists and farmers are still arguing about where.

In winter, green fees hover around €80, but in midsummer they could be half that. Renting a golf cart will cost you up to €40 and club rental can cost up to €25.

Cycling routes, including photos, are online at www.amigosdelciclismo .com in Spanish.

CYCLING

If you've got strong legs, cycling may be the perfect way to see the Canary Islands. Bike rental is available across the islands, and numerous companies offer guided excursions of a day or even longer. If you think you're in very good shape, try the climb up to El Teide or the Alto de Garajonay. If constantly heading uphill on a bicycle isn't your idea of a good time, sign up with a guided excursion; they'll often cart your bike up to the top of the hill then turn you loose to zip down. Recommended outfitters can be found on Tenerife (see p164) and La Gomera (see p188).

Less-extreme routes can be found on the eastern islands, especially Gran Canaria, which has a strong cycling community. Outside Maspalomas on Gran Canaria there are a few excellent bike trails, and Fuerteventura also has decent cycling areas.

The price of renting a bike depends largely on what kind of bike you get – suspension and other extras will cost more. In general, a day's rental starts at about €15, and a guided excursion will be around €40.

For cycle touring information, see p261.

Food & Drink

Canary cuisine is all about simple pleasures. Grilled fish served with a zesty herb sauce. Boiled potatoes with crinkly, salted skin. Juicy grilled kid. Green salads served with buttery avocado grown in the neighbouring town. The islands' traditional dishes are those made with ingredients produced on the islands, and although restaurants can now get any and every kind of exotic ingredient flown in, there is still no beating unfussy traditional cooking.

The single best advice we can offer is to eat local, fresh food whenever possible. If you're not picky, you might as well just set aside the menu and ask your server for the *plato del día* (daily special) or *pescado del día* (catch of the day); these dishes are almost sure to be the house's best offering.

Through the years, traditional Canary dishes have rubbed shoulders with mainland Spanish cuisine and even South American specialities, giving way to unique Canary spins on recipes from elsewhere. And, of course, these days you'll find everything from Chinese to Italian to pub fare in the big resorts. The very best dining experiences, however, are usually to be had away from the tourist swarms and in the cosy, farmhouse restaurants that dot the islands' interiors.

Pleasures of the Canary Islands: Wine, Food, Beauty, Mystery by Ann and Larry Walker is one of the few introductions to Canarian cuisine in English.

STAPLES & SPECIALITIES

The staple product *par excellence* is *gofio,* a uniquely Canario product. A roasted mixture of wheat, maize or barley, *gofio* takes the place of bread in the traditional Canary diet. There is no shortage of bread these days, but *gofio* remains common. It is something of an acquired taste and, mixed in varying proportions, is used as a breakfast food or combined with almonds and figs to make sweets.

Other basic foods long common across the islands are bananas and tomatoes, but nowadays the markets are filled with a wide range of fruit and vegetables. Beef, pork and lamb are widely available (more often than not, imported), but the traditional *cabra* (goat) and *cabrito* (kid) remain a staple animal protein. Most local cheeses also come from goats' milk.

Canarian cuisine owes a lot to the New World; it was from South America that elementary items such as potatoes, tomatoes and corn were introduced. From there also came more exotic delights such as avocados and papayas, while sweet mangoes arrived from Asia. Look out for all three in the valleys and on supermarket shelves.

The most-often-spotted Canarian contribution to the dinner table is the *mojo* (spicy salsa sauce made from coriander, basil or red chilli peppers). This sauce has endless variants and is used to flavour everything from chicken legs to cheese.

Papas arrugadas (wrinkly potatoes) are perhaps the next-best-known dish, although there is really not much to them. They're small new potatoes boiled and salted in their skins. They really come to life when dipped in one of the *mojos.*

Of the many soups you'll find, one typically Canarian variant is *potaje de berros* (watercress soup). Another is *rancho canario,* a kind of broth with thick noodles and the odd chunk of meat and potato – it's very hearty.

Some of the classic mainland Spanish dishes widely available include paella (saffron rice cooked with chicken and rabbit or with seafood – at its best with good seafood), tortilla (omelette), gazpacho (a cold, tomato-based soup usually available in summer only), various *sopas* (soups) and *pinchos morunos* (kebabs).

Todos los Mojos de Canarias by Flora Lilia Barrera Álamo and Dolores Hernández Barrera is a book to look out for if you get hooked on mojo (salsa sauce). The various recipes, which will let you practise your skills when you get back home, are to be treasured.

Dining in the Canary Islands

Breakfast *(desayuno)* is usually a simple meal, with juice, coffee or tea, cereal or *gofio*, and toast with ham or cheese. Many hotels serve heartier, German-style breakfasts. Locals may have a simple coffee at home and then have a midmorning *bocadillo* (baguette sandwich) when out. Breakfast can be served up until around 10am.

The serious eating starts with lunch *(la comida* or, less commonly, *el almuerzo)*. While Canarios tend to eat at home with the family, there is plenty of action in the restaurants too, starting at about 1pm and continuing until 4pm. In many restaurants, a set-price *menú del día* (see the boxed text, below) is served at lunchtime.

Dinner is served late, from about 9pm until 11pm (perhaps later on weekends). If you turn up for dinner mid-evening, you'll be eating alone – if the restaurant is even open. Of course, in the most popular tourist areas the restaurants cater for the strange habits of foreigners, but you'll be unlikely to see a single Canario dining in them. At-home dinners tend to be light for locals, but on weekends and special occasions they eat out with gusto.

Snacks are an important part of the Spanish culinary heritage. You can usually pick up a quick bite to eat to tide you over until the main meal times swing around. Standard snacks (or *meriendas*) include tapas and *bocadillos*. Typically, this will be a rather dry affair with a slice of *jamón* (ham) and/or *queso* (cheese), or a wedge of *tortilla española* (potato omelette).

> Potatoes were introduced to the Canary Islands from Peru in the 1600s, and connoisseurs identify at least 23 varieties.

Desserts

Canarios have a real sweet tooth. Some of the better-known sticky sweets are *bienmesabes* (a kind of thick, sticky goo made of almonds and honey – deadly sweet!), *frangellos* (a mix of cornmeal, milk and honey), *tirijaras* (a type of confectionery), *bizcochos lustrados* (a type of sponge cake) and *turrón de melaza* (molasses nougat).

Don't miss the *quesadillas* from El Hierro – they've been making this cheesy cinnamon pastry (sometimes also made with aniseed) since the Middle Ages. *Morcillas dulces* (sweet blood sausages), made with grapes, raisins and almonds, are a rather odd concoction; perhaps the closest comparison is the Christmas mince pie.

DRINKS
Coffee

The Canary Islanders like coffee strong and bitter, then made drinkable with thick sweetened condensed milk. It takes some getting used to, and many visitors consider the coffee here downright vile.

A *café con leche* is about 50% coffee, 50% hot milk; ask for *sombra* if you want lots of milk. A *café solo* is an espresso (short black); *café cortado* (or just *cortado*) is an espresso with a splash of milk. If you like your coffee piping hot, ask for any of the above to be *caliente*.

MENÚ DEL DÍA

The travellers' friend in the Canary Islands, as in mainland Spain, is the *menú del día,* a set meal available at most restaurants for lunch and occasionally in the evening too. Generally, you get a starter (salad, soup or pasta) or side dish followed by a meat, fish or seafood dish and a simple dessert, which can include local specialities (see Desserts, above) or Spanish favourites such as *flan* (crème caramel), *helado* (ice cream) or a piece of fruit. Drinks and coffee may or may not be included.

There are some local variations on the theme: *cortado de condensado* is an espresso with condensed milk; *cortado de leche y leche* is the same with a little standard milk thrown in. It sometimes comes in a larger cup and is then called a *barraquito*. You can also have your *barraquito con licor* or *con alcohol,* a shot of liquor usually accompanied by a shred of lemon and sometimes some cinnamon – this is the authentic *barraquito,* as any Canario will tell you. In the easternmost islands you may be asked if you want your milk *condensada* or *líquida.*

For iced coffee, ask for *café con hielo:* you'll get a glass of ice and a hot cup of coffee to be poured over the ice – which, surprisingly, doesn't all melt straight away.

Wine

The local wine-making industry is relatively modest, but you can come across some good drops. Wine comes in *blanco* (white), *tinto* (red) or *rosado* (rosé). Prices vary considerably. In general, you get what you pay for and can pick up a really good tipple for about €5.

One of the most common wines across the islands is the *malvasía* (Malmsey wine, also produced in Madeira, Portugal). It is generally sweet *(dulce),* although you can find the odd dry *(seco)* version. It is particularly common on La Palma.

Tenerife is the principal source of wine, and the red Tacoronte Acentejo was the first Canarian wine to earn the grade of DO *(denominación de origen;* an appellation certifying high standards and regional origin). This term is one of many employed to regulate and judge wine and grape quality. Other productive vineyards are in the Icod de los Vinos, Güímar and Tacoronte areas of Tenerife. In Lanzarote, the vine has come back into vogue since the early 1980s, and in late 1993 the island's *malvasías* were awarded a DO.

The La Dorada brewing company makes a thoroughly local beer from *gofio* called Volcan.

Beer

The most common way to order a beer *(cerveza)* is to ask for a *caña,* which is a small draught beer *(cerveza de barril* or *cerveza de presión).* La Dorada, brewed in Santa Cruz de Tenerife, is a very smooth number. Tropical, which is produced on Gran Canaria and is a little lighter, is a worthy runner-up and the preferred tipple of the eastern isles.

Spirits

Apart from the mainland Spanish imports, which include the grape-based *aguardiente* (similar to schnapps or grappa), *coñac* (brandy) and a whole host of other *licores* (liqueurs), you could try some local firewater if you come across it. One to try is *mistela* from La Gomera, a mixture of wine, sugar, rum and sometimes honey – a potent taste!

WHERE TO EAT & DRINK

Café culture is a part of life here, and the distinction between cafés and bars is negligible; coffee and alcohol are almost always available in both.

Bars take several different forms, including *cervecerías* (beer bars, a vague equivalent of the pub), *tabernas* (taverns) and bodegas (old-style wine bars). Variations on the theme include the *mesón* (traditionally a place for simple home cooking).

Sitting inside rather than on the outdoor terrace can often save you 10% to 20% of the bill. Inside or outside, you should leave a tip, simply rounding up if the bill is very small, but leaving up to 10% in a nice place.

Restaurants generally open for lunch and dinner, from 1pm to 4pm and then 9pm to midnight, unless they have a bar attached, in which case they

The Best of Canary Island Cooking, produced by the Centro de la Cultura Popular Canaria, is a great little volume that is readily available at various shops around the islands in a number of languages.

may be open right through the day. Most restaurants close one day per week and advertise this fact with a sign in the window.

VEGETARIANS & VEGANS

The Canary Islands may seem like paradise to some, but they can be more like purgatory for vegetarians, and worse still for vegans. This is meat-eating country, so you will find your choices (unless you self-cater) a little limited. Salads are OK, and you will come across various side dishes such as *champiñones* (mushrooms, usually lightly fried in olive oil and garlic). Other possibilities include *berenjenas* (aubergines), *menestra* (a hearty vegetable stew), *espárragos* (asparagus), *lentejas* (lentils) and other vegetables that are sometimes cooked as side dishes.

Restaurants that cater particularly well for vegetarians are noted in this book with a Ⓥ.

EATING WITH KIDS

Eating with children is no hassle in the Canary Islands. Places will often include a children's menu (especially in tourist resorts) at a very reasonable price (say, €6 for a burger with chips or portion of spaghetti). Children are treated with a mix of indulgence and respect – like special little adults, really. Many rural or isolated places will not have highchairs, although tourist resorts will be able to accommodate them and set them up for you at the table. All the usual baby-food products are readily available at the supermarkets and pharmacies.

EAT YOUR WORDS

Want to know the difference between a *salchida* and a *salchichón*? Get behind the cuisine scene by getting to know the foodies' language. For pronunciation guides, see the Language chapter (p266).

Useful Phrases

Table for..., please.
oo·na *me*·sa *pa*·ra..., por fa·*vor*   Una mesa para..., por favor.
Can I see the menu please?
pwe·do ver el me·*noo*, por fa·*vor*   ¿Puedo ver el menú, por favor?
Do you have a menu in English?
tye·nen oon·a *kar*·ta en een·gles   ¿Tienen una carta en inglés?
What is today's special?
kwal es el *pla*·to del *dee*·a   ¿Cuál es el plato del día?
What's the soup of the day?
kwal es la *so*·pa del *dee*·a   ¿Cuál es la sopa del día?
What do you recommend?
ke me re·ko·*myen*·da   ¿Qué me recomienda?
I'll try what she/he's having.
pro·*ba*·ray lo ke e·lya/el es·*ta* ko·*myen*·do   Probaré lo que ella/él está comiendo.
What's in this dish?
ke een·gre·*dyen*·tes tye·ne es·te *pla*·to   ¿De qué es este plato?
Can I have a (beer) please?
oo·na (ser·*ve*·sa) por fa·*vor*   ¿Una (cerveza) por favor?
Is service included in the bill?
el ser·*vee*·syos es·ta een·kloo·ee·do en la *kwen*·ta   ¿El servicio está incluido en la cuenta?
Thank you, that was delicious.
moo·chas *gra*·syas, es·*ta*·ba bwe·*nee*·see·mo   Muchas gracias, estaba buenísimo.
The bill, please.
la *kwen*·ta, por fa·*vor*   La cuenta, por favor.

I am a vegetarian.
    soy ve·khe·ta·*rya*·na/o   *Soy vegetariana/o.*
Do you have any vegetarian dishes?
    tye-nen al-*goon pla*-to ve-khe-ta-*rya*-no   *¿Tienen algún plato vegetariano?*
I'm allergic to ...
    ten-go a·lair·*jee*·ya a   *Tengo alergía a ...*

Food Glossary

Deciphering a menu in the Canaries is always tricky. However much you already know, there will always be dishes and expressions with which you're not familiar. The following list should help you with the basics at least.

PESCADO & MARISCOS (FISH & SHELLFISH)

almejas	al·*me*·khas	clams
anchoas	an·*cho*·as	anchovies
atún	a·*toon*	tuna
bacalao	ba·ka·*lao*	salted cod
bonito	bo·*nee*·to	tuna
boquerones	bo·ke·*ro*·nes	raw anchovies pickled in vinegar
calamares	ka·la·*ma*·res	squid
cangrejo	kan·*gre*·kho	crab
gambas	*gam*·bas	shrimps
langostinos	lan·gos·*tee*·nos	large prawns
lenguado	len·*gwa*·do	sole
mejillones	me·khee·*lyo*·nes	mussels
ostra	*os*·tra	oyster
pez espada	pes es·*pa*·da	swordfish
pulpo	*pool*·po	octopus
vieira	vee·*ey*·ra	scallop

CARNE (MEAT)

cabra	*ka*·bra	goat
cerdo	*ser*·do	pork
chorizo	cho·*ree*·so	spicy red cooked sausage
conejo	ko·*ne*·kho	rabbit
cordero	kor·*de*·ro	lamb
hígado	*ee*·ga·do	liver
jamón	kha·*mon*	ham
lomo	*lo*·mo	pork loin
pato	*pa*·to	duck
pavo	*pa*·vo	turkey
riñón	ree·*nyon*	kidney
salchicha	sal·*chee*·cha	fresh pork sausage
salchichón	sal·chee·*chon*	peppery cured white sausage
sesos	*se*·sos	brains
vacuno	va·*koo*·no	beef

FRUTAS & NUECES (FRUIT & NUTS)

aceituna	a·sey·*too*·na	olive
aguacate	a·gwa·*ka*·te	avocado
almendras	al·*men*·dras	almonds
cacahuete	ka·ka·*we*·te	peanut
cereza	se·*re*·sa	cherry
fresa	*fre*·sa	strawberry
lima	*lee*·ma	lime

limón	lee-*mon*	lemon
mandarina	man-da-*ree*-na	tangerine
manzana	man-*sa*-na	apple
melocotón	me-lo-ko-*ton*	peach
naranja	na-*ran*-kha	orange
piña	*pee*-nya	pineapple
plátano	*pla*-ta-no	banana
sandía	san-*dee*-a	watermelon
uva	*oo*-va	grape

HORTALIZAS (VEGETABLES)

calabacín	ka-la-ba-*seen*	zucchini, courgette
cebolla	se-*bo*-lya	onion
champiñones	cham-pee-*nyo*-nes	mushrooms
espárragos	es-*pa*-ra-gos	asparagus
espinaca	es-pee-*na*-ka	spinach
guisante	gee-*san*-te	pea
haba	*a*-ba	broad bean
lechuga	le-*choo*-ga	lettuce
lentejas	len-*te*-khas	lentils
pimiento	pee-*myen*-to	pepper, capsicum
puerro	*pwe*-ro	leek
zanahoria	sa-na-o-rya	carrot

TARTAS & POSTRES (CAKES & DESSERTS)

flan	flan	crème caramel
galleta	ga-*lye*-ta	biscuit, cookie
helado	e-*la*-do	ice cream
pastel	pas-*tel*	pastry, cake
torta	*tor*-ta	round flat bun, cake
turrón	too-*ron*	almond nougat

TÉCNICAS (COOKING TECHNIQUES)

a la brasa	a la *bra*-sa	to barbecue
a la plancha	a la *plan*-cha	grilled
al horno	al *or*-no	baked
asar	a-*sar*	to roast
frito	*free*-to	fried
rebozado	re-bo-*sa*-do	battered
relleno	re-*lye*-no	stuffed

Drinks Glossary

CAFÉ (COFFEE)

café con leche	ka-fe kon *le*-che	50/50 coffee and hot milk
café cortado	ka-fe kor-*ta*-do	short black with a splash of milk
café solo	ka-fe *so*-lo	a short black
café con hielo	ka-fe kon *ye*-lo	iced coffee

REFRESCOS (SOFT DRINKS)

agua potable	a-*gwa* pot-*ab*-le	drinking water
agua mineral	a-*gwa* mee-ne-*ral*	bottled water
con gas	kon gas	fizzy
sin gas	sin gas	still
batido	ba-*tee*-do	flavoured milk drink/milk shake
zumo de naranja	*soo*-mo de na-*ran*-kha	orange juice

VINO (WINE)

blanco	*blan*·ko	white
de la casa	de la *ka*·sa	house
rosado	ro·*sa*·do	rosé
tinto	*teen*·to	red

CERVEZA (BEER)

botellín	bo·tel·*yin*	bottled
caña	ka·*nyah*	draught
jarra	*kha*·ra	in a pint glass

OTHER ALCOHOLIC DRINKS

aguardiente	a·*gwa*·*dyen*·te	grape-based spirit (similar to schnapps or grappa)
coñac	ko·*nyak*	brandy
licor	*lee*·kor	liqueur
ron	ron	rum
sangría	san·*gree*·a	a wine and fruit punch usually laced with red wine

Gran Canaria

Gran Canaria is the third-largest island in the Canaries archipelago but accounts for almost half the population. It lives up to its cliché as a continent in miniature, with a dramatic variation of terrain, ranging from the green and leafy north to the mountainous interior and desert south. This is a rare Canary Island where you feel that there are still secret places to explore.

To glean a sense of this impenetrable quality, head to the centre where the sheer drama of the mountains more resembles the Tibetan highlands than a relatively small island. Alas, all too frequently, the perception of Gran Canaria is one of mass beach-front tourism, with few visitors ever discovering the riches of the natural hinterland. Considering this diversity in landscape, the good news is that, with your own wheels, you can get a reasonable look at the entire island in just three days or so, while the trip is equally feasible, if more time-consuming, by bus.

The flip side to all that bucolic mountainous terrain is a rugged coastline interspersed with white sandy beaches and, more famously (and depressingly), a garish tiara of purpose-built holiday resorts. Fortunately, there's no need to hang around. For active travellers Gran Canaria can keep the adrenalin pumping, with scope for hiking, horse trekking and water sports. Culture vultures can be similarly satiated by the museums, churches and historic towns, as well as by getting under the skin of the colourful, cosmopolitan capital of Las Palmas de Gran Canaria.

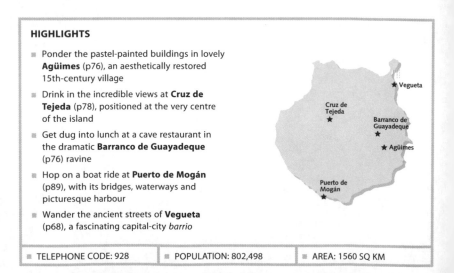

HIGHLIGHTS

- Ponder the pastel-painted buildings in lovely **Agüimes** (p76), an aesthetically restored 15th-century village
- Drink in the incredible views at **Cruz de Tejeda** (p78), positioned at the very centre of the island
- Get dug into lunch at a cave restaurant in the dramatic **Barranco de Guayadeque** (p76) ravine
- Hop on a boat ride at **Puerto de Mogán** (p89), with its bridges, waterways and picturesque harbour
- Wander the ancient streets of **Vegueta** (p68), a fascinating capital-city *barrio*

■ TELEPHONE CODE: 928   ■ POPULATION: 802,498   ■ AREA: 1560 SQ KM

ITINERARY 1
KIDS' GRAN CANARIA

Gran Canaria is a kiddie wonderland with plenty of natural, manufactured or theme-parked stuff to do. The beaches are the most obvious attraction, and those in the southern resorts come complete with all variety of boat rides. In Puerto Rico you can go dolphin spotting with **Spirit of the Sea** (**1**; p89). Further west in **Taurito** (**2**; p89), the whole place resembles a family-themed park with several pools (and pool tables) plus all variety of amusements geared towards kids and accommodating grown-ups. Theme parks are prolific in these parts, particularly around **Playa del Inglés** (**3**; p83), where you can choose from camel rides, zoos, water parks, Wild West shows and a few more things besides. On a more highbrow note, even the most museum-jaded tot cannot fail to be impressed by the model galleons at the **Casa/Museo de Colón** (**4**; p68), in Las Palmas, with its colourful Columbus history. For a more hands-on, how-the-hell-does-it-work experience, tag after the school trips at the superb **Museo Elder de la Ciencia y la Tecnología** (**5**; p71) science museum, also in the island's capital.

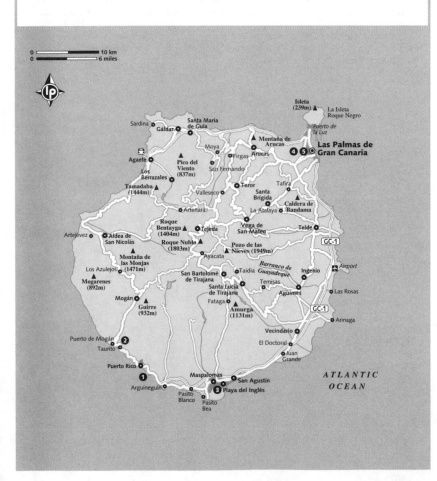

ITINERARY 2
GRAN CANARIA OUTDOORS

This island offers some fabulous activities, ranging from strolling through fragrant pine forests to adrenalin-charged mountain biking and diving. Lace up those trainers and inhale the sea breezes on Las Palmas' lovely 3km *paseo marítimo* (seaside promenade), hugging the golden sands of the **Playa de las Canteras (1**; p71). For a lofty experience, head for **Roque Nublo (2**; p78) a four-million-year-old rock that is the remains of an ancient volcano. You can hike the circuit, or park nearer the peak, which cuts the puffing and panting to around half the time. (Rock climbing is also popular here, with several routes of varying levels of difficulty). Aside from these, Gran Canaria has 32 protected natural areas and is cobwebbed with paths and signposted trails.

Water sports are the athletic biggie on the island, particularly windsurfing, with Gran Canaria considered one of the top international destinations for surfing the breeze. A suitably blustery beach is **Pozo Izquierdo (3**; p85). Diving, sailing and deep-sea fishing are also widely available, particularly in the southern resorts. Check the activity sections in the respective destinations. Kite boarders may want to consider ferrying over to Fuerteventura and **Playa de Sotavento de Jandía (4**; p113) with its 22km of white sand and perfect leeward winds for this rapidly growing sport.

Cycling the interior of Gran Canaria can be challenging; this is hilly terrain. Pedal power can be more fun when you are sweating it out (or competing!) with others; a whizzo choice for organising tours is **Free Motion (5**; p86) in Playa del Inglés.

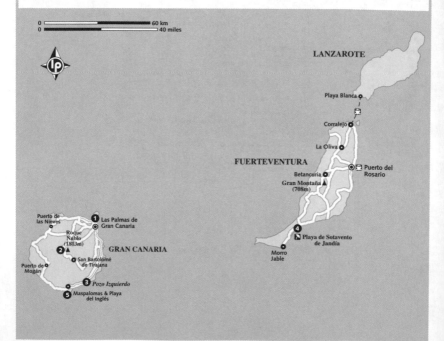

HISTORY

Gran Canaria was known to its original inhabitants as Tamarán, linked to the Arabic name for date palms *(tamar)*, whereas the Romans christened the island Canaria (see the boxed text, p62).

Conquest began in earnest in 1478 with the landing of a Spanish force led by Juan Rejón. Despite beating off a furious counter-attack by Doramas, the *guanarteme* (chief) of the island's Telde kingdom, Rejón was supplanted by Pedro de Vera, who stayed put for the following five years. The turning point was the conversion of the Guanche chief, Tenesor Semidan, to Christianity. In April 1483 he convinced the islanders to surrender.

The island was soon colonised by a ragtag assortment of adventurers and landless hopefuls from as far away as Galicia, Andalucía, Portugal, Italy, France, the Low Countries and even Britain and Ireland.

Initially, the island boomed from sugar exports and transatlantic trade between Spain and the Americas. But, as the demand for Canary Islands sugar fell and the fortunes of wine grew, the island declined before its main rival and superior wine grower, Tenerife. It was not until the late 19th century that Gran Canaria recovered its position.

To this day the two islands remain rivals and, between them, are home to most of the islands' permanent populace.

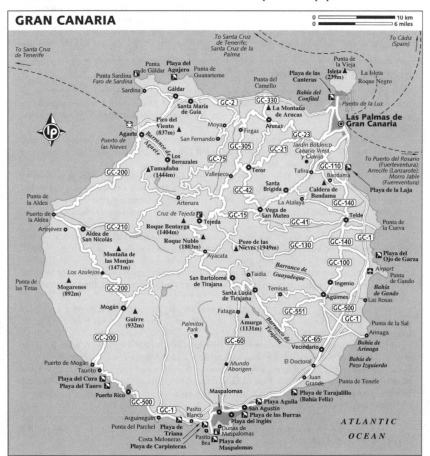

GRAN CANARIA

INFORMATION
Books & Maps
An excellent map is *Gran Canaria*, published by Distrimapas Telstar, containing accurate city maps of Las Palmas, Maspalomas, Playa del Inglés and various other towns.

Michelin map No 220 *Gran Canaria* can be found in souvenir and bookshops throughout the island.

Discovery Walking Guides produces two titles for hikers: *Gran Canaria Mountains Walking Guide* and *Gran Canaria South & Mountains Walking Guide*, both written by DA Brawn.

Landscapes of Gran Canaria by Noel Rochford includes walks, car tours and picnic sites.

Newspapers
The most widely read local newspapers on Gran Canaria and the two most eastern islands are *Canarias 7* and *La Provincia* (www .laprovincia.es).

Of the English-language weeklies, *Island Connections* – on sale at newsagents but available free from most tourist offices – is the most widely distributed. Another freebie is *Round Town News* (RTN), a fortnightly paper with plenty of what's-on information.

ACCOMMODATION
Las Palmas and the southern coastal resorts have plenty of accommodation, although many hotels in the latter tend to get block-booked by tour companies. Among the top recommendations is Hotel Madrid (p72) in the old part of Las Palmas and the most delightful budget choice on the island. Only marginally more expensive, but exuding wheelbarrows full of rustic elegance, the Hotel Rural Casa de los Camel-

---

DOGS, BIRDS & PURPLE PROSE

To the ancient Greeks, the fabled islands beyond the Pillars of Hercules (today's Straits of Gibraltar) were known as the Atlantes, after the daughters of Atlas whom Hercules supposedly visited. Long thought to be filled with fruit trees, the islands were also often referred to as the Garden of Hesperides.

The Romans, who apparently never set foot on the islands, knew them as the Insulae Fortunatae (Fortunate Isles). The Spaniards, when they set about conquering them in the 15th century, also began by calling them the Islas Afortunadas.

Juba II, the North African king who informed Pliny the Elder about the islands, referred to them as the Insulae Purpuriae (Purple Isles), due to the purple dyes extracted from the orchid lichens on Fuerteventura and Lanzarote. The Guanches (the islands' original inhabitants) had their own names for the islands, including Gomera (La Gomera) and Hero (El Hierro), which are basically preserved to this day.

Why Canaria? One improbable tale tells of a Latin couple, Cranus and Crana, who, while out adventuring, bumped into what is now Gran Canaria (as you do) and liked it so much they stayed. They dubbed the island Cranaria, later simplified to Canaria.

Another theory suggests the name was inspired by the trilling canary birds, thought by some to be native to the islands. However, most ornithologists claim the bird took the name from the islands rather than vice versa.

Others reckon the name came from the Latin word for dog *(canus)* because members of Juba's expedition discovered what they considered unusually large dogs. Still others held that the natives of the island were dog eaters!

Unsurprisingly, probably none of these fanciful solutions is near the mark. A more plausible theory claims that the people of Canaria, who arrived several hundred years before Christ, were in fact Berbers of the Canarii tribe living in Morocco. The tribal name was simply applied to the island and later accepted by Pliny. How Canaria came to be Gran (Big) has a couple of predictably feeble explanations: either because the islanders put up a big fight while resisting conquest, or the island was thought to be the biggest in the archipelago.

Equally unclear is at precisely what point the islands came to be known collectively as Las Islas Canarias, although this probably came with the completion of the Spanish conquest of the islands at the end of the 15th century.

PLAIN SAILING

In the 1880s, when Puerto de la Luz (Las Palmas) was developing as a port, merchant and passenger ships had to moor some way from the docks. A quasi-rowing boat–cum-yacht was developed to ferry people and goods from ship to shore.

Like any business, these little *botes* (boats) suffered both busy and slack times. During the latter, their captains and crews organised regattas in the port area. This idea, born to ease the boredom of long days before Sudoku, eventually developed into a regular competition, and the tradition continues.

Eighteen of these curious craft remain today and regularly gather for an afternoon's racing on Saturday (usually from 5pm) and Sunday (around noon) from April to October. Crewed by eight to 12 people, each boat represents a district of Las Palmas.

Apart from the odd appearance of the participating vessels, the race itself is delightfully eccentric in that competitors race only *en bolina* (against the wind), but in such a way as to get maximum power from it. The fact that the prevailing wind remains pretty much the same off the east coast of Gran Canaria makes it the ideal spot for such races. The *botes* start at Playa de la Laja, a few kilometres south of the southern suburbs of Las Palmas, and finish at Playa de Alcaravaneras.

---

los (p76) is located in one of the island's prettiest towns. Another gem is Teror, and the warm hospitality at lovely colonial-style Casa Rural Doña Margarita (p80). At the other end of the design scale is the stylishly modern Palm Beach (p87), designed in stunning retro-chic style. Topping the lot for setting, with its surround of palm plantations, Hacienda del Buen Suceso (p80) is just gorgeous.

For something a thousand metaphorical miles from the package-tour resorts, consider renting a *casa rural* (country house). Check the **Acantur** (www.ecoturismocanarias.com) website or contact **Gran Canaria Rural** (☎ 928 46 25 47; www.grancanariarural.com), **AECAN** (☎ 922 24 08 16; www.aecan.com) or **RETUR** (☎ 928 66 16 68; www.returcanarias.com). For overall accommodation, log onto www.lonelyplanet.com/accommodation.

ACTIVITIES

Many visitors come to flop on the beach and relax, but if you're looking for something more active, there is ample potential (see p60). Pozo Izquierdo (p85), on the southeastern coast, has demanding, world-class windsurfing, while Maspalomas (p83) and Playa de las Canteras (p71) are popular for kite boarding and have more gentle waves. **Zoco Boardriding Adventures** (www.zocoboardriding.com) organises windsurfing and kite-boarding camps for beginners and more experienced enthusiasts.

There are several diving and deep-sea-fishing outfits in the southern resorts, while landlubbers can bike or trek, independently or in a guided group. Details are provided under specific towns.

Eurotrekking (☎ 928 14 11 87; www.trekkingcanarias .com) also organises excellent half-day hikes twice a week with a minimum of six people.

Thalassotherapy

This fashionable health treatment, based on warmed-up sea water, is designed to relieve stress and other more physical aches and pains. Whether or not it works (some of its claims for cellulite control seem a little bit dubious), it is still a sensual experience in its own right and often does wonders for skin ailments. There are centres throughout the island, including at the Hotel Puerto de las Nieves (p82), the Hotel Gloria Palace (p85) near Playa del Inglés and at the magnificent Villa del Conde (p87) in Maspalomas.

FESTIVALS & EVENTS
February–March

Carnaval Celebrated throughout the island, but particularly in Las Palmas. Three to four weeks of madness and fancy dress mark the first rupture with winter in February (the dates move depending on when Lent falls), with the bulk of the action taking place around Parque de Santa Catalina.

GRAN CANARIA

Festival del Sol (mid-February) A gay and lesbian film festival that takes place in Las Palmas and Playa de Inglés simultaneously.

June
Fiesta de San Juan (23 June) Las Palmas festival to honour the city's patron saint. Cultural events are staged across the city, while fireworks and concerts take place on Playa de las Canteras.
Corpus Christi This feast with movable dates takes place around June and is marked by the laying out of extraordinary floral 'carpets' in some of Las Palmas' historic old streets.

August
Fiesta de la Rama (around 4 August) Takes place in Agaete, with origins that lie in an obscure Guanche rain dance. Nowadays, locals accompanied by marching bands parade into town brandishing tree branches and then get down to the serious business of having a good time.

September
Fiesta de la Virgen del Pino (first week of September) The Virgin is the patron of the island and Teror is the religious capital. The festival is not only a big event in Teror, it's the most important religious feast day on the island's calendar.

GETTING THERE & AWAY
Air
Along with the two airports on Tenerife, Gran Canaria's **Gando airport** (☎ 928 57 91 30), 16km south of Las Palmas, is the biggie in the islands. From here, there are connections to all other islands, as well as regular flights to mainland Spain and beyond.

Binter Canarias (☎ 902 39 13 92; www.binternet .com) flies between Gran Canaria and Tenerife Norte (30 minutes, five daily), Tenerife Sur (30 minutes, twice daily), La Palma (50 minutes, three daily), El Hierro (45 minutes, two daily), La Gomera (40 minutes, twice daily), Fuerteventura (35 minutes, 11 daily) and Lanzarote (40 minutes, nine daily).

Islas Airways (☎ 902 47 74 78; www.islasairways .com) has flights to Fuerteventura (35 minutes, two daily) and Tenerife Norte (35 minutes, two daily).

Iberia (www.iberia.com) has six flights daily to Madrid, while **Spanair** (www.spanair.com) has three and **Air Europa** (www.aireuropa.com) has five. Iberia and Spanair fly daily to Barcelona.

At the airport, there's a tourist office on the ground floor (open whenever flights arrive), car-rental offices, a post office, a

pharmacy (☺ until 10pm) and money-changing facilities (including a Western Union representative). Disabled access is good.

Boat
Ferries and jetfoils link Gran Canaria with Tenerife, Lanzarote and Fuerteventura, using Las Palmas and Agaete ports. See the Getting There & Away sections under each port for more details and p260 for details of the ferry to/from Cádiz (mainland Spain).

GETTING AROUND
To/From the Airport
Taxis and buses service the airport and cover the whole island. See individual town listings for further details.

Bus
Blue, turquoise or green **Global** (☎ 902 38 11 10; www.globalsu.net in Spanish) buses provide the island with a network of routes, although the service to many rural areas is pretty thin. In Las Palmas, yellow municipal buses provide an efficient citywide service.

Car
Car rental is abundant and can work out very economical if you book in advance. All the usual international companies have representation at the airport. An excellent choice is **Cicar** (Map p66; ☎ 928 27 72 13; Calle Nicolas Estevanez 18, Las Palmas; www.cicar.com), with offices throughout Gran Canaria and cars from €35 a day.

Taxi
Taxis are plentiful, especially in Las Palmas and tourist resorts. Fares are more than reasonable for local trips, but soon clock up if you're travelling longer distances.

LAS PALMAS DE GRAN CANARIA

pop 376,953

Las Palmas has a mainland-Spain feel, spiced up with an eclectic mix of other cultures, including African, Chinese, and Indian, plus the presence of container-ship crews and the flotsam and jetsam that tend to drift around port cities. It's an intriguing place with the sunny languor and energy you would normally associate with the Mediterranean or North Africa. The hooting taxis, bustling shopping districts, chatty bars and thriving port all give off the energy of a city: Spain's seventh largest.

Vegueta, the oldest quarter and declared a Unesco World Heritage site in 1990, is both atmospheric and fashionable; many of the best bars and restaurants are here. At the other end of town, the sweeping arc of Playa de las Canteras is a lot cleaner than many city beaches and provides you with the tantalising possibility of having a plunge in between your sightseeing and shopping. Above all, Las Palmas is an authentic Spanish working city that doesn't warrant its somewhat seedy image. Sure, like any port, there are areas where you wouldn't walk at night with an expensive camera slung round your neck but, overall, you should feel perfectly safe here and the city is well-deserving of at least a couple of days of exploration.

HISTORY

Although Jean de Béthencourt's partner in mischief, Gadifer de la Salle, sailed past here in 1403, it wasn't until 1478 that Europeans actually landed in the area. That year Juan Rejón and his troops set up camp just south of La Isleta, naming it Real de las Palmas. As the conquest continued, the original military

---

FOOD & DRINK

Local cuisine is renowned for making use of every part of the *cochino* (pig). That cute, curly tail, or *templero,* was traditionally hung from the kitchen doorway to be periodically dipped into the cooking pot as a stock. A typical tapa here, generally accompanied by the traditional rum aperitif, is *caracajas* (pieces of fried pork liver doused in a spicy sauce). Goat is also popular, along with rabbit and veal, while seafood is, naturally enough, always a good bet – this is an island, after all. Try the much-prized *vieja* (parrot fish), a member of the sea-bream family, plus, if it's included on the menu, the local crustacean *santorra,* which is similar in appearance to the common lobster but has a distinctive rich (some would say, gourmet) flavour.

Goats' cheese is produced on several islands, though one of the best known soft cheeses, Gran Canaria's *queso de flor,* is made from a combination of cows' and sheep's milk. The cheese, which is produced exclusively in the northern Guía area, is then infused with the aroma of flowers from the *cardo alcausí* thistle. Another scrumptious winner is the similarly tasting *pastor* cheese, produced in the Arucas region.

The towns and villages are the scene of some interesting small markets, most of which sell local cheeses, cold meats and bakery goods, as well as local souvenirs and trinkets. They make for an easy-going morning away from the bustle of the resorts. Markets generally last from 9am to 2pm and include the following:

- **Puerto de Mogán** (Friday) One of the most touristy.
- **San Fernando** (Wednesday and Saturday)
- **Arguineguin** (Tuesday and Thursday)
- **Teror** and **Vega de San Mateo** (Saturday and Sunday)
- **San Bartolomé de Tirajana** (Sunday)

Among the outstanding Gran Canaria wines is the fruity Del Monte, a perfect, if tiddly, accompaniment to meat dishes with an alcohol content over 11.5%. Aside from *ron miel* (honey rum), which is more liqueur than rum, try the banana-based *cobana,* also produced in Gran Canaria. ¡Salud!

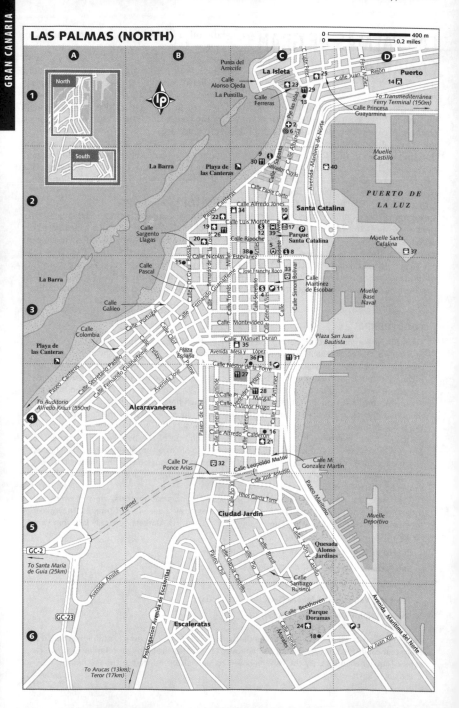

LAS PALMAS (NORTH)

0   400 m
0   0.2 miles

INFORMATION		
French Consulate.................................1 C4	Museo Elder de la Ciencia y la	Natural Burguer.............................31 C3
Inter Clinic.......................................2 C1	Tecnología...................................17 C2	
Netherlands Consulate......................3 D6	Museo Néstor ....(see 18)	ENTERTAINMENT
Office Services.................................4 C3	Pueblo Canario.............................18 C6	Casino las Palmas....................(see 24)
Police Station...................................5 C2		Estadio Insular.............................32 B4
Teleminutos.....................................6 C1	SLEEPING	Pacha..33 C3
Tintorería Avenida............................7 C3	Apartamentos Playa Dorada............19 B2	
Tourist Information Kiosk...................8 C2	Aparthotel Las Lanzas....................20 B2	SHOPPING
Tourist Information Kiosk...................9 C2	Hostal Fallow................................21 C4	Boxes & Cigars.............................34 C2
Tourist Office...........................(see 18)	Hotel Concorde............................22 B2	El Corte Inglés Department
UK Consulate..................................10 C1	Hotel Imperial Playa......................23 C1	Store...35 C3
US Consulate..................................11 C3	Hotel Santa Catalina......................24 C6	El Corte Inglés Department Store........36 C3
Viajes Insular..................................12 C2	Hotel Tenasoya.............................25 C1	
		TRANSPORT
SIGHTS & ACTIVITIES	EATING	Acciona - Trasmediterránea Ferry
7 Mares Las Canteras........................13 C1	Casa Pablo...................................26 B2	Terminal....................................37 D2
Castillo de la Luz.............................14 D1	Covered Market.............................27 C4	Cicar...38 C2
Gran Canaria School of Languages......15 B3	El Olivo.......................................28 C4	Fred Olsen Bus for Agaete.............39 C2
Lavy Sub..16 C4	Mesón Condado............................29 C1	Naviera Armas Ferry
	Molinet.......................................30 C2	Terminal....................................40 C2

camp expanded into the *barrio* (district) of San Antonio Abad, later known as Vegueta.

By the time Christopher Columbus sailed by on his way to the Americas in 1492, the busy little hub of the old town had already been traced out. Everybody likes to claim a hero for their very own and the Gran Canarian version of history has it that Columbus briefly stopped here for repairs before pushing on to La Gomera.

Las Palmas grew quickly as a commercial centre and, in recognition of its importance, the seat of the bishopric of the Canary Islands was transferred here from Lanzarote in the mid16th century.

The city, along with the rest of the archipelago, benefited greatly from the Spanish conquest of Latin America and subsequent transatlantic trade. But, inevitably, the islands became a favourite target for pirates and buccaneers. In 1595 Sir Francis Drake raided Las Palmas with particular gusto. Four years later a still more determined band of Dutch adventurers reduced much of the town to ruins.

In 1821, Santa Cruz de Tenerife was declared capital of the single new Spanish province of Las Islas Canarias. This left the great and good of Las Palmas disgruntled but redress was some time in coming.

The fortunes of the port city fluctuated with those of the islands as a whole, as boom followed bust in a chain of cash-crop cycles. However, towards the end of the 19th century Las Palmas began to prosper, due to the growing British presence in the city.

The Miller and Swanston trading families were already well established by the time Sir Alfred Lewis Jones set up the Grand Canary Coaling Company in Las Palmas. The city flourished as a crucial refuelling stop for transatlantic shipping, which continued until just before the outbreak of WWII, when coal-fired ships gradually made way for more modern vessels.

It was the British who introduced the first water mains, electricity company and telephone exchange in the early 20th century. The city's prosperity had become such that Madrid could no longer resist calls for the islands to be divided into two provinces. Las Palmas thus became capital of Gran Canaria, Fuerteventura and Lanzarote in 1927.

It was from Las Palmas that Franco launched the coup in July 1936 that sparked the Spanish Civil War.

Since the 1960s tourism boom, Las Palmas has grown from a middling port city of 70,000 to a bustling metropolis of close to 400,000 people. And, while it shares the status of regional capital evenly with Santa Cruz de Tenerife, there is no doubt that Las Palmas packs the bigger punch in terms of influence and size.

ORIENTATION

Las Palmas stretches from the historical centre in the south, centred on the Vegueta and Triana districts, up a series of long boulevards towards bustling Santa Catalina and the port, Puerto de la Luz – a good 3km. From there, it continues up to what was once an islet off the island, still called La Isleta.

The most interesting sights are concentrated in Vegueta, while the heavier, more international action is around Santa Catalina. The bulk of the hotels are here, close to the 3km-long golden sands of Playa de las Canteras, plus the bars, shops and port.

Maps

El Corte Inglés (p75) department store produces a good city map, which is readily available at hotels. For bus routes, pick up the local public-transport map, *Guaguas Municipales* (yellow cover), available at tourist offices, which also produce their own city map.

INFORMATION
Bookshops

Librería del Cabildo Insular de Gran Canaria (Map p70; ☎ 928 38 15 39; Calle Travieso 15) Stocks lots of titles about the Canary Islands. Most are in Spanish but there are a few shelves of English guides (including Lonely Planet) and similar.

Emergency

Police station (Map p66; ☎ 928 44 64 00; Parque Santa Catalina) Just west of the tourist office.

Internet Access

Teleminutos (Map p66; ☎ 928 22 30 22; Paseo Canteras 66; per hr €2; ⓣ 10am-10pm)

Laundry

There are loads of laundries where you can leave a pile of washing and collect it the next day.

Tintorería Avenida (Map p66; ☎ 928 24 42 67; Calle Nestor de la Torre; per load around €6; ⓣ 8.30am-1.30pm & 4-8pm Mon-Fri, 9-11am Sat) Near Plaza de España.

Medical Services

Inter Clinic (Map p66; ☎ 928 27 88 26; Calle Sagasta 62) A 24-hour clinic with an ambulance service and multilingual practitioners, including dentists and surgeons, and is savvy on the international insurance front.

Money

Office Services (Map p66; Calle Martínez de Escobar 5) Represents Western Union and also has an office at the airport.

Viajes Insular (Map p66; ☎ 928 22 79 50; Calle Luis Morote 9) Represents American Express.

Post

Main post office (Map p70; ☎ 928 36 21 15; Avenida Primero Mayo 62)

Tourist Information

Bus station information office (Map p70; ☎ 928 36 83 35; Estación San Telmo, Parque San Telmo; ⓣ 6.30am-8.30pm Mon-Fri, 7.30am-1pm Sat & Sun) Great for island-wide transport and general info.

Main tourist office (Map p70; ☎ 928 21 96 00; Calle León y Castillo 17; ⓣ 8am-3pm Mon-Fri) Has island-wide information.

Tourist information kiosk (Map p70; Parque San Telmo; ⓣ 10am-8pm Mon-Fri, 10am-3pm Sat)

Tourist information kiosk (Map p66; Playa de las Canteras; ⓣ 10am-7.30pm Mon-Fri, 10am-1pm Sat)

Tourist information kiosk (Map p66; Parque Santa Catalina; ⓣ 9am-2pm Mon-Fri)

Tourist office (Map p66; Pueblo Canario, Ciudad Jardin; ⓣ 9am-2.30pm Mon-Fri)

DANGERS & ANNOYANCES

Las Palmas is the largest city in the islands, as well as a major port, so it does have a mildly seamy side, particularly around the docks. That said, it has clearly had a scrub-up of late and there is no reason for you to feel particularly threatened, provided you take the standard city precautions and don't stand in dark alleys late at night waving maps and money. Similarly, don't leave anything of value in your car, especially a rental.

Parque San Telmo and Parque Santa Catalina are safe enough in daylight, though you can expect a fair quota of down-and-outs, which increases after dark. If hookers with attitude hanging around in doorways are your type of scene, head for Calle Molinos de Viento, a block west of Calle León y Castillo. Otherwise, it's best to avoid this louche zone.

SIGHTS
Vegueta & Triana

This is the most historic and architecturally rich city district. Take the time to stroll the streets, ducking into the atmospheric bars and restaurants along the way (see p73).

CASA/MUSEO DE COLÓN

This **museum** (Map p70; ☎ 928 31 23 73; Calle Colón 1; admission free; ⓣ 9am-7pm Mon-Fri, to 3pm Sat & Sun) is a superb example of Canarian architecture, built around two balconied patios, complete with fountains, palm trees and parrots. The exterior is a work of art itself, with some showy *plateresque* (silversmithlike) elements combined with traditional heavy wooden balconies.

Although called Columbus' House (it's possible he stopped here to present his credentials to the governor in 1492), most of what you see dates from the time this was the opulent residence of Las Palmas' early governors.

The museum's four sections include fascinating accounts of Columbus' voyages, the Canary Islands role as a staging post for transatlantic shipping, pre-Columbian America and the city of Las Palmas. Don't miss the model galleon on the ground floor. Upstairs is an art gallery with some striking canvases from the Hispanic-Flemish school.

CATEDRAL DE SANTA ANA & MUSEO DIOCESANO

The city's brooding, grey **cathedral** (Map p70; ☎ 928 33 14 30; Calle Obispo Codina 13; ☺ 10am-5pm Mon-Fri, to 2pm Sat) was begun in the early 15th century, soon after the Spanish conquest, but took 350 years to complete. The neoclassical façade contrasts with the interior, which is a fine example of what some art historians have denominated Atlantic Gothic. The retable above the high altar comes from Catalunya (mainland Spain) and the exquisite lamp hanging before the altar was made in Genoa (Italy). The cathedral also displays several paintings by Juan de Miranda, the islands' most respected 18th-century artist.

The **Museo Diocesano** (Map p70; ☎ 928 31 49 89; Calle Espíritu Santo 20; admission €3; ☺ 10am-5pm Mon-Fri, to 2pm Sat) is set on two levels around the Patio de los Naranjos, once home to The Inquisition. It contains a fairly standard collection of religious art and memorabilia, including centuries-old manuscripts, wooden sculptures and other ornaments.

You can also access the cathedral's **tower** (admission €1.50; ☺ 10am-4.30pm Mon-Fri, to 1.30pm Sat) if you fancy a stunning and wide-ranging view of the surrounds from the city to the coast.

IGLESIA DE SAN ANTONIO ABAD

Just behind the Casa/Museo de Colón, heading towards the waterfront, this small **church** (Map p70; Plaza San Antonio Abad 4) of modest Romanesque-Canarian design is where, according to tradition, Columbus prayed for divine help before sailing for the Americas.

MUSEO CANARIO

The island's main **museum** (Map p70; ☎ 928 33 68 00; www.elmuseocanario.com; Calle Dr Verneau 2; adult/under 12/concession €3/free/1.20; ☺ 10am-8pm Mon-Fri, to 2pm Sat & Sun) chronicles Gran Canaria's preconquest history. It claims the heady boast of having the largest collection of Cro-Magnon skulls in the world. There are also several mummies, plus a collection of pottery and other Guanche implements from across the island. The gift shop stocks some excellent children's educational material.

CENTRO ATLÁNTICO DE ARTE MODERNO

The city's main **museum of modern art** (CAAM; Map p70; ☎ 902 31 18 24; www.caam.net; Calle Balcones 11; admission free; ☺ 10am-9pm Tue-Sat, to 2pm Sun) hosts some superb temporary exhibitions, while its permanent collection focuses on 20th-century art from both Canarian and international artists. The museum is housed in a tastefully rejuvenated 18th-century building, which is flooded with natural light. Local artists include Eduardo Gregorio, Santiago Santana and César Manrique.

GABINETE LITERARIO

This sumptuously ornate **historical building** (Map p70; Plazoleta Cairasco) was the island's first theatre and is a national monument. It's an old-world display of faded elegance, with a gracious interior patio and rooms lined with bookcases crammed with learned-looking volumes. The place now functions as a private club, although the pricey French restaurant (La Galeria) is open to all.

CALLE MAYOR DE TRIANA

This **street** (Map p70), now pedestrianised, has long been the main shopping street in Las Palmas. In between window shopping, look skyward to enjoy some real architectural gems, including several striking examples of modernism.

CASA/MUSEO DE PÉREZ GALDÓS

In 1843 the Canary Islands' most famous writer, Benito Pérez Galdós, was born in this **house** (Map p70; ☎ 928 36 69 76; Calle Cano 6; admission free; ☺ 9am-7pm Mon-Fri, 10am-5pm Sat, 10am-2pm Sun) in the heart of old Las Palmas. He spent the first 19 years of his life here before moving on to Madrid and literary greatness.

The house contains a reconstruction of the author's study, various personal effects and other objects related to his life. It is a delightful place with a pretty central courtyard. Guided tours take place hourly, but only in Spanish.

PARQUE SAN TELMO

The **Iglesia de San Telmo** (Map p70), on the southwestern side of the park, was one of the first religious buildings in town. Beside

GRAN CANARIA

LAS PALMAS (SOUTH)

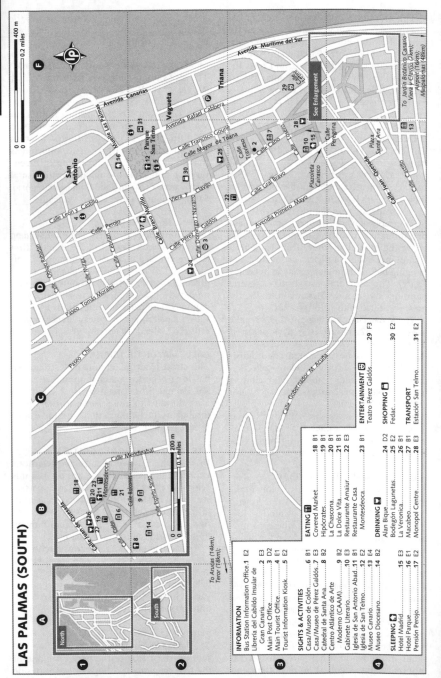

INFORMATION

Bus Station Information Office..1	E2
Librería del Cabildo Insular de Gran Canaria................2	E3
Main Post Office....................3	D2
Main Tourist Office.................4	E1
Tourist Information Kiosk..........5	E2

SIGHTS & ACTIVITIES

Casa/Museo de Colón..............6	B1
Casa/Museo de Pérez Galdós....7	E3
Catedral de Santa Ana............8	B2
Centro Atlántico de Arte Moderno (CAAM)............9	B2
Gabinete Literario.................10	E3
Iglesia de San Antonio Abad..11	B1
Iglesia de San Telmo.............12	E2
Museo Canario....................13	F2
Museo Diocesano.................14	B2

SLEEPING

Hotel Madrid......................15	E3
Hotel Parque.....................16	E1
Pensión Perojo...................17	E2

EATING

Covered Market..................18	B1
Hipócrates........................19	B1
La Chascona......................20	B1
La Dolce Vita.....................21	B1
Restaurante Amaiur...............22	E3
Restaurante Casa Montesdeoca...................23	B1

DRINKING

Alan Bique........................24	D2
Bodegón Lagunetas..............25	E2
La Verónica.......................26	B1
Macabeo..........................27	B1
Monopol Centre..................28	E3

ENTERTAINMENT

Teatro Pérez Galdós.............29	F3

SHOPPING

Fedac..............................30	E2

TRANSPORT

Estación San Telmo..............31	E2

it is a tourist information kiosk and, in the northwestern corner, a beautiful modernist **kiosk**, which these days functions as an ice-cream stall and open-air *terraza* (terrace).

Ciudad Jardín

This leafy, upper-class suburb is an eclectic mix of architectural styles, ranging from British colonial to whitewashed Andalucian. Also here is lovely Parque Doramas with its fine *dragos* (dragon trees; see the boxed text, p42). The park was designed by the British towards the end of the 19th century, when the UK dominated the economic life of Las Palmas.

PUEBLO CANARIO

Designed by artist Néstor Martín Fernández de la Torre, and built by his brother Miguel, the **Pueblo Canario** (Map p66) borders the gardens of the Parque Doramas. With a restaurant, central plaza, handicraft shops and children's playground, it is designed as a pleasant bit of escapism in a quasitraditional Canarian village.

MUSEO NÉSTOR

This **art gallery** (Map p70; ☎ 928 24 51 35; Pueblo Canario; adult/student €2/free; ☻ 10am-8pm Tue-Sat, 10.30am-2.30pm Sun) is dedicated to the works of symbolist painter Néstor, who died in 1938, and includes a modest collection of works by fellow Canarian artists.

Santa Catalina

Santa Catalina is an intriguing mix of city beach, multicultural melting pot, edgy port and business hub. At times you'll feel like you're in the developing world; at other times you're firmly in mainland Spain.

PLAYA DE LAS CANTERAS

The fine 3km stretch of yellow, sandy **beach** lies a few hundred metres west of the centre, creating a holiday-resort border to the city. There's an attractive *paseo marítimo* (seaside promenade) – the Paseo Canteras – which allows walkers, cyclists, joggers and rollerbladers to cover the entire length of the beach, free from traffic. The whole area hums with the activity of bars, restaurants, nightclubs and shops.

MUSEO ELDER DE LA CIENCIA Y LA TECNOLOGÍA

This 21st-century **museum of science and technology** (Map p66; ☎ 928 01 18 28; www.museoelder .org; Parque Santa Catalina; adult/under 18yr €3.50/2.50; ☻ 11am-9pm Tue-Sun) is full of things that whirr, clank and hum. It occupies a revamped docks' warehouse to the east of Parque Santa Catalina and is a great space to spend a few hours. Children will be rapt at some of the displays – a space pod, interactive chromakey screen and graphic depiction of a baby's birth – while adults may be equally fascinated by the 'how the internet functions' exhibit.

CASTILLO DE LA LUZ

Built in the 16th century to ward off pirate attacks, this **castle** (Map p66) is a venue for art exhibitions, but was closed for restoration at the time of research.

Jardín Botánico Canario Viera y Clavijo

About 9km southwest of the city, just before the village of Tafira Alta, this vast **botanical garden** (Map p61; ☎ 928 35 36 04; admission free; ☻ 9am-6pm) – Spain's largest, encompassing 27 hectares – hosts a broad range of Macronesian flora from all seven Canary Islands, including many species on the verge of extinction.

Buses 301, 302 and 303 all pass by the garden's upper entrance. By car, take the C-811 road from Las Palmas.

ACTIVITIES
Surfing

Playa de las Canteras is not the world's greatest surf break but you can catch some good waves, and plenty of locals are out here at the weekend. You'll need your own board.

Diving

7 Mares Las Canteras (Map p66; ☎ 928 26 27 86; www .7mares.es; Calle Tenerife 12; 1hr dive €29, 2hr initiation dive €60) has English-speaking diving instructors and offers courses at all levels, plus wreck dives and equipment rental.

Lavy Sub (Map p66; ☎ 928 23 25 30; Calle Alfredo Calderón 20) offers similar.

LANGUAGE COURSES

The **Gran Canaria School of Languages** (Map p66; ☻ 928 26 79 71; www.grancanariaschool.com; Calle Dr Grau

GRAN CANARIA

Bassas 27) offers intensive courses from €127 per week. It has a good reputation and has been in business for more than 40 years. Lodging may also be arranged.

SLEEPING

The bulk of the accommodation is around Santa Catalina beach and the port.

Vegueta & Triana

BUDGET

Pensión Perojo (Map p70; ☎ 928 37 13 87; Calle Perojo 1; s/d without bathroom €17/26) A late-19th-century building with grand old doors and high ceilings, and the scrupulously clean rooms washed in pale peach. The management is young and energetic, and the only downside is its position on an intersection that cops the full brunt of the peak-hour-traffic noise.

ourpick Hotel Madrid (Map p70; ☎ 928 36 06 64; fax 928 38 21 76; Plazoleta Cairasco 4; s/d €30/40, without bathroom €25/30) Thoroughly recommended, this place has almost as much charm as history: General Franco spent the night of 17 July 1936 in room No 3 here (and reputedly left without paying!). The next day he flew to Spain and the rest is history: his dictatorship governed the country for 40 years. Run by a couple of enthusiastic brothers, the interior is a beguiling mix of agreeable tat, priceless antiques and hanging plants. The rooms have an old-world feel with antique bed heads and china; No 1 has great plaza views. The downstairs bar and restaurant is atmospheric and generally crowded, though the menu is clearly geared for tourists and a tad overpriced.

MIDRANGE

Hotel Parque (Map p70; ☎ 928 36 80 00; www.hparque .com; Muelle Las Palmas 2; s/d with breakfast €68/79; P ⊠ ▯ ▧) This six-storey hotel is excellently positioned overlooking the Parque San Telmo, a short stroll from the historic Vegueta and Triana *barrios*. The best views are from the rooftop solarium and breakfast room. Rooms are large but dated, with floral curtains and a predominance of brown furnishings. More colour and style could make this a real winner, but for the moment we'll push the comfort rather than class.

Ciudad Jardín

TOP END

Hotel Santa Catalina (Map p66; ☎ 928 24 30 40; www .hotelsantacatalina.com; Calle León y Castillo 227; s/d €139/180;

P ⊠ ▯) At the heart of Parque Doramas, this historic hotel is truly magnificent with traditional Canarian balconies, showy turrets and a red-carpetstyle arcaded entrance. The rooms won't disappoint; there are king-size beds, antique bed heads, oriental carpets and plush furnishings. It exudes the class of another era, with its own casino and *hammam* (Turkish bath) and delightful views of either the sea or subtropical gardens.

Santa Catalina & the Port

BUDGET

Hostal Fallow (Map p66; ☎ 928 23 48 94; Calle Alfredo Calderón 25; s/d without bathroom €15/18, s/d with bathroom €20/22) A pretty turquoise building with basic clean rooms on a quiet, mainly residential street. Romancing couples be warned, the makeshift bathrooms have separating walls that don't reach the ceiling.

Aparthotel Las Lanzas (Map p66; ☎ 928 26 55 04; fax 928 26 55 08; Bernardo de la Torre 79; s/d with breakfast €36/45, 2-person apt €50) This place is comfortably homey. The apartments are well kitted-out with a breakfast bar, small fridge and thoughtful extras like a bread board and bottle opener. The bedrooms could do with a few splashes of colour, but the sitting room is pleasant enough, overlooking a quiet pedestrian street.

MIDRANGE

Apartamentos Playa Dorada (Map p66; ☎ 928 26 51 00; fax 928 26 51 04; Calle Luis Morote 69; apt for 1-2 people €60, 3-4 people €75) This place has space, lots of it, from the vast lobby to the apartments, which have enough kitchen cupboards for a family of four. There are plenty of cosy touches like clocks, baby mobiles and a jolly tablecloth. The bedrooms have a spare-room feel, with murals and colourful bedspreads.

Hotel Tenesoya (Map p66; ☎ 928 46 96 08; fax 928 46 02 79; Calle Sagasta 98; s/d/t €60/71/82) The colourful lobby and downstairs sitting area are boldly decorated with a combination of burgundy and canary-yellow colouring accentuated by bright, abstract paintings and fresh flowers. The bedrooms are roomy and light-filled; get your money's worth by going for one with a terrace and sea view.

Hotel Concorde (Map p66; ☎ 928 26 27 50; www.hotel concorde.org; Calle Tomás Miller 85; s/d €115/157; P ⊠ ▧) Constantly being updated, this is one of the city's time-tested hotels, dating back to the '60s and popular with German guests. The rooms have panoramic sea views, with quality marble-and-honey-coloured timber fittings. There's a rooftop pool.

TOP END

Hotel Imperial Playa (Map p66; ☎ 928 46 88 54; www.nh-hoteles.com; Calle Ferreras 1; s/d €125/175; P 🏊 🖳 🏄) The lobby here sets the tone with its black tubular lamps, chocolate-brown paintwork, sage green sofas and chairs and a magnificently quirky version of Velázquez' *Las Meninas* executed in colourful tiles. The rooms are perfectly co-ordinated with their striped navy blue–and-white curtains and fabrics coupled with cool, pale parquet floors. The terraces overlook the harbour.

EATING

The choice of restaurants in Las Palmas reflects its stylish big-city feel. For the most atmosphere, head to the Vegueta and Triana *barrios*. If you are after Asian cuisine, there are plenty of Japanese and Chinese restaurants (and supermarkets) around Calle Valencia, southwest of Plaza España.

Vegueta & Triana

La Dolce Vita (Map p70; ☎ 928 31 04 63; Calle Agustín Millares 5; mains €5-10; 🕒 closed Sun; V) The home-made pasta here is the real thing and the décor is fun, with Italian film posters papering the walls.

Hipócrates (Map p70; ☎ 928 31 11 71; Calle Colón 4; mains €6-9; 🕒 closed Mon; V) Across from Casa/Museo de Colón, in an old cottage, this charming vegetarian restaurant has a generous €9 *menu del día*, sparkling green-and-white décor and a small patio, complete with a bubbling fountain. All the vegetarian mainstays are here, including seitan kebabs, vegetarian lasagne and imaginative salads.

La Chascona (Map p70; ☎ 928 33 34 35; Calle Pelota 15; mains €7-10; V) This restaurant has the lot: cutting-edge design, innovative food, young, fashionable staff and even super-stylish loos. Try the healthy *cazuelita de verduras salteadas* (a casserole of briskly steamed vegetables), made with market-fresh veg seasoned to perfection.

Restaurante Amaiur (Map p70; ☎ 928 37 07 17; Calle Pérez Galdós 2; mains €12-17; 🕒 closed Mon) Next to a 19th-century palace, this special-occasion place is of similar vintage with elegant dining rooms, parquet floors and high ceil-

ings. Dishes like peppers stuffed with codfish, monkfish with prawns, and caviar should placate the most discerning gourmet.

Restaurante Casa Montesdeoca (Map p70; ☎ 928 33 34 66; Calle Montesdeoca 10; mains €14-18; 🕒 closed Sun) A romantic restaurant set in an exquisite 16th-century house. Dine in the gorgeous, leafy patio with its traditional wooden balconies and sunny, yellow walls. Any of the meat or seafood dishes can be recommended.

Santa Catalina & the Port

our pick **Natural Burguer** (Map p66; ☎ 928 29 78 67; Avenida Mesa y López 3; mains €2.50-2.75; V) South of Santa Catalina, this eco-McDonald's burger joint is justifiably popular with budget-seekers and students. Veggie burgers with a choice of toppings are on the menu, as well as the regular beef burgers (although you are penalised with a white bun rather than wholemeal). Extras include watercress salad, corn on the cob and *papas del abuelo* (thick-cut potato chips). Go all out with a papaya-and-guava juice on the side.

Mesón Condado (Map p66; ☎ 928 46 94 43; Calle Ferreras 22; mains €5-15) This better-than-decent, middle-of-the-road (décor-wise) restaurant serves up a combination of Galician food from northwestern Spain, Canarian fare and more mainstream Spanish dishes. A very satisfying *menú del día* (set menu) will set you back a piffling €6 or so.

Casa Pablo (Map p66; ☎ 928 26 81 58; Calle Tomás Miller 73; mains €9-41; 🕒 closed Mon; P) A grand old restaurant with a knight in armour lording it over the front door. Plenty of Spanish celebrity pics adorn the walls to leave you in no doubt that this is *the* place to come in Las Palmas for solid traditional cuisine. You can be a lightweight with an excellent tapas menu if you prefer.

El Olivo (Map p66; ☎ 928 24 49 08; Calle Pi y Margal 10; mains €12-16; 🕒 closed Sun) This stylish restaurant is well worth seeking out. There are just four tables in the tiny dining room, which has a minimalist green-and-yellow décor. Think pyramids, drizzle and *nouvelle* taste sensations. Reservations essential.

Molinet (Map p66; ☎ 928 26 30 19; Paseo Canteras 6; mains €13-15) Italian-owned, the wine-red-and-black interior is as original as the menu, which includes ostrich with a muscatel sauce. Or go for a home-style dish like fresh pasta topped with *porcini* mushrooms. There are outside tables overlooking the beach.

GRAN CANARIA

Self-Catering

For the freshest and cheapest produce check out the covered markets: the best are located between Calles Barcelona and Néstor de la Torre (Map p66) and on the corner of Calle Mendizabal and Calle Juan de Quesada (Map p70) in Vegueta.

DRINKING
Bars & Pubs

There is no shortage of watering holes in Las Palmas. There are popular *terrazas* on Plaza España (Map p66) and lining Parque Santa Catalina (Map p66), and both are good for a day or dusk drink. The Vegueta area, with its low-key ambience, is the most fashionable place for a night-time tipple.

Macabeo (Map p70; ☎ 928 32 17 28; Calle La Pelota 15) This place oozes atmosphere and style with its cavernous interior decorated with intriguing childlike drawings and shelves of dusty bottles. A second, smaller bar with dim lighting and stone walls is perfect for locked-eyes-over-cocktails time.

La Veronica (Map p70; ☎ 928 33 34 35; Calle La Pelota 18; closed Sun) The sort of place you would go to before swishing off for a night at the opera. It's sophisticated and stylish, with natural stone, arty giant photos and an interesting, iridescent emerald-green light behind the bar, which sounds awful but somehow works.

Bodegón Lagunetas (Map p70; ☎ 928 36 30 94; Calle Constantino 16) One of several tapas bars on this street, this one also has a restaurant. Hang out in the bar with a *caña* (beer) and enjoy the fascinating sepia-photo exhibition of late-19th-century Las Palmas.

Alan Bique (Map p70; Avenida Primero Mayo 57; 9pm-3am Tue-Sat) Easy to miss, so look for the Mahou beer sign. This place has a chill-out setting and attracts effortlessly stylish regulars.

One great entertainment space is the **Monopol Centre** (Map p70; La Plazuela), which has a cinema, *terrazas*, bars and small clubs. Our favourite is the Lounge Bar, which doesn't get going until after midnight, but has funky DJ sounds and a spacey, industrial vibe.

ENTERTAINMENT
Late-Night Bars & Discos

The late-night bars and discos are mostly in the area around Santa Catalina beach and Puerto de la Luz. Drinks cost around €5.

Pacha (Map p66; ☎ 928 27 16 84; Calle Simón Bolivar 3; 11pm-5.30am) Part of the Pacha empire and a super-cool place to see and be seen, the club attracts a slightly more mature crowd than the usual bump-and-grind discos.

Live Music

You can enjoy free performances of Canarian folk music in the Pueblo Canario (p71) every Sunday morning from about 11.30am.

Classical Music & Opera

Auditorio Alfredo Kraus (Map p66; ☎ 928 49 17 70; www.auditorio-alfredokraus.com; Avenida Principe de Asturias) A spectacular auditorium, designed by the Catalan architect Óscar Tusquets, and striking in its geometric modernity. Constructed partly of volcanic rock, with a huge window with broad ocean views, it is the dominant feature of the southern end of Playa de las Canteras. This is one of the venues for the annual summer **Jazz Festival** (www.canariasjazz.com).

Theatre

Teatro Pérez Galdós (Map p70; ☎ 928 36 15 09; www.teatroperezgaldos.es; Calle Letini 1) has some theatrical performances and more frequent music recitals.

Casino las Palmas

If you feel like a flutter, don the glad rags, grab your passport and head for the **casino** (Map p66; ☎ 928 23 39 08; www.casinolaspalmas.com; 8pm-4am) within the city's prestigious Hotel Santa Catalina (p72), built in 1904 in the heart of Parque Doramas.

Football

The **Union Deportiva de Las Palmas** (UD; www.udlaspalmas.net in Spanish) is Gran Canaria's premier football team. To see it in action, join the throng heading for the 20,000-seat **Estadio Insular** (Map p66; ☎ 928 24 09 10; Calle Pio XII).

SHOPPING

Fedac (Foundation for Ethnography & the Development of Canarian Handicrafts; Map p70; ☎ 928 36 96 61; Calle Domingo J Navarro 7) Head to this government-sponsored, nonprofit store for handicrafts, including pottery, baskets and leather work.

Boxes & Cigars (Map p66; ☎ 928 41 16 50; Calle Tomás Miller 80) If it's cigars you're after, this place has a dazzling range on offer, with the boxes just about as attractive as the smokes.

The long-time traditional shoppers' street is Calle Mayor de Triana (Map p70), which is as interesting for its architecture as its idiosyncratic shops. Other recommended shopping strips include Calle Cano, Calle Viera y Clavijo and the surrounding streets.

Las Palmas' super-chic shoppers' hang-out is Avenida Mesa y López (Map p66). Here you'll find the mammoth department store **El Corte Inglés** (Map p66; ☎ 928 26 30 00; Avenida Mesa y López 15 & 18), as well as numerous shops and boutiques. Nearby, around Parque Santa Catalina, there are plenty of cheap electronic-goods and discount shops with great deals on cameras, watches, computer equipment and mobile phones.

GETTING THERE & AWAY
To/From the Airport
Bus 60 runs between the airport and Estación San Telmo (Map p70) twice hourly between 7am and 7pm and hourly thereafter (€1.90, 25 minutes), continuing onto Santa Catalina (€2.40, 35 minutes). A taxi between the airport and central Las Palmas costs about €20.

Boat
For details of the weekly ferry to/from Cádiz (mainland Spain), see p260.

The quickest way to Santa Cruz de Tenerife is by **Acciona-Trasmediterránea** (Map p66; ☎ 902 45 46 45; www.trasmediterranea.com) ferry (€51, one hour 20 minutes), which departs at least twice daily.

For a bus/ferry combination to Santa Cruz de Tenerife with Fred Olsen, see p82. The Fred Olsen bus (Map p66) for Agaete leaves from Parque Santa Catalina.

Trasmediterránea ferries (€40, seven hours, three weekly) serve Puerto del Rosario on Fuerteventura, while a Friday service (from €47, five hours) heads for Arrecife on Lanzarote at 8am.

Naviera Armas (Map p66; ☎ 928 26 77 00; www .navieraarmas.com) has a daily ferry (€42, 3¾ hours) at 7.10am (2pm on Sunday) to Morro Jable on Fuerteventura, 12 weekly (€24, two hours, 45 minutes) to Santa Cruz de Tenerife, two weekly (€32, 6½ hours) to Puerto del Rosario and a daily ferry (€40, 7¼ hours) to Arrecife at 11.50pm.

Bus
Estación San Telmo (Map p70; ☎ 902 38 11 10; www.glo balsu.net in Spanish; Parque San Telmo) is located at the northern end of the Vegueta district and can provide an island-wide schedule.

Buses 30 and 44 (€5.50, about 50 minutes) go express to Maspalomas, buses 91 and 1 (€7.50, two hours) to Puerto de Mogán, buses 12 and 80 (€1.10, about 20 minutes) to Telde and buses 103 and 105 (€2.50, one hour) to Santa María de Guía and Gáldar. There are frequent services to all these destinations.

The night-owl bus 5 links the capital and Maspalomas. It leaves on the hour, from 8pm to 3am, from Estación San Telmo station in Las Palmas, and on the half-hour, from 9.30pm to 4.30am, from Maspalomas. If you plan to travel much outside Las Palmas, economise with a Tarjeta Insular (see the boxed text, p64).

Car
There are many car rental firms at the airport, at the jetfoil terminal and scattered across the Santa Catalina district.

GETTING AROUND
Bus
Yellow buses serve the metropolitan area. Pick up a route map from the tourist office, kiosks or the bus station.

The Tarjeta Insular (see the boxed text, p64) also works on urban routes, saving around 30%. A standard single ticket, bought on the bus, costs €1.

Yellow buses 1, 12, 13 and 15 all run from Triana northwards as far as the port and the northern end of Playa de las Canteras, calling by the bus station and Parque Santa Catalina.

For €8.50 (free for children under four) you can buy a ticket giving you unlimited hop-on-hop-off travel for one day on the **Guagua Turística** (Tourist Bus; ☎ 928 30 58 00; www .guaguas.com). It departs from Parque Santa Catalina irregularly 12 times daily and is an excellent way of getting an initial overview of the city.

Car
Driving in Las Palmas is a pain, with the normal big-city rush-hour traffic jams and a baffling one-way street system. Most of the centre operates meter parking. Otherwise, there are several private car parks, where you pay around €2 per hour.

Taxi
If you need a **taxi** (☎ 928 46 00 00, 928 46 56 66, 928 46 22 12), you can call, flag one down or head for one of the plentiful taxi stands across the city.

AROUND LAS PALMAS

Charming as Las Palmas is, it is still a noisy and chaotic city. Thankfully, if you are seeking some more mellow surroundings, you won't have far to travel.

Starting from Las Palmas, an enjoyable one-day circuit heads first south and then cuts inland to take in the mountainous Tejeda region before swinging northeast back towards the capital.

TELDE
pop 104,900

Telde is the island's second city and, although generally bypassed by tourists, the historic centre has all the cobblestone charm of Vegueta, once you look beyond the gloomy industrial surroundings. The city was founded before the Spanish conquest, by monks from Mallorca seeking to set up a bishopric in the Fortunate Isles, and is known for its production of string instruments, above all the *timple* (a kind of ukulele) – the islands' musical emblem.

The **tourist office** (☎ 928 13 90 55; Calle León y Castillo 2; ☼ 8am-3pm Mon-Fri) is just off Plaza de San Juan.

Among the grand old houses of the San Juan area is the 15th-century **Basílica de San Juan.** You can't miss the gloriously kitsch 16th-century altarpiece, all gilt and gold, with a Crucifixion at its heart. The Christ figure is made from a corn-based plaster (nothing to do with toes!) by Tarasco Indians in Mexico.

The **Museo León y Castillo** (Calle León y Castillo 43; admission free; ☼ 8am-2pm Mon-Fri) is devoted to the city's most famous resident, a late-19th-century politician. The building, his former home, is lovely but the exhibits may fail to thrill.

More interesting for most is the short walk to the **Iglesia de San Francisco**. From the Plaza San Juan, take cobbled Calle Inés Chanida west as it runs alongside an old aqueduct with orange and banana groves below. In the church, note the three polychrome stone altars on the northernmost of the twin naves and the fine *artesonado* (coffered ceiling).

Buses 12, 80 and 86 (€1.35, about 20 minutes, every 20 minutes) run to/from Las Palmas.

INGENIO & AGÜIMES

A short bus ride south of Telde brings you to the towns of Ingenio and Agüimes, separated from each other by the Barranco de Guayadeque (below). Ingenio is best known for its ceramics but, otherwise, is a plain Jane compared to its neighbour.

The historic centre of Agüimes is one of the most perfectly restored and prettiest on the island; so much so that the mega-luxury hotel Villa del Conde (p87) in Maspalomas is a pastiche of the old town centre. Agüimes' helpful **tourist office** (☎ 928 12 41 83; www.aguimes.es; Plaza de San Antón 1; ☼ Mon-Fri 8am-3pm) has plenty of local information.

Sights

The pedestrian streets are lined with superb examples of vernacular Canarian architecture; they surround shady Plaza del Rosario. The **Iglesia de San Sebastián** (☼ 9.30am-12.30pm & 5-7pm Tue, Thu, Sat & Sun), with its dome of 12 large windows (symbolising the 12 apostles), is considered one of the best examples of Canarian neoclassicism. The **Centro de Interpretación** (Plaza de San Antón 1; ☼ Mon-Fri 8am-3pm) shares the tourist-office building and has well-documented exhibits on the evolution of the town's urban structure through the centuries.

Sleeping & Eating

Hotel Rural Casa de los Camellos (☎ 928 78 50 53; www.hecansa.com; Calle Progreso 12; s/d €51/70) A lovely place that doubles as a catering school, so the restaurant (in a former camel stable) is worth staying in for. The rooms are elegant yet rustic, with antiques and wooden beams and balconies.

El Populacho (☎ 928 78 41 51; Plaza de Rosario 17; tapas €2.50; ⓥ) On the corner of the main square, this atmospheric tapas bar is housed in a former grocer's shop (1933), as depicted in the lively murals that cover the walls.

Getting There & Around

A number of buses connect the two towns with Telde and Las Palmas. From Agüimes, bus 22 (€1.10, 20 minutes, hourly) heads southeast to Arinaga, a popular coastal swimming spot even though it lacks a real beach.

BARRANCO DE GUAYADEQUE

The Barranco de Guayadeque (Guayadeque Ravine) rises up into central Gran Canaria in a majestic sweep of crumpled ridges. For most of the year, the vegetation here is lush and green; if you can, visit in early spring when the almond trees are in blossom and the landscape is stunningly verdant and beautiful. At the entrance of the *barranco*, the **Centro de Interpretación** (☎ 928 78 37 99; admission €2.40; ✆ 9am-5pm Tue-Sat, 10am-6pm Sun) is built into a cave and includes exhibits and explanations on the original inhabitants, including a mummy found in a local cave in the 19th century.

Around 4km from here, watch for the inhabited caves with their quirky exteriors, and stop for a drink at **Bar Guayadeque** (☎ 928 17 22 12; Cueva Bermeja 23), housed in a cave next door to a tiny underground chapel. Continuing on, there is a picnic ground for self-caterers or a couple of evocative cave restaurants, including the excellent **El Centro** (☎ 928 17 21 45; mains €4-9) with its warren of dining rooms reaching deep into the cave. Try the *carne de cerdo frita con alioli de la casa* (fried pork with homemade garlic mayonnaise), which won first prize in a local culinary contest. This is a superb area for walking – continue until the road peters out by Restaurante Tagoror, from where there are a couple of trails and stunning views that stretch right to the sea.

TEMISAS

If you're driving, you can take a back road that weaves across the mountains from Agüimes to Santa Lucía de Tirajana. As the road approaches the tiny village of Temisas, set on a natural balcony, note the terracing up each side of the centre and incised into the valleys below. These terraces were worked until relatively recently. Then came mass tourism along with less-gruelling, better-paid work.

The impressive setting for Temisas, with its backdrop of impenetrable cliffs, has views across a ravine that falls away down to the sea. The village itself is sleepy and atmospheric, with original stone houses and cottages.

SANTA LUCÍA DE TIRAJANA

This village has a similarly attractive position to Temisas, positioned in the upper reaches of a palm-filled valley with gleaming white houses blinkered by traditional wooden shutters. It is also home to an extraordinary museum.

Don't be put off by the gaudy leaflets at the tourist office, the **Castillo de la Fortaleza** (☎ 928 79 80 07; admission €2), located on the main street at the entrance to the village, is well worth a stop. The miniature castle with its grey stone turrets was built around 50 years ago, not for tourism purposes but as a folly, as well as the home of local archaeologist, writer, artist and collector Vicente Sanchez Araña, who died in 1997, aged 77. The museum has 16 rooms that reflect the eclectic interests and energy of this veritable Renaissance man. The most impressive room houses a well-labelled (in several languages) archaeological display of Guanche artefacts found in nearby caves. These include a tiny carved female idol; a Guanche symbol and one of only two in the world (the other is exhibited in a museum in France). Another room displays ancient armaments, including a 16th-century crossbow, while still another concentrates on local botany. Upstairs there is an art gallery with some particularly impressive watercolours by Canarian artists. This labour of love is well worth the modest admission price.

Bus 34 (€2.60, 40 minutes, seven daily) connects Santa Lucía with San Bartolomé de Tirajana and El Doctoral.

SAN BARTOLOMÉ DE TIRAJANA

pop 3620 / elevation 850m

San Bartolomé has no notable sights, but the views out over the Tirajana valley are stunning and the town makes a good base for hiking and exploring the surrounding mountainous countryside – along with the endearing Germans and their hiking sticks. If you're planning a visit, make it on Sunday morning when there's a lively farmers' market.

La Hacienda del Molino (☎ 928 12 73 44; www.lahaciendadelmolino.com; Calle Los Naranjos 2; d from €80) is run by an enthusiastic young couple. The bar, restaurant and rooms have a warm, vernacular look with lots of wood and stone. There is also a restored mill where you can see how *gofio* is made and a more-up-to-date sitting room complete with plasma TV and plush white sofas and chairs.

German owned **Aldiana** (☎ 928 12 30 00; www.aldiana.de; Calle Oficial Mayor Jose Rubio s/n; s/d €65/130; Ⓟ ▣ ▨) has a mildly bizarre African-hunting-lodge look with its zebra-striped upholstery and mounted animal heads on the wall. The rooms are more mainstream luxurious, however, with four-poster bed, spa and DVD and video player – plus a spa and fitness centre. Located on a bluff above the town, there are spectacular views of San Bartolomé cupped by soaring mountains.

FATAGA

A 7km detour south from San Bartolomé brings you to the charming hamlet of Fataga, sitting squat on a small knoll humbled by lofty cliffs to the west. Its cobbled lanes are a joy to roam, especially as there are at least three bodegas in this vine-growing centre – all are well signposted but, less happily, all have sporadic opening hours.

About 1.5km north of the village, parts of **El Molino del Agua** (☎ 928 17 23 03; Carretera Fataga; s/d with breakfast €40/52) hacienda date back to the 16th century. Hidden among a grove of around 1000 palm trees, the accommodation is in simply furnished stone cabins with wicker chairs on the terraces and painterly views of orchards and distant mountains. The restaurant (mains from €7) has tables under the orange trees and a reasonable Canarian menu. The new owners have plans to introduce more activities, including hiking, and to restore the nearby namesake mill to full working order.

Located on the main road, **Bar Restaurante La Albericoque** (☎ 928 79 86 56; Calle Nestor Álamo 4; mains €5-7) has good local and international fare, including veal in breadcrumbs and filled jacket potatoes. The main draw, however, is the outside terrace with its wall-to-wall mountain views.

Bus 18 (€2.85, 50 minutes, four times daily) from Maspalomas to San Bartolomé stops here.

TEJEDA & AROUND

pop 2347 / elevation 1050m

Tejeda is 33km north of San Bartolomé, along a road that twists its way through splendidly rugged scenery of looming cliffs and deep gorges. It is a lovely hill village with a handsome church and steep, winding streets lined with balconied houses.

The gastronomic highlight in town is **Dulceria Nublo Tejeda** (☎ 928 66 60 30; Calle Hernández Guerra 15), a sublime pastry shop with delicious local treats freshly baked on the premises. Try the chestnut-and-almond cakes coated in chocolate and take home a jar of delicious *bienmesabe* (almond-and-honey spread).

If you want to stay in the area, the quaintly named Fonda de la Tea hotel and restaurant was on the verge of opening when

we visited; it is located on the main street, east of the church.

Cruz de Tejeda

The greenish-greyish stone cross from which this spot takes its name marks the centre of Gran Canaria and its historic *caminos reales* (king's highways), along which it is still possible to cross the entire island. The site is usually swarming with tourists, hence the souvenir stalls and donkey rides.

From the lookouts here you can contemplate the island's greatest natural wonders: to the west is the sacred mountain Roque Bentayga (below) and, in clear weather, the towering pyramid of Teide on Tenerife; to the southeast, the island's highest peak, Pozo de las Nieves (opposite), and the extraordinary emblem of the island Roque Nublo (1803m), which as often as not is enveloped in cloud. Dropping away to the northeast is Vega de San Mateo (opposite).

Walking here doesn't present any great challenges, but take water, dress warmly and leave the Jimmy Choos at home. Generally, you'll follow well-paved and signposted paths that snake their way around rock formations often obscured by cloud. The half-hour walk from Cruz de Tejeda to Roque Nublo is especially recommended. You can get information and tips from Hotel El Refugio (below).

Hotel Rural El Refugio (☎ 928 66 65 13; www.hotel ruralelrefugio.com; Cruz de Tejeda s/n; s/d €60/74; P ✗ ♨) is a cheery hotel that makes a great base for a few days' walking. It has rustic, comfortable rooms and a restaurant and bar that do a brisk business with sightseers.

Bus 305 (€3.20, two hours, five daily) from Las Palmas (via Santa Brígida and Vega de San Mateo) passes by on its way to Tejeda. From Tejeda you're better off with a bike or car, although bus 18 connects it to Las Palmas.

Roque Bentayga

A few kilometres west of Tejeda village rises the Roque Bentayga (1404m). It's signposted but you will need your own transport. Around the Roque and surroundings there are various reminders of the Guanche presence here – from rock inscriptions to granaries and a sacred ritual site.

Pozo de las Nieves

Those with their own wheels can drive 15km southeast of Tejeda to this, the highest peak on the island at 1949m. Follow the signs for Los Pechos and keep an eye on the military communications post that sits atop the rise. On a clear day the views are breathtaking. Due southwest of here stands the distinctive Roque Nublo.

VEGA DE SAN MATEO

Descending from the barren, chilly heights of Tejeda, the landscape shifts and changes and, as you approach San Mateo, the sweeping *vega* (plain) becomes a gently undulating sea of green. As with most of the northern strip of the island (especially the northeast), the area is busily cultivated and agriculturally rich, as well as an important vine-growing region.

This area is densely populated; most of the island's population lives in the north. The town is memorable mainly for its dramatic setting, along with the farmers' market held every Saturday and Sunday behind the bus station (just follow the shopping baskets). If you are here in September, try to come on the 21st for the *romería* (pilgrimage) and celebrations of the patron saint, St Matthew.

Bus 303 (€2, 30 minutes) comes up from Las Palmas every 30 minutes.

SANTA BRÍGIDA & CALDERA DE BANDAMA

En route to Las Palmas, the next town of any note is Santa Brígida, about 9km east of Vega de San Mateo. A rather drab place, it's lifted by a pretty park and narrow, tree-lined streets at its heart. There are sweeping views from the parish church over fields and palm groves to the central mountains. Stop at the **Casa del Vino** (☎ 928 64 42 45; Calle Calvo Sotelo 26; admission free; ☼ 10am-6pm Tue-Fri, to 3pm Sat & Sun) with its modest display of wine-making implements, plus the more entertaining option of tasting (and purchasing) local wines.

Back on the road to Las Palmas, after 4km, there's a turn-off for the **Caldera de Bandama**, one of the largest extinct volcanic craters on the island, 1km in diameter, with superb views. Close by is **La Atalaya**, the prime pottery-producing village on the island, where you can buy lovely ceramics, then stress about transporting them home.

Bus 311 (€1.25, 30 minutes) leaves virtually hourly from Las Palmas to the village of Bandama, passing through La Atalaya, which takes you close to the crater.

THE NORTH

As on most of the islands, Gran Canaria's fertile north presents a gently shifting picture from its rugged, mountainous interior and the southern beach resorts and dunes. Dramatic ravines, intensively tilled fields and terraces and forests of pine trees covered with mossy lichen typify the landscape as you wind along twisting roads and past myriad villages and hamlets. Only as you reach the west does the green give way to a more austere, although no less captivating, landscape: the west coast is the most dramatic on the island.

TEROR

pop 1095 / elevation 543m

In spite of its name, Teror, 22km southwest of Las Palmas, does anything but inspire fear. The central Plaza Nuestra Señora del Pino and Calle Real are lined with picturesque old houses with leaning walls and wooden balconies. The only jarring building is the new and modern Auditorio de Teror, just west of the basilica. Aesthetics aside, it has admirably provided the town with a new cultural venue. There's a farmers' market in the plaza on Saturday mornings with stalls selling wheels of local goat's cheese (ask for a taste). The Sunday market is larger and more commercial.

One of the loveliest houses is the 17th-century **Casa de los Patronos de la Virgen** (Plaza Nuestra Señora del Pino 3; admission €3; ☼ 11am-6pm Mon-Fri, 10am-2pm Sun). Pleasantly musty, this house is devoted to preserving 18th-century life and is full of intriguing odds and ends, mostly from the Las Palmas family who used it as a second home.

Dominating the square is the **Basílica de la Virgen del Pino** (☼ 8am-noon & 2-6pm), a neoclassical 18th-century church, and home to Gran Canaria's patron saint. According to legend, the Virgin was spied atop a pine tree in the nearby forest in the 15th century, which turned Teror into a quasi-Fatima pilgrimage site. The church interior, a lavishly gilt-laden affair, sees the enthroned

Virgen de la Nieve illuminated in her place of honour at the heart of a lavishly ornate altarpiece, surrounded by angels. It's a pity about the piped religious music, but the sign to turn off your mobile phone is spot on, stating that 'you don't need a mobile to talk to God'.

Sleeping & Eating

Casa Rural Doña Margarita (☎ 928 35 00 00; www.margaritacasarural.com; Calle Padre Cueto 4; 2-/4-person apt €75/120) A beautifully restored, colonial-style 18th-century house run by lovely Queta and her husband in her late grandmother's home. There are three large and homey apartments with fully equipped kitchens, pleasant bedrooms and large sitting-cum-dining rooms with wooden beams and stone walls. There is a minimum three days' stay.

El Rincón de Magüi (☎ 928 63 04 54; Calle Diputación 6; mains €6-12) Very popular pizzeria and restaurant with outside tables, plus a brick-clad dining room decorated with ceramic plates and photos of well-fed celeb diners like former Spanish PM Aznar.

Getting There & Away

Buses 216, 220 and 229 (€1.90, 30 minutes, hourly) connect with Las Palmas and buses 215 and 235 (€2.15, 20 minutes, hourly) with Arucas.

ARUCAS

pop 33,800

Nicknamed the 'pearl of Gran Canaria', Arucas is a great day out from Las Palmas. It is a handsome, compact town with pedestrian streets lined with elegant historic buildings. The **tourist office** (☎ 928 62 31 36; municipal gardens; ☾ 8am-4pm Mon-Fri) can assist with accommodation.

Sights

The extraordinary, neo-Gothic **Iglesia de San Juan** (☾ 9.30am-12.30pm & 4.30-7.15pm) stands sullen watch over the bright white houses of Arucas in a striking display of disproportion. The church has a Sagrada Familia (Gaudí) look with its elaborate pointed spires and was, fittingly, designed by a Catalan architect. Construction started in 1906 on the site of a former *ermita* (chapel) and was completed 70 years later. Within, a fine 16th-century Italian Crucifixion hangs above the altar; the wooden Cristo Yacente (Reclining Christ) is similarly

impressive, together with three magnificent rose windows.

From the church, walk down Calle Gourié to lovely Calle León y Castillo, flanked by colourful colonial-style buildings. Turn right into Plaza Constitución, home of the late-19th-century modernist **ayuntamiento** (town hall), which was being restored at the time of research. Opposite are the gracious **municipal gardens**, laid out in French style with fountains, pavilions, sculptures and magnificent dragon palm trees. The gardens house the **Municipal Museum** (☎ 928 60 11 74; ☾ 10am-8pm Mon-Fri, to 1pm Sat), which has a permanent exhibition by Canarian painters and sculptors, plus temporary shows.

Calle Heredad flanks the gardens on the southern side of the plaza, dominated by the neoclassical **Heredad de Aguas de Arucas y Firgas** building, completed in 1908.

More to the taste of many visitors is the **Destilerías Arehucas** (Arehucas Rum Distillery; ☎ 928 93 29 00; www.arehucas.com; ☾ 10am-2pm Mon-Fri). Free guided visits, culminating in a tipple, take place during opening hours.

Northwest of town, on the road to Bañaderos, the **Jardín de las Hespérides** (Jardín de la Marquésa; admission adult/under 18yr €6/3; ☾ 9am-1pm & 2-6pm Mon-Sat) botanical garden is owned by the Marquésa de Arucas (along with the Hacienda del Buen Suceso; see below). Lushly planted with more than 2500 different plants, trees and cacti, there are ponds, places to sit and a greenhouse with banana trees. The admission fee includes a detailed guide identifying the plants on display.

Sleeping & Eating

ourpick Hacienda del Buen Suceso (☎ 928 62 29 45; www.haciendabuensuceso.com; Carretera de Arucas a Bañaderos; s/d €105/150; P ❊ ⊠) Set among lush banana plantations about 1.5km west of town. This aesthetically renovated country estate dates back to 1572; the oldest in the Canary Islands. The rooms are rustic yet elegant, with lashings of white linen, beamed ceilings and parquet floors. The spa is luxuriously marbled and the whole place has an ambience of utter tranquillity. The restaurant (mains from €8) dishes up exquisitely prepared traditional dishes that change according to what is in season.

La Bodega de Arucas (☎ 928 60 17 69; Calle Párroco Cárdenes 5; mains from €6; V) The most stylish place in town with its trendy cocktail bar, complete with music videos and chic dining space aloft. The menu includes lots of healthy salads and a decadent caramel tart (as a reward).

Getting There & Away
Buses 205 and 206 (€1.90, 25 minutes) provide an hourly service to/from Las Palmas, while bus 215 (€1.05, 15 minutes) runs hourly to Teror.

AROUND ARUCAS
If you have wheels (preferably four), take the steep, well-signposted route to **La Montaña de Arucas**, 2.5km north of town. From here there's a splendid panorama of Las Palmas, the northern coast of the island, orchards, banana groves and, less happily, hectare upon hectare of plastic greenhouses. The restaurant here, **El Meson de la Montaña** (☎ 928 60 14 75; mains from €7), has fabulous views and is touristy but good. Solid choices include onion pie with cured ham, and fillet steak with truffles. Vegetarians have slim pickings, aside from lavish salads and a fine apple cake.

MOYA
pop 8300 / elevation 490m
The spectacular 13km drive between Arucas and Moya hugs the flank of the mountain, providing gee-whiz views of the northern coast. Moya is an unpretentious working town with some traditional Canarian architecture, including the lovely **Casa/Museo Tomás Morales** (☎ 928 62 02 17; admission free; ☺ 8am-8pm Mon-Fri, 10am-2pm & 5-8pm Sat), opposite the 16th-century church on Plaza de la Candelaria, with its stunning views of the *barranco* (ravine). Once home to the Canarian poet, who died in 1922, aged just 37, the museum includes a music room with a 170-year-old clavichord, a small hall used for classical concerts and a pretty walled garden with grapefruit trees and cacti.

Buses 116 and 117 (€2, one hour, 15 daily) run to/from Las Palmas.

SANTA MARÍA DE GUÍA
pop 8430
Just off the main C-810 highway, 25km west of Las Palmas, Santa María de Guía (or just Guía) was temporarily home to the French composer Camille Saint-Saêns (1835–1921), who used to tickle the ivories in the town's 17th-century neoclassical church.

In the 18th century, the town and surrounding area were devastated by a plague of locusts. To rid themselves of this blight, the locals implored the Virgin Mary for help. This remains a tradition and on the third Sunday of September the townsfolk celebrate La Rama de las Marías by dancing their way to the doors of the church to make offerings of fruits. The town is also known for its *queso de flor* (flower cheese).

Buses 103 and 105 (€2.30, 50 minutes) pass by roughly every half-hour on their way from Las Palmas.

GÁLDAR
pop 22,763 / elevation 124m
One of the most important archaeological finds on the islands is the **Cueva Pintada** (Painted Cave), near the Agaete exit of town. The walls bear deteriorating designs, in red, black and white, left behind by the Guanches. The surrounding area, which includes remains of a Guanche settlement, contains the **Cueva Pintada Museum & Archaeological Park** (☎ 928 89 57 46; adult/child €6/3.90; ☺ 9.30am-8pm Tue-Sat, 11am-8pm Sun). You can only visit by calling ahead to book.

A couple of kilometres away, at Playa del Agujero, is the **Necrópolis de Gáldar**. Mummies, objects used in Guanche funeral rites and domestic items have been discovered among these tombs. The area has, however, been fenced off and seems likely to stay that way.

Gáldar's **tourist office** (☎ 928 89 58 55; Edificio Heredad de Agua, Plaza Heredamientos s/n; ☺ 8am-2.30pm Mon-Fri) has plenty of brochures on the area.

Buses 103 and 105 (€2.50, one hour) head east for Las Palmas roughly every half-hour. Southbound, buses 101, 102 and 103 (€1.10, 20 minutes, hourly) link Gáldar with Agaete and Puerto de las Nieves.

AGAETE & PUERTO DE LAS NIEVES
pop 5640
The town of Agaete, 10km southwest of Gáldar, is a relaxing small place with a handful of seafood restaurants and some low-key sights. Nearby, Puerto de las Nieves was the island's principal port until the 19th century and is now the terminal for the ferry to Santa Cruz de Tenerife. It's nothing to go overboard about, and the beaches are small, black and pebbly, but the buildings, with their brilliant blue trim against dazzling white stucco, look as though they have been transplanted from

GRAN CANARIA

some Greek island. There are also several unpretentious and good seafood restaurants by the port, mainly frequented by locals in the know.

Just in from the beach is the **Iglesia de Nuestra Señora de la Concepción**. Built in 1874, it is strikingly Mediterranean in style. Inside are two parts of a 16th-century Flemish triptych by Joos van Cleve. The centre panel is preserved in the nearby chapel, **Ermita de las Nieves**.

Around Agaete the coast takes on a sterner countenance than further north. From the jetty you can see the see the stump of the **Dedo de Dios** (God's Finger), a basalt monolithic rock that was a serious tourist attraction until it took a tumble in a 2005 hurricane. Take a look at the photos outside its namesake restaurant (below).

Sleeping & Eating

Hotel Puerto de las Nieves (☎ 928 88 62 56; Avenida Alcalde José de Armas s/n; s/d €63/98; P ✸ ☐) This hotel has an old-fashioned lobby but superb large, modern rooms washed in pale peach with parquet and tile floors. Choose between large rooms with sofas and chairs or smaller ones with large terraces with sun-bed space. There is a classy Thalassotherapy centre with all the treatments, including an intriguing-sounding chakra stone massage.

Restaurante el Cápita (☎ 928 55 41 42; Calle Nuestra Señora de las Nieves 37; mains €5-12) A slightly smarter proposition, with a reasonable €6 *menú del día*. The fresh fish dishes can't be faulted, though the service may see you twiddling your thumbs when it's crowded.

Restaurante Las Nasas (☎ 928 89 86 50; Calle Nuestra Señora de Las Nieves 7 s/n; mains €7-9; ⌚ closed Tue) There's a great atmosphere in this former warehouse with its old-fashioned black-and-white interior, jolly model boats, high ceilings and a small walled terrace overlooking the ocean. It's also usually the busiest along this seafood strip; a good sign.

Cofradía de Pescadores (☎ 928 88 62 50; Muelle Puerto de las Nieves; mains €7-10) Next to the port, with an outdoor terrace, you can dine on catch-of-the-day along with the fishermen – and there's no better recommendation than that. Try the speciality, *fritura de pescado* (lightly fried seafood), or one of 30 tapas *para picar* (to taste).

Restaurante Dedo de Dios (☎ 928 89 85 81; Carretera Puerto de las Nieves s/n; mains €7.50-9; ⌚ closed Tue) A cavernous restaurant hung with ferns in a lovely old building overlooking the beach

and the rocky remains of the poor old Dedo. It fills up with large, boisterous families at weekends and has a vast menu of mainly fish and seafood dishes.

Getting There & Away

Bus 103 (€3.60, 1¼ hours) links the town and port with Las Palmas at least hourly. Bus 101 (€3.20, 50 minutes, four daily) heads south for Aldea de San Nicolás.

Fred Olsen (☎ 928 55 40 05; www.fredolsen.es) operates eight fast ferries (adult/under 12 years/12 to 26 years €40/20/31) a day from Puerto de las Nieves for the hour-long trip to Santa Cruz de Tenerife. There is a free bus connection to Las Palmas (Parque Santa Catalina). Returning, the bus leaves Las Palmas 1½ hours before the ferry is due to depart.

ALDEA DE SAN NICOLÁS

Usually known as San Nicolás de Tolentino, this rather scruffy town has little to excite the senses – it's the sort of place you only hang around in because the arse has fallen out of your car. The lure here is the travelling, not the arriving. The road between Agaete and San Nicolás takes you on a magnificent cliff-side journey. If you head southwest in the late afternoon, the setting sun provides a soft-light display, marking out each successive ridge in an ever-darker shadowy mantle. There are numerous lookouts along the way to take in the rugged views.

The approach from Mogán and the south (see North of Puerto de Mogán, p91), though lacking the seascapes, is almost as awesome.

Bus 38 (€3.20, one hour, five daily) runs between Puerto de Mogán and Aldea de San Nicolás. Bus 101 (€3.40, 50 minutes, four daily) runs between Agaete and San Nicolas.

AROUND ALDEA DE SAN NICOLÁS

Heading north out of town, take a detour to **Puerto de la Aldea**, with its small harbour, couple of seafood restaurants and, for self-caterers, the shady **Parque Ruben Día** with its stone tables and benches set under the pine trees. After your blow-out meal of bread, cheese and *cerveza* (beer), take a stroll along the promenade and check out the small black stony beach.

Also just out of town, in the hamlet of Artejévez, is the well-signposted **Cactualdea** (☎ 928 78 90 57; admission adult/under 18yr €6/3), which claims to be the largest cactus park in Europe, with over 1200 species of the prickly plant, plus a replica Guanches' cave. Expect the usual insipid theme-park eating options; take a picnic if you can.

ARTENARA

A back road climbs eastwards up the valley from Aldea de San Nicolás to the hilltop village of Artenara, from where you are close to Tejeda. The sparsely populated countryside of bare ridges and rugged hills is dotted with **troglodyte caves**, some still inhabited.

Bus 220 (€4.20, two hours) runs hourly from Las Palmas. No buses connect the village with Aldea de San Nicolás.

PLAYA DEL INGLÉS & MASPALOMAS

pop around 40,000

This is Gran Canaria's most famous holiday resort and a sun-splashed party place for a mainly northern-European crowd. That said, during the day (and out of season) it has a more upmarket appearance than you may expect. This is not Benidorm, or even Los Cristianos in Tenerife. In the centre you are more likely to stumble across expensive hotels or smart apartment blocks than Dot-and-Alf-style English pubs. On the downside, there is virtually nothing that is even halfway Spanish here; everything is tourist driven and the only languages you'll need are German or English. The town plan is also undeniably soulless, with the neatly traced boulevards and roundabouts betraying all the town-design spontaneity of a five-year plan.

At night, most of the action takes place in and around the Yumbo Centrum, with the leather handbags and wallets in the stores replaced by leather gear in steamy gay bars. The vaguely wholesome, bustling family atmosphere evaporates as the discos (both straight and gay) swing until dawn, barrels and bottles are drained by the dozen in bars, and the drag shows, saunas and sex shops all do a roaring trade.

The only natural items of genuine interest are the impressive dunes of Maspalomas, also home to some of Gran Canaria's most luxurious hotels and the island's largest golf course. The dunes fold back from the beach and cover 400 hectares, and their inland heart has been declared a nature reserve with restricted access.

ORIENTATION

The Playa del Inglés is next to the centre of the triangle-shaped urban area, while to the southwest are the beaches and dunes of Maspalomas. East of Playa del Inglés the resort continues, but thins out in the areas known as Veril and San Agustín. The main shopping centres are north of the centre in San Fernando and Bellavista.

There are bus stops all over the resort, including a couple beside Yumbo.

INFORMATION

Emergency

Local police (☎ 928 14 15 72; Plaza de la Constitución 2) Near the dunes of Maspalomas.

Internet Access

Free Motion (☎ 928 77 74 79; www.free-motion.net; Hotel Sandy Beach, Avenida Alfereces Provisionales s/n; per 30min €2; ☺ 9am-8pm Mon-Fri, to 6pm Sun)

Laundry

Laundrette (Lot 411, 4th fl, Yumbo Centrum; ☺ 8am-8pm Mon-Fri, to 1pm Sat) Drop your washing off and collect it the next day.

Medical Services

The resort is swarming with clinics, their business no doubt enhanced by shattering hangovers and third-degree sunburn.

24-hour clinic (☎ 928 76 12 92; cnr Avenida España & Avenida EE UU) Multilingual clinic opposite the tourist office.

Money

Viajes Insular (☎ 928 76 05 00; Avenida Moya 14; ☺ closed Sun) Represents American Express.

Post

Post office (Avenida Tirajana)

Tourist Information

Cabildo tourist office (☎ 928 77 15 50; www.gran canaria.com; cnr Avenida España & Avenida EE UU; ☺ 9am-2pm & 3-8pm Jul-Sep, 9am-9pm Mon-Fri & 9am-1pm Sat Oct-Jun) Just outside the Yumbo Centrum, with maps, helpful staff and public toilets.

SIGHTS & ACTIVITIES

Dunas de Maspalomas

In 1994 these fabulous **dunes** were designated a national park. The best view of them is from the bottom of Avenida Tirjana. Stroll through the arches of the Hotel Riu Palace Maspalomas to the balcony, which is

GRAN CANARIA

PLAYA DEL INGLÉS & MASPALOMAS

INFORMATION
24-Hour Clinic....................1 C2
Cabildo Tourist Office..........2 C2
Free Motion....................(see 8)
Laundrette....................(see 23)
Local Police......................3 A2
Post Office........................4 C2
Viajes Insular....................5 C2

SIGHTS & ACTIVITIES
Camello Safari....................6 C3
Canarias Extreme................7 C2
Free Motion........................8 C2
Happy Biking....................9 D2

SLEEPING
Europalace........................10 D2
Palm Beach......................11 A4
Parque Tropical Hotel 12 D2
Pensión San Fernando........13 C2
Respect Los Almendros........14 C3
Sahara Beach Club..............15 C3

EATING
Casa Vieja 16 C1
Mundo..............................17 C2
Restaurante La Liguria........18 C2
Restaurante La Toja............19 C2
Restaurante Rías Bajas.......20 C2

DRINKING
Hard Rock Café..................21 C2
Heaven..........................(see 23)
Kasbah Centre....................22 C2

SHOPPING
Fedac..............................(see 2)
Yumbo Centrum.................23 C2

surrounded by a botanical garden displaying many shrubs and plants endemic to
the Canaries. There is a small information
office here with sporadic opening hours.
Although the dunes look too pristine to
blight with footprints, you *can* walk on the
sand, but do respect the signs and keep to
the designated trails. Alternatively, you can
go the full Sahara and opt for a camel trip
with **Camello Safari** (☎ 928 76 07 81; adult/under 12yr
€30/15; ☽ 9am-4.30pm).

Theme Parks

There's a multitude of theme parks with brochures and advertising everywhere.
　　Palmitos Park (☎ 928 14 02 76; www.aspro-ocio
.es; adult/under 12yr €17/12; ☽ 9.30am-6pm) is a few

kilometres north of the resort area, this is a
subtropical oasis crammed with exotic flora
and 1500 species of birds, along with an
aquarium, orchid exhibit, reptile house, petting farm and animals such as wallabies and
orang-utans. Buses run here regularly from
various stops in Playa del Inglés, Puerto Rico
and Maspalomas.
　　Mundo Aborigen (☎ 928 17 22 95; Carretera Playa
del Inglés-Fataga; adult/under 12yr €10/5; ☽ 9am-6pm) is
located 6km along the road north to Fataga,
where around 100 model Guanches stand in
various ancient poses designed to give you
an idea of what life was like here before the
conquistadors turned up to build theme
parks. Take bus 18 from San Fernando or
San Bartolomé.

An enormous water park, **Aqualand** (☎ 928 14 05 25; www.aqualand.es; Carretera Palmitos Park; adult/under 18yr €20/14; ☼ 10am-5pm Oct-Jun, to 6pm Jul-Sep) boasts its own surf beach with seven types of waves and miles of rides and slides. Take bus 45 or 70 to get here from Playa del Inglés or Puerto Rico respectively.

After the water rides and Guanches, how about a trip to the Orient? **Camel Safari Park La Baranda** (☎ 928 79 86 80; Carretera Playa del Inglés-Fataga; 1hr ride €25; ☼ 9am-6pm) has 70 camels and is located in a lush property with palms and avocado and citrus trees and also has a restaurant, bar and small zoo.

Diving

Dive Academy Gran Canaria (☎ 928 73 61 96; www.dive academy-grancanaria.com; Calle La Lajilla s/n, Arguineguín; initiation dives from €46, advanced open water 5 dives €270) has a free minibus to pick up plungers from their hotels and take them to the dive academy, due west of town. Both boat and shore dives are available.

Swimming

For many, the only energy left after partying at night will be for getting down to the beach and collapsing for the day. Beaches, from east to west, are Playa de las Burras, Playa del Inglés and Playa de Maspalomas. They all link up to form the one beach.

Surfing & Windsurfing

Although surfing is possible here (the best waves tend to break off the western end of Maspalomas by the lighthouse), this is not mind-blowing surfing territory. Windsurfers are better off heading east, beyond the resorts to Bahía Feliz, Playa Aguila, and, best of all, **Pozo Izquierdo**, which is for experienced windsurfers. **Club Mistral** (☎ 928 15 71 58; www.club-mistral .com; Carretera General del Sur, km 47, Playa de Tarajalillo; 6hr beginner's windsurfing course €120), in Bahía Feliz, rents boogie boards, surfboards, ocean kayaks and windsurfing boards and equipment. It also organises windsurf safaris.

In Playa Aguila, world windsurfing champion Bjorn Dunkerbeck runs the **Dunkerbeck Windsurfing Center** (☎ 928 76 29 78; www.dunker beck-windsurfing.com) with several courses available, including a 10-hour initiation course for €190.

Thalassotherapy

Centro de Talasoterapía (☎ 928 76 56 89; www.hotel gloriapalace.com; Hotel Gloria Palace, Calle Las Margaritas s/n) is Europe's largest Thalassotherapy centre, occupying a huge complex attached to Hotel Gloria Palace, and is nothing short of breathtaking. Fabulous sea-water treatments leave your skin as smooth as a baby's bum and your mind as light as a feather. A day's dunking and use of the various appliances costs from €50.

Golf

Don those plaid Bermudas and head off to **Meloneras Golf** (☎ 928 14 53 09; www.lopesanhr .com; Costa Meloneras; green fees plus buggy €100-120), which opened late 2006, in between Maspalomas and the harbour of Pasito Blanco, in an area earmarked for yet another luxury development.

IT'S A GAY OLD LIFE

Gran Canaria is the gay honey-pot of the Canaries, and Playa del Inglés is Europe's winter escape playground. There are several hotels and apartment blocks that cater towards gay and lesbian guests. One of the classiest, close to the dunes, is **Respect Los Almendros** (☎ +00 44 20 74 28 37 37; www.respect-holidays.co.uk; Avenida Francia 3; ☒) – book through the UK company. The bungalows are set in lush, landscaped gardens and facilities include a gym, spa, bar and restaurant.

A seemingly endless string of bars, discos and clubs are crammed into the Yumbo Centrum (p88), which is predominantly a gay scene, although this doesn't stop small numbers of lesbians and straights from wading in. Little happens before midnight. From then until about 3am the bars on the 4th level of the Yumbo Centrum bear the brunt of the fun, after which the nightclubs on the 2nd level take over.

At dawn, people stagger out for some rest. Some make for the beach at Maspalomas, across the dunes, which are themselves a busy gay cruising area.

For more information about gay clubs, events, accommodation and personal classifieds, check the following websites www.colectivogama.com (in Spanish), www.gaymap.info and www.gran canariagay.com.

Cycling

Happy Biking (☎ 928 76 68 32; www.happy-biking.com in German; Hotel Continental, Avenida Italia 2; bike hire per day from €7; ⏰ 8.30am-7pm Mon-Sat); now there's a nice name! Happy Biking rents out a range of cycles and also organises cycle tours, mostly quite gentle, which start at €30, including bike hire, transport and a picnic.

The slickly run **Free Motion** (☎ 928 77 74 79; www.free-motion.net; Hotel Sandy Beach, Avenida Alféreces Provisionales s/n; bike hire per day from €9, tours per day from €45; ⏰ 9am-8pm Mon-Fri, 9am-6pm Sun) also offers a range of tours for small groups and has bikes and quads for rental.

Horse Riding

Another happy (and unrelated) lot is **Happy Horse** (☎ 679 86 70 57; www.happy-horse.org; 3hr trek €54), with horse treks in the hinterland southeast of town. Pick up from your hotel is included in the price.

Kayaking

If you are looking for a watery pursuit more adrenalin-boosting than a glass-bottom boat, check out **Canarias Extreme** (☎ 606 58 01 03; www .canariasextreme.com; Avenida EE UU 43; kayak tours per day €75), which organises single- and double-kayak tours all around the coast.

Walking

Away from the coast you find a complete contrast to the beaches: untamed country-side with a dramatic variance in terrain, ranging from rocky and wild to gently undulating hills.

Free Motion (above) has a choice of four hiking trips: Roque Nublo, Green North, Lake Tour and the daunting-sounding Summit Tour; all priced at around €45. The company will arrange transport to/from various resorts on the coast, including Puerto Rico and Puerto de Mogán for a small fee. Happy Biking (above) offers gentler day walks from €40, including pick up from your hotel.

To enjoy an exhilarating (and free) 5km walk, simply follow the promenade that extends eastwards from Playa del Inglés. The path follows a track that is sometimes at shore level and sometimes above it.

SLEEPING

There are more than 500 hotels, apartment blocks and bungalows in Playa del Inglés and Maspalomas; in peak periods many are full to bursting. Consider booking a package outside Spain; you may save considerably more than what a tour operator offers. Travel agents in Britain, Ireland, Germany and the Netherlands brim with deals and last-minute offers.

If you're going it alone, it's almost impossible to assess where you should head. You get, in reasonable measure, what you pay for. In shoulder to high season you are unlikely to find an apartment (which is generally cheaper than a hotel) for less than €60 for two people.

All we can do is give some indicative places and prices. With no taxi fare in the urban area above €8 – and taxis rolling through the night – consider taking a place away from the beach, even away from Playa del Inglés itself.

If you haven't reserved in advance, pick up an accommodation list and town map from one of the tourist offices and let your fingers do the walking. Many apartments don't have anyone in permanent attendance so it's often useless to simply turn up with hope in your heart.

Budget

A true budget scene doesn't exist in these parts.

Pensión San Fernando (☎ 928 76 39 06; Calle La Palma 16; d without bathroom €18) There's precisely one *pensión* (guesthouse) in town and, if you can get in, it's tidy, if spartan, and located in a quieter part of town.

Midrange

The bulk of apartments and hotels will fall into this category but remember, they're usually booked by tour operators.

Sahara Beach Club (☎ 928 76 07 76; www.sahara -beach-club.com; Avenida de Alemania 53; bungalows from €54; P ⟨⟩) This low-rise complex overlooks the dunes and has a tranquil, homey atmosphere with well-equipped bungalows and lovely gardens. There are private terraces with small lawns and rose bushes. The minimum stay is four days; most guests stay for several weeks.

Europalace (☎ 928 77 41 81; reservas_europalace@ hotmail.com; Calle Hamburgo 12; d with half-board from €70; ⟨⟩) One of the best situations in town, across from the beach. If you don't feel like sharing the sand, don't worry, this giant concrete honeycomb of a place has three pools on various levels, plus all the extras you could possibly want – except tranquillity, that is.

Parque Tropical Hotel (☎ 928 77 40 12; Avenida Italia 1; s/d/tr €75/125/175; P ⟨⟩ ⟨⟩) A real gem in this sea of generic high-rise hotels. Dating

---

STREETSCAPES

In Maspalomas the street names are revealing – Avenida del Touroperador Saga Tours, Avenida del Touroperador Alpitours, Neckermann, Tui, Thomson and so on and so on. No plain old streets (calles) either – all avenues, no matter how small.

---

back to the '60s, this hotel has a traditional Canarian look with wooden balconies, white stucco exterior and lush, mature gardens set amid small pools and fountains. The rooms have an Andalucian feel, with terracotta tiles, dark-wood fittings and beams combined with soothing pastel-coloured paintwork.

Top End

The premier top-end establishments are out by the dunes in Maspalomas.

our pick **Villa del Conde** (☎ 928 56 32 00; www .lopesanhr.com; Mar Mediterrañneo 7; s/d/ste €102/132/234; P ⊠ ☐ ☎ ☐) One of the latest luxury hotels to open here, Villa del Conde is modelled on the historic centre of the town of Agüimes (p76), including its neoclassical church, which has been emulated (complete with bell tower, central dome and peeling-plaster effect) as the hotel's main lobby. The rooms are set in the 'village houses', which are centred around a main plaza, complete with bandstand and terrace restaurant. It could be like Disneyland, but the architecture is executed so tastefully that it somehow works. Facilities include six pools, several restaurants and bars, a mini club and a Thalassotherapy spa. There's a minimum one-week stay in July and August.

Palm Beach (☎ 928 72 10 32; www.seaside-hotels .com; Avenida Oasis s/n; d from €185; P ⊠ ☐ ☎ ☐) This hotel has recently been refurbished by international interior designer Alberto Pinto in a retro-chic style. Despite a mildly unprepossessing exterior, step within and it is a riot of colour and exciting modern design. In the main hall, the striped sofas are topped off with bright, colour-coordinated cushions, with massive abstracts on the walls, white tubular lambs and glass bowls of green apples. Get the picture? The rooms are all different and similarly snazzy.

EATING

The resort is predictably swarming with restaurants, with the normal mix of Chinese

buffets, Argentinian grills, bland international and that increasingly rare breed – authentic Spanish.

Restaurante La Liguria (☎ 928 76 03 36; Avenida Tirajana 24; pizza €6-9, pasta €5.50-10; V) Serving up a better class of pizza than the cardboard-base norm, the flamboyant Genoese owner also whips up tasty pasta dishes, including a vegetarian choice. Sit outside on the attractive terrace, thankfully separated from the main road by shrubs and trees.

Casa Vieja (☎ 928 76 90 10; Calle El Lomo 139, Carretera de Fataga; mains €7-18; ☾ 1pm-midnight) Just north of the GC-1 motorway, along the road to Fataga, this restaurant is run with passion. The 'Old House' has a real campo (countryside) feel. Plants festoon the low roof, canaries trill and the menu is unwaveringly authentic; try the grilled meat. There is live traditional music most weekends.

Restaurante La Toja (☎ 928 76 11 96; Edificio Barbados II, Avenida Tirajana 17; mains €8-13; ☾ closed Sun lunch) A quality establishment blending the best of cuisines from France and Galicia. Try the veal in Marsala wine or troubling-sounding elephant's ear with chips (actually a thin fillet of steak). The prices are reasonable given the fancy atmosphere and food.

Mundo (☎ 928 76 10 63; Apartamentos Tenesor, Avenida Tirajana s/n; mains €12-15; ☾ closed Mon; V) An oasis of fashionable sophistication, Mundo opened in 2005 and has seriously raised the culinary game in these parts. Think American diner-meets-Japanese, with a spruce-minimalist dining room with retro black-and-white tiles and cherry-red chairs. Try the black pasta with king prawns if it's on the menu.

Restaurante Rías Bajas (☎ 928 76 40 33; cnr Avenida Tirajana & Avenida EE UU; mains €13-27) Within stumbling distance of the Yumbo Centrum, the tank of tentacle-waving crustaceans at the entrance gives it all away: the fish and seafood dishes here have an island-wide reputation. There's a sister restaurant in Urbanisation Meloneras in Maspalomas.

Self-Catering

Three large supermarkets, including the economical Mercadona, are situated in the Centro Comerciál Bellavista, just beyond San Fernando, to the north of town.

DRINKING & ENTERTAINMENT

The Yumbo Centrum transforms into a pulsating clubbers' heaven at night – and the aptly named Heaven (an offshoot of the London club) is the flashiest and best of the gay discos here. There are straight and gay places in the centre and you could stagger around Yumbo Centrum – as many do – for weeks and not sample all the nightlife options. The Kasbah Centre is another buoyant nightlife hot spot for party animals.

Ease into your evening with a cocktail at the nearby **Hard Rock Café** (☎ 928 76 78 14; Avenida Alféreces Provisionales 29; ☼ 11am-late) with its standard red Cadillac, elegant terrace and fancy cocktails.

Check the online party guide at www.maspalomas-tonight.com for a virtual club and disco tour.

SHOPPING

About the only interruption to the hectares of apartments, hotels, restaurants and bars comes in the form of the shopping centres. In them you can buy everything from children's wear to electronics. A good tip is to keep on looking, despite the enormous temptation to buy everything as soon as you see it – you may well save even more money if you shop around.

Yumbo Centrum (www.cc-yumbo.com; Avenida EE UU; ☼ 24hr) There are more than 200 businesses in this four-level commercial centre. You can buy shoes, leather goods, perfume and anything else you fancy, tax-free, although the quality should be checked. There are also supermarkets on the premises.

Fedac (☎ 928 77 24 45; Centro Insular del Turismo, cnr Avenida España & Avenida EE UU; ☼ 10am-2pm & 4-7.30pm Mon-Fri) If you're after local handicrafts, visit the small Fedac shop located with the Cabildo tourist office. Fedac is a government-sponsored nonprofit store, with prices and quality that are a good standard by which to measure those of products sold elsewhere. You'll also get a guarantee with your purchase.

GETTING THERE & AWAY
To/From the Airport

Bus 66 (€3.30, one hour, hourly) runs to/from Gando airport until about 9.15pm. For a taxi, budget for about €30 for Playa del Inglés and €35 for Maspalomas.

Bus

Buses link regularly with points along the coast, westwards as far as Puerto de Mogán and eastwards to Las Palmas. For Las Palmas (€5.50, about 50 minutes), take bus 5 (night bus), 30 or 44 (nonstop). Pick up *horarios* (timetables) at the tourist office – one for the south of the island and one for the north.

GETTING AROUND
Bus

Global (☎ 902 38 11 10; www.globalsu.net in Spanish) runs buses to many of the theme parks listed earlier. The fare for a standard run within town is €1. If you plan to travel out of town, a Tarjeta Insular (see the boxed text, p64) is a good investment.

Car

If you must take your car down to the beach, there's a large paying car park beside Playa del Inglés. Street parking costs a reasonable

---

DETOUR

If you want more space on the sand, there are several choice beaches on the coast-hugging GC-500 road, west of Playa del Inglés. Follow the signs to the town hospital and Puerto de Mogán from the centre (top of Avenida Tirajana), passing Holiday World on your left. The road climbs past palm plantations and the new golf course, Meloneras Golf (p85). At Km7 watch for the **Pasito Bea** sign, turning left on the rough approach that leads to a small black sandy cove secluded by rocks, which is mixed nude and clothed. After a quick dip, continue along the road, which winds around arid hills and, after 1.2km, comes to **Playa de Carpinteras**. Follow the track east of the main beach here, park on the cliffs and you will discover an idyllic, little-known (until now!) broad arc of sand with shallow water backed by sloping dunes. You can clamber around the rocks due east of here to reach the beach, which again is mixed nude and clothed. The third beach worth recommending is at Km 9.2. **Playa de Triana** is a black pebbly beach, with parking on the main road; note that you are expected to wear your togs here!

Follow the road a further 4km to a roundabout, where it rejoins the GC-1 heading towards the vastly more commercial beaches of Puerto Rico and beyond.

€0.50 for 30 minutes up to €3 for four hours (between 10am and 9pm).

Taxi

You can call a **taxi** (☎ 928 76 67 67), and taxi stands abound and are reliable. From Playa del Inglés, no destination within the urban area costs more than €8.

AROUND PLAYA DEL INGLÉS & MASPALOMAS

PUERTO RICO & ARGUINEGUÍN

While Maspalomas has redeeming features, in the shape of its natural dunes and superbly unnatural nightlife, its resort cousins further west are a good example of how greedy developers can destroy a coastline that shares a similar setting to Italy's Amalfi coast. Around every corner it seems there is yet another resort surrounded by steep banks of apartment blocks stretching into the hinterland. How some of these poor tourists get to the beach is a puzzle; crossing the main road is hazardous enough, and then it can be a long walk – especially if you have to return for your sunblock!

Parts of the port area of Arguineguín still remain true to its roots as a small, active fishing settlement, but it's a nondescript town with a couple of rather scrubby beaches. If you are here at lunchtime, check out the **Cofradía de Pescadores** (☎ 928 15 09 63; mains from €7; ☉ closed Wed & Sep), which, despite the plastic tablecloths and disarming six-language menu, buys its catch of the day direct from the fishing boats. Arguineguín is also home to a well-respected diving school (see p85).

Puerto Rico is a good example of appalling town planning; the original fishing village has all but disappeared under a sea of concrete, with the apartment blocks stacked up like stadium seats against the mountains. The beach is pleasant but certainly not large enough to cater to the number of beds here. The only escape is the multitude of boat trips that depart from the harbour, including the dolphin-spotting **Spirit of the Sea** (☎ 928 56 22 29; www.dolphin-whale.com; adult/under 12yr €22/12.50), offering two-hour trips in glass-bottom catamarans. A percentage of your ticket price goes towards marine research and conservation. **Lineas Salmon** (☎ 649 91 93 83; return €10) offers similar, with eight hourly services on a glass-bottom ferry to/from Puerto de Mogán from 10am and 5pm and eastwards to Arguineguín from 9.30am to 4.30pm. It also runs a daily two-hour dolphin-spotting trip for the same price as the ferry, departing from Puerto Rico at 10.30am.

The resorts further west. including Playa del Cura, Playa del Tauro and **Taurito**, are of a similar ilk. At least the latter has made an effort to gear itself to families with a vast landscaped lido with lagoon-style pools, tennis courts, minigolf, gym equipment, bars and sun beds. The waters here are flat, smooth as glass and safe for swimming.

Buses connect Puerto Rico and Arguineguín with Maspalomas and Playa del Inglés (€1.60, 30 minutes) and with Puerto de Mogán (€1.25, 15 minutes) and Las Palmas (€6.15, 1 hour 50 minutes), roughly every half-hour.

PUERTO DE MOGÁN

After Taurito, a couple of kilometres of rugged coastline recall what this whole southern stretch of the island must have been like 40 years ago, before mass tourism descended on the Canaries.

Finally you round a bend; below you is a smallish crescent of sandy beach and next to it, a busy little yacht harbour and fishing port. Puerto de Mogán, although now largely given over to the tourist trade, is light years from its garish counterparts to the east. Thankfully, even the recent construction inland is more aesthetically pleasing, including the luxury new Hotel Cordial Mogán Playa (p90).

Although its nickname, 'Venice of the Canaries', may be a tad of an exaggeration, the architecture and bridged waterways are as pretty as a chocolate box and the whole place exudes an air of opulence and charm. In the heart of the port, low-rise apartments have wrought-iron balconies, brightly coloured trim and are covered in dazzling bougainvillea.

On the downside, the place gets packed with envious tourists from the other resorts during the day, particularly on Friday morning when a street market takes over most of the town. Stalls sell the usual overpriced belts, bags and shell jewellery and, if you are staying here, it's a good day to leave.

LOCAL VOICES

For diving instructor Jerry O'Connor, being six foot under is nothing new; he comes from a family of well-known undertakers in Ireland's County Cork.

'Did you hear the one about the two Paddies who opened the dive centre Canary Diving Adventures (below) in Gran Canaria without knowing a word of Spanish?' he quips. 'Well, here it is!' The centre opened nearly 10 years ago and is one of the longest-established under the same owners on the island. It is also one of the few to have gained PADI 5 Star Gold Palm Resort status.

So, what's so special about diving here?

'The warm waters are fed by the Gulf Stream, which means there is a fabulous range of marine life, with more than 553 species of fish. We can also offer a shore dive to the El Cabron Reserve created with the aim of controlling overfishing, and terrific with shoals of different species of fish, and an extensive reef system. Plus there are two shipwrecks near here, including the *Alagranza*, which was sunk about 15 years ago and has become home to large shoals of barracuda and yellow snapper.

'Diving is also year-round in Gran Canaria and it's really noticeable how people are starting to want to get involved with sports and activities here, rather than just sit on the beach and sunbathe all day.'

Who are your typical divers?

'It varies. During the winter our customers are considerably more 'mature', whereas in the summer the clientele is far younger'

So you're happy here?

'I love it. Gran Canaria has so much variety in its landscape, the climate is superb and the people are as friendly as the Irish! I wouldn't want to live anywhere else.'

Sights & Activities

Tucked among the restaurants and bars on Calle Los Pescadores, the simple **Ermita de San Fernando** church dates back to 1955. You can take a peek inside during Mass at 6pm on Tuesday and Saturday.

Puerto de Mogán is the main centre for diving on Gran Canaria, with caves and wrecks just offshore. **Atlantik Diving** (☎ 689 35 20 49; www.clubdemar.com; Hotel Club de Mar, Playa de Mogán s/n; single dive with full equipment €40) offers courses at all levels, from a Discover Scuba experience (three hours, €90) to Dive Master (minimum 20 days, €570).

Canary Diving Adventures (☎ 928 56 54 28; www .canary-diving.com; Hotel Taurito Princess, Playa de Taurito) is run by a couple of Irish brothers, (see the boxed text, above). It offers guided boat dives (from €30), four-hour (and longer) PADI certification courses from €360 and one-day beginner courses for €75.

Submarine Adventure (☎ 928 56 51 08; adult/under 12yr €28/14) has a yellow submarine that submerges for 40 minutes eight times daily – and its owners run a free bus as far as Playa del Inglés to pick up punters. If you're expecting coral and sharks, you'll be disappointed; the submarine scarcely leaves the harbour and the fish you see are less impressive than those in any fish market.

Sleeping

Pensión Eva (☎ 928 56 52 35; Calle Lomo Quiebre 35; s/d without bathroom €20/25) About 750m inland, heading north from town, this excellent-value place has straightforward, light-filled rooms, a spacious rooftop terrace and – best news of all – a communal kitchen with a couple of fridges that makes self-catering (and socialising) a breeze.

La Venecia de Canarias (☎ 928 56 56 00; www .laveneciadecanarias.net; Local 328, Urb Puerto de Mogán; 1-/2-bedroom apt €70/105) Right in the thick of the resort's 'Venetian' quarter, with a truly lovely frontage surrounded by terrace bars, this well-managed complex has attractive, if smallish, apartments that sleep between three and five people. There are low-season reductions.

Hotel Club de Mar (☎ 928 56 50 66; www.clubdemar .com; Playa de Mogán s/n; d €95, apt from €105; ❄ ☐ ☎) Beside the yacht-filled harbour, this hotel complex has a spa, large, airy doubles, and apartments (between two and four people) with all the trimmings. Bag a room with a terrace overlooking the infinity pool with the beach beyond. The hotel's new Patio Canario restaurant (mains from €7) is good for fish dishes.

Hotel Cordial Mogán Playa (☎ 928 72 41 00; www.cordialcanarias.com; d with half-board from €175;

Ⓟ Ⓧ ▣ ⓖ) The most recent addition to the town but, happily, the architecture is stunning and low-rise, with the accommodation set around a central lobby, complete with stained-glass dome. Echoing the harbour with waterways and bridges, the public areas are a delight, while the rooms are all earth colours, expensive marble and gold-and-cream striped wallpaper. This is a truly stylish hotel that has succeeded in blending well with the environment. May it be a lesson to them all.

Most of Puerto de Mogán's apartments are rented out by locals; ask for Pepita at the **Supermercado Venencia** (☎ 928 56 55 63; Avenida Castillete Mogán; apt €50; ☯ 8am-8pm), opposite the entrance to the La Venencia de Canarias hotel, who owns a small, well-positioned apartment block that is cheaper than the norm. **Apartmentos Puerto de Mogan** (☎ 928 56 50 66; www .apartamentosmogan.com; around €420 a week), located a street back from the harbour, is another good source. It also arranges rental cars.

Eating
There are plenty of cafés and restaurants with pleasant *terrazas* offering fresh fish.

La Cucina (☎ 639 46 71 14; Calle Corriente 8; pizzas €5-7) Run by Italians, this tiny place is predominantly a takeaway with a couple of outside tables. The pizzas come highly recommended, and there is also a limited range of pasta dishes and salads, plus the obligatory creamy tiramisu.

Restaurante Cofradía (☎ 928 56 53 21; Muelle s/n; mains €10-22) This fishing cooperative restaurant is situated in the southwestern corner of the quay. Although the white tablecloths and multilingual menus mean the tourists have arrived, the fish is as fresh as ever. Tuck into a plate of grilled sardines; you'll never open a tin again.

La Bodeguilla Juananá (☎ 928 56 50 44; Plaza Mayor s/n; mains €12-20) Tucked into the corner of grandly named Plaza Mayor, in front of the yacht harbour, this restaurant is run with passion. The décor has an African theme and the gastro-flair dishes include daily specials like smoked swordfish served with avocado and a sauce made from the sap of canary palms.

Getting There & Away
There is no shortage of buses heading east to Puerto Rico and Playa del Inglés (€1.25,

15 minutes). Bus 1 (€7, two hours) departs hourly for Las Palmas. Ferries also run between the port and Puerto Rico (see p89).

NORTH OF PUERTO DE MOGÁN
Just as Puerto de Mogán is a relief from the south coast's relentless armies of apartments, bungalows and Guinness on tap, so the GC-200 road north from the port is another leap away from the crowds.

As it ascends gradually up a wide valley towards Mogán, you pass craggy mountains and orchards of avocados, the main crop in these parts. **Mogán** is a relaxed, unspoilt small town in a lovely mountainous setting with several pleasant restaurants and bars and a traditional small church.

our pick **El Sirocco B&B** (☎ 928 56 93 01; www.elsiroco .com; Calle San Antonio 8; d €50) is a charming B&B in an 18th-century former schoolhouse, creatively transformed by a German-English couple according to feng shui principles. The rooms are large and boldly colourful (think raspberries and cream), with Andrea's evocative landscape photos on the walls. There are four plant-filled patios and a hearty cooked breakfast is included in the price.

To press on, you have two choices. The GC-200 winds off to the northwest, travelling 26km through some spectacularly craggy mountains to Aldea de San Nicolás (p82), blighted when you get close to town by the sea of plastic greenhouses. Stop for a glass of fresh papaya juice at **Las Cañadas** (☎ 928 17 25 80; www.restaurantelascanadas.com), around 8km from Mogán on your left-hand side. This is an agreeably quirky restaurant and bar with stunning views plus the added appeal of turtles, a chameleon and a small museum with old agricultural equipment, radios and the like. You can also buy local honey and the largest avocados you have ever seen (when in season). The winding road continues through **Los Azulejos**, a colourful rock formation created by different coloured minerals of brilliant greens, yellows and ochres. To avoid a head-on collision, take your photos from the signposted **Fuente de los Azulejos Mirador** lookout.

Alternatively, a minor turn 2.5km north of Mogán heads northeast up to Ayacata, from where you can head to Tejeda p78 and the highest peaks on the island.

Fuerteventura

The second-largest island in the archipelago (after Tenerife), Fuerteventura is also the clos-est of the Canaries to the African coast: Morocco's Cape Juby is just 100km away. There are striking similarities in the landscape, particularly in the houses with their North African–style flat roofs for collecting rainfall. Communities are sprawled across the plains like tossed dice, often with no discernable centre, and punctuated by cacti, scrub and goat farms. In other ways, Fuerteventura emulates its neighbour Lanzarote, only with more colours. The volcanoes resemble piles of saffron, chilli and coriander; surreal triangles of exotic spices.

Most visitors, however, are more interested in mastering the waves and the wind than contemplating the abstract aesthetics of its scenery. Fuerteventura has year-round sunshine and the biggest and best beaches in the Canaries. The Atlantic winds that once propelled hundreds of windmills here now serve as the power for world-class windsurfing and kite boarding.

Fuerteventura has its main tourist resorts at opposite ends of the island. At the northern tip is Corralejo, beloved of the British sun seekers, while deep down south lies Morro Jable, largely frequented by Germans, and a markedly staider place.

Locals are known as Majoreros, or Maxoreros, from the Guanche (the islands' original inhabitants) name for the northern kingdom of the island – Maxorata.

HIGHLIGHTS

- Be a culture vulture and check out the cutting-edge modern art at La Oliva's **Casa de los Coroneles** (p106)

- Dine on catch-of-the-day seafood while gazing over the waves at pretty **Corralejo** (p106)

- Catch the waves at **Isla de Lobos** (p108), just one of the super-cool surfing spots here

- Kick off your shoes and do cartwheels in the soft, powdery sand at the **Parque Natural de Corralejo** (p108) sand dunes

- Be dazzled by the rare verdant green of the evocative valley location of lovely **Betancuria** (p101)

Corralejo ★★
Isla de Lobos ★
Parque Natural de Corralejo ★
La Oliva ★
Betancuria ★

- TELEPHONE CODE: 928
- POPULATION: 69,500
- AREA: 1660 SQ KM

ITINERARY 1
BEST BEACHES

Fuerteventura is famous for its glorious beaches, the best of which are in the south of the island, where the endless stretches of sand resemble more the Caribbean than the Canaries. **Morro Jable** (**1**; p114) has a spectacular wide arc of sand, an excellent water-sports centre and a long promenade for dodging joggers. The Península de Jandía's top windsurfing beach is **Playa de Sotavento de Jandía** (**2**; p113) with its 22km of white sand and leeward winds; kite boarding is also taking flight here. **Costa Calma** (**3**; p113) and **Caleta de Fuste** (**4**; p103) have superb family beaches with golden sands, shallow waters and kids' activities (like camel rides), while in the north, **Corralejo** (**5**; p106) sports a small sandy beach at its centre and, south of town, blindingly white sand dunes where you can find secluded beaches and pretty rocky coves. Still in the north, head beyond the castle at **El Cotillo** (**6**; p111) to discover a wilder beach, complete with sculptures, seagulls and thundering surf.

FUERTEVENTURA

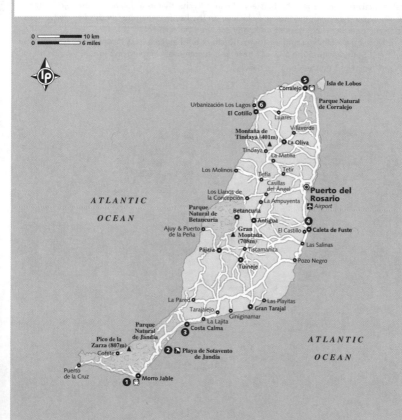

FUERTEVENTURA

ITINERARY 2
BE A GOOD SPORT

Fuerteventura is a superb destination for the sports enthusiast and, as a year-round destination, there is something to do in every season. Although catching the waves or sailing the breeze are the most famous sports here, there are less adrenaline-spiked activities available. Fuerteventura's peaceful but stark landscape offers some great walking opportunities, with oases, volcanic craters, abandoned haciendas and rugged coastlines available to the intrepid. The **Isla de Lobos** (1; p108) nature reserve is also excellent for walkers; turning right as you get off the ferry will take you on a circular tour of the island. There's also a climb up Caldera de la Montaña here – well worth the dizzying views.

Leaving behind those soggy muddy trails, mountain biking in Fuerteventura is a completely different experience. 'Cycling in the interior is a bit like cycling on the moon,' one enthusiast was heard remarking. Most resorts, including **Corralejo** (2; p109), have bicycle rental outfits.

If you fancy swinging a golf club, Caleta de Fuste is home to the island's first and only PGA championship-rated golf course, the **Fuerteventura Golf Club** (3; p104). A more unusual, if predictable, activity here (given the blustery climate) is kite flying. If you're in Corralejo in early November you may catch the three-day festival on the beach, when hundreds of colourful kites speckle the blue sky like a flock of brilliantly coloured butterflies.

Finally, if you are feeling seriously energetic, check out **Las Tres Islas** (4; opposite), which kicks off in neighbouring Lanzarote and will have you swimming, climbing, cycling and windsurfing and lands you right on the Corralejo beach.

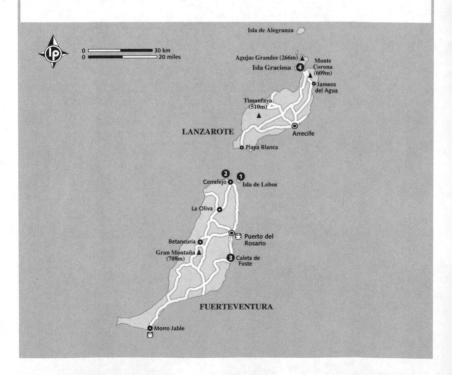

HISTORY

The island was known to the Romans as Planaria, due to its flatness. What the Europeans came to dub Fuerteventura (Strong Adventure) was in fact divided into two tribal kingdoms separated by a low, 6km-long wall: Jandía, on the southern peninsula, as far north as La Pared; and Maxorata, which occupied the rest of the island.

In January 1405 Fuerteventura was the second island to fall to the initial wave of conquerors under Jean de Béthencourt. He established a permanent base, including a chapel, in the mountainous zone of what came to be known as Betancuria, with Santa María de Betancuria evolving as the island's capital. The choice of location was determined due to the natural water supply, while the terrain gave a measure of natural defence against attacks from Guanches and pirate raids.

New settlements spread slowly across the island and, in the 17th century, Europeans occupied El Cotillo, once the seat of the Guanche Maxorata kingdom. At this time, the Arias and Saavedra families took control of the *señorío* (the island government deputising for the Spanish crown). By the following century, however, officers of the island militia had established themselves as a rival power base in La Oliva. Los Coroneles (the Colonels) gradually took virtual control of the island's affairs, enriching themselves at the expense of both the *señores* and the hard-pressed peasantry.

The militia was disbanded in 1834 and in 1912 the island, along with others in the archipelago, was granted a degree of self-administration with the installation of the *cabildo* (local authority).

INFORMATION
Books & Maps

Landscapes of Fuerteventura by Noel Rochford provides ideas for drives and walks around the island. Good city and island maps are available from the tourist offices.

Magazines

The free monthly magazine *Fuerteventura Gazette* can be found in tourist offices and contains lifestyle information. The monthly *Fuerteventura Magazine*, in Span-ish, German and English, has current affairs and classifieds.

ACCOMMODATION

Finding a place to stay in the coastal resorts can be problematic as many apartments and hotels are block-booked by tour operators.

If things look grim, head for Puerto del Rosario, where you should be able to find a room. Camp sites are few and far between; check www.campinguia.com for a list. Plenty of people seem content to pitch a tent or plonk a caravan near the beaches, but this is illegal and you risk being moved on in the middle of the night.

To assist with advance booking, check out www.haystack.lonelyplanet.com, www.catalogorural.com (in Spanish), www.casas-rurales.info (in Spanish) and www.ecoturismocanarias.com. The latter three specialise in *casas rurales* (rural accommodation).

Among the top recommended places to stay on the island is the brilliantly located budget choice Hotel Corralejo (p109), overlooking the beach; the rustic tranquillity of Hotel Rural Mahoh (p112), complete with stone-clad bedrooms; handsome and elegant Hotel Fuerteventura (p100); the lovely retreat feel of Casa Isaítas (p103) and sumptuously luxurious Hotel Atlantis Duna Park (p110) with all its pampering extras.

ACTIVITIES

The sea offers most of the action. From Caleta de Fuste, Morro Jable and Corralejo, you can both dive and windsurf. The waters off Corralejo are good for deep-sea fishing and the nearby curling waves draw in surfers. Kite boarding is gaining in popularity, too, thanks to regular wind gusts on the coast. Water-sports tuition and equipment rental are listed throughout the chapter.

The island has a good selection of walking options. Companies that offer guided walks include **Caminata** (☎ 928 53 50 10; Calle Tabaiba 27, Villaverde) and **Sendifuer** (☎ 928 16 23 85; Calle Victor Carmona, Las Playitas, Tuineje). Lunch plus transport is included.

If this all sounds a tad tame, consider signing up for **Las Tres Islas** (www.lastresislas.com) annual event. Participants start off on neighbouring Lanzarote with a swim, a hike and a bicycle ride, before rowing, canoeing or even windsurfing to Corralejo and a grand finale party on the beach.

FUERTEVENTURA

FUERTEVENTURA

FESTIVALS & EVENTS
July–August
Día de San Buenaventura (14 July) Locals in Betancuria honour the patron saint in a fiesta dating from 1456.
Windsurfing World Championship Held at Playa de Sotavento de Jandía at the end of July and early August, this mega-event attracts windsurfers and kite boarders from around the world.

September
Nuestra Señora del Pino (8 September) Antigua's local feast day.

October
Fiesta de la Virgen del Rosario (first Sunday of October) Puerto del Rosario dons its party threads to celebrate this festival honouring the capital's patron.

FUERTEVENTURA FOR CHILDREN
The main attraction has to be the beaches, many of which have fine white sand and shallow waters that are safe for paddling tots. For a watery manmade adventure, the massive **Baku Water Park** (☎ 928 86 72 27; admission adult/under 12yr €18/12; ☷ 10am-7pm) in Corralejo has ten-pin bowling, crazy golf and a driving range, as well as wave pools and kamikaze-style slides and rides.

There are plenty of boat trips on offer throughout the resorts, which families may enjoy. At Puerto Castillo, Catamaran Excursions (p104) has a daily four-hour trip at 12.30pm. El Majorero (p109) and the Celia Cruz Catamaran (p109) do similar trips from Corralejo to the Isla de Lobos, where there

are some superb beaches or the possibility (for older children) of renting bikes and exploring the island via pedal power. For something different, you can head down to the watery depths with the submarine *Nautilus* (p104), or save a few euros and see a wider range of marine life at the El Brasero aquarium (p105).

If you don't object to zoos, Oasis Park (p105) has mammals, birds and sea life, plus shows and camel rides; the latter are also available at the Zoo Safari (p112).

GETTING THERE & AWAY
Air
El Matorral airport (☎ 928 86 05 00) is 6km south of Puerto del Rosario.

Binter (☎ 902 39 13 92; www.binternet.com) has 10 flights daily to Gran Canaria (€62, 40 minutes) and at least six daily to Tenerife Norte (€86, 50 minutes). **Islas Airways** (☎ 902 47 74 48; www.islasairways.com) is considerably cheaper and has five flights daily to Gran Canaria (€30, 30 minutes).

Otherwise, charter flights connect the island with mainland Spanish cities and several European cities, including London, Amsterdam, Munich and Frankfurt.

There is a **tourist office** (☎ 928 85 12 50; 9am-7pm Mon-Sat, 11am-4pm Sun) in the airport arrivals hall.

Boat
Five weekly ferries link Puerto del Rosario and Las Palmas de Gran Canaria, while faster jetfoils speed between Morro Jable and Las Palmas. For details, see p116.

There *are* boats between Puerto del Rosario and Arrecife on Lanzarote, but you're better off taking one of the regular ferries that make the 25-minute crossing between Corralejo and Playa Blanca in Lanzarote's south (see p142).

GETTING AROUND
Given the scant public transport, renting a car is recommended and a whole lot cheaper than catching taxis.

To/From the Airport
You can get taxis (€8) or buses to Puerto del Rosario and, from there, buses to other parts of the island. For details on the airport bus, see p100.

Taxis from the airport to Corralejo cost around €35; to El Cotillo, around €37; to Costa Calma, around €55; and to the Jandía beaches, around €75.

Bus
Tiadhe (☎ 928 85 09 51, 928 85 21 62; www.tiadhe.com) provides a limited service, with 17 routes operating around the island. The most frequent are bus 6 (€2.75, 40 minutes, every half-hour), which links Puerto del Rosario with Corralejo, and bus 3 (€1.20, 20 minutes, hourly), which runs from Caleta de Fuste via the airport to the south. Bus 5 (€2.20, 20 minutes, 11 daily) runs from Morro Jable to Costa Calma.

On other routes, check times carefully before setting out. A number have only one service daily, primarily to transport school children and workers to and from Puerto del Rosario.

If you intend to use the buses fairly frequently, it is worth investing in a **Tarjeta Dinero** (€12) discount card. Tell the driver your destination and he will endorse your card; it represents about a 30% saving on each trip.

Buses do not accept €20 or €50 notes, so it's a good idea to stock up on change if buying individual tickets.

Car
You can belt around in taxis, but it soon becomes costly. It's far better to hire a car from one of the many rental offices at the airport.

PUERTO DEL ROSARIO

pop 35,110
Puerto del Rosario, the island's capital – and the only place of consequence that exists for reasons other than tourism – is home to more than half the island's population. It's a relatively modern little port town that only really took off in the 19th century. If you fly to the island, or use the buses, you may well find yourself passing through. It's a strange city with no discernable centre, which makes finding shops, restaurants and bars a frustrating business.

The good news is that the town hall has ambitious plans to make the city more tourist-friendly with a revamp of the promenade and surrounding streets. In the absence of

FOOD & DRINK

More than any other Canary island, Fuerteventura's traditional cuisine is simple and essentially the result of poverty. One of the keys remains the quality and freshness of the ingredients, particularly the seafood, although, sadly, with the increase in so-called international cuisine, the distinctive ping of the devil's tumble dryer can occasionally bear witness to preprepared dishes in the more touristy resorts.

Given that there are more goats than people on Fuerteventura (honest!), goat stew is very popular here. But it is the cheese that is the real winner. In fact, so renowned is the Majorero cheese that, just like a fine wine, it bears a *denominación de origen* (proof of origin) label, certifying that it is indeed from the island and the genuine product. It's the first Canary Island cheese to receive this accolade, and the first goat's cheese in Spain to bear the label.

At the heart of the process is the Majorero goat, a high-yielding hybrid of goat originally imported from the Spanish mainland, which can give as much as 750L of milk in one year. Whole cheeses weigh between one and six kilograms, but shop assistants will happily cut you a slice as thick or thin as you like; and you can usually taste before you buy. The cheese is ideally purchased young and soft, with a powdery white rind that becomes yellow with age. Cheeses that are to be stored for some time are often given a coating of oil, corn meal or paprika to preserve them.

Majorero is not easy to obtain outside Fuerteventura, so if you're a *queso* (cheese) fan, stock up before you leave – and perhaps add an extra slab for friends back home.

Unlike neighbouring Lanzarote, Fuerteventura is not known for its wine, though the island could soon be producing its own olive oil; the trees have recently been introduced here and an oil mill established.

Try the popular local tipple *ron miel*, a dark, syrupy rum with honey added, or stick to the freshly squeezed juices at the *zumerías* (juice bars).

any significant art museum, the city has also recently been graced by more than 100 sculptures by local and international artists. These are located throughout the capital and another positive sign that Puerto is trying to gild its somewhat tarnished image.

HISTORY

Puerto del Rosario, once little more than a handful of fishermen's cottages, became the island's capital in 1860, due to its strategic position as a harbour.

Until 1956 it was known as Puerto de las Cabras, named after the goats for which it had long been a watering hole (before becoming the main departure point for their export in the form of chops). In an early rebranding exercise, it was renamed the more dignified Puerto del Rosario (Port of the Rosary).

When Spain pulled out of the Sahara in 1975, it sent about 5000 Legión Extranjera (Foreign Legion) troops to Fuerteventura to keep a watch on North Africa. The huge barracks in Puerto del Rosario are still in use, although troops now number less than 1000.

ORIENTATION

The straggly city centre backs away from the port with the main street, Calle León y Castillo, being the artery that links the two. Running across this is Avenida Primero de Mayo, something of a commercial hub (don't get your hopes up though).

INFORMATION

Emergency
Police station (☎ 928 85 06 35; Calle Fernández Castañeyra 2)

Medical Services
Cruz Roja (Red Cross; ☎ 928 85 13 76; Avenida Constitución 19) Near the tourist office.
Hospital General (☎ 928 53 17 99; Carretera al Aeropuerta s/n) On the highway towards the airport.

Money
Banks with multilanguage ATMs line Avenida Primero de Mayo.

Post
Post office (☎ 928 85 04 12; Calle 23 de Mayo 76)

Telephone

There are plenty of public telephones throughout town and near the port area.

Tourist Information

Provincial tourist office (☎ 928 53 08 44; www
.fuerteventuraturismo.com; Almirante Lallermand 1;
🕑 8am-3pm Mon-Fri) Information on the island, as well
as the capital and a good city map.
Tourist office (☎ 928 85 01 10; www.puertodelrosario
.org in Spanish; Avenida Marítimo s/n; 🕑 8am-3pm Mon-
Fri) Small office on the seafront, opposite Hotel Roquemar.

Travel Agencies

Viajes Marsans (☎ 928 53 20 44; www.marsans.es;
Calle Profesor Juan Tadeo Cabrera 3; 🕑 9.30am-2pm &

5-8pm Mon-Sat) Good for charter flights and tours to the
other islands.

SIGHTS

About the only sight, as such, is the modest **Casa Museo de Unamuno** (☎ 928 85 14 00; Calle Rosario 11; admission free; 🕑 9am-2pm Mon-Fri). The philosopher Miguel de Unamuno, exiled for his opposition to the dictatorship of Primo de Rivera, stayed here in 1924. He later escaped to France before returning to his position at Salamanca University when the Republicans came to power in 1931.

The ground-floor house has been turned into a period piece, with four rooms furnished from Unamuno's day, including the bedroom (complete with potty!) and his study with

FUERTEVENTURA

PUERTO DEL ROSARIO

0 _____ 400 m
0 _____ 0.2 miles

INFORMATION
Cruz Roja.................................1 B2
Hospital General.....................2 A4
Police Station..........................3 C2
Post Office...............................4 B3
Provincial Tourist Office.........5 C2
Tourist Office..........................6 C2
Viajes Marsans........................7 B3

SIGHTS & ACTIVITIES
Casa Museo de Unamuno 8 B2

SLEEPING 🛏
Hostal Tamasite 9 C2
Hotel JM Puerto Rosario.......10 C2
Hotel Roquemar...................11 C2

EATING 🍴
Artesanos del Gofio..............12 B3
El Cangrejo Colorao..............13 D2
La Manduka...........................14 C2
Mercado................................15 C3
Mesón Las Brasas..................16 D1

DRINKING 🍷
Camelot.................................17 C2
Coyote ....(see 17)

TRANSPORT
Acciona-Trasmediterránea....18 B2
Bus Station.............................19 B2
Estación Marítima 20 C3
Main Bus Stop.......................21 B2
Naviera Armas........................22 C2
Taxi Rank...............................23 C3
Taxi Rank 24 B2

original desk. You'll get a warm smile at the entrance, but if you're after information in anything other than Spanish, you're short on luck.

SLEEPING

There are few good reasons for staying but if you have a hard time getting a room elsewhere on the island, you're likely to find something here.

Budget

Hotel Roquemar (☎ 928 53 15 47; hotelroquemar@hotmail .com; Avenida Marítima s/n; s/d €30/40; 🗶) Located on a busy corner across from the promenade, this 12-room hotel has been tastefully refurbished and is excellent value. The rooms are comfortable and bright, with fridges and sea views. Go for corner room No 103 with its two balconies.

Hostal Tamasite (☎ 928 85 02 80; fax 928 85 03 00; Calle León y Castillo 9; s/d from €35/45; 🗶) The Tamasite is a well-situated, two-star *pensión* (guesthouse) that was in the throes of being transformed into a chic boutique hotel when we visited. You may have to pay more than the listed prices; call first or be prepared to shift your credit card into overdrive.

Midrange

Hotel Fuerteventura (☎ 928 85 11 50; Calle Playa Blanca 45; s/d €55/75; P 🗶 🗟) Previously a *parador* (state-run) hotel but now privately owned, this good-looking hotel overlooks Playa Blanca, 3km south of the city centre. Unfortunately, it's also right under the flight path for the nearby airport, which can mean earplugs on lie-in mornings. Still, the rooms have old-fashioned charm with glossy wooden floors and high ceilings. The effortlessly stylish restaurant (mains from €7) also has an excellent reputation.

Hotel JM Puerto Rosario (☎ 928 85 94 64; www.jm hoteles.com; Avenida Ruperto González Negrín 9; s/d with breakfast €55/83; 🗶 🖳) A solid choice, this corporate-style hotel comprises 88 rooms that are far more attractive than its looming modern exterior would suggest. Beds are big, bathrooms are plush and facilities are good. The public areas have wi-fi access.

EATING

Eating out in Puerto del Rosario can be rewarding, with some good choices and modest prices. The **mercado** (market; Calle García Escámez s/n)

is a good place to pick up a wheel of *queso artesanal de cabra* (organic goat's cheese), costing around €9 a kilo.

Artesanos del Gofio (☎ 928 53 38 80; www.artesanosdel gofio.com; Calle Dr Fleming 7; biscuits from €1) The place to come for local gourmet goodies, including tasty chocolate *gofio* (a roasted mixture of wheat, maize or barley) biscuits.

Mesón Las Brasas (☎ 928 53 09 98; Calle Juan XXIII 68; mains €6.50-11) A family-friendly place, serving a fair range of unpretentious and tasty fish and meat dishes. The *menú del día* (set menu) is a €6 bargain.

El Cangrejo Colorao (☎ 928 85 84 77; Calle Juan Ramón Jiménez 2; mains €10-18) There's a pleasing old-fashioned elegance about this seafront restaurant with its bow-tied, white-tablecloth ambience. The menu is only in Spanish – always a good sign – and includes *cazuela de champiñones y jamon* (meat stew with mushrooms and ham) and *mejillones rellenos de cordero* (mussels filled with lamb). There is a €17 *menú del día*.

La Manduka (☎ 928 34 46 57; Calle León y Castillo 3; mains €15-20) Think of stepping into an Andy Warhol painting when you eat here. The dining rooms are all intense colours, large abstract paintings and dazzling tableware. Thankfully, the food rises to the challenge with an innovative menu that includes dishes like *solomillo de Ibérico con salsa de dátiles y sabrosa jardinera al sesámo* (fillet steak with a date sauce and fresh vegetables with sesame).

DRINKING

Puerto del Rosario has a modest nightlife scene geared for the locals.

Camelot (Calle Ayose 6; 🕒 11pm-3am Mon-Sat) This bar has a medieval theme and a bank of music-video screens mixed in with DJs and disco. You can catch live music performances here, too, although the quality can be patchy.

Coyote (☎ 670 85 08 30; Calle León y Castilla 14; 🕒 9pm-3am Mon-Wed, to 5am Thu-Sat) Right next door to Camelot, this is an enticing little spot with a good list of cocktails, some live music and a boisterous weekend crowd post-midnight.

GETTING THERE & AWAY
To/From the Airport

Take bus 3 (see opposite). The trip to the airport takes 10 to 15 minutes and costs €0.90. A taxi will rack up about €7.

Boat

Acciona-Trasmediterránea (☎ 928 85 00 95; www.tras
mediterranea.com; Calle León y Castillo 58) ferries
(€41, seven hours) leave from the *estación
marítima* (ferry terminal) for Las Palmas de
Gran Canaria at 1pm Tuesday, Thursday
and Saturday from June to September.

Naviera Armas (☎ 928 85 00 32; www.navieraarmas
.com) runs to Las Palmas (€41, 6½ hours)
daily at midday. The office is just east of
the port entrance.

Bus

Tiadhe (☎ 928 85 09 51; www.tiadhe.com) buses leave
from the main bus stop just past the corner
of Avenida León y Castillo and Avenida
Constitución. The following services oper-
ate from Puerto del Rosario:
Bus 1 Morro Jable via Tuineje (€8.50, two hours, at
least 12 daily)
Bus 2 Vega del Río de Palmas via Betancuria
(€2.70, 50 minutes, two daily Monday to Saturday)
Bus 3 Caleta de Fuste via the airport (€1, 20
minutes, at least 14 daily)
Bus 6 Corralejo (€2.70, 40 minutes, at least 18 daily)
Bus 7 El Cotillo (€3.50, 45 minutes, three daily)
Bus 10 Morro Jable direct (€8, 1½ hours, three daily
Monday to Saturday)

GETTING AROUND
Bus

One municipal bus does the rounds of the
city every hour. Catch it at the bus station
(*Estación de Guaguas*).

Taxi

If you need a **taxi** (☎ 928 85 00 59, 928 85 02 16),
call or grab one from the two taxi ranks –
one near Casa Museo de Unamuno, the
other near the entrance to the port area.

THE CENTRE

Central Fuerteventura offers the most
geographically diverse landscape on this
overwhelmingly desert-covered island. The
soaring mountains of the Parque Natural
de Betancuria are contrasted in the south
by the wadi-style palm-tree oasis of Vega
del Río de Palmas. The west and east coasts
are characterised by rocky cliffs interspersed
with small black pebble beaches and stuck-
in-a-time-warp fishing hamlets. In contrast,
the central copper-coloured plains around

Antigua are dotted with old windmills dating back a couple of centuries. If you're driving, it's the sort of landscape that makes you
wish you had invested in that wide-angle
camera lens.

BETANCURIA
pop 688

Wonderfully lush, this pretty hamlet is tucked
into the protective folds of the basalt hills
and is a patchwork of dry-stone walls, palm
trees and simple whitewashed cottages. Lording over it all is a magnificent 17th-century
church and courtyard

Jean de Béthencourt thought this the ideal
spot to set up house in 1405, so he had living
quarters and a chapel built. To this modest
settlement he gave his own name, which,
with time, was corrupted to Betancuria (or
the Villa de Santa María de Betancuria, in
the unexpurgated version). During the course
of the 15th century, Franciscan friars moved
in and expanded the town, which amazingly
(given its size) remained the island's capital
until 1834. The island's proximity to the North
African coast made it easy prey for Moroccan
and European pirates who, on numerous occasions, managed to defy Betancuria's natural
mountain defences and sack it.

Sights

If you approach from the north, look for the
ruins of the island's first **monastery** on your
left, built by the Franciscans.

The **Iglesia de Santa María** (☎ 928 87 80 03; Calle Alcalde Carmelo Silvera s/n; admission €1.50; ⏰ 11am-4.20pm
Mon-Sat) dates from 1620 and has a magnificent stone floor, wooden ceiling and elaborate
baroque altar. Pirates destroyed its Gothic
predecessor in 1593.

A short walk away is the **Museo de Arte
Sacro** (☎ 928 87 80 03; Calle Alcalde Carmelo Silvera s/n;
⏰ 10am-4.20pm Mon-Sat), containing a mixed bag
of religious art, including paintings, gold and
silverware. Admission is included with entry
to the Iglesia de Santa María.

Of modest interest also is the **Casa Museo
de Betancuria** (☎ 928 87 82 41; Calle Roberto Roldán s/n;
admission €1; ⏰ 10am-5pm Tue-Sat, 11am-2pm Sun),
which houses a simple collection of Guanche
artefacts, but was closed for restoration at
the time of research. Across from the church,
the **Museo Artesania** (adult/under 10yr €5/3; ⏰ 11am-
4pm) is a museum and craft centre where you
can see weavers and similar at work, taste the

FUERTEVENTURA

local cheese, watch a 20-minute film about local culture and visit the small exhibition of antique agricultural and domestic implements and appliances. There is also a shop selling such goodies as the local *licor de hierbas* (herb liquor).

Eating

Casa Princess Arminda (☎ 928 87 89 79; Calle Juan de Bethencourt 2; tapas €2.50-4) This bar, with another lovely terrace, has been in the same family since the 15th century and is named after a Guanche princess who died defending Gran Canaria. The atmosphere and tapas are suitably memorable.

Casa de Santa María (☎ 928 87 82 82; Plaza Santa María de Betancuria 1; mains €9-18; ☽ closed Sun night & Mon) Opposite the main portal of the church, this restaurant looks like it has been transplanted from Andalucía. The interior is set around several courtyards with bubbling fountains, plants and flowers. The menu includes all manner of goaty offerings – from roasted to fried cheese with apple chutney.

Getting There & Away

Bus 2 (€2.30, 50 minutes) passes through here twice daily (except Sunday) on its way between Puerto del Rosario and Vega del Río de Palmas, a short distance south.

AROUND BETANCURIA

A couple of kilometres north of Betancuria, there's a handy **lookout** (on both sides of the road) that explains the various mountain peaks that loom on the horizon. Further on, the **Mirador Morro Velosa** offers mesmerising views across the island's weird, disconsolate moonscape. If the barrier to the lookout is closed, the view is almost as spectacular at the col over which the FV-30 highway climbs before it twists its way north through Valle de Santa Inés, a hiccup of a village. Stop at the central **La Casa del Queso** (☎ 928 87 88 05) to pick up a chunk of *queso de cabra;* you can taste it first at the adjacent bar.

In the pretty **Casillas del Ángel** village, the petite **Iglesia de Santa Ana** contains an 18th-century wooden carving of St Anne.

For a superb meal, try **La Era** (☎ 928 53 81 80; Carretera General de Casillas del Ángel; mains €8-15) at the western end of the town. A long, low ochre building, the elegant dining room attracts business bods from all around with its menu of traditional, superbly prepared local dishes.

Heading south of Betancuria for Pájara, you soon hit the small oasis of **Vega del Río de Palmas**. As you proceed, the reason for the name becomes clear – the road follows the course of a near-dry watercourse still sufficiently wet below the surface to keep alive a stand of palms.

ANTIGUA
pop 7000

This is one of the larger inland villages but it's a fairly dull place with not much to retain you, aside from a quick dip into the 18th-century **Nuestra Señora de Antigua** (☽ 10am-2pm). One of the island's oldest churches, it has a pretty pink-and-green painted altar.

Scarcely 1km north of here is the **Molino de Antigua** (☎ 928 87 80 41; adult/under 12yr €1.80/0.90; ☽ 10am-6pm Tue-Fri & Sun), a fully restored windmill with cacti garden, audiovisual display and a bar and restaurant. There is also a gift shop, with all proceeds going directly to the craftsmen and women, which makes a pleasant change.

Bus 1 (€1.80, 30 minutes) passes through here en route between Puerto del Rosario and Morro Jable.

AROUND ANTIGUA

You'll require your own transport to access these small towns.

La Ampuyenta

If it's open, the 17th-century **Ermita de San Pedro de Alcántara** merits a quick stop. The *ermita* (chapel) is surrounded by a stout protective wall built by the French from the Normandy area. Within, the walls of the nave are decorated with large, engagingly naive paintings, contrasting with the more sophisticated works embellishing the wooden altarpiece.

Tiscamanita
pop 260

Visit this tiny hamlet, 9km south of Antigua, to see a working mill (and find out what a hard grind it all was). The **Windmill Interpretation Centre** (☎ 928 85 14 00; admission €1.80; ☽ 10am-6pm Mon-Sat) highlights a praiseworthy restoration project and all the information about windmills you could possibly want to know; there's a free guide in English. If there is wind, you can sit under the lovely pomegranate tree and try freshly ground *gofio*.

DETOUR

If you have your own wheels, a 9km side trip from Pájara takes you northwest to **Ajuy** and contiguous **Puerto de la Peña**. A blink-and-you'll-miss-it fishing settlement, its black-sand beach makes a change from its illustrious golden neighbours to the south on the Península de Jandía. The locals and fishing boats take pride of place here, and the strand is fronted by a couple of simple seafood eateries serving up the day's catch.

There's a low-key coastal walking track heading right (north) as you face the water, leading for a few minutes along the windy rocks, with some lovely views.

PÁJARA
pop 3100

What makes the 17th-century **Iglesia de Nuestra Señora de Regla** unique in the islands is the Aztec-inspired exterior with its animal motifs, and the simple retables behind the altar, which are more subdued than the baroque excesses of mainland Spain (stick a coin in the machine on the right at the entrance to light them up). They are an example of influences flowing back from Latin America – in this case, Mexico. Don't forget to look up; there's a magnificent carved wooden ceiling.

Across the road from the church is **Restaurante La Fonda** (☎ 928 16 16 25; Calle Nuestra Señora de Regla 25; mains €6.50-12.50), which has a beguiling rustic ambience, with stone walls and wooden ceilings as well as ropes of garlic, legs of ham and strings of chilli hanging from the ceiling. The food here is good, honest and hearty.

our pick **Casa Isaítas** (☎ 928 16 14 02; www.casaisaitas .com; Calle Guize 7; s/d with breakfast €66/84) One of the loveliest *casas rurales* is run by two delightful women, Mercedes and Pilar. The lovingly restored 18th-century stone house has two plant-filled central courtyards, traditional wooden galleries and balconies and an outside barbecue complete with giant paella pan; evening meals are an optional extra. There are just four simply rustic rooms, a couple of which were part of the original house.

Bus 13 (€1.90, 30 minutes, daily at 12.45pm) runs between Pájara and Gran Tarajal then on to La Lajita, stopping at villages en route. There are no services to the north.

AROUND PÁJARA

The drive directly north towards Betancuria is one of the most spectacular on the island, while the journey south towards Península de Jandía via La Pared is almost as attractive. Fuerteventura ranks as relatively flat when compared to Lanzarote and the other islands to the west, but you would never think so as you wend your way through this lonely and spectacularly harsh terrain.

CALETA DE FUSTE

This smart well-landscaped resort, exudes an opulent southern-California feel, particularly around the sprawling Barceló minivillage, which fronts the main beach. Caleta is convenient for the airport and, if you're travelling with a young family, the wide arc of sand and shallow waters are ideal. However, if you are seeking somewhere intrinsically Canarian, then look elsewhere; this is yet another of Fuerteventura's purpose-developed tourist resorts, although, in all fairness, it is a relaxing place with some good hotels and restaurants.

Information

The **tourist office** (☎ 928 16 32 86; Centro Comercial Castillo; 🕑 9am-3pm Mon-Fri) shares a space with the police station and is surprisingly sparse on information, given the popularity of the place.

Sights & Activities

The squat, round tower known grandly as **El Castillo** has been turned into an appendage of the Barceló Club El Castillo bungalow complex. In front of here, the white sandy beach, complete with volleyball net and **camel rides** (30min ride €10), is ideal for families, although a poor relation compared to the rolling dunes and endless sands of Corralejo and Jandía. There are plans to extend the promenade, which will enhance the area, although the continuous development may do the exact opposite.

DIVING & SNORKELLING

Deep Blue (☎ 928 16 37 12, 606 27 54 68; www.deep -blue-diving.com; orientation dive €18) is conveniently situated beside the port. For up to four dives, each dive costs €33, reducing to €21 for more than 12 dives. There are beginner courses for Professional Association of Diving Instructors (PADI) certification and a wide range of specialist courses, including ones for children (€41). You can also go snorkelling with **Aqua Ventura** (☎ 630 16 76 92; adult/under 12yr €28/20), located adjacent to Deep Blue.

SURFING & WINDSURFING

For a surf, head to the **Surf School** (☎ 620 84 64 15; www.fuerteventurasurfschool.com; 1-3-day courses €40-100), located behind the tourist office. On the far side of the main beach, in front of Los Pescadores restaurant, **Fanatic Fun Center** (⏱ 10am-5pm) offers six-hour beginner courses for €95, including windsurfing equipment hire. Gear hire alone costs €30/50/170 per half-day/day/week.

SAILING & SUBMARINING

From the port, **Catamaran Excursions** (☎ 928 16 35 14; Puerto Castillo; adult/under 12yr €50/25) sails daily at 12.30pm, returning at 4.30pm. The price includes lunch on board, the use of snorkelling equipment and a visit to the company's small oceanarium. With any luck (well, quite a bit, actually), you might catch sight of dolphins and whales.

Nautilus (adult/under 4yr/4-12yr €20/free/10), a small yellow submarine, sets out on the hour each day for a 45-minute dive.

GOLF

Covering a vast 1.5 sq km, the **Fuerteventura Golf Club** (www.fuerteventuragolfclub.com; 18 holes €52) has top-wack facilities, including a pro shop and resident PGA professional. It was the venue for the 2004 Spanish Open.

THALASSOTHERAPY

You can't miss the glass building behind the beach with its giant 'Thallaso' sign. At **Balneario Thalasso** (☎ 928 16 09 61; www.spabalnearia .com; Calle Savila 2; ⏱ Jun-Sep), a relaxing massage with chocolate will cost you a lip-smacking €59, while an aromatic face massage will set you back just €24. Thalassotherapy is also available at the Barceló Club El Castillo (right).

Sleeping

As in other resorts, most places here fill with tourists on all-in package deals.

Aparthotel Castillo de Elba (☎ 928 16 36 00; www.hotelselba.com; Urbanazion Costa Antigua; studios/apt €55/63; P ⊠ ⊠) Energetic souls will love this place with its tennis, squash and paddle courts, plus a golf course a couple

of kilometres away. The three-star apartments and studios are bright and attractive with pine furnishings and balconies (for recovery time). Low-season reductions are available.

Barceló Club El Castillo (☎ 928 16 31 00; www.bar celo.com; Avenida Castillo s/n; bungalows from €76; P ⊠ ⊠ ⊠ ⊠) This franchise is so large it deserves its own postcode. The whole place has a sumptuous feel, with bougainvillea-draped bungalows, a Thalassotherapy centre and gardens fronting onto the beach.

Eating

Frasquita (☎ 928 16 36 57; Playa de Caleta de Fuste; mains €7-10; ⏱ closed Mon) This is one of the best restaurants on the island for fresh seafood, despite its very plain appearance with white plastic tables and chairs. Sit in the glassed-in dining room overlooking the beach rather than the front terrace, which mysteriously overlooks the car park out back.

Puerto Castillo Restaurante (☎ 928 53 19 45; Avenida Castillo s/n; mains €9-12; ⏱ closed Sun) Beside the *castillo*, this 1st-floor restaurant has sea views from a vast terrace and an elegant ambience in the dining room. Try the mussels with green *mojo*, or red peppers with seafood for a memorable taste-bud treat.

La Paella (☎ 928 16 31 00; Caleta de Fuste; mains €9.50-17) This beach-side restaurant has comfortable wicker armchairs and real cosmopolitan character. The menu includes fried chicken with dates, leek and prawn pie and a delicious cheese platter with fig puree. It's part of Barceló (what isn't?) but has distinctive, individual flair.

AROUND CALETA DE FUSTE

Just south of Caleta, in Las Salinas, is the **Museo de la Sal** (Salt Museum; ☎ 928 17 49 26; adult/under 12yr €5/free; ⏱ 10am-6pm Tue-Sat; ⊠) with audiovisual displays that explain the history of salt and demonstrate how it is extracted from the sea. A few kilometres south of here, follow the signs to **Pozo Negro**, which will take you past palm plantations. This relatively unspoilt fishing village has two popular seafood restaurants, including **Los Pescadores** (☎ 928 17 46 53; mains €7), which dishes up excellent fish dishes and has a terrace on the beach. Pozo Negro is popular with windsurfers, but bring your own gear.

THE SOUTHEAST

GINIGINAMAR & TARAJALEJO

These two quiet fishing hamlets go about their business largely undisturbed by tourists, though Tarajalejo, with a couple of hotels and apartment blocks at its southern limit, is under siege: a four-star Bahia Playa hotel was under construction when we visited. Their small, grey beaches are nothing spectacular but reasonably uncrowded. Stop for a drink at the simple Tofio Chiringuito, with its straw umbrellas on the beach at Tarajalejo. This is a popular spot for windsurfers.

Just west of the FV-2 highway outside Tarajalejo, El Brasero has a tiny **aquarium** (☎ 928 87 20 70; adult/under 12yr €4.50/2.30; ⏰ 10am-7pm) with around 120 species of fish. There is also a restaurant and bar. Adjacent is the **Centro Hípica** (☎ 699 24 46 23; per hr €20) for horse riding and trekking.

Camping El Brasero (☎ 928 16 10 01; fax 928 16 10 28; camp site per person/tent €8/3; ⚓) is also here with reasonable shady sites, two small swimming pools and even a modest gym. There are discounts for stays over 15 days.

Bus 1 (€5.20, one hour 20 minutes, hourly) between Puerto del Rosario and Morro Jable stops at Tarajalejo but not in Giniginamar.

LA LAJITA

This little fishing village presents yet another black-sand and pebble beach and cove with colourful fishing boats and an unspoiled waterfront. However, stretching all the way to the highway is a sprawl of unimaginative apartment blocks. At its southern exit is one of the island's largest theme parks: at **Oasis Park** (☎ 928 16 11 35; Carretera General de Jandía s/n; adult/under 11yr €18/9; ⏰ 9am-6pm) you can wander around the little zoo, populated by monkeys, exotic birds and other caged unfortunates, with various shows, including sea lions, birds of prey and parrots. You can also join a 35-minute camel trek (adult/child €8/4). If plant life is more your thing, visit the park's botanical garden, with more than 2300 types of cacti.

Bus 1 (€5.20, one hour 20 minutes, hourly) stops at the highway exit to town, from where it's a short walk south to the complex.

THE NORTH

ROAD TO LA OLIVA

The FV-10 highway shoots westwards away from Puerto del Rosario into the interior where ochre-coloured soil and distant volcanoes create a barren, otherworldly landscape.

FUERTEVENTURA

LOCAL VOICES

The following couple are the grandparents of a family friend and it was a privilege to have a glimpse into the hardships of their world.

Pedro Cabrero Curbelo (85) and his wife, Magdalena (84), were both born on Fuerteventura and lived through the island's endemic poverty before the arrival of tourism. 'There was no electricity or mains water until 1979 and this town (Giniginamar) only had four houses and a church,' explains Pedro.

'We had a *pozo* (well) but the water was very salty. In the old days a lot of people left for Venezuela to make their fortunes, because life was so hard here and the land supplied little food. I went to work in the southern Sahara in the sulphate mines for several years and when I returned, I married. It was still hard; there was only one doctor on the whole island. We lost two children and, if there was a death in the village, we had to carry the deceased over our shoulders to the cemetery, as there were virtually no surfaced roads.

'We started rearing goats to make cheese that was sold door to door. It was the only way to make a living here.'

Today the farm is thriving with around 600 goats and a flock of sheep. According to daughter Theresa, her mother is still up at 7am every morning to look after the goats. The milk is collected daily for transport to a cheese-making factory.

'Do you like cheese?' I ask innocently.

'No!' Pedro and Magdalena answer in unison, before bursting into gales of laughter.

Before crossing the ridge that forms the island's spine, it passes through the sleepy hamlets of **Tetir** and **La Matilla**. The tiny 1902 chapel in the latter is a good example of the simple bucolic buildings of the Canaries – functional, relatively unadorned and aesthetically pleasing.

About 7km south of La Matilla, along the FV-207, and 1km beyond the village of Tefía, is the **Ecomuseo la Alcogida** (☎ 928 85 14 00; adult/under 12yr €4.50/free; ☒ 10am-6pm Tue-Sat), a restored agricultural hamlet complete with furnished houses, outbuildings and domestic animals (though the chained-up dogs have a troubling un-eco feel). Overall, it's an interesting glimpse into the tough rural life of the not-too-distant past, with local artisans working in some of the settlement's buildings making lace and wicker baskets. There's a gift shop and an optional audio commentary in English (€3).

Follow the road out of Tefía and swing right (west) on the FV-211 for **Los Molinos**. On the way you can't miss the old windmill used to grind cereals for the production of *gofio*, sitting squat across from a distinctive white-domed observatory. Los Molinos itself is little more than a few simple houses overlooking a small, grey, stony beach with cliff trails to the east and plenty of goats, geese and stray cats. If you do stop here, make a point of having a seafood lunch at **Restaurante Casa Pon** (mains €6-10; ☒ 11am-6pm) while gazing over Atlantic breakers.

Tindaya is a sprawling village where much of the island's Majorero goat cheese is produced, although you wouldn't know it; there are no high-street delis selling the cheese here (in fact, there's no high street!). See the boxed text on p98 for more information on this renowned cheese.

Bus 7 from Puerto del Rosario to El Cotillo passes through all but Tefía and Casa de los Molinos three times daily. Bus 2 (€1.25, 20 minutes, twice daily), between Puerto del Rosario and Vega del Río de Palmas, passes by Tefía. There are no buses to Los Molinos.

LA OLIVA
pop 2300
One-time capital of the island, in fact if not in name, La Oliva still bears a trace or two of grander days. The weighty bell tower of the 18th-century **Iglesia de Nuestra Señora de la Can-** delaria is the town's focal point of sorts, with its black volcanic bulk contrasting sharply with the bleached-white walls of the church itself. To the south, the 18th-century **Casa de los Coroneles**, (☎ 928 86 19 04; admission free; ☒ 10am-2pm & 4.30-7pm Tue-Sun) looks more like a child's toy fort than a simple *casa* (house). In fact, its name means House of the Colonels and it has an interesting history: from the early 1700s, the officers who once presided here virtually controlled the affairs of the island. Amassing power and wealth, they so exploited the peasant class that, in 1834, Madrid, faced with repeated bloody mutinies on the island, disbanded the militia.

The building has been aesthetically restored, retaining its traditional central patio and wooden galleries, and opened in November 2006 as a space for displaying world-class modern art. Temporary exhibitions include audiovisual installations, as well as paintings and photography. Adjacent to the *casa*, the perfect cone of the volcano is an example of nature's art as opposed to human's.

Another highlight here is the **Centro de Arte Canario** (☎ 928 37 12 66; www.centrodeartecanario .com; admission €4; ☒ 10.30am-2pm Mon-Sat) with its garden of sculptures, and galleries containing works by such Canarian artists as César Manrique and Alberto Agullo. There are also temporary exhibitions and paintings by owner Manuel Delgado Camino. To find the gallery, follow the signs from the centre of town.

About 250m north of the church, on the road to El Cotillo, is the **Casa Cilla Museo del Grano** (admission adult/under 12yr €1.20/free; ☒ 9.30am-5.30pm Tue-Fri & Sun), a small museum devoted to grain – both its production and the harsh life of the farming cycle in general.

Bus 7 (€1.90, 35 minutes) between Puerto del Rosario and El Cotillo passes through three times daily.

CORRALEJO
pop 12,000
Your opinion of this place will depend wholly upon where you are standing. The former fishing village near the harbour and main beach still has charm, despite the tourists, with narrow, uneven streets, good seafood restaurants and even a fisherman's cottage or two. Venture inland a couple of blocks and you find the predictable could-be-anywhere-resort with Slow Boat buffets,

CORRALEJO

0 — 300 m
0 — 0.2 miles

INFORMATION
Centro de Salud.......................**1** B4
Clínica Médica Brisamar.........**2** C6
Oceana.....................................**3** B4
Police Station..........................**4** C4
Post Office...............................**5** B4
Tourist Office..........................**6** C4

SIGHTS & ACTIVITIES
Celia Cruz Catamaran Ticket
    Kiosk.................................**7** D3
Dive Centre Corralejo............**8** C3
El Majorero Ticket Kiosk........**9** C3
Matador Surf School..............**10** B5
Siña Maria 111........................**11** C3
Ventura Surf Center...............**12** C5
Vulcano Biking......................**13** B4

SLEEPING
Apartamentos Corralejo
    Beach...............................**14** C4
Fuente Park..........................**15** B5
Hesperia Bristol Playa............**16** B3
Hotel Atlantis Duna Park.......**17** C5
Hotel Corralejo.....................**18** C4

EATING
Café de Viena.......................**19** C5
El Andaluz............................**20** C3
La Cabaña Asturiana.............**21** C4
La Factoria...........................**22** C4
Poco Loco............................**23** C5

DRINKING
Antiguo Café del Puerto........**24** C3

Cafe Latino...........................**25** C3
Centro Comercial Atlántico....**26** C4
Dubliner.........................(see 26)
Rock Island Bar....................**27** B5
Waikiki................................**28** C5

SHOPPING
Market.................................**29** C6
No Work Team......................**30** C5

TRANSPORT
Bus Station...........................**31** B4
Cicar...................................**32** C4
Fred Olsen...........................**33** C3
Naviera Armas......................**34** D3
Rent A Bike Club..................**35** B4
Taxi Rank.............................**36** C4

FUERTEVENTURA

ATLANTIC OCEAN

Punta de Corralejo

Paseo Marítimo Bristol

Calle Atalaya

To Fuerte Snorkelling (2km)

Calle Nuestra Señora del Carmen

Calle General Prim

Calle Iglesia

Calle Pérez Galdós

Calle Pizarro

Calle Milagrosa

To El Cotillo (17km)

Calle General García Escámez

Plaza Grande de Corralejo

Carrero Blanco Calle Almirante

Calle Lepanto

Calle Fahía

Calle Juan Sebastián Elcano

Paseo Atlántico

Avenida Juan Carlos

Calle Palangre

Calle Churruca

Calle Acorazado España

Calle Anzuelo

Calle Carabela

Calle Fragata

ATLANTIC OCEAN

Calle Anguila

Calle Red

Calle Acacia

Nuestra Señora del Carmen

Avenida Grandes Playas

Calle Marcelino Camach

To Bike Center (400m);
Grandes Playas (3km);
Parque Natural de Corralejo (5km);
Flag Beach Windsurf Center (5km)

Calle Palmeras

Calle Anzuelo

Calle Gran Canaria

Calle Hibisco

To Baku
Water Park (50m);
La Oliva (13km)

DETOUR

The bare, 4.4-sq-km **Isla de Lobos** takes its name from the *lobos marinos* (sea wolves) that lived there. They were, in fact, *focas monje* (monk seals), which have since disappeared thanks to the hungry crew of French explorer de la Salle, which ate them to stave off starvation in the early 15th century.

You can go on an excursion to the islet from Corralejo. Once you've disembarked there's little to do but go for a short walk, order lunch at the quay-side *chiringuito* (kiosk) – reserve when you arrive if you intend to lunch there – and head for the pleasant little beach.

It's a popular bird-watching destination and there are hammerhead sharks in the waters around the island. Surfers often carve up the mean breaks when the waves are pumping.

The cheapest and fastest way to get there is on the **Isla de Lobos ferry** (adult/child return €15/7.50). Departing Corralejo at 10am, it leaves the island at 4pm. A minicruise is another option; see opposite.

---

fish and chips and a grid system of streets. It could be worse: the buildings are low-rise and you can still find the occasional local Spanish bar.

What makes Corralejo, however, are the blindingly white sand dunes to the south of town, sweeping back into gentle sugar-loaf rolls from the sea and fabulous broad sandy beaches. Protected as a nature park, no one can build on or near them…for now, that is. Unfortunately, a couple of monolithic concrete eyesores from the Riu hotel chain managed to get here before the regulation was in place.

Orientation

Corralejo's east is bordered by its small passenger harbour, which is the oldest part of town. The streets of the new, modern part of town are easy to navigate, while the main surfing beaches are accessible by taxi.

Information

EMERGENCY
Police station (☎ 928 86 61 07; Paseo Atlántico s/n)

INTERNET ACCESS
Oceana (Avenida Nuestro Señora del Carmen 14; per 30min €2.70; ☼ 10am-11pm)

MEDICAL SERVICES
Centro de Salud (☎ 928 86 61 43; Avenida Juan Carlos I) Next to the main bus station.
Clínica Médica Brisamar (☎ 928 53 64 02; Avenida Nuestro Señora del Carmen; ☼ 24hr) One of several private clinics geared towards tourists.

POST
Post office (☎ 928 53 50 55; Calle Isaac Peral 55)

TOURIST INFORMATION
Tourist office (☎ 928 86 62 35; www.corrale jograndesplayas.com; Avenida Marítimo 2; ☼ 8am-3pm Mon-Fri) Located on the seafront near the harbour with shelves full of brochures.

Sights & Activities
PARQUE NATURAL DE CORRALEJO
The beach dunes of this protected **nature park** stretch along the east coast for about 10km from Corralejo. It can get breezy here, hence the popularity with windsurfers and kite boarders. The locals have applied their ingenuity to the sand-sticking-to-the-suntan-lotion problem by erecting little fortresses of loose stones atop shrub-covered sandy knolls to protect sun-worshippers from the wind. The area is free to enter, and sun lounges and umbrellas are available for hire in front of the luxury hotels.

DIVING & SNORKELLING
Dive Center Corralejo (☎ 928 53 59 06; www.dive centercorralejo.com; Calle Nuestra Señora del Pino 22; dives from €29), is a respected dive operator, operating since 1979. Located just back from the waterfront, you can take the plunge with a beginner course. It also rents out equipment and can accommodate disabled divers with an advanced booking.

You can go snorkelling on the Isla de Lobos with **Fuerte Snorkelling** (☎ 680 85 61 22; www.fuerte services.com; Paseo Marítimo Bristol s/n; adult/under 12yr €35/30), visiting two sites with a maximum of eight people per excursion.

WINDSURFING & KITE BOARDING
Conditions along much of the coast and in the straits between Corralejo and Lanzarote – the

Estrecho de la Bocaina – are ideal for both wind-surfing and kite boarding. The **Ventura Surf Center** (☎ 928 86 62 95; www.ventura-surf.com; Calle Fragata s/n; 1½hr course from €45, gear hire per hr from €23) is one of several in the area that cater for beginners. The centre is on the beach at the end of the street.

Out at Grandes Playas, **Flag Beach Windsurf Center** (☎ 928 86 63 89; www.flagbeach.com; Calle General Linares 31) has beginner windsurfing courses for €120 for three days and windsurf hire from €25 per hour. The staff are also excellent kite boarding instructors, with an introductory two-day course costing €220. Check it out also for accommodation arrangements.

SURFING

Corralejo is a justifiably popular base for surf-ers, with phrases like 'the Hawaii of Spain' commonly bandied about. **Matador Surf School** (☎ 928 86 73 07; www.matadorsurfschool.com; Calle Pal-angre 4; 3-day course €120; ⏰ 10am-noon & 6-8pm Mon-Sat) offers courses, including equipment and insurance plus transport to the waves.

Flag Beach Windsurf Center (☎ 928 86 63 89; www .flagbeach.com; Calle General Linares 31) also rents out boards (from €12 per day) and boogie boards (from €10 per day), plus it has a great beginner course for €45.

BOAT TRIPS

Three-hour minicruises aboard **El Majorero** (☎ 619 30 79 49; Estacíon Marítimo; adult/under 12yr €18/9) allow a couple of hours on the Isla de Lobos (see the boxed text, opposite). They leave at 10am and noon. Alternatively, sim-ply use the boat to get across to the islet (adult/child return €15/7.50). The last boat back leaves at 4pm. Buy your tickets from the kiosk at the port.

The **Celia Cruz Catamaran** (☎ 928 86 64 99; Es-tacíon Marítimo; adult/under 12yr return €15/7.50) sails to the Isla de Lobos daily at 10am, noon and 3.30pm.

FISHING

You can sign up for deep-sea-fishing trips at the port with **Siña Maria 111** (☎ 617 78 22 49; angler/spectator €60/50). Trips take place between 8am and 1.30pm Monday to Saturday, and the skipper will cook your catch for lunch and keep the beer flowing.

CYCLING

Vulcano Biking (☎ 928 53 57 06; Calle Acorazado España 10; per day/3 days/week €6/15/30; ⏰ closed Sun) rents

bikes. For guided excursions contact the **Bike Center** (☎ 928 53 53 62; www.extreme-animals.com; Calle Las Dunas s/n; 4hr trip €29; ⏰ 10am-5pm).

Sleeping

It can be a real hassle finding somewhere to stay in Corralejo. Without wheels it can be worse, as a lot of the apartments are strung out along the beach south of town. Still more of a pain, many deal only with tour operators. So if you don't come on a package, be prepared to move on to, say, Puerto del Rosario until you can organise something in one of the resorts.

BUDGET

Hotel Corralejo (☎ 928 53 52 46; Calle Colón 12; s/d/t €30/35/40) A one-star seaside bargain right in the heart of town with pleasant, albeit small, rooms washed in ochre and with bathrooms; go for one with a balcony and the five-star views overlooking the delightful small beach. It's a mite shabby but everything works and several rooms overlook the town beach.

MIDRANGE

Apartamentos Corralejo Beach (☎ 928 88 63 15; www.corralejobeach.com; Avenida Nuestro Señora del Car-men 3; studios €54, apt €60-75; 🖳) These studios and apartments in between the old and new parts of town were in the throes of being updated during research. That said, they are well worth checking out. The accommodation is centred around a pool and there is a host of activities on offer, with gym, sauna, squash and mini-golf available. Discounts of 20% are available for stays of a week or longer.

Fuente Park (☎ 928 53 53 10; www.fuentepark.com; Calle Anguila 1; 2-person apt from €75; P 🖳 🖳) Well located just off the main *avenida*, within stroll-ing distance of the old harbour and beach, this place has superb facilities and a veritable five-star feel. There are colourful landscaped gardens, two pools, satellite TV and wi-fi in the lobby. The whitewashed apartments are modern and attractive with balconies and separate kitchens.

TOP END

Hesperia Bristol Playa (☎ 928 86 70 20; www.hesperia -bristolplaya.com; Urbanizacion Lago de Bristol 1; apt €83; P 🖳 🖳 🖳 🖳) Surrounded by bougainvil-lea, hibiscus and palms, this aparthotel is a green oasis of luxury and style. The slick, modern apartments are set around three swimming pools, with a handy supermarket

FUERTEVENTURA

for self-catering. There is a miniclub to keep the kiddies happy.

Hotel Atlantis Duna Park (☎ 928 53 61 51; www.atlantishotels.com; Calle Red 1; s & d €90-162; P ⌧ ℞) The quality is up there with the best of them at this centrally located hotel. The rooms are large and comfortable with terracotta tiles, shiny marble bathrooms and large balconies overlooking the two palm-fringed pools. There is satellite TV, wi-fi access and tennis courts, plus a gym and health club offering all the usual pampering delights like spa, massage and sauna.

Eating

The pedestrian area around the town's small port is home to plenty of restaurants with outside terraces for ultimate people-watching potential.

Café de Viena (Calle Juan de Austria 27) Possibly the best place in town for breakfast. Choose between Spanish, German, English or vegetarian – with all the trimmings and freshly squeezed orange juice.

La Factoria (☎ 928 53 57 26; Avenida Marítimo 9; mains €6-9; V) Situated right on the beach in the old harbour, the owner is from Bologna, so knows a thing or two about pasta, which is freshly made daily and delicious. The pizzas are similarly good with thin, crispy bases and tasty toppings – *mama* would definitely approve.

El Andaluz (Calle La Ballena 5; mains €9-16; ☻ closed Sun & Mon; V) The chef-owner is from Córdoba – and it shows. The menu includes *salmorejo* (thick, gazpacho-style soup) and *gambas al ajillo* (shrimps in garlic sauce). Vegetarians are catered to (rare in Andalucía!) with a tasty leek pie with vegetables.

Poco Loco (☎ 928 86 66 62; Avenida Nuestro Señora del Carmen 16; mains €10-14) You can expect a good grilling at this Argentinean-style steak house with its T-bone steaks, lamb chops and – good heavens – vegetarian lasagne! The orange-and-black interior is a mite macho, however, while the mountain stag's head looks suitably benign.

La Cabaña Asturiana (Avenida Marítimo 3; mains €12-14) This restaurant has a superb position on the seafront with an attractive chunky wood furnished interior. The menu here offers something different: traditional Asturian cuisine with dishes like Asturian stew, rabbit or sausages in cider and tuna-stuffed onions. Tastier than they sound – promise!

Drinking

Finding a drink in Corralejo doesn't pose a problem. Bars take up much of the **Centro Comercial Atlántico** (Avenida Nuestro Señora del Carmen) as well as the custard-yellow shopping centre further down the road, on the corner of Calle Anguila.

Dubliner (☎ 928 86 66 35; Centro Comercial Atlántico, Avenida Nuestro Señora del Carmen; ☻ 9pm-2am) An English-run Irish bar with live music nightly, including '60s music, rock and blues. If you are not ready for cocoa when it closes, you can shimmy over to the Mafasca Buddha club across the way.

our pick **Waikiki** (Calle Arístides Hernández Morán 11; ☻ 10am-11.30pm) An excellent place to party, where a mix of surfers, party animals, families and friends gather in a hibiscus-fringed beach-side setting to scoff pizza (€5 to €6), sip cocktails and even indulge in a Caribbean dance lesson (10.30pm Tuesday and Thursday). There is late-night music and the piña coladas are sublime.

Rock Island Bar (☎ 928 53 53 46; www.rockislandbar.com; Calle Crucero Baleares s/n; ☻ 7.30pm-late) Over the last 17 years, Mandy and musician husband Gary have made this bar one of the most popular in town. There is acoustic music nightly, played to a predominantly expat crowd.

Antiguo Café del Puerto (Calle Ballena 10; tapas €1.50-4.20) A classy place with rag-washed walls and some tasty tapas. It's a great choice for a drink and a snack without being deafened by Euro-cheese music.

Cafe Latino (Calle Ballena; cocktails €5; ☻ closed Wed afternoon) For coffee, ice cream, a cocktail or snack, this place on the waterfront has a French Riviera feel with its stripy umbrellas and classy look.

Shopping

No Work Team (☎ 928 53 51 11; Avenida Nuestro Señora del Carmen 46; ☻ 10am-2pm & 5-8pm Mon-Sat) One local surf-wear label to check out is No Work Team. In its shop you'll find good-quality, comfy duds for men, women and children, with an unmistakeable surfing feel.

Market (cnr Calle Gran Canaria & Avenida Nuestro Señora del Carmen; ☻ 9am-1pm Mon & Fri) Rather tame local market that is heavier on African arts and crafts than it is on Canarian specialities.

Getting There & Away
BOAT
Fred Olsen (☎ 902 53 50 90; www.fredolsen.es) ferries leave seven times daily for Playa Blanca

(adult/child/12 to 26 years/car €21/10/14/27, 35 minutes) in Lanzarote. You can buy tickets at the port. Otherwise, hop onto one of the **Naviera Armas** (☎ 928 54 21 13; www.navieraarmas .com) boats (adult/child/12 to 26 years/car €16/8/13/18, six or seven daily).

At the Lanzarote end, Fred Olsen puts on a free connecting bus as far as Puerto del Carmen for its 9am and 5pm services. The 9am run continues to Lanzarote's airport. This free bus also operates in the other direction (see p142).

BUS
The bus station is located on Avenida Juan Carlos I. Bus 6 (€2.75, 40 minutes) runs regularly from the bus station to Puerto del Rosario.

Bus 8 (€2.50, 40 minutes, 13 daily) heads west to El Cotillo via La Oliva.

CAR & MOTORCYCLE
There's a string of car-rental companies near the Centro Comercial Atlántico on Avenida Nuestro Señora del Carmen. **Cicar** (☎ 928 82 29 00; www.cicar.com) has an office right at the commercial centre's entrance and good prices, with an economy car from around €100 for three days.

If you want just two motorised wheels, stop by the originally named **Rent A Bike Club** (☎ 928 86 62 33; Avenida Juan Carlos I 21; ☯ 9am-1pm & 5-8pm Mon-Sat, 9am-1pm Sun), opposite the bus station. You can rent scooters and motorcycles from €35 and €60 per day respectively, with full insurance.

Getting Around
TAXI
Call ☎ 928 86 61 08 or ☎ 928 53 74 41 for a taxi. A trip from the town centre to the main beaches will cost about €6. There's a convenient taxi rank near the Centro Comercial Atlantico.

EL COTILLO
pop 4400
This former fishing village has real character; it's a bit scruffy in places, but that's all part of the charm. Unfortunately, the cranes have arrived – and not the winged variety. At least the development continues to be low-rise and, particularly around Las Lagos, the architecture is more imaginative than most. Head for the *muelle* (harbour), the most atmospheric

part of town, and continue north to El Cotillo's only veritable sight: tubby **Castillo del Tostón** (☯ 9am-noon & 1-4pm Mon-Fri, 9am-1pm Sat & 9am-3pm Sun), which is not really a castle, more a Martello tower. There's a sight-and-sound exhibit, a display of arsenal and you can climb to the top for sweeping views of the surf beach with its bizarre clump of sculptures by French artist Kadir Attia.

Once the seat of power of the tribal chiefs of Maxorata (the northern kingdom of Guanche Fuerteventura), El Cotillo has been largely ignored since the conquest. The exceptions to the rule were cut-throat pirates who occasionally sought to land here, and the slowly growing invasion of less-violent sun seekers who prize the area's unaffected peacefulness.

Activities
DIVING
The friendly and supremely helpful staff at **Dive Inn** (☎ 928 86 82 63; Calle Felix de Vera Guerra s/n; single dive €35) will take you to all the best spots for scuba diving (courses and equipment hire available) and can help out with tips about the surrounding area. Snorkelling gear is available for those who prefer to float on the water's surface, and there's also a nifty snorkelling course available (€25).

SURFING
Experienced surfers should make for a spot known as Bubbles, which is not as innocuous as it sounds. Waves break over reef and rocks; you can pick out the casualties on the streets of El Cotillo and Corralejo during the surfing season. To get here, you'll need your own transport. If you need to hire gear, including surfboards, body boards and wetsuits, visit the **Cycle & Surf Shop** (☎ 610 31 69 86; Calle Guillermo Gutierrez s/n; surfboards per day €12.50, body boards per day €7.50, wetsuits per day €5; ☯ 10am-2pm & 5-7pm), a friendly little shop beside the Last Resort bar. It also rents out bicycles (per day €10).

Shopping
Stop by the **Clean Ocean Project** (www.cleanocean project.org; 11 Calle del Muelle de Pescadores) with its cool surf wear in soft greens and blues. The business donates a percentage of all profits to beach-cleaning days and anti-pollution awareness. There are branches in Menorca and Barcelona; check the website for more info about this cool ecofriendly company.

FUERTEVENTURA

Sleeping

There are several central places to stay in El Cotillo.

ourpick La Gaviota (☎ /fax 928 53 85 67; www .la-gaviota.de; studios €37, d from €37) This laid-back, neohippy place, which flies the Jolly Roger, has been lovingly created by a German couple; Ralf made most of the furniture and has scavenged ruins for old doors and the like. Every apartment is different, including one with a bedroom built into a cave. The result is very special, but word is out so book in advance. It's a shame about the construction going on next door, but the views out to sea are unaffected and sublime.

Hotel Maria Hierro (☎ 928 53 85 98; hotelmariquita hierro@wanadoo.es; Calle Maria Hierro s/n; s/d with breakfast €38/54; P ⊠ ⊠) Located on a square near the harbour, this pleasant hotel has impressive public areas with a glass atrium, rooftop swimming pool and wall of glistening copper-coloured tiles. The rooms are a slight letdown in the originality stakes, but sufficiently comfortable and spacious.

Apartamentos Juan Benítez (☎ 629 17 63 48; www .apartamentosjbenitez.com; Calle La Caleta 4-6; 2-person apt €50; ⊠) This jaunty and colourful block has well-equipped modular apartments built around a central pool. All apartments have sea views and satellite TV.

Eating

Restaurante La Vaca Azul (☎ 928 53 86 85; mains €6-12; ☙ closed Tue; V) Enjoys prime position overlooking the pebbly beach, although the surreal rooftop cow (floodlit in lurid blue at night) has the best spot. The menu includes paella, vegetarian kebabs and mixed fish grill (minimum two people). The place doubles as a gallery for local photographers and artists.

ourpick Restaurante Fusion (☎ 687 20 88 40; Calle Santiago Apostol 7; mains €7.50) Enjoys a good, central location with a solid traditional menu, outside tables and a pleasant indoor dining space with a quirky wall display of ancient nails. Kick-start your appetite with a dish of *ropa vieja* (literally, 'old clothes'), made with beef, peppers and chickpeas from a peasant recipe. Grilled tuna, garlic with octopus and grilled aubergine slices with goat's cheese and honey are similar culinary winners.

Aguayre (Calle La Caleta 5; mains €7.50; V) This is a trendy Tex Mex–cum-Italian-cum-vegetarian restaurant. Come here with an appetite and tuck into one of the piled-high salads, California wraps or a sizzling volcano pizza with chilli, mushrooms and hot peppers.

Heaven (Calle 23 de Abril de 1973 50; ☎ 9.30am-2am Wed-Mon) Come here for your HP sauce fix. Fish and chips, kebabs and chicken tikka are also on the menu, plus Guinness on tap. The name says it all: this place is heaven for deprived Brits.

Azzurro (☎ 928 17 53 60; Carretera Al Faro; mains €12; ☙ closed Mon) The restaurant is located near the lighthouse in the Los Lagos part of town with its shallow pools and scrubby desert setting. At this place overlooking the beach, with a pretty peach-painted interior, the menu includes fish fillet in lemon and basil and a tasty pasta dish with mushrooms and prawns in a nest of parmesan cheese.

Getting There & Away

Bus 7 (€3.60, 45 minutes) for Puerto del Rosario leaves daily at 6.45am, noon and 5pm. Bus 8 (€2.50, 40 minutes, 13 daily) leaves for Corralejo.

AROUND EL COTILLO

Located 1.5km northwest of the village of Lajares and 12km from Corralejo, **Zoo Safari** (☎ 928 86 80 06; ☙ 10am-5pm Mon-Sat) offers half-hour camel rides (adult/child €6/3) and a 1½-hour trip into the caldera of the long-extinct Calderón Hondo volcano (adult/child €15/7.80). The latter trip departs from Zoo Safari at noon and 2pm Monday to Saturday.

The nearby town of **Villaverde** is nothing special, although the surrounding wide plains are colourfully impressive.

ourpick Hotel Rural Mahoh (☎ 928 86 80 50; www.mahoh.com; Sitio de Juan Bello; s €61-77, d €96-144, tr €162-180; P ⊠) is stunning, if you fancy sticking around. Set in an early-19th-century stone-and-wood building, it's surrounded by a stunning cacti garden. Mahoh means 'My Land, My Country' and is also the name of a local environmental group set up by hotel owners Tinín and Zaragoza Martínez. There are nine romantic bedrooms decorated with antiques and warm colours, plus the modern conveniences of ADSL and a wi-fi zone. That said, the cockerel, which is part of a small farmyard with goats, will serve as your morning alarm. The attached restaurant (mains €8 to €10, closed Tuesday) is reason enough to stay, although it's also possible to just drop in for a filling Canarian meal. There's live traditional music on Saturday nights.

PENÍNSULA DE JANDÍA

Most of the Península de Jandía is protected by its status as the Parque Natural de Jandía. The southwest is a canvas of craggy hills and bald plains leading to cliffs west of Morro Jable. Much of the rest of the peninsula is made up of dunes, scrub and beaches.

Somewhere along this peninsula, it is said, German submarine crews used to hole up occasionally during WWII. You think these beaches are paradise now? Just imagine them with not a single tourist, not one little apartment block; only you and your mates from the U-boat!

According to other stories, Nazi officials passed through here after the war to pick up false papers before heading on to South America. One version of the story even has hordes of Nazi gold buried hereabouts – so bring your bucket and spade.

COSTA CALMA

Costa Calma, about 25km northeast of Morro Jable, is a confusing muddle of one-way streets interspersed with apartments, commercial centres (at least eight!) and the occasional hotel. The long and sandy beach is magnificent, but the whole place lacks soul or anything historic; its lifeline being the (mostly) German tourists.

Activities

If catching the breeze with a sail and a board appeals, **Fanatic Fun Centre** (☎ 928 53 59 99; www .fanatic-surf.com; 🕙 9.30am-6pm summer, 10am-5pm winter) on the beach runs windsurfing courses (from €40 per hour) and also rents equipment (from €15 per hour). English and German are spoken.

Sleeping

The majority of apartments and hotels here cater to German package tourists. If you want to stay in one of the larger, resort-style complexes, contact www.sbhoteles.es.

H10 Playa Esmeralda (☎ 928 87 53 53; www.h10 .es; Punta del Roquito 2; s/d with breakfast €71/92; [P] [⚡] [💻] [♨]) Opened in 2005, this luxurious hotel enjoys prime position above the beach and has superb facilities, including a state-of-the-art health and fitness club. The rooms are restrained chic, decorated in earth colours.

Apartamentos Maryvent (☎ /fax 928 87 55 28; www .maryvent.de; Caleta Mansa 13; 2-/3-person apt €72/77) Cascading down the cliff with superb views of the beach, this upmarket place has self-contained modern apartments with satellite TV and private balconies with sun beds.

Eating & Drinking

Galería (☎ 928 87 54 16; Comercial Centre Bahia Calma; mains €7-12; 🕙 closed Sun; [V]) A good choice on a sunny day (and there are plenty), this restaurant has a lovely terrace with sea views and a varied Mediterranean and German menu with plenty of vegetarian choices.

For a cocktail, head to **Bar Synergy** (Centro Comercial Costa Calma; 🕙 7pm-3am Mon-Sat), which is about as hip as Costa Calma gets, with a dark-pink interior and lightweight mainstream music.

PLAYA DE SOTAVENTO DE JANDÍA

The name is a catch-all for the series of truly stunning beaches that stretch along the east coast of the peninsula. For swimming, sunbathing and windsurfing, this strand is a coastal paradise, with kilometre after kilometre of fine, white sand that creeps its way almost imperceptibly into the turquoise expanse of the Atlantic.

For 10 hyperactive days each July, its drowsy calm is shattered by daytime action and frantic nightlife as the beach hosts a leg of the **Windsurfing World Championship** (www.fuerteventura-worldcup.org). Kite boarding is also a part of this wind-powered display of prowess.

Various driveable trails lead down off the FV-2 highway to vantage points off the beach – its generous expanses mean you should have little trouble finding a tranquil spot on the sand.

If you want to do a bit of cyberspace research before arriving, you could check out www.playasdejandia.com.

LA PARED

Located on the west coast, this is another hot spot for surfers. As you approach the mottled black basalt and sandy beach, look for the *queso artesano* sign on your right where you can pick up a wheel of local organic goat's cheese. For surfing courses and board rental, stop by the oddly named **Cowabunga** (☎ 619 80 44 47; www.cowabunga.de; 17 Avenida del Istmo; 4hr beginner course €48, rental per day €10). Overlooking the beach, **Restaurante Bahía**

La Pared (☎ 928 54 90 30; mains from €8) specialises in fresh fish and seafood paella. The restaurant also runs an adjacent swimming-pool complex, complete with kiddie slides, which is free for diners.

MORRO JABLE

pop 9040

More staid than its northern counterpart, Corralejo (even if you wanted roast beef and Yorkshire pud you'd be hard pushed to find it), Morro Jable is almost exclusively German. The beach is the main attraction, stretching for around 2km from the older part of town and fronted by low-rise, immaculately landscaped apartments and hotels. Back from the beach, the charm palls somewhat with a dual carriageway lined with commercial centres and hotels.

Orientation

Approaching Morro Jable from the north, you'll arrive via Avenida Saladar. The older town centre, up the hill, is a maze of narrow, steep streets with limited parking.

Information

EMERGENCY

Police station (☎ 928 54 10 22; Calle Laurel)

INTERNET ACCESS

Cosmo Office (☎ 928 54 50 67; Cosmo Centro Comercial, Avenida Saladar; per hr €4; ⏲ 9am-1pm & 5-10pm Mon-Fri, 5-10pm Sun) Offers speedy connection.

MEDICAL SERVICES

Centro Medico Jandía (☎ 928 54 15 43; Cosmo Centro Comercial, Avenida Saladar; ⏲ 24hr) A multilingual medical clinic.

POST

Post office (☎ 928 54 03 73; Calle Gambuesas)

TOURIST INFORMATION

Tourist office (☎ 928 54 07 76; turismo@playadejandia.com; Cosmo Centro Comercial, Avenida Saladar; ⏲ 8am-3pm Mon-Fri) Lots of brochures and helpful staff.

Tourist office (☎ 928 16 64 08; Calle San Juan s/n; ⏲ 8am-3pm Mon-Fri) Smaller office in the old town.

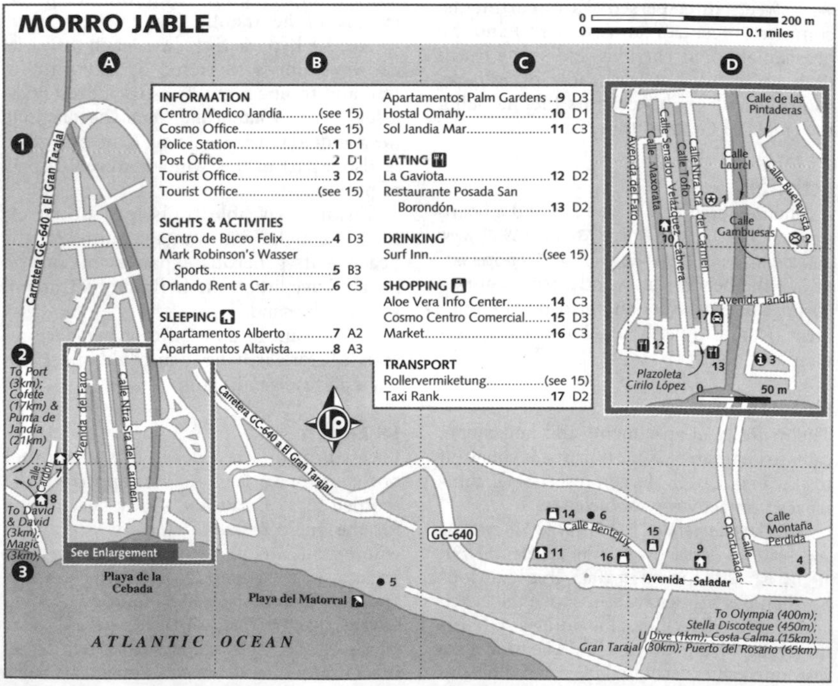
MORRO JABLE
0 200 m
0 0.1 miles
A
B
C
D
1
2
3
INFORMATION
Centro Medico Jandía..........(see 15)
Cosmo Office....................(see 15)
Police Station........................1 D1
Post Office.............................2 D1
Tourist Office.........................3 D2
Tourist Office....................(see 15)
SIGHTS & ACTIVITIES
Centro de Buceo Felix.............4 D3
Mark Robinson's Wasser Sports.............5 B3
Orlando Rent a Car.................6 C3
SLEEPING
Apartamentos Alberto 7 A2
Apartamentos Altavista............8 A3
Apartamentos Palm Gardens ..9 D3
Hostal Omahy........................10 D1
Sol Jandia Mar.......................11 C3
EATING
La Gaviota.............................12 D2
Restaurante Posada San Borondón.........................13 D2
DRINKING
Surf Inn.............................(see 15)
SHOPPING
Aloe Vera Info Center............14 C3
Cosmo Centro Comercial.......15 D3
Market..................................16 C3
TRANSPORT
Rollervermiketung................(see 15)
Taxi Rank..............................17 D2
Carretera GC-640 a El Gran Tarajal
To Port (3km); Cofete (17km) & Punta de Jandía (21km)
Calle Cardón
To David & David (3km); Magic (3km)
Avenida del Faro
Calle Ntra Sra del Carmen
See Enlargement
Playa de la Cebada
Playa del Matorral
ATLANTIC OCEAN
GC-640
Calle Bentejuy
Calle Oportunidadas
Avenida Saladar
Calle Montaña Perdida
To Olympia (400m); Stella Discoteque (450m); U Dive (1km); Costa Calma (15km); Gran Tarajal (30km); Puerto del Rosario (65km)
Calle de las Pintaderas
Calle Laurel
Calle Buenavista
Calle Gambuesas
Avenida Jandía
Plazoleta Cirilo López
Avenida del Faro
Calle Maxorata
Calle Senador Velázquez Cabrera
Calle Toño
Calle Ntra Sra del Carmen
50 m

Sights & Activities

BEACHES

The magnificent **Playa del Mattoral**, stretching eastwards for over 4km from Morro Jable, is great for indulging in a variety of water sports, churning a pedalo or just collapsing on the sand. The beach rarely gets crowded, but for true solitude head for the beaches 7km further east, although they are only accessible with some kind of transport.

DIVING

Divers can explore the sea bottom with **U Dive** (☎ 629 10 51 91; Hotel Occidental Gran Fuerteventura, Urbanización Esquinzo Butihondo s/n; initiation dive €25), which offers daily dives with small groups in 12 diving spots, as well as dive safaris, PADI courses at all levels and free try-dives in a swimming pool.

If you speak German, check out the **Centro de Buceo Felix** (☎ 928 54 14 18; www.tauchen -fuerteventura.de; Avenida del Sakvadir 27; 1hr dive €26), which organises daily dives at 1pm.

WINDSURFING

The newest place in town is **Mark Robinson's Wasser Sports** (www.robinson.de; 10-12hr beginner course €167, board rental per hr €20), part of the luxurious Robinson's resort, situated on Playa del Matorral.

BOAT TRIPS

Magic (☎ 928 15 02 48; 5hr cruise adult/under 12yr €54/28) operates a couple of smart catamarans out of the port. Sailing at 10am or 10.30am (also at 4pm from May to October), cruises include a barbecue lunch and allow plenty of time for swimming and snorkelling.

David & David (☎ 928 87 61 68; info@david-david .net) organises sport fishing (per person €90) and sea excursions for nudists (no smirking please) for €70 per person.

CYCLING

Orlando Rent a Car (☎ 928 54 00 65; Apartmentos El Matorral bajo, Avenida Jandía; per day €8) is conveniently located near the Cosmo Centro Comercial and rents out bikes for one day or longer, including insurance.

Sleeping

BUDGET

Hostal Omahy (☎ 928 54 12 54; Calle Maxorata 47; d €30) Rooms here have a threadbare appearance but are clean and comfortable enough if all you are after is a cheap sleep.

Apartamentos Altavista (☎ 928 54 01 64; Calle Abubilla 8; 1-/2-person apt €40/50) Easy to find (but not so easy to park) beside the church in the old town; you can't miss the multicoloured exterior. The apartments are large and modern and most have sea views.

MIDRANGE

Sol Jandia Mar (☎ 902 14 44 44; www.solmelia.com; Avenida Jandía s/n; d €48; P X 🖳 🖳) Part of the Melia hotel chain, and providing excellent value with spacious, modern apartments, brightly furnished with dark-blue fabrics and wood fittings. The gardens surround a pool and are colourfully landscaped; there is a miniclub for tots.

Apartamentos Alberto (☎ 928 54 51 09; Avenida del Faro 4; studios €40-48, 2-/4-person apt €50/65; P) Located in a quiet spot in the old town, these apartments have a sunny Mediterranean look with their white stucco and colourful hibiscus. Apartments include kitchenette, sitting room and a terrace. Go for a sea view if you can, or hang out in the pretty rooftop garden.

Apartamentos Palm Gardens (☎ 928 54 10 00; fax 928 54 10 40; Avenida Saladar s/n; 2-/4-person apt €65/80; 🖳) Cascading like a ziggurat down the hillside, this huge apartment complex has airy, attractive apartments with small kitchenettes, satellite TV and terraces. If you are tired of sand in your swimsuit, there's an inviting freshwater pool.

Eating

You can get the usual bland international cuisine and fast food at innumerable places among the apartments, condos and shopping centres along Avenida Saladar. Head into the older part of town for seafood and more authentic choices.

Restaurante Posada San Borondón (☎ 928 54 14 28; Plazoleta Cirilo López 1; mains €7.50-18) Somewhere a little more interesting, and offering a variety of Spanish food, is this restaurant where the grilled sole touched our soul. It's easy to find, right next to the steamship exterior, complete with portholes and funnels, of Bar Barco.

La Gaviota (☎ 928 54 20 97; Calle Tomas Grau s/n; mains €8-12) One of the better restaurants on this seaside strip. Go for a plate of *mojo* potatoes as a starter, followed by a plate of freshly grilled sardines.

Drinking

The main nightlife action is along the beachfront part of the resort. A cluster of pubs is concentrated in the Cosmo Centro Comercial.

Surf Inn (☎ 928 54 22 72; Cosmo Centro Comercial; ☿ 7pm-3am Mon-Sat) This place is aimed at a younger late-night crowd who like to check out surfing and snowboarding videos in between quaffing cocktails.

Olympia (☎ 928 16 60 12; Centro Comercial Playa Paradiso, Avenida Saladar s/n; ☿ 10am-1am) With comfortable wicker furniture, a central bar and picture windows overlooking the seafront, this place is perfect for post-dinner cocktails; the music is pretty chilled out, as well.

You could also head for **Stella Discoteque** (Avenida Saladar s/n), 450m further on – look for the twin bronze lions and you are nearly there.

Shopping

Cosmo Centro Comercial (Avenida Saladar) This large centre has plenty of shops selling tax-free goodies.

There's a small Thursday **market** (Avenida Saladar; ☿ 9am-1.30pm) in a car park due west of the tourist office. With most stalls run by Moroccans, Africans and German dropouts, you'll be lucky to find anything that smacks particularly of the Canaries. The **Aloe Vera Info Center** (☎ 928 16 63 29; aloe-vera-canarias@web .de; Avenida Jandía s/n) can tell you everything you ever wanted to know about this healing species of cacti.

Getting There & Away

TO/FROM THE AIRPORT

Bus 10 (€6.95, 1½ hours, three daily) connects the town with the airport; taxis will cost around €75.

DETOUR

Much wilder than their leeward counterparts, the long stretches of beach on the windward side of the Peninsula de Jandía are also harder to get to. You really need a 4WD to safely negotiate the various tracks leading into the area.

The wild length of coast that is the **Playa de Barlovento de Jandía** can get very windy, though the flying sand doesn't seem to deter the nude bathers, who are as common as the partly clothed variety. Take care swimming here: the waves and currents can often be more formidable than the generally calmer waters on the other side of the island.

BOAT

The port, Puerto de Morro Jable, is 3km by road from the centre of town.

Naviera Armas (☎ 928 54 21 13; www.navieraarmas .com) ferries head for Las Palmas (€42, 3¾ hours) at 6.30pm daily.

You can get tickets for both services at the port or at the town's many travel agents.

BUS

The first bus 1 (€8.50, two hours, at least 12 daily) for Puerto del Rosario leaves at 6am (weekdays) and the last leaves at 10.15pm. Bus 10 (€8, 1¾ hours, three daily), via the airport, is faster. Bus 5 (€2.20, 40 minutes) to Costa Calma runs frequently.

Getting Around

There is a taxi rank in the town centre just off Avenida Jandía. To call a taxi, ring ☎ 928 54 12 57.

TURTLE BIRTHDAY

In January 2007, 145 loggerhead turtles were successfully hatched on the Cofete beach in the Parque Natural de Jandía. The beaches of Fuerteventura are only the second site in the world selected for such a translocation of eggs; the first being in Mexico. The eggs came from a turtle colony in Cape Verde, which has similarities to the beaches and environment here, namely in the quality of the water, the sand and, above all, the consistently warm climate. The loggerhead turtle is fast becoming an endangered species and is in urgent need of protection due to the same old story: indiscriminate fishing, accidental capture in nets and pollution. This sanctuary is essentially a nursery where the turtles will remain until they are a year old, at which time they will be released back into the ocean. The project organisers hope to repeat the hatching at least every five years in an attempt to reverse the depletion of this species of marine turtle. Check out the website www.gobiernodecanarias.org/medioambiente.

You can rent a scooter from **Rollervermiketung** (☎ 928 54 50 67; Cosmo Centro Comercial) for €39 per day with full insurance.

AROUND MORRO JABLE
Punta de Jandía
Twenty kilometres of graded but unsealed road winds out along the southern reaches of the peninsula to a lone lighthouse at Punta de Jandía.

Puerto de la Cruz, found a couple of kilometres east of the lighthouse, is a tiny, bedraggled fishing settlement and weekend retreat for locals. Two fairly modest *chiringuitos* (beach-side restaurants), open only during lunchtime, serve up the local catch to tourists passing en route to the island's westernmost point. There's little to choose between them; go for the one with a table free.

Cofete
About 10km along the same road from Morro Jable, a turn-off leads northeast over a pass and plunges to Cofete (7km from the junction), a tiny peninsula hamlet at the southern extreme of the Playa de Barlovento de Jandía. Sandy tracks, negotiable on foot or by 4WD, snake off to this wind-whipped strand. **Restaurante Cofete** (☎ 928 17 42 43; mains €6-12; ☽ 11am-7pm) does drinks and excellent snacks and has a more sophisticated menu than you'd expect from a restaurant that's literally at the end of the road. It does fresh fish as well as *carne de cabra en salsa* (goat in sauce) – maybe a close relative of the semiwild creatures you pass on the journey here.

FUERTEVENTURA

Lanzarote

Lanzarote is an intriguing island that has an extraordinary geology of 300 volcanic cones, and ticks all the right good-time boxes. There are great beaches, intriguing sights and plenty of restaurants and hotels. Its largely volcanic landscape has a stark and otherworldly appearance, with the occasional bucolic, palm-filled valley juxtaposed with surreal crinkly-black lava fields. The island also has a refreshing lack of neon-blazing entertainment, which helps preserve its uniqueness and integrity.

In other ways, however, Lanzarote resembles a giant, albeit tasteful, theme park. The island's approach to tourism has been shaped by the inspiration of artist César Manrique, who saw the commercial potential of the island's striking landscape, and aesthetically developed several sites. The careful adherence to traditional rural architecture, with its distinctive green paintwork, is also largely due to the vigilance of Manrique and his successors. Unfortunately, developers in a couple of the coastal resorts succumbed to greed over such aesthetic ideals and have gone for the pack-in-maximum-punters approach. An exception is the luxurious new harbour in Playa Blanca, which, while not traditional, at least has a cohesive architectural look.

Lanzarote is the fourth-largest and most northeasterly island of the Canaries, measuring around 60km north to south and a mere 21km at its widest east-west point. The island's name is assumed to be a corruption of Lanzarotto (or Lancelotto) Malocello, the Genoese seafarer who landed on the island in the early 14th century.

Unesco has declared the entire island a biosphere reserve.

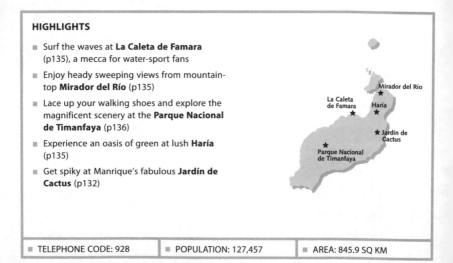

HIGHLIGHTS

- Surf the waves at **La Caleta de Famara** (p135), a mecca for water-sport fans
- Enjoy heady sweeping views from mountain-top **Mirador del Río** (p135)
- Lace up your walking shoes and explore the magnificent scenery at the **Parque Nacional de Timanfaya** (p136)
- Experience an oasis of green at lush **Haría** (p135)
- Get spiky at Manrique's fabulous **Jardín de Cactus** (p132)

| ■ TELEPHONE CODE: 928 | ■ POPULATION: 127,457 | ■ AREA: 845.9 SQ KM |

ITINERARY 1
CÉSAR MANRIQUE

Try to visit as many of the following sights as you can and, if you don't have your own wheels, don't worry, you can always join a tour. The best-known of Manrique's famous sculptures marks the entrance of the **Monumento al Campesino** (**1**; p130), dedicated to the hard grind of the agricultural workers. Not many folk would set up house in a lava field, and the **Fundación César Manrique** (**2**; p129), in Manrique's former home outside Tahiche, is appropriately extraordinary…as is the **Jardín de Cactus** (**3**; p132) with its myriad of prickly cacti, north of Guatiza. Many consider Manrique's first project, the **Jameos del Agua** (**4**; p133), his pinnacle achievement. The take-your-breath-away drama of the **Cueva de los Verdes** (**5**; p132) comprises a natural work of art. Take in the magnificent views from the **Mirador del Río** (**6**; p135), experience the awesome force of nature with a trip to the extraordinarily beautiful **Montañas del Fuego** (**7**; p136) and don't miss out on a milder, more-painterly visit to the **Museo de Arte Contemporáneo** (**8**; p126), another crowning Manrique project, this time housed in a castle in Arrecife.

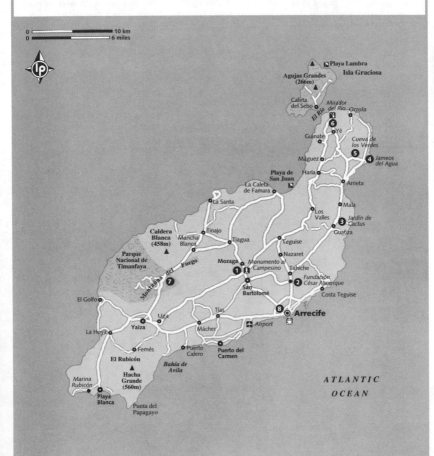

ITINERARY 2
THE WINE (& CHEESE) TRAIL

Lanzarote's volcanic terrain is far removed from your typical lush, green vineyards, but the determined locals have managed to make the black earth work in their favour. These days the local *vino* (wine) is definitely something to get sniffy about.

You could start your tipple trail near San Bartolomé at the **Monumento al Campesino** (**1**; p130), with its excellent restaurant serving traditional local cuisine. Close by, **Bodega Mozaga** (**2**; p131) dates back to 1880 and has won awards for its deliciously fruity *malvasía*. Another excellent wine cellar, **Bodega Tinache** (**3**; p130), has 20 hectares of vines en route to Timanfaya; go for the dry Malmsey and Moscatel. A smaller cellar, **Bodega Vega de Yuco** (**4**; p131), has its vineyards dug into a hillside near the small town of Tías. Again, white wines are the winners, particularly the dry or semisweet *malvasía*. Founded in 2001, **Bodega La Vegueta** (**5**; p130) may be the youngster, but goes the traditional wine-making route and has won several prestigious awards. The dry Malmsey liquor is well worth the extra weight in your hand luggage.

The perfect accompaniment, Fuerteventura, is a speedy half-hour ferry ride away, and produces the Canaries' best goat's cheese (see the boxed text, p98) – the only *queso* (cheese) to have earned Spain's prestigious *denominación de origen* label. Pop into the local **Corralejo** (**6**; p106) supermarket and pick up a wheel of the soft, nutty Majorero, together with a *barra* (loaf) of fresh bread (you've already got the wine!) for a picnic on the glorious white sandy beach – just one more good reason for travelling the high seas to get here.

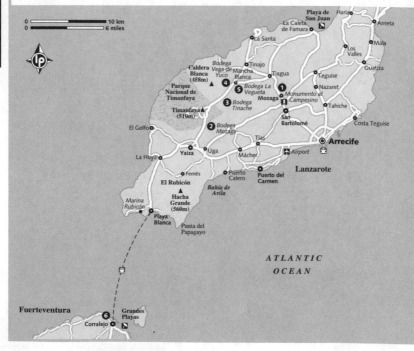

HISTORY

Lanzarote was the first Canary Island to fall to Jean de Béthencourt in 1402, marking the beginning of the Spanish conquest. Along with Fuerteventura, the island was frequently raided by Moroccan pirates based along the northwest African coast, barely 100km away. The problem accelerated during the 16th century, but the Moroccans weren't the only source of grief. British buccaneers such as Sir Walter Raleigh, Sir John Hawkins and John Poole also plundered the island, as did French bearers of the skull and crossbones such as Jean Florin and Pegleg le Clerc.

By the middle of the 17th century, misery, piracy and emigration had reduced the number of islanders to just 300.

As if they hadn't suffered enough, in the 1730s massive volcanic eruptions destroyed a dozen towns and some of the island's most fertile land. But the islanders were to discover an ironic fact: the character of the volcanic soil proved a highly fertile bedrock for farming (particularly wine grapes), which brought relative prosperity to the descendants of those who had fled from the lava flows to Gran Canaria.

Today, with tourism flourishing alongside the healthy, if small, agricultural sector, the island is home to around 127,000 people, not counting all the holiday blow-ins who, at any given time, can more than double the population.

INFORMATION
Books & Maps

Noel Rochford's *Landscapes of Lanzarote* includes useful suggestions for drives and walks of varying duration around the island.

Michel Houellebecq's *Lanzarote* has a haunting Camus quality. This taut, fictionalised account covers a package tour to the island taken by a Frenchman. In the volcanically charred landscape of Lanzarote the main character appears to see the hint of rebirth; a renewal by fire.

Michelin map No 221, *Lanzarote & Fuerteventura*, is good to have, although the free tourist map will usually suffice and includes functional maps of Arrecife, Puerto del Carmen, Playa Blanca and Costa Teguise. You can pick it up at tourist offices and hotels.

Newspapers & Magazines

The semi-official *Lancelot* (available free), published weekly in Spanish and quarterly in English and German, is available at many newsstands. A monthly glossy, the *Lanzarote Gazette* includes what's-on information.

ACCOMMODATION

Most accommodation is in apartments and bungalows, the majority concentrated in the resorts of Puerto del Carmen, Playa Blanca and Costa Teguise. The main problem for independent travellers is that the majority get block-booked by tour operators months in advance.

Arrecife may not blow you away as a capital, but can make a good base and there are usually rooms available, even in high season.

To assist you with advance booking, check out www.lanzaroteaccommodation.com, http://lanzaroteisland.com/hotels, www.lanzaroterural.com (in Spanish), www.lanzaroteisland.com/casas_rurales and www.ecoturismocanarias.com; the latter three specialise in *casas rurales*.

Among the top recommended accommodation is the beautiful 18th-century hacienda of Finca de Las Salinas (p137); the rustic authenticity of Caserío de Mozaga (p131); Cardona (p126), a particularly good-value *pensión* in the capital; the unparalleled opulence of Hotel Meliá Salinas (p129); and the tranquil location coupled with superb facilities of Finca de la Florida (p131).

ACTIVITIES

If lolling on the beach turning the pages of the local bonkbuster starts to pall, it may be time for something marginally more active. The wild and rugged north coast sports some of Europe's finest surfing beaches. Check out the surf school at La Caleta de Famara (p135) or, if you're confident to go solo, head further east to La Santa, which has a wave-crashing beach just outside town.

The beaches of the south coast are also excellent for kite boarding, windsurfing and diving. The sea temperature rarely drops below 18°C and underwater visibility ranges between 6m and 20m, depending on the season.

Cycling, whether it be a gentle pedal around your resort or a more strenuous outing along the lightly trafficked roads, is also possible, while the best hiking can be found around Parque Nacional de Timanfaya (p136), although you must reserve in advance.

LANZAROTE

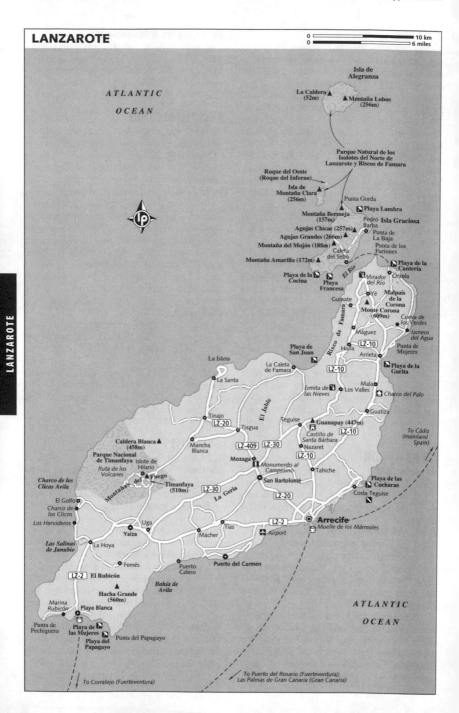

LANZAROTE

0 _____ 10 km
0 _____ 6 miles

ATLANTIC OCEAN

Isla de Alegranza

La Caldera (52m) ▲ ▲ Montaña Lobos (256m)

Parque Natural de los Isolotes del Norte de Lanzarote y Riscos de Famara

Roque del Oeste (Roque del Inferno)

Isla de Montaña Clara (256m)

Punta Gorda

Montaña Bermeja (157m)

Playa Lambra

Pedro Barba

Isla Graciosa

Agujas Chicas (257m) ▲

Punta de La Baja

Agujas Grandes (266m) ▲

Montaña del Mojón (188m) ▲

Punta de los Fariones

Montaña Amarilla (172m) ▲

Caleta del Sebo

Playa de la Cocina

El Río

Playa de la Cantería

Orzola

Playa Francesa

Mirador del Río

Malpaís de la Corona

Guinate

Yé

Monte Corona (609m) ▲

Cueva de los Verdes

Máguez

Jameos del Agua

Playa de San Juan

Haría

LZ-10

Punta de Mujeres

Arrieta

Playa de la Garita

La Isleta

La Caleta de Famara

LZ-10

Mala

Los Valles

La Santa

Ermita de las Nieves

Charco del Palo

Guatiza

Tinajo

LZ-20

Tiagua

El Jable

Teguise

Guanapay (447m) ▲

Castillo de Santa Bárbara

LZ-10

To Cádiz (mainland Spain)

Caldera Blanca (458m) ▲

Mancha Blanca

LZ-409

LZ-30

Nazaret

Parque Nacional de Timanfaya

Islote de Hilario

Mozaga

LZ-10

Ruta de los Volcanes

Fuego

Monumento al Campesino

Tahiche

Charco de los Clicos Avila

Montañas del

Timanfaya (510m)

San Bartolomé

Playa de las Cucharas

El Golfo

LZ-30

La Geria

Costa Teguise

Charco de los Clicos

Uga

Los Hervideros

Yaiza

Tías

LZ-2

Arrecife

Las Salinas de Janubio

La Hoya

Mácher

Airport

Muelle de los Mármoles

Femés

Puerto Calero

LZ-2

El Rubicón

Puerto del Carmen

Hacha Grande (560m) ▲

Bahía de Avila

Marina Rubicón

Playa Blanca

ATLANTIC OCEAN

Punta de Pechiguera

Playa de las Mujeres

Playa del Papagayo

Punta del Papagayo

To Corralejo (Fuerteventura)

To Puerto del Rosario (Fuerteventura); Las Palmas de Gran Canaria (Gran Canaria)

LANZAROTE

FESTIVALS & EVENTS

February–March

Carnaval Celebrated with gusto, particularly in Arrecife, although it is slightly less rambunctious than the revelry in Las Palmas de Gran Canaria and Santa Cruz de Tenerife. Festivities kick off the week before Ash Wednesday.

July

Fiesta de Nuestra Señora del Carmen (16 July) Takes place annually in Teguise in celebration of the town's saint, with plenty of dancing in the street and general merriment.

August

Fiesta de la Vendimia (mid-August) A jolly festival that takes place at Bodega.La Geria. Newly harvested grapes are poured into a vast vat for everyone to have a good trample upon (fortunately, they don't find their way into a wine bottle!).

Día de San Ginés (25 August) The day of the island's patron saint is a major fiesta in even the smallest *pueblo* (village). In Arrecife, the streets surrounding the Iglesia de San Ginés are home to the most boisterous celebrations.

October

César Manrique-Puerto Calero International Regatta (mid-October) Prestigious yachting regatta that takes place off the southern coast. It includes the TP 52 racing class – the Formula 1 of the international regatta world.

LANZAROTE FOR CHILDREN

There's plenty going on for children on the island; several of the Manrique sights (see p119) should keep them suitably gobsmacked, while the southern resorts have plenty of kiddie-geared activities. The island's most touted attraction is the Guinate Tropical Park (p135) with its birds, aquarium, botanical garden and various shows. There are plenty of sea-themed activities, aside from the ubiquitous glass-bottom boats. Submarine Safaris (p140) submerge to the watery depths and the company also runs a kids club where, according to the brochure, the children learn how to build a submarine. **Paracraft** (☎ 928 51 26 61; www.lanzarote.com/paracraft; Playa Chica, Puerto del Carmen; ⊙ 10am-6pm) offers parascending (10 minutes, €70) and jet-ski rental (20 minutes, €45). If the sea starts to pall, Costa Teguise's **Aquapark** (☎ 928 59 21 28; Avenida De Teguise s/n; adult/2-12yr €21/15; ⊙ 10am-6pm) has the usual watery assortment of rides and slides.

GETTING THERE & AWAY

The following provides a brief overview of air and boat options. For more comprehensive information, see the Getting There & Away sections for specific towns.

Air

From **Guasimeta airport** (☎ 928 84 60 00; www.aena .es), 6km southwest of Arrecife, **Binter** (☎ 902 39 13 92; www.binternet.com) has at least 10 daily flights to Las Palmas de Gran Canaria (45 minutes), at least four daily to Tenerife Norte (50 minutes) and two weekly to Tenerife Sur (50 minutes). Operators from the mainland include **Air Europa** (www.aireuropa.com), **Iberia** (www .iberia.com) and **Spanair** (www.spanair.com).

Budget airlines from various airports in the UK, including **Easyjet** (www.easyjet.com), **Ryan Air** (www.ryanair.com), **Thomson Fly** (www.thomsonfly.com) and **Excel Airways** (www.xl.com), fly to Lanzarote.

Boat

For details on the ferry services from Arrecife to Gran Canaria, see p127. For details on Fred Olsen ferry services between Playa Blanca and Corralejo (Fuerteventura), see p142.

GETTING AROUND

To/From the Airport

Buses 22 and 23 (€1, 20 minutes) connect the airport and Arrecife twice hourly between 7.20am and 10.50pm Monday to Friday. Services run between 8.50am and 10.50pm on weekends. A taxi to/from the airport and Playa Blanca costs around €35.

Bus

Arrecife Bus (☎ 928 81 15 22; www.arrecifebus.com) has a frequent service around the Arrecife area, especially to Puerto del Carmen and Costa Teguise. Other routes connect with Playa Blanca in the south and inland towns such as Teguise. Otherwise, services are minimal or nonexistent.

Car

Car-rental offices are widespread. A reasonable local choice is **Cabrera Medina** (☎ 928 51 11 26; www.cabreramedina.com; Calle Ruperto González Negrín 8), which has a central Arrecife office and good prices (from €35 per day). Street parking is relatively easy to find in Arrecife.

LANZAROTE

Taxi

Recommended only for shorter trips, a **taxi** (☎ 928 52 22 11) will cost considerably more than the average car rental.

ARRECIFE

pop 53,920

Arrecife is a small, manageable city with a pleasant Mediterranean-style promenade, an inviting sandy beach and – it has to be said – a disarming backstreet hotchpotch of sun-bleached, peeling buildings, elegant boutiques, rough bars and good (and bad) restaurants. The sights are scarce yet interesting and include a couple of castles, a fashionable cultural centre and a pretty lagoon. If anything, Arrecife's most notable quality is that it's a no-nonsense working town that earns its living from something other than tourism.

HISTORY

The single biggest factor behind Arrecife's lack of pizzazz is that it only became the island's capital in 1852. Until then, Teguise ruled supreme. Although Teguise is today a relatively modest town, its architectural heritage shows what Arrecife missed out on by being a port for the erstwhile capital.

In 1574 the Castillo de San Gabriel was first constructed (it was subsequently attacked and rebuilt) to protect the port. Its sister further up the coast, the Castillo de San José, was raised in 1771.

By the close of the 18th century, a semblance of a town had taken uncertain shape around the harbour. As its commerce grew and the threat of sea raids dropped off in the 19th century, Arrecife thrived. As the defensive imperatives for keeping the capital inland receded, the move of the island's administration to Arrecife became inevitable.

ORIENTATION

Arrecife is easy to navigate. With the notable exceptions of the Castillo de San José and the port, everything of interest is located in a tight area around the centre. If you arrive by bus, alight at Playa del Reducto and walk eastwards to the centre of town.

The main streets for shops and restaurants are La Marina and the pedestrianised Avenida León y Castillo.

INFORMATION
Emergency

Bomberos (Fire Brigade; ☎ 928 81 48 58)
Cruz Roja (Red Cross; ☎ 928 81 22 22) Ring for an ambulance.

FOOD & DRINK

The Lanzarote cuisine does not vary dramatically from that of its neighbouring islands. The Canary staple, *gofio* (toasted grains), is common here, as are the addictive *papas arrugadas* (wrinkly potatoes) accompanied by a *mojo* sauce, including *mojo verde* (with parsley), *mojo de cilantro* (with fresh coriander) and the classic *mojo picón* (with spicy-hot paprika). An excellent traditional restaurant is La Era (p138) in Yaiza.

San Bartolomé is the geographical centre of Lanzarote and an important agricultural region where vegetables grow in the sandy *jable* soil, unique to the island. The main crops are watermelons, squash and *batatas* (sweet potatoes); the latter were introduced into the Canaries from the Antilles and, owing to a typing error, initially confused with regular potatoes. They are an important ingredient in the ubiquitous black pudding.

Lanzarote has an indigenous seafood, the *lapa*, which is a species of limpet traditionally grilled (which releases the flesh from the shell) and accompanied by a green *mojo*. Note that, although they do not look as appealing, the black-fleshed *lapas* are tastier than the orange variety.

Do try the local wines while you are here (see the itinerary on p120); the vines flourish in the black volcanic soil and are planted in small craters to protect them from the wind. The grapes are planted and harvested manually, resulting in high labour costs. When you buy a bottle of Lanzarote-origin wine you actively contribute to the preservation of a traditional method of viniculture in danger of dying out. Interestingly, Lanzarote vines were not afflicted by the phylloxera disease that destroyed many European vineyards in the mid-19th century. Thus, the Lanzarote grapes you enjoy in your wine today are the very same variety drunk by inhabitants here over 200 years ago.

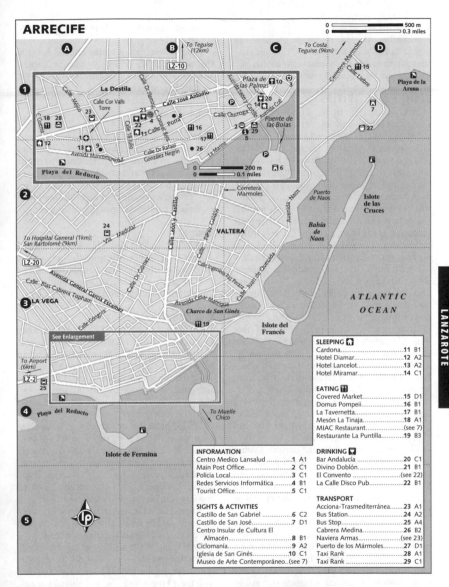

ARRECIFE

0 — 500 m
0 — 0.3 miles

INFORMATION
Centro Medico Lansalud 1 A1
Main Post Office.......................2 C1
Policia Local...........................3 C1
Redes Servicios Informática 4 B1
Tourist Office..........................5 C1

SIGHTS & ACTIVITIES
Castillo de San Gabriel 6 C2
Castillo de San José...................7 D1
Centro Insular de Cultura El
    Almacén...............................8 B1
Ciclomanía............................9 A2
Iglesia de San Ginés.................10 C1
Museo de Arte Contemporáneo..(see 7)

SLEEPING
Cardona...............................11 B1
Hotel Diamar.........................12 A2
Hotel Lancelot.......................13 A2
Hotel Miramar.......................14 C1

EATING
Covered Market.....................15 D1
Domus Pompeii......................16 B1
La Tavernetta........................17 B1
Mesón La Tinaja....................18 A1
MIAC Restaurant...................(see 7)
Restaurante La Puntilla...........19 B3

DRINKING
Bar Andalucía 20 C1
Divino Doblón........................21 B1
El Convento.........................(see 22)
La Calle Disco Pub..................22 B1

TRANSPORT
Acciona-Trasmediterránea.......23 A1
Bus Station............................24 A2
Bus Stop..............................25 A4
Cabrera Medina......................26 B2
Naviera Armas......................(see 23)
Puerto de los Mármoles...........27 D1
Taxi Rank 28 A1
Taxi Rank 29 C1

LANZAROTE

Policía Local (Police; ☎ 928 81 13 17; Avenida Coll 5)

Internet Access
Redes Servicios Informática (☎ 928 81 22 09; Calle Coronel Bens 17; per hr €1.80; ◷ 9am-1.30pm & 5-8pm Mon-Fri, 9am-1pm Sat)

Medical Services
Centro Medico Lansalud (☎ 928 80 50 79; Calle Coronel Ildefonso Valls de la Torre 4) Use this in town.
Hospital General (☎ 928 80 16 36) To the northwest of the city centre, on the highway to San Bartolomé.

Post
Main post office (La Marina 8) Has fax facilities.

Tourist Information

Tourist office (☎ 928 81 31 74; www.turismolanzarote .com; La Marina s/n; ☺ 8am-3pm Mon-Fri) Located in a fabulous band rotunda–meets–tourist office building on the promenade and has good city maps.

SIGHTS & ACTIVITIES

Converted in 1994 by the Fundación César Manrique into a sleek modern-art museum, the **Museo de Arte Contemporáneo** (MIAC; ☎ 928 81 23 21; Carretera de Puerto Naos; admission free; ☺ 11am-9pm) is housed in the **Castillo de San José**, which was built in the 18th century to deal with pirates and, at a time of famine on the island, to provide unemployed locals with a public-works job scheme. Today it houses the most important collection of modern art in the Canaries. Aside from a couple of early works by Manrique himself (which may help explain why he turned to architecture), artists such as Miró, Millares, Rivera, Gerardo Rueda, Sempere and Tápies are on show. Both gallery and restaurant (opposite) are well worth the 30-minute walk or €3.50 taxi ride from the city centre.

Another vibrant gallery space is the **Centro Insular de Cultura El Almacén** (☎ 928 81 01 21; Calle José Betancort 33; admission free; ☺ 8am-3pm Mon-Fri), a cultural centre housed in a former warehouse that has had a stylish makeover, once again influenced by Manrique. There are exhibitions, a cinema (showing original-version films) and a bar and restaurant named after César's old buddy, Picasso, where you can enjoy live music at weekends.

The city's second castle, the curiously squat 16th-century **Castillo de San Gabriel** was sorely tested on several occasions by Moroccan and European pirates. Today it is home to occasional exhibitions, but generally closed to the public.

The **Iglesia de San Ginés** (Plaza de San Ginés), an attractive church consecrated to the island's patron saint, was built in 1665 and features a statue – which originated in Cuba – of said saint. Opening hours vary. The nearby **Charco de San Ginés** is an attractive lagoon that could be a commercialised, Portofino-style place but, thankfully, it's not (yet). The buildings and restaurants here are a beguiling combo of mildly down-at-heel and freshly whitewashed with blue trim.

If you fancy a dip, **Playa del Reducto** is a superb white sandy beach, a thong's throw from Calle Dr Rafael González Negrín. It's safe for children, reasonably clean and, generally, surprisingly empty.

Pedal-power aficionados should head to **Ciclomanía** (☎ 928 81 75 35; www.ciclomania.es; Calle Almirante Boado Endeiza 9; mountain bikes per day €10; ☺ closed Sun), which rents out mountain bikes and all the extras, including children's seats and helmets.

SLEEPING

Arrecife can make a handy base, especially given the welcome proliferation of bars and restaurants at the end of a long sightseeing day. Note that business travellers often base themselves here, meaning that accommodation at weekends can be cheaper than midweek.

Budget

Cardona (☎ 928 81 10 08; Calle 18 Julio 11; s/d €27/33) A dapper central *pensión* (guesthouse) with a sparkling marble lobby and bright rooms. The institution-green colour scheme could go, but the staff are gracious and the price is right.

Midrange

Hotel Miramar (☎ 928 80 15 22; www.hmiramar.com; Avenida Coll 2; s/d/tr €48/63/80; ℗ ⊠ ⊒ ⑆) Waterfront Miramar has been subjected to an adventurous paint palette in the public spaces, while the rooms are more subdued with blue-and-gold décor, fitted carpets and small balconies. Breakfast is a high, with its ocean views from the roof terrace.

our pick Hotel Diamar (☎ 928 81 56 56; www.hotel diamar.com; Avenida Fred Olsen 8; s with breakfast €59-64, d with breakfast €70-77; ⊠ ⊒) Opened in 2006, privately owned Diamar has a boutique feel and is a welcome addition to Arrecife's hotel scene. Overlooking the beach, the rooms are good-looking and large and set around a central atrium with traditional Canarian balconies. Those with a sea view cost slightly more. There is wi-fi, a cafeteria and an elegant restaurant (mains from €7).

Hotel Lancelot (☎ 928 80 50 99; hlancelot@terra.es; Avenida Mancomunidad 9; s/d €63/78; ⊠ ⊠ ⑆) Recently revamped rooms have a five-star feel with their king-size beds, sexy abstract prints, plush décor and ample balconies with ocean views. There's a rooftop pool and wi-fi access, plus live, smoochy jazz in the bar.

EATING

Mesón La Tinaja (☎ 928 81 44 96; Calle Guenia 2; raciones €3-12; ☺ closed Sun night) This restaurant specialises in traditional Basque dishes like black pudding from Burgos, red peppers stuffed with codfish and red sausage from Bera. More international fare includes tasty curried rice with vegetables.

Domus Pompeii (☎ 928 81 42 16; Calle José Betancourt 19; mains €7-10; **V**) The owner of this trattoria is from Pompeii so expect faux-Roman surroundings and delicious thin-crust Neapolitan pizza, plus homemade pasta with simple, fresh sauces. The house wine is superb.

Restaurant La Puntilla (☎ 928 81 36 13; El Charco de San Ginés; mains €7-14) The breezy blue-and-white colour scheme adds to the charm of this lake-side restaurant with its view of the bobbing boats. The menu includes seafood dishes like octopus with potatoes in *mojo* and fried squid.

MIAC Restaurant (☎ 928 81 23 21; Castillo de San José; mains €11-43; 1-3.45pm & 7.30-11pm, bar 11am-midnight) Situated in the Castillo de San José, along with the art gallery (see opposite), is Arrecife's greatest gastronomic-cum-visual experience. Glide down the spiral staircase and order some wonderful meat and fish dishes in the grooviest possible setting. The huge wraparound windows overlook the port and the décor is the usual Manrique mix of airy and inventive. The bow-tied service completes the dress-for-dinner feel.

There's a smattering of breezy outdoor cafés and restaurants on Calle Ruperto González Negrín and La Marina. **La Tavernetta** (☎ 928 80 75 09; cnr La Marina & Calle Tresguerra; mains €5-7; **V**) is a winner with its picture windows and vast menu, including bacon-and-egg breakfasts, healthy salads, fish and meat dishes and a heavenly chocolate soufflé. For self-catering, there's a modest **covered market** (Calle Liebre; 9am-1pm Mon-Sat).

DRINKING

There's plenty of nightlife choice in town, ranging from gritty local bars to intimate chill-out cafés – and just about everything in between. The main moving-and-shaking clubs are located on one short strip of central Calle José Antonio.

Bar Andalucía (☎ 928 08 36 07; Calle Luis Martín 5; closed Sun) Right off the main shopping strut and sporting Andalucian tiles, paintings for sale and straight-from-Seville tapas

like stuffed peppers and *patatas alioli* (fried potatoes with garlic mayonnaise).

Divino Doblón (Calle José Antonio 57; 11pm-4am) A nautical-themed cavernous place attracting throngs of young revellers with its three bars and energetic mix of music.

La Calle Disco Pub (Calle José Antonio 74; 10pm-late) has regular live bands along with neighbour **El Convento** (Calle José Antonio 76; 10pm-late), which has arches and columns but little else ecclesiastical. Both clubs get going around midnight, with DJs spinning a mix of music, including funky house, retro and rocky Latino.

GETTING THERE & AWAY
To/From the Airport

Lanzarote's airport is 6km south of Arrecife. Buses 22 and 23 (€1, 20 minutes) run between the airport and Arrecife every 30 minutes or thereabouts between 7.10am and 10.40pm Monday to Friday (between 8.40am and 10.40pm on weekends). A taxi will cost about €9.

There's a **tourist office** (☎ 928 84 60 73; 9am-7pm Mon & Wed, 9.30am-9.30pm Tue & Thu, 9am-9.30pm Fri & Sat, 10.30am-9.30pm Sun) in the arrivals hall.

To/From the Port

Puerto de los Mármoles is about 4km northeast of central Arrecife. The Arrecife–Costa Teguise bus calls in at the port. A taxi costs about €3.50.

Boat

The weekly **Acciona-Trasmediterránea** (☎ 902 45 46 45; www.trasmediterranea.es) ferry (adult/child €256/128, 28 hours) to Cádiz on mainland Spain stops at Arrecife on the way from Las Palmas de Gran Canaria. Accommodation is in cabins and it leaves at 3pm on Friday. The company frequently has two-for-one special fares.

Naviera Armas (☎ 902 45 65 00; www.navieraarmas .com) has daily ferries (adult/child €40/16, 7¼ hours) to Las Palmas de Gran Canaria. There are seven daily ferries (five on Sundays) from Playa Blanca to Corralejo on Fuerteventura (€16, 25 minutes).

You can get tickets at the *estación marítima* (ferry terminal) or at the **Acciona-Trasmediterránea/Naviera Armas office** (☎ 928 81 10 19; Calle José Antonio 90; 8.15am-1.30pm Mon-Fri, 8.15-10.45am Sat), or up to one hour before embarkation.

BONO BUS

If you are planning on making a few trips, invest in a **Bono Bus** card, which can save you around 30% off the fare. The cards cost €12 and €22 and are purchased at bus stations. Tell the driver your destination and the amount will be deducted from your card via a stamping machine.

Bus

Arrecife Bus services crisscross the island from the **bus station** (Vía Medular). Many westbound buses also stop at Playa del Reducto. Bus 2 (€1.40, 40 minutes, about every 20 minutes) runs to Puerto del Carmen, while bus 1 (€1, 20 minutes, about every 20 minutes) serves Costa Teguise. Bus 6 (€2.95, 1½ hours, 12 daily) goes to Playa Blanca via Puerto del Carmen and buses 7 and 9 (€1, 30 minutes, up to nine daily) go to Teguise via Tahiche. Three buses on weekdays (two daily on weekends) head north for Orzola (€2.95, 1½ hours), from where you can get a boat out to the islet of Graciosa.

Car & Motorcycle

You will find plenty of rental companies, especially around Avenida Mancomunidad and Calle Dr Rafael González Negrín.

GETTING AROUND
Bus

A couple of *guaguas municipales* (local buses) follow circuits around town, but you're unlikely to need them.

Taxi

There's a taxi rank beside the tourist office on La Marina and another on Calle José Antonio. Otherwise call ☎ 928 80 31 04.

AROUND ARRECIFE

COSTA TEGUISE

Northeast of Arrecife is Costa Teguise, which is perfectly pleasant, provided you are not expecting cobbled streets and crumbling buildings. This is a purpose-built holiday resort, built on a grid system, with bustling shopping centres, good beaches and water sports, plenty of mediocre (and better) bars and restaurants but, inevitably perhaps, no real soul. There's not even an original fishing village at its heart.

The most appealing beach is Playa de las Cucharas. Those further south suffer unfortunate views of the port and industry near Arrecife. The Centro Comercial Las Cucharas shopping centre is the resort's focal point.

Information

Clínica Lanzarote (☎ 928 59 02 21; Avenida Islas Canarias 13) A 24-hour medical clinic in the Apartamentos Lanzarote Gardens complex.
Internet Access (☎ 928 34 68 16; Apartmento Celeste, Avenida Islas Canarias; per hr €1.60; ☷ 10.30am-midnight)
Post office (☎ 928 82 72 68; Avenida Islas Canarias 12) In the Centro Comercial Las Maretas.
Tourist office (☎ 928 59 25 42; Avenida Islas Canarias s/n; ☷ 10am-5pm) Has piles of brochures.

Sights

The Thursday **craft and produce market** (Centro Pueblo Marinero; ☷ 11am-4pm) deservedly draws the crowds. The Friday market is more mainstream and naff.

Activities
DIVING

Sign up at long-established **Calipso Diving** (☎ 928 59 08 79; www.calipso-diving.com; Centro Comercial Calipso; one dive €25) for courses and dives; there is equipment hire for experienced divers. The **Aquatis Diving Center** (☎ 928 59 04 07; www.diving-lanzarote.net; Playa de las Cucharas; dive €25) offers similar.

WINDSURFING

Take advantage of the steady local winds with **Windsurf Paradise Lanzarote** (☎ 928 34 60 22; www.windsurflanzarote.com; Calle La Corvina 8; 1½hr beginner course €35), on Playa Las Cucharas, which also rents out equipment.

CYCLING

For bicycle hire, check out **Bike Station** (☎ 628 10 21 77; www.mylanzarote.com; CC Maretas s/n; rental day/week €11/70), which also arranges tours (from €30) of the island.

GOLF

If you fancy a hit of golf, **Costa Teguise Golf** (☎ 928 59 05 12; www.lanzarote-golf.com; Avenida Golf s/n) has 18 holes (from €55) and offers lessons (from €180 for nine lessons). Club hire is available.

DETOUR

En route from Tahiche to Teguise you reach the unassuming small town of **Nazaret**. In the centre, look for a sign to Lagomar. Follow this up through the sleepy side streets until you come to the **Lagomar** restaurant. Stop for a drink in the bar, set around a white puddle of a pool with tunnels and cosy seating. The architecture has a New Mexico–meets-Moroccan look with its towers, cupolas and interesting angles built into the side of a cliff. It was designed by Manrique for Omar Sharif and was supposedly lost by the actor in a spectacularly unsuccessful game of bridge.

WALKING

Olita Treks (☎ 619 16 99 89; www.olita-treks.com; Centro Comercial Mareta; walks from €35) conducts excellent local walks, which cover turf such as Isla Graciosa, the island's volcanoes or various coastal stretches. Walks are either half- or full-day, and the price includes pick-up and transport. English is spoken.

Sleeping & Eating

Hotel Meliá Salinas (☎ 928 59 00 40; Avenida Islas Canarias 16; www.solmelia.com; s/d €357/462, ste €699-974; villa €1362-2160; P 🅿 🛏 🖥 🏊 🚫) You may not have the funds to stay here, but do drift in for a drink and enjoy the botanical blast of the soaring central atrium with its trees, waterfalls, bridges, flowers and ponds designed by (who else?) César Manrique. The rooms are predictably sumptuous and the villas are glorious. Low-season reductions are available.

There's no shortage of restaurants, although Chinese, Indian and English pub fare are troublingly more prevalent than traditional Canarian cuisine.

Patio Canario (☎ 928 34 62 34; Plaza de Pueblo, Avenida Islas Canarias; mains €6-12) This place specialises in fresh fish and seafood from the Isla de la Graciosa. The outside terrace is set in an attractive courtyard, with a handy German bakery across the way for that a slice of strudel for afters.

Getting There & Away

Bus 1 (€1, 20 minutes, about every 20 minutes) connects with Arrecife (via Puerto de los Mármoles) from 7am to midnight.

TAHICHE

Fundación César Manrique (☎ 928 84 31 38; adult/under 12yr €7.50/free; ☉ 10am-6pm daily Jul-Oct, 10am-6pm Mon-Sat & 10am-3pm Sun Nov-Jun) is an art gallery and a centre for the island's cultural life. Only 6km north of Arrecife, it was home to César Manrique, who enjoys a posthumous status on the island akin to that of a mystical hero. He built his house, Taro de Tahiche, into the lava fields just outside the town. The subterranean rooms are, in fact, huge air bubbles left behind by flowing lava. It's a real James Bond hideaway, with white leather seats slotted into cave-like dens and a sunken swimming pool. There's a whole gallery devoted to Manrique, plus minor works by some of his contemporaries, including Picasso, Chillida, Miró, Sempere and Tàpies. Tragically, in September 1992, only six months after the foundation opened its doors, César Manrique was killed a few yards away in a car accident.

At least seven buses a day stop here on their way from Arrecife to Teguise. Look for the huge mobile sculpture by Manrique dominating the roundabout, and walk 200m down the San Bartolomé road.

TEGUISE

pop 15825

Teguise, 12km north of Arrecife, has a North Africa–meets-Spanish-pueblo feel. It is an intriguing mini-oasis of low-rise buildings set around a central plaza and surrounded by the bare plains of central Lanzarote. Firmly on the tourist trail, there are several shops here selling flowing garments and handmade jewellery, plus restaurants, bars and a handful of monuments testifying to the fact that the town was the island's capital until Arrecife took the baton in 1852.

Maciot, the son of Jean de Béthencourt, moved here when it was a Guanche settlement and married Teguise, daughter of the one-time local chieftain. Various convents were founded and the town prospered. But with prosperity came other problems, including pirates who plundered the town several times, hence the ominously named Calle de la Sangre (Blood Street).

Teguise has a large and touristy Sunday morning market. Surprisingly, there is a dearth of places to stay in town.

Sights

Sprawling **Palacio Spínola** (Plaza de la Constitución; admission €3; 9am-3pm Mon-Fri, 10am-3pm Sun) was built between 1730 and 1780 and passed to the Spínolas, a prominent Lanzarote family, in 1895. Nowadays it serves as both museum (of sorts) and the official residence of the Canary Islands government. It deserves a leisurely perusal, although many of the furnishings are clearly a few decades more modern than their surrounds.

Across the plaza is the eclectic **Iglesia de la Virgen de Guadalupe** (9am-1.30pm Mon-Sat), which has suffered numerous remodellings since it was first built in the 16th century, leaving it in a rather confused state.

Several monasteries dot the town, and wandering Teguise's pedestrianised lanes is a pleasure in itself. Keep your eyes peeled for the Franciscan **Convento de Miraflores**, the **Convento de Santo Domingo** and the **Palacio de Herrera y Rojas**.

The **Castillo de Santa Bárbara** is not only the oldest fort on the Canaries, but the only castle that really looks the part. Perched up on Guanapay peak, with sweeping views across the plains, it was erected in the 16th century by Sancho de Herrera, consequently expanded and then fell into disuse. Since being restored, it houses the modest, yet fascinating, **Museo del Emigrante Canario** (928 84 59 13; admission €3; 10am-4pm daily summer, 10am-5pm Mon-Fri, 10am-4pm Sat & Sun winter), a poignant collection relating to the long history of migration from the islands to Spain's American colonies.

Eating

our pick **Casa Leon** (928 84 59 31; Calle Leon y Castillo s/n; mains €8-10; closed Mon; **V**) Run by affable Frenchman Philippe and his Canarian partner José, this small restaurant shares its locale with a health-food shop and alternative-therapy centre. The cuisine is essentially Moroccan, with a few healthy international options; there is a generous buffet on Sunday. The ambience is laid-back and cosy with warm colours, Moroccan lamps and provocative artwork.

Acatife (928 84 50 37; Calle San Miguel 4; mains €8-16) A memorable traditional restaurant; look for the ancient wooden door. The interior continues the rustic theme, with beams and chunky wooden furniture, while the food is down-to-earth and hearty, as befits the surroundings.

Getting There & Away

Numerous buses, including 7 and 9 (€1, 30 minutes) from Arrecife, stop in Teguise en route to destinations such as Orzola and Haría. There are also Sunday buses to the town's market from Costa Teguise, Puerto del Carmen and Playa Blanca.

SAN BARTOLOMÉ & AROUND

Starting life as the Guanche settlement of Ajei, San Bartolomé (population 17,452) ended up in the 18th century as the de facto private fiefdom of a militia leader, Francisco Guerra Clavijo y Perdomo, and his descendants.

A couple of kilometres northwest of town, on the Tinajo road, rises up the modernistic, white **Monumento al Campesino** (Peasants' Monument), erected in 1968 by (surprise, surprise) César Manrique to honour the thankless labour that most islanders had endured for generations. Adjacent stands the **Museo del Campesino** (928 52 01 36; admission free; 10am-6pm), which is more a scattering of craft workshops, including weaving and ceramics, that may or may not be open. Most people come here to eat – ironic for a monument dedicated to those who habitually endured hunger – at the **restaurant** (928 52 01 36; mains €5-11; 12.30-4pm). The dining room is vast, circular and sunken, complete with tunnel. There is a good wine and rum list and well-prepared local cuisine, accompanied by Canarian music. Try the stone bass in coriander sauce or chicken casserole with garlic and potatoes.

Three kilometres southwest, en route to pretty Yaiza, is the **Museo del Vino El Grifo** (928 52 49 51; www.elgrifo.com in Spanish; admission incl glass of wine €3; 10.30am-6pm). This is the former bodega (old-style wine bar) and winery of the El Grifo company, where you can see wine-making equipment, some of it dating back to 1775, buy all sorts of wine-drinking requisites and indulge in a little wine tasting (€0.90 to €1.10 for a half-filled glass). We recommend grabbing a seat and quaffing through the five different wines on offer (€7.50), as long as you're not driving.

This region has several excellent winery routes, including one between San Bartolomé and Tinajo, which includes the excellent **Bodegas La Vegueta** (jquevedo@faycan.es), **Bodega Tinache** (www.tinache.com), **Bodega Vega de**

Yuco (bodegavegadeyuco@hotmail.com) and **Bodega Mozaga** (bodegasmozaga@hotmail.com); see p120.

In San Bartolomé itself, the **Museo Etnográfico Tanit** (☎ 928 52 23 34; www.museotanit.com; Calle Constitución 1; admission €6; ☻ 10am-5pm Mon-Fri, to 3pm Sat), set in an 18th-century Canarian house, concentrates on the last 200 years of local life, with artefacts, equipment and exhibitions. English explanations are available.

Sleeping

If you want to stay in these parts, there are a couple of delightful rural options.

our pick Caserío de Mozaga (☎ 928 52 00 60; www.caseriodemozaga.com; Calle Mozaga 8; d with breakfast €115; ☒) Northwest of San Bartolemé, in the village of Mozaga, this 18th-century family home retains its rustic authenticity with a central courtyard complete with original *aljibe* (water system). The rooms have high ceilings and are graced with family heirlooms. The restaurant (mains from €10) has an excellent reputation.

Finca de la Florida (☎ 928 52 11 24; www.hotelfinca delaflorida.com; El Islote 90; s/d with breakfast €66/120, mains from €7; ℗) Located just off the road to Yaiza, this traditional house with decorative wooden balconies has large rooms washed in Canary yellow with wood furnishings and sky-blue textiles. The property is surrounded by vineyards with volcano views. There is plenty to entertain, including a gym, tennis court, spa, sauna and minigolf.

THE NORTH

Lanzarote's northern towns and villages are typically clusters of whitewashed buildings surrounded by a felt-covered landscape of lichen and lava fields. The principal attractions are the combined works of nature and César Manrique: his house (now a gallery), a pair of breathtaking lava caves, cactus

CÉSAR MANRIQUE

Born on 24 April 1919, César Manrique grew up in relative tranquillity by the sea in Arrecife. After a stint as a volunteer with Franco's forces during the 1936–39 Civil War, he enrolled in Madrid's Academia de Bellas Artes de San Fernando in 1945, having already held his first exhibition five years earlier in his home town of Arrecife.

Influenced by Picasso and Matisse, Manrique held his first major exhibition of abstract works in 1954. In the following years, his opus toured most of Europe, and in 1964 he was invited by one of his admirers, Nelson Rockefeller, to the USA where he exhibited in New York's Guggenheim Museum. But Manrique never forgot his birthplace and returned home in 1968, after his successful US tour, brimming with ideas for enhancing what he felt to be the incomparable beauty of Lanzarote.

He began with a campaign to preserve traditional building methods and another to ban the blight of advertising billboards. A multifaceted artist, Manrique subsequently turned his flair and vision to a broad range of projects, with the whole of Lanzarote becoming his canvas. In all, he carried out seven major projects on the island and numerous others elsewhere in the archipelago and beyond. At the time of his death, he had several more on the boil. See p119 for an itinerary of Manrique's sites.

On the grand scale, it was primarily Manrique's persistent lobbying for maintaining traditional architecture and protecting the natural environment that prompted the *cabildo* (government) to pass laws restricting urban development. The growing wave of tourism since the early 1980s has, however, threatened to sweep away all before it. But Manrique's ceaseless opposition to such unchecked urban sprawl touched a nerve with many Conejeros and led to the creation of an environmental group known as El Guincho, which has had some success in revealing – and at times even reversing – abuses by developers. Manrique was posthumously made its honorary president.

As you pass through villages across the island, you'll see how traditional stylistic features remain the norm. The standard whitewashed houses are adorned with green-painted doors, window shutters and strange onion-shaped chimney pots. In such ways, Manrique's influence and spirit endure.

LANZAROTE

SEEING RED

Fields of cacti, their leaves green, fleshy and the shape of giant rabbit ears, are about all that grows around the small village of Guatiza. And grow they do, in profusion, hemming in the *pueblo* (village). They're a last reminder of what was once a thriving trade on Tenerife and the eastern islands.

Much more than a harsh desert plant, they're home and food to *la cochinilla* (cochineal insects). To this day, these tiny insects are collected in the tens of thousands. Each one contributes a blood-red droplet of the dye cochineal, used as a colouring in food and cosmetics.

Elsewhere, the once-thriving cochineal trade has long since withered, killed off by competition from synthetic dyes. But in Guatiza a centuries-old cottage industry still just manages to persist.

---

gardens and a stunning lookout. We recommend as a minimum the Jameos del Agua cave (opposite).

GUATIZA & CHARCO DEL PALO

Just north of tiny Guatiza is the **Jardín de Cactus** (Cactus Gardens; ☎ 928 52 93 97; admission €5; ☯ 10am-6pm; ♿), signalled by an 8m-high spiky metal cactus, the work of – you've guessed it – César Manrique. Built in an old quarry, it comes over as more a giant work of art than a botanical garden. There are nearly 1500 different varieties of this prickly customer, every single one labelled. The entrance fee includes a hot or cold drink at the on-site restaurant.

If you fancy bathing (or even shopping!) in the buff, a few kilometres north of here is the naturist resort of **Charco del Palo** (d from €55) with pleasant sandy beaches and rocky coves. To get here, take the narrow road to the beach just south of Mala. There is bungalow-style accommodation available if you want to stay a few days with like-minded souls (mainly Germans). Contact **Obona** (☎ 928 17 31 76; Calle Cabrera Peraza 6, Charco del Palo).

ARRIETA

pop 1929

Next northwards is the fishing village of Arrieta. Its main attraction is the small beach, **Playa de la Garita**, a combination of volcanic rock and sand with a congenial beach bar and restaurant, Chiringuito Beach, where you can kick back with a beer and tapas.

You'll find blue-balconied **Apartamentos Arrieta** (☎ 928 84 82 30; Calle Garita 25; 2-person apt €30) on the main street. It's a well-maintained place with good-sized, pine-furnished apartments and a vast rooftop terrace. Rafael, the elderly owner, only speaks Spanish.

Smack bang on Arrieta's jetty is **Restaurante El Charcón** (☎ 928 84 81 10; Muelle Arrieta; mains €6-10; ☯ closed Wed), which dates from 1988. The menu is fish-based, including grilled octopus for under €8. There is outdoor seating for catching the rays.

Bus 9 (€2.95, 1½ hours, three daily Monday to Friday, two on weekends) from Arrecife to Orzola calls in here.

MALPAÍS DE LA CORONA

The 'badlands of the crown' are the living (or dead) testimony to the volcanic upsurges that shook the north of the island thousands of years ago. Plant life is quietly, patiently, winning its way back, and it is here that you can visit two of the island's better-known volcanic caverns.

Cueva de los Verdes & Jameos del Agua

More obviously than on any of the other islands, lava is the hallmark of Lanzarote. So, unsurprisingly, after the lunar wonders of the Parque Nacional de Timanfaya (p136), the flow of visitors is strongest here, at the site of an ancient lava slide into the ocean. The cavernous Cueva de los Verdes and, further 'downstream', the hollows of the Jameos del Agua – adapted by César Manrique into a kind of New Age retreat-meets-bar – are an easy 1km walk from one another.

Cueva de los Verdes (☎ 928 84 84 84; adult/under 12yr €8/free; ☯ 10am-6pm) is a yawning, 1km-long chasm, which is the most spectacular segment of an almost-8km-long lava tube left behind by an eruption that occurred 5000 years ago. As the lava ploughed down towards the sea (more than 6km of tunnel is above sea level

LOCAL VOICES

Tila Braddock hurtles along the beach on a quad bike for our rendezvous at an Arrieta beach bar. No surprises there; one of Tila's passions is promoting extreme sports in Lanzarote.

'We have to get away from this Lanzagrotty image! Unfortunately, the best-known southern resorts have been overbuilt and exploited, but there is a lot more to this island than sun, sea and karaoke! I am urging those in power to promote Lanzarote as an extreme sports destination as it is perfect, with a dramatic landscape, fantastic beaches and great climate.'

Tila really is a mover and shaker here. He was instrumental in starting both the Dash (see the boxed text, p139) and **Las Tres Islas** (www.lastresislas.com) events; the latter was first held in 2004 and covers four disciplines, three islands and two sea crossings.

'Participants have to swim from Isla Graciosa to the Lanzarote shore, and then run up the cliff to the Mirador del Río. Next, they bicycle to Playa Blanca before canoeing or windsurfing to Fuerteventura. No fuel is allowed and it culminates with a big party on the beach.'

Competitors are urged to raise sponsorship for ADAPH, an independent registered charity based in Morocco that helps disabled children and adults in the Sahara. 'I feel we have an obligation to these people who were abandoned by Spain after the death of Franco.'

Tila arrived in Puerto de Carmen from England 22 years ago as a windsurfing instructor. When he discovered the north of the island, he stayed put. 'I had discovered the *real* Lanzarote. It's greener, the food is fantastic and the locals are so friendly and laid-back.'

Together with his wife, Michelle, and their four children, Tila is slowly restoring a 100-year-old farmhouse just inland from Arrieta. The house uses solar and wind energy and is made from all natural materials, including stones wheelbarrowed in from the surrounding terrain. That doesn't mean any lack of luxury, however, as attested by the outside spa that was happily bubbling away when we arrived there later in the day.

'We're having a barbecue and party tonight, do stay!' Tila enthuses, children and dogs underfoot. A tempting offer indeed…

Check out www.youthsunited.com to learn more about Tila's fund-raising sports events on Lanzarote, together with details about how you can sign up.

LANZAROTE

today, and another 1.5km extends below the water's surface), the top layers cooled and formed a roof, beneath which the liquid magma continued to slither until the eruption exhausted itself.

You will be guided through two chambers, one below the other. The ceiling is largely covered with what look like mini-stalactites, but no water penetrates the cave. The odd pointy extrusions are where bubbles of air and lava were thrown up onto the ceiling by gases released while the boiling lava flowed; as they hit the ceiling and air, they 'froze' in the process of dripping back into the lava stream.

In spite of the name '*verde*', there's nothing green about this cave – 200 years ago it was considered the property of a shepherd family, the Verdes. At other times it served as a refuge for locals during pirate assaults on the island.

Anyone with severe back problems might think twice about entering the cave – there are a few passages that require you to bend at 90 degrees to get through. Similarly, it's no place for claustrophobes.

The visit is worthwhile in itself for a great visual gag deep inside the cave. No, we're not telling – and urge you in turn to keep it quiet from your friends. Guided tours, lasting about 45 minutes and available in English, take place when there are 50 people waiting, which usually doesn't take long to happen. Concerts of mainly jazz and blues are held here from September to April, organised by **Musical Candelaria** (☎ 649 99 09 56).

The first cavern of the **Jameos del Agua** (☎ 928 84 80 20; adult/under 12yr €8/free) resembles the nave of a vast marine basilica. Molten lava seethed through here en route to the sea, but in this case the ocean leaked in a bit, forming the startling azure lake at the heart of the Jameos. Manrique's idea of installing bars and a **restaurant** (⏱ 7.30-11.30pm) around the lake, adding a pool, a concert hall seating 600 (with wonderful acoustics) and the subtly didactic Casa de los Volcanos, was a pure brainwave.

Have a closer look into the lake's waters. The tiny white flecks at the bottom are crabs. Small ones, yes, and the only known examples of *Munidopsis polymorpha* (blind crabs) away from the deepest oceans. Do heed the signs and resist the temptation to throw coins into the water – their corrosion could kill off this unique species. Like the Cueva, access for the mobility impaired is not really possible – there are a lot of steps.

Bus 9 (€2.95, 1½ hours) between Arrecife and Orzola stops at the turn-off for Jameos del Agua, but only runs three times daily Monday to Friday (7.40am, 10.30am and 3.30pm) and twice on weekends (7.40am and 3.30pm). It's better to have your own car or join a tour.

ORZOLA

Most people just pass through this northern fishing town on their way to the Isla Graciosa. Some stop for a food break in one of several restaurants flanking the port, where you can be sure that the seafood is flapping fresh, but relatively few get wind of the **beach** a couple of kilometres west of the town – about the only one in this part of the island, which is otherwise dominated by steep, uncompromising cliffs.

MINOR CANARIES

The string of tiny islets flung out north of Lanzarote are known as the Minor Canaries, and minor they certainly are. All except Isla Graciosa (aka La Graciosa) are part of a nature reserve, with access generally limited to researchers.

Isla Graciosa

This island is recommended for the ultimate stress-busting break. A day should do it, however, with anything longer being strictly for the keenest surfers (and the surfing here is world-class) or for those seeking longer-term peace and quiet.

About 600 people live on the island, virtually all in the village of Caleta del Sebo, where the Orzola boat docks. Behind it stretches 27.5 sq km of largely barren scrubland, interrupted by five minor volcanic peaks ranged from north to south. About a 30-minute walk southwest of Caleta del Sebo is delightful little Playa Francesa; there's also Playa Lambra at the northern end of the islet.

On a windy day Caleta del Sebo can seem a cross between a bare Moroccan village and a sand-swept Wild West outpost. This place is worlds away from the tourist mainstream. There are no sealed roads and the main form of transport seems to be battered old Land Rovers.

There's a smattering of places to stay.

Pensión Girasol (☎ 928 84 21 18; www.graciosaonline .com in Spanish; Avenida Virgen del Mar s/n; d €17-20), about 100m on the left from the ferry, has recently been renovated and offers standard, clean rooms. Those with sea-view balconies are well worth the few extra euros. You'll find a breezy, casual restaurant (mains €7.50 to €10) downstairs; try the delicious grilled parrot fish. Accommodation in nearby apartments (€36) can also be arranged.

Pensión Enriqueta (☎ 928 84 20 51; fax 928 84 21 29; Calle Mar de Barlovento 6; d with/without bathroom €20/17) is a block back from the waterfront. It has simple, clean doubles that leave little lasting impression. The downstairs restaurant (mains €5) is a notch up from the norm, however, with plenty of local atmosphere and good seafood dishes.

Signs offering accommodation are posted in windows throughout town. Generally, you'll get a smart little apartment sleeping up to four people for about €38 to €45 per night.

If you feel like accelerating out of first gear, boogie on down to **Las Arenas** (Calle Mar de Barlovento s/n; ☽ from 12.30am Fri & Sat), a disco pub at the back of the Enriqueta that only opens its steamy doors to revellers after midnight.

Líneas Marítimas Romero (☎ 928 84 20 70; www .geocities.com/lineas_romero; Calle García Escámez 11) runs three boats daily (four between July and September) from Orzola across to the islet (adult/child €15/8, 20 minutes). It can get very rocky between Orzola and Punta Fariones, so you may want to pop a seasickness pill. Unless you want to be Robinson Crusoe for the night, take the outbound 10am or noon sailing, which allows time to explore before taking the last boat back at 4pm (6pm July and August).

To get around the island, consider hiring a bike. **Bike Graciosa Island** (☎ 928 84 21 38; Muelle; bike per day from €8; ☽ 10am-1pm) has its office right in the harbour and can provide a rudimentary map to help you find those far-off beaches.

THE NORTHWEST

The island's northwest arguably offers visitors the most rewarding look at Lanzarote's natural beauty. It's a place of attractive, unspoiled towns, some great escapes and stunning panoramic views.

MIRADOR DEL RÍO

About 2km north of Yé, the Spanish armed forces set up gun batteries at the end of the 19th century at a strategic site overlooking El Río, the strait separating Lanzarote from Isla Graciosa. Spain had gone to war with the USA over control of Cuba, and you couldn't be too careful! In 1973 the ubiquitous César Manrique left his mark, converting the gun emplacement into a spectacular bug-eyed lookout point.

Mirador del Río (☎ 928 52 65 51; adult/under 12yr €4.70/free; ☼ 10am-6pm) has a good bar and souvenir shop; a drink is included in the entrance price. There are vertiginous views of the sweeping lava flows – frozen in time – that fall to the ocean, Isla Graciosa and the surrounding volcanic islets. Pay €1 to get up close and personal with a telescope.

GUINATE

The main reason for visiting the village of Guinate, about 5km south of Mirador del Río, is the **Guinate Tropical Park** (☎ 928 83 55 00; www.guinatepark.com; adult/under 12yr €14/5; ☼ 10am-5pm; ☒), home to around 1300 rare and exotic birds, a cacti garden and some animals, including monkeys and lemurs. The parrot show is best avoided, unless you enjoy birds on bicycles and the like.

Just beyond the park is another fine (and completely free) **lookout** across El Río and the islets.

HARÍA
pop 4894

Possibly the prettiest village in Lanzarote. Set in a lush and bucolic palm-filled valley punctuated by splashes of brilliant colour from (rare) bougainvillea and poinsettia plants, this North African–style oasis was a spa for wealthy Canarios in the past. The central pedestrian avenue, Plaza León y Castillo, is shaded by eucalyptus trees and the site of a Saturday morning craft market.

Dos Hermanos (☎ 928 83 54 09; Plaza León y Castillo; mains €7.50-10) is in a choice location with tables outside on the plaza. The menu has it all, it seems, including traditional goat and lamb dishes and (if you must) cheese omelette with chips. Check out the superb sand sculptures at the craft shop next door.

If it's local atmosphere you seek, head into **Bar Ney-ya** (cnr Calle Cilla & Calle Hoya), in an old-fashioned building with high ceilings, some dark corners and outside tables; inexpensive tapas are available.

Bus 7 (€2.65, 45 minutes) connects Haría to Arrecife via Teguise and Tahiche four times daily Monday to Friday and three times a day on weekends.

LA CALETA DE FAMARA

Years before he hit the big time, Manrique whiled away many a childhood summer on the wild beach of La Caleta de Famara. It's one of the best beach spots on Lanzarote and a place where you don't have to fight for towel space on the sand. This low-key seaside hamlet, with its dramatic cliff views, has a youthful, bohemian vibe and makes few concessions to the average tourist, aside from a few choice restaurants overlooking the surf.

Famara's excellent waves offer some of Europe's finest breaks. Pedro Urrastarazu at **Famara Surf Shop** (☎ 928 52 86 76; www.famarasurf.com; El Marinero 39; 1-day surf school €39; ☼ 10am-8pm) rents boards and offers courses at various levels.

Sleeping & Eating
Apartments Famara Surf (☎ 928 52 86 76; www.famarasurf.com; El Marinero 39; 2 person apt €42) Owned by the surf shop, these are clean, well-equipped apartments with TV and fridge, whether you're here to surf or sunbathe.

Playa Famara Bungalows (☎ 928 84 51 32; www.bungalowsplayafamara.com; Urbanización Famara; bungalows from €55; ☒) This distinctive complex is located 2km north of the main town, and is a modern step-terraced arrangement of semicircular holiday homes constructed from rock and lots of white stucco. Bungalows sleep between two and six, and longer stays (or low season) equal good discounts.

our pick El Risco (☎ 928 52 85 50; Calle Montaña Blanca 30; mains €6-11.50; ☼ closed Mon) A superb location, with a terrace overlooking the sea and a nautical blue-and-white interior. Owner Gustavo recommends his fish and goat dishes, but has also introduced a menu of pizzas and savoury crepes to appeal to the less intrepid diner. The result makes this a winner for fussy families. The dining-room is pleasantly informal and there's a small terrace for catching the breeze.

Restaurante Sol (Calle Salvavidas 48; mains €6-13; ☑ closed Mon) Located in a simple blue-and-white building fronting the sea. Try the grilled fish or fried baby squid. This place gets packed out at weekends with noisy local families – always a good sign.

Getting There & Away

Bus 20 (€1.80, 50 minutes) connects Arrecife with La Caleta de Famara. It leaves La Caleta de Famara at 7.30am, 9am and 5.30pm and sets off from the capital at 7am, 8.30am, 2pm and 5pm, Monday to Friday only.

TIAGUA

About 10km south of La Caleta, and 8km northwest of San Bartolomé, the ecologically aware, open-air **Museo Agricola El Patio** (☎ 928 52 91 34; admission €6; ☑ 10am-5.30pm Mon-Fri, to 2.30pm Sat; ⓖ) recreates a 19th-century traditional farmer's house (complete with wine cellar!) and provides an insight into traditional aspects of the island's culture. Signage – including some irritatingly edifying texts – is in English. You'll see loads of old equipment and furniture, a windmill and the odd camel or donkey chewing the cud.

Tiagua is on the bus 16 (€1.10, 30 minutes) route from Arrecife to La Santa. Bus 20 (€1.10, 25 minutes) to La Caleta de Famara also calls in here.

PARQUE NACIONAL DE TIMANFAYA

The eruption that began on 1 September 1730 and convulsed the southern end of the island was among the greatest volcanic cataclysms in recorded history. A staggering 48 million cu metres of lava spurted and flowed out daily, while fusillades of molten rock were rocketed out over the countryside and into the ocean. When the eruption finally ceased to rage after six long years, over 200 sq km had been devastated, including 20 villages and 30 hamlets.

The **Montañas del Fuego** (Mountains of Fire), at the heart of this eerie 51-sq-km **national park** (☎ 928 84 00 57; admission €8; ☑ 9am-

5.45pm, last bus tour at 5pm), are appropriately named. When you reach the Manrique-designed lookout and Restaurante del Diablo (note his wonderful light fittings in the form of giant frying pans) at a rise known as the Islote de Hilario, try scrabbling around in the pebbles and see just how long you can hold them in your hands. At a depth of a few centimetres, the temperature is already 100°C; by 10m it's up to 600°C. The cause of this phenomenon is a broiling magma chamber 4km below the surface.

Some feeble (or rather, given the harsh environment, decidedly robust) scraps of vegetation, including 200 species of lichen, are reclaiming the earth in a few stretches of the otherwise moribund landscape of fantastic forms in shades of black, grey, maroon and red. Fine copper-hued soil slithers down volcanic cones, until it's arrested by twisted, swirling and folded mounds of solidified lava – this is one place where you really must remember to bring your camera.

The people running the show at Islote de Hilario, near the restaurant, gift shop and car park, have a series of endearing tricks. In one, they shove a clump of brushwood into a hole in the ground and within seconds it's converted by the subterranean furnace into a burning bush. A pot of water poured down another hole promptly gushes back up in explosive geyser fashion; you have exactly three seconds to take that impressive snap.

The **Restaurant del Diablo** (☎ 928 84 00 56; menú del día €15; ☑ noon-3.30pm; Ⓟ) is a gag in itself – whatever meat you order you can watch sizzling on the all-natural, volcano-powered BBQ out back. The food's none-too-impressive but, hey, who's here for the cuisine? Vegetarians might feel a bit left out, though, what with all the smoking rabbit, T-bones and chicken. In the midst of all this carnivorous activity, there's a good list of local wines, some available by the half-bottle.

Included in the admission price of the national park, tan-coloured buses take you along the exciting 14km **Ruta de los Volcanes**, an excursion through some of the most spectacular volcanic country you are ever likely to see. The trilingual taped commentary includes a fascinating eyewitness account by local priest Don Agustín Cabrera including the following truly surreal-sounding scene: '...the earth suddenly opened near Timan-

---

FIRE WALKS

It is possible to walk within Parque Nacional de Timanfaya – but you'll need to plan in advance and you'll be part of a select group of just seven people. The 3.5km, two-hour Tremesana guided walk (Spanish and English) leaves from the **Mancha Blanca Visitors Centre** (☎ 928 84 08 39; Carretera de Yaiza a Tinajo Km11.5; ⏰ 9am-5pm) at 10am on Monday, Wednesday and Friday. Reserve a spot by phone or in person – at the time of research, you needed to reserve at least three weeks in advance if you wanted to walk in the summer high season. Try calling a day or two before and see if there's been a cancellation. The much more demanding Ruta del Litoral (9km, six hours) takes place once a month (no fixed date) and you need to reserve in person and be judged fit enough to handle the pace and the terrain. Both walks are free.

---

faya. The first night an enormous mountain rose up from the depths of the earth and from its point issued flames which continued to burn for 19 days'.

Buses leave every hour or so and the trip takes about 30 minutes. By about 10am there can be long queues to get into the park, so you may find yourself waiting for a tour.

North of the park, on the same road, is the informative **Mancha Blanca Visitors Centre** (☎ 928 84 08 39; www.mma.es; Carretera de Yaiza a Tinajo Km11.5; ⏰ 9am-5pm), which has excellent audiovisual and informative displays about the park.

INLAND & WEST COAST

The interior and west coast of Lanzarote are within easy reach of popular tourist haunts to the south, but can seem a world away in terms of crowds, infrastructure and activities. These are reasons enough to explore this area, along with its striking abstract landscape of towering black mountains and odd stone circles that have more to do with growing vines than any pagan cult.

LA GERIA

Near San Bartolomé (p130) the LZ-30 winds through the southwest, passing what has to be one of the oddest-looking vine-growing regions around. The viticulturists of Lanzarote have found the deep, black lava-soil, enriched by the island's shaky seismic history, perfect for the grape. The further south you go, the more common are these unique vineyards consisting of little dugouts nurtured behind crescent-shaped stone walls, known as *zocos*, implanted in the dark earth.

The *malvasía* (Malmsey wine) produced here is a good drop and along the road you pass a good half-dozen bodegas where you can buy the local produce at wholesale prices.

Try **Bodega La Geria** (☎ 928 17 31 78; www.lageria .com), where you can pick up bottles of dry or semi-*dulce* (sweet) *malvasía* (among others) for around €5.50. There's also a good little bar/café.

our pick **El Chupadero** (☎ 659 59 61 78; www.el -chupadero.com; tapas €4-8.50), which lies 4km north of Uga on the LZ-30, is one stunning little place you should head for. This German-owned farm/bodega does great tapas like garlicky prawns, which can be washed down with dry local *malvasía* wines from a terrace overlooking the vineyards. The simple whitewashed décor, with beamed ceilings and black-and-white photos, is one of the most stylish in these parts.

YAIZA

pop 9664

Yaiza is something of a southern crossroads, so you'll probably pass through on your travels. There's no specific reason for hanging about, but if you arrive at lunchtime and are feeling peckish, you'll be able to find a few pleasant-enough restaurants, including one excellent place (you'll need to book ahead).

It's a tidy, whitewashed town and the recipient of numerous awards for cleanliness. For sights, try the local church, **Nuestra Señora de los Remedios**, which was built in the 18th century and features a lovely blue-white-and-gold painted altarpiece and a folkloric painted wooden ceiling.

Sleeping & Eating

Finca de las Salinas (☎ 928 83 03 25; www.fincasalinas .com; Calle La Cuesta s/n; s/d €142/218, ste €266-328;

LANZAROTE

(P X R)) This beautifully converted 18th-century hacienda is a definite treat. The vibrant colours and cactus gardens give it a Mexican feel. The rooms are spacious and tasteful, with several located in converted stables. There is a gym, spa, sauna, tennis courts and bicycle hire on offer.

La Era (☎ 928 83 00 16; www.la-era.com in Spanish; Calle El Barranco 3; mains €10-15; ☽ closed Mon) Reservations are essential at this atmospheric restaurant set in a converted 300-year old farmhouse with the dining rooms set around a central courtyard. Another Manrique project, the dishes are firmly traditional and include de-boned rabbit with dates and César Manrique *torrijas* (a type of pancake with cane syrup and pumpkin jam), apparently from an old family recipe.

EL GOLFO & AROUND
This former fishing village has a laid-back, bohemian feel with its cluster of traditional buildings and lack of tourist-geared tat for sale. It's a fabulous place to come at sunset, with several bars overlooking the sea.

Just south of the village begins a string of small black-sand beaches. The one fronting the **Charco de los Clicos** is popular with sightseers. The Charco itself is a small, emerald-green pond, just in from the beach and overshadowed by wonderfully colourful and textured volcanic rocks. It is not safe to swim here though, as it can get very rough.

Along the coast road, which eventually leads to La Hoya, stop by **Los Hervideros**, a pair of caves through which the sea glugs and froths. After about 6km you reach the long Playa de Janubio, behind which are **Las Salinas de Janubio**, salt pans from where sea salt is extracted.

There is just one hotel in El Golfo and it's the charming **Hotelito del Golfo** (☎ /fax 928 17 32 72; Avenida Marítima 10; d €55; ☒), a friendly, family-run hotel and restaurant (mains from €6) that hasn't raised its prices in years. Tuck into a bowl of seafood soup for just €3 before bedding down in one of the bright, well-kitted-out rooms.

You will find no shortage of eating options beyond the hotel. On the waterfront there is a string of inviting bars and restaurants, including **Casa Torano** (☎ 928 17 30 58; Avenida Marítima), **Lago Verde** (☎ 928 17 33 11; Avenida

Marítima 46), where you can also enquire about renting an apartment, and **Mar Azul** (☎ 928 17 31 32; Calle Mayor 42).

THE SOUTH

The island's south is home to the most popular resorts and attracts family groups after an easy-going, sunny time punctuated with a deep-sea-fishing excursion or boozy night out.

PUERTO DEL CARMEN
With sunshades four lanes deep, this is the island's most popular beach and its oldest purpose-built resort. That said, if you are seeking an iota of Canarian atmosphere, head for the El Varadero harbour, at the far west of the beachfront, which still has a faint fishing-village feel with its bobbing boats and uninterrupted ocean views. Otherwise the centre remains a primarily Brit-geared resort with restaurants and bars competing for the cheapest bacon-and-eggs breakfast or largest (and loudest) Sky Sports screen.

Orientation
Lanzarote's premier resort straggles for 6km beside mostly golden sand. Its main street is Avenida Playas, a gaudy ribbon hugging the beach with shops, bars and restaurants.

Information
BOOKSHOPS
Bookswop (Calle Timanfaya 4; ☽ 9.30am-6pm Mon-Fri, to 1.30pm Sat) The best source for new and secondhand English-language books.

EMERGENCY
Policía Local (Police; ☎ 928 84 52 52; Avenida Juan Carlos I) Directly behind the post office.

INTERNET ACCESS
Most amusement arcades, including the Centro Commercial La Peñita near the El Varadero harbour, have internet terminals.
Network Xpress (☎ 928 51 52 54; Centro Comercial Marítimo, Avenida Playas; per hr €2)

MEDICAL SERVICES
Clínica Lanzarote (☎ 928 51 31 71; Avenida Playas 5) A well-staffed 24-hour medical centre.

POST

Post office (☎ 928 51 03 81; Avenida Juan Carlos I s/n) Beside the roundabout at the junction of Avenida Juan Carlos I and Calle Guardilama, in the western part of town.

TOURIST INFORMATION

Tourist office (☎ 928 51 53 37; www.puertodelcarmen .com; Avenida Playas s/n; ⌚ 10am-9pm Mon-Fri, to 1pm Sat) Halfway along Playa Grande.

Activities

The main activities seem to be kicking back with a beer or flaking out on the beach, but there's no lack of opportunity for something less supine. Diving is popular, as well as jet skiing and banana and paracraft rides.

CYCLING

For bicycle hire, contact **Renner Bikes** (☎ 629 99 07 55; www.mountainbike-lanzarote.com; Centro Comercial Marítimo, Avenida Playas s/n; per day €24).

DIVING & SURFING

Among several enterprises, tried and trusted operators are **Safari Diving** (☎ 928 51 19 92; www .safaridiving.nl; Playa de la Barrilla 4), **Canary Island Divers** (☎ 928 51 54 67; www.canaryislanddivers.com; Calle Alemania 1) and **Manta Dive Centre** (☎ 928 51 68 15; www .manta-diving-lanzarote.com; Calle Juan Carlos I 6). Prices start at around €25 per dive with your own equipment, and €35 including rental.

You can rent surfboards (€6 per hour) and buy the latest colour-coordinated lycra at **El Niño** (☎ 928 59 60 54; CC La Hoya), just up from the harbour.

HORSE RIDING

Horseback rides are available from **Lanzarote a Caballo** (☎ 928 83 03 14; www.lanzaroteacaballo.com; Carretera Arrecife-Yaiza; rides per hr €30). It's a great way to see the landscape, and hotel pick-up is available.

Sleeping

At last count there were around 200 hotels, apartment blocks and bungalow complexes in Puerto del Carmen. Many only deal with tour operators but may oblige the independent blow-in – if there is a room free.

Pensión Magec (☎ /fax 928 51 38 74; www.pension magec.com; Calle Hierro 11; s/d €25/30) There's just one standard *pensión* in Puerto del Carmen and it's a good one. Housed in a blue-and-white traditional house there are sea views from several rooms; go for No 21, with its private balcony, if you can. There are a few cheaper rooms available with shared facilities.

Apartamentos Isla de la Graciosa Lanzarote (☎ 928 51 33 86; Calle Reina Sofía 20; apt €55) These two-star modern apartments are located in the older part of town. They are spotlessly clean and the kitchens have pale wood fittings. There are reductions for stays of more than a night.

Hotel Los Fariones (☎ 928 51 01 75; www.grupofariones .com; Calle Roque del Este 1; s/d €95/145; P ⌂ ☐ ☒) This is the *grande dame* on the hotel scene;

LANZAROTE

THE DASH

Described as 'a great sailing adventure' by former Spanish windsurf champion, Nino Navarro, the Dash from Lanzarote to Tarfaya Sahara in Morocco was initiated in 2003, in part by Tila Braddock (see the boxed text, p133), to 'create a bridge between Christian and Muslim, rich and poor and two continents'.

The owners of large yachts were approached and asked whether they would be interested in sailing to the former Spanish colony of Tarfaya Sahara, a mere 100km across the ocean. More than just a race, the boats were loaded up with wheelchairs and equipment for the disabled, as well as clothing, baby supplies and just about anything that could be collected and carried.

'These people are very poor,' laments Tila. 'The Spanish left the region 30 years ago. One of the motivations behind the Dash is to create an interest again, so people will see the potential in the Sahara and invest. We have already been instrumental in setting up a windsurfing school in Tarfaya called Surfaya.'

Initially, participants stayed just one night in large Saharan tents in North Africa, but this has been increased to two or three as the people have grown to fully appreciate just what Tarfaya has to offer with its beautiful beaches and the wonderful hospitality of the local people.

Currently an annual event, there are plans to increase the frequency of the race. For more information, check www.youthsunited.com.

the very first hotel to be built here, around 40 years ago. The rooms are comfortable, if old-fashioned, with the main perk being the location right on the beach and close to the more atmospheric older part of town. Facilities include tennis courts and minigolf.

Eating

Among all the sauerkraut, fish and chips and other delights on offer along the Avenida Playas pleasure zone, you'll occasionally stumble across a place offering some local cuisine. For a cluster of worthwhile restaurants serving essentially Spanish cuisine, take a walk to the old port.

Casa Roja (☎ 928 51 58 66; Avenida Varadero s/n; mains €8-18) Enjoying possibly the best location in town, this is a low-key place overlooking the pretty harbour. The menu is appropriately seafood-based, with the obligatory tank of potential dinner mates at the entrance.

Puerte Bahia (☎ 928 51 37 93; Avenida Varadero 5; mains €9-18) Come here for the uninterrupted sea views from a vast terrace and a menu that is predictably multinational but includes some treats, such as vegetable risotto with mushrooms and seaweed, and an above-average seafood *zarzuela* (stew).

Restaurante La Cañada (☎ 928 51 04 15; Calle César Manrique 3; mains €12-15; ☒ closed Sun) Located just off the Avenida Playas, this restaurant lovingly prepares Canarian specialities, including oysters (from €3.60 cach), roasted goat and delicious *papas arrugadas* (wrinkly potatoes).

Drinking & Entertainment

The bulk of the bars, discos and nightclubs in Puerto del Carmen are lined up along the waterfront Avenida Playas. If you're after maximum-density partying, try the Centro Comercial Atlántico, where you'll find such bars and disco pubs as Waikiki, Paradise and Dreams.

Cervecería San Miguel (☎ 928 51 52 65; Avenida del Varadero s/n; ☒ 10.30am-3am) A good spot for a plate of steamed mussels washed down with a cold beer, of which there are several available on tap, including Guinness, Fosters and John Smith's Bitter.

César's (www.cesars.net; Avenida Playas 14; ☒ 10pm-6am) A very popular nightclub that attracts a breezy, hedonistic young crowd that appreciates populist DJs, flashing lights and lots of shooters amid a faux-Roman décor.

Buddy's (Calle Tenerife 18; ☒ 10pm-3.30am) A cool, laid-back club that attracts a mixed-age clientele with its nightly live jazz and blues.

Getting There & Around

Buses run the length of Avenida Playas, making frequent stops and heading for Arrecife (€1.80) about every 20 minutes from 7am to midnight.

A free **Fred Olsen** (☎ 901 10 01 07; www.fredolsen .es) bus leaves from the Varadero (the port jetty) in Puerto del Carmen at 9am and 5pm, linking with the ferry (adult/child/12 to 16 years €21/10/15, 20 minutes), which runs from Playa Blanca to Corralejo on Fuerteventura. In the reverse direction, free buses for Puerto del Carmen meet the 9am and 5pm ferries from Corralejo on their arrival in Playa Blanca. The morning run continues to Lanzarote's airport.

PUERTO CALERO

A few kilometres west of Puerto del Carmen, and its complete antithesis, Puerto Calero is a pleasant, relatively tranquil yacht harbour lined with cafés and restaurants sporting a jaunty maritime vibe that sees plenty of locals in deck shoes.

Sights & Activities

One of the newest worthwhile sights on the island, the **Museo de Cetáceos** (☎ 928 84 95 60; www.museodecetaceos.org; ☒ 10am-6pm; ☒) is a natural history museum devoted to 24 species of whales to be found in the surrounding waters. The exhibit includes audiovisual displays, life-size exhibits, photographs and whale sounds.

You can book a range of activities, including kayaking, bungee jumping and caving, at the Puerto Calero glass-surrounded **office** (☎ 928 84 95 39; ☒ 9am-9pm) in the centre of the marina.

SUBMARINE

The yellow sub of **Submarine Safaris** (☎ 928 51 28 98; www.submarinesafaris.com; adult/2-14yr €48/28; ☒ 10am, noon, 2pm & 4pm) makes one-hour dives, reaching a depth of 27m.

DEEP-SEA FISHING

Skippered by the well-regarded Tino García, **Mizu I** (☎ 609 88 69 80; www.sportfishinglanzarote .com; angler/companion €75/50) will transport you to the nearby depths as you search for mako sharks and other big fish. You'll be picked up from your hotel and taken to Puerto Calero. All equipment is included in the price.

DIVING

The English-run **Squalo Diving Center** (☎ 928 84 95 78; www.squalodiving.com) offers PADI courses, including a night diver course (€270) and a digital underwater photography course (€190).

Eating

Keep walking with your nose in the air, past all the English-themed bars and restaurants, until you reach **Amura** (☎ 928 51 31 81; mains €10-25) with its vast terrace commanding sweeping sea views. The menu includes quietly gourmet treats like a salad of prawns, scallops and sautéed artichokes, and suckling pig with gnocchi and green-apple foam.

PLAYA BLANCA

If you are looking for sand between the toes rather than a rollicking nightlife, Playa Blanca is not a bad choice. Despite the presence of an American fast-food chain at the beach, it is a quiet resort that has not yet spiralled completely out of control. That said, you're better off crossing the ocean to Corralejo on Fuerteventura, where the beaches and dunes easily outclass Playa Blanca's. The best beaches here are at Punta del Papagayo to the east (p142), which are pretty and relatively isolated. Check out also the new swanky port, Marina Rubicón, to the west of the town centre, which must have emptied the municipal piggy bank.

The **tourist office** (☎ 928 51 77 94; ⏲ 8.30am-12.30pm & 2-5pm Mon-Fri, 8.30am-12.30pm Sat) in the port, at the rear of the ferry booking office.

Activities
BOAT TOURS

The 33m-long **César II** (☎ 928 81 36 08; adult/under 12 yr €47/23) sails to the Isla de Lobos off Fuerteventura from Monday to Friday. Tours run between 10.15am until 5.45pm and include a light lunch.

Marea Errota (☎ 928 51 76 33; mareaerrota@retemail .es; adult/child €42.50/24) is a handsome swashbuckling galleon that does twice-daily coastal cruises down to the Papagayo beaches. Pick-

up from your accommodation is included in the price.

Rubicat (☎ 928 51 90 12; Marina Rubicón; adult/under 12yr €55/free) has day-long tours on a catamaran, including lunch, drinks and a 50% discount for the second passenger.

DIVING

Friendly and extremely professional, **Cala Blanca** (☎ 928 51 90 40; www.calablancasub.com; Centro Comercial el Papagayo) offers individual dives, courses and a charmingly named 'Sea Baptism' option (€50) for absolute beginners.

At the new marina, the **Rubicon Diving Center** (☎ 928 34 93 46; www.rubicondiving.com) has courses at all levels, including a six-dive package for €200.

Sleeping

Apartamentos Gutiérrez (☎ /fax 928 51 70 89; Plaza Nuestra Señora del Carmen 8; apt €40) Just by the town church, and one of the cheapest places to stay in this area. Tidy, attractive apartments (six in all) are available, but no English is spoken, so brush up on your Spanish or your sign language.

Apartamentos Bahía Blanca Rock (☎ 928 51 70 37; www.h10.es; Calle Janubio s/n; apt per person €58; P ⌘ ⌨ ⛶) For something more stylish, this place has natty, well-run, Canarian-style apartments (sleeping up to four) in a complex just off Avenida Papagayo and a 100m stroll from the main beach. The Daisy Mini Club keeps the kiddies amused, while you can enjoy a snooze in the solarium. Prices vary hugely, according to season.

Princesa Yaiza (☎ 928 51 92 22; www.princesayaiza .com; Avenida Papagayo s/n; s/d €180/250, s/d ste from €210/280; P ⌘ ⌨ ⛶) Distinctive for its domes, cupolas, towers and exotic greenery, the whole complex oozes good taste, with sensitive architectural flourishes and silky-smooth service. The list of amenities could fill a slim volume. Low-season discounts knock about 30% off the above rates.

Villas Kamezí (☎ 928 51 86 24; Calle Mónaco s/n; bungalow for up to 8 people €230-290; P ⌘ ⌨ ⛶) A discreet, environmentally friendly complex of 31 stunning villas with two to four bedrooms and tastefully decorated with real *Ideal Home*–style décor. it's within easy strolling distance of the Papagayo beaches, if you can be bothered tearing yourself away from the private saltwater pool. Fabulous.

LANZAROTE

Eating

Restaurante Casa José (Plaza Nuestra Señora del Carmen 8; mains €5-11; ☒ closed Sun lunch) Opposite the church, this modest restaurant with its traditional green paintwork has a kitchen-sink informal atmosphere and excellent seafood dishes.

El Maño (☎ 928 51 87 12; Marina Rubicón; mains €10-15) Trip along the long wooden bridge to reach this rare Spanish restaurant, which includes dishes from all over the country, including *salmorejo* (a thick, garlicky gazpacho) from Cordoba, black pudding from Burgos and a Valencian-style paella.

El Almacen de la Sal (☎ 928 51 78 85; Paseo Marítimo 12; mains €12-35; ☒ closed Tue; Ⓥ) An excellent waterfront restaurant, with fish dishes being the pick of the bunch (although a good vegetarian selection is also tempting). It's about halfway between the port and the main beach and has a cheaper lunchtime menu.

Getting There & Away

Bus 6 (€3, 1½ hours) runs at least six times daily between Playa Blanca and Arrecife via Puerto del Carmen.

Fred Olsen (☎ 902 53 50 90; www.fredolsen.es) ferries (adult/child/12 to 26 years €21/10/15, 20 minutes, four to five times daily) link Playa Blanca with Corralejo on Fuerteventura. **Naviera Armas** (☎ 902 45 65 00; www.navieraarmas.com) has five to six sailings daily (adult/child/12 to 26 years €16/8/13, 25 minutes).

Free Fred Olsen buses leave Puerto del Carmen (9am and 5pm) to connect with the 10am and 6pm ferry departures. A free service also meets the 9am and 5pm ferries from Corralejo. The morning run continues to Lanzarote's airport.

PUNTA DEL PAPAGAYO

The southeast coast leading up to Punta del Papagayo is peppered with a series of pretty golden-sand coves. The promontory is a *reserva natural protegido* (protected nature reserve). The road beyond the rickety toll barrier (€3 per vehicle) is dirt, but quite manageable even in a small car. Or take the easy way and hop aboard the **Princess Yaiza Taxi Boat** (☎ 928 51 43 22; adult/child €15/7.50), which sets out four times daily from Playa Blanca.

LANZAROTE

Tenerife

Tenerife is the biggest and best-known Canary Island, with over 10 million visitors a year, and finally the word is out that the landscape, sights and attractions here go way beyond beaches, lap dancers and best bitter on tap.

The potpourri of experiences includes 350km of coast; tropical-forest walks and designer-shop struts; dark forays into volcanic lava; traditional Canarian cuisine and (if you must) egg and chips. As for the drama, this is where Tenerife really does soar high and above its neighbouring islands. At 3718m the Pico del Teide is Spain's tallest peak, surrounded by a moonscape of rock formations and intense volcanic colours. It's fabulous walking territory; pack your lace-ups.

Tenerife is also diverse enough to allow an authentic Canarian experience. Simply put, the further you head away from the southwestern resorts, the fewer tourists you find. For example, the capital, Santa Cruz de Tenerife, is delightfully untainted by camera-wielding coach loads, although Carnaval gets packed with a clued-in crowd here for an experience second only to Rio in terms of raw fiesta spirit.

Putting pleasure before business is an appealing quality of the Tinerfeños, which means there is plenty of nightlife choice, ranging from spit-and-sawdust local bars to big bad discos with international DJs and foam parties.

In short, Tenerife is a happening, well-rounded and lively destination that caters just as happily to rucksack-toting types as sozzled sun worshippers.

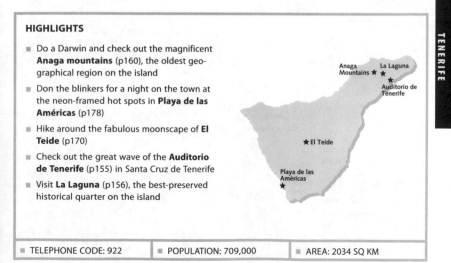

HIGHLIGHTS

- Do a Darwin and check out the magnificent **Anaga mountains** (p160), the oldest geographical region on the island
- Don the blinkers for a night on the town at the neon-framed hot spots in **Playa de las Américas** (p178)
- Hike around the fabulous moonscape of **El Teide** (p170)
- Check out the great wave of the **Auditorio de Tenerife** (p155) in Santa Cruz de Tenerife
- Visit **La Laguna** (p156), the best-preserved historical quarter on the island

Anaga Mountains ★   La Laguna ★
Auditorio de Tenerife ★
★ El Teide
Playa de las Américas ★

TENERIFE

| ■ TELEPHONE CODE: 922 | ■ POPULATION: 709,000 | ■ AREA: 2034 SQ KM |

ITINERARY 1
STRIDING OUT: FROM TENERIFE TO LA GOMERA & EL HIERRO

Tenerife has a diverse and varied scope for walkers. You could start at the heart and soul of the island, **Pico del Teide** (**1**; p170) and the gentle, yet rewarding, 16km Las Siete Cañadas day walk between the two visitor centres, allowing four to five hours.

Hightail it (on wheels) to Los Cristianos and hop on one of the daily ferries for La Gomera. Head inland from your disembarkation point of San Sebastián de la Gomera to **Parque Nacional de Garajonay** (**2**; p195), a green oasis in the centre of this mountainous island. Follow the trail, surrounded by laurel trees, to the **Alto de Garajonay** (**3**; p196) where, if it is clear, you can swoon at the stunning views of Tenerife and El Teide. Hike down to lush **Valle Gran Rey** (**4**; p202) and stride out through the palms.

Catch the ferry to El Hierro, skip the capital Valverde and head straight for **La Restinga** (**5**; p239) and a gentle stroll through **El Pinar** (**6**; p238), a protected pine forest. Head to **El Sabinar** (**7**; p244) further west, where twisted juniper trees create a ghostly yet captivating landscape.

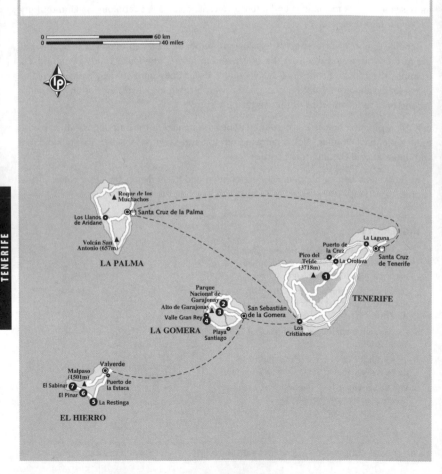

ITINERARY 2
ACE ARCHITECTURE: FROM CLASSIC TO CUTTING EDGE

Tenerife has some striking examples of traditional Canarian architecture. One of the finest historical quarters can be found in **La Orotava** (**1**; p165), its cobbled streets studded with grand 17th-century mansions, distinctive for their ornate wooden balconies. For the largest concentration of historic buildings, meander down Calle Colegio, where 12 mansions – the former homes of noble local families – stand. Don't miss the appropriately named Casa de los Balcones, which is sumptuously over the top. Due south, **Garachico** (**2**; p168) is another frozen-in-time town with stately historic buildings interspersed with simple fishermen's cottages. Check out the classic San Roque and La Quinta Roja hotels, as well as the contrasting, scaled-down simplicity of the native architecture of **Masca** (**3**; p173); this is how villages are supposed to look, with stone houses and a refreshing lack of concrete. There's not much to stop you on the southern coast, where the architecture tends towards the upturned-egg-carton look. There are exceptions, however, with luxury hotels like **Villa Cortés** (**4**; p182) in Playa de las Américas with its Mexican-hacienda look and fabulous palette of colours. Head through Parque Nacional del Teide, stopping briefly at lovely **Vilaflor** (**5**; p173) with its traditional buildings surrounding the main square, and take an obligatory gawp at El Teide. In the north, **La Laguna** (**6**; p156) heaves with fine 16th- and 17th-century Renaissance mansions. Take a leisurely stroll around the historic central plaza, surrounded by stately buildings fronted by wooden balconies and porches. The island's capital, Santa Cruz de Tenerife, holds the island's most exciting modern building, the **Auditorio de Tenerife** (**7**; p155), which shimmers on the seafront like a giant wave about to break, providing the city with a world-class venue for concerts and the arts.

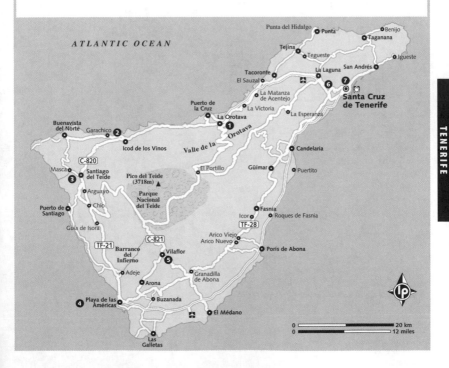

TENERIFE

HISTORY

The original inhabitants of Tenerife were primitive cave-dwellers called Guanches who arrived from North Africa around 200 BC. Tenerife was the last island to fall to the Spanish (in 1496) and subsequently became an important trading centre. As such, it was subject to invasions by marauding pirates and, in 1797, from the British in the famous battle of Santa Cruz, when Nelson lost his arm during the fight.

In 1821 Madrid declared Santa Cruz de Tenerife, by then the island's main port, the capital of the Canaries. The good and great of Las Palmas de Gran Canaria remained incensed about this until 1927 when Madrid finally split the archipelago into two provinces, with Santa Cruz as provincial capital of Tenerife, La Palma, La Gomera and El Hierro. As economic links between the Canaries and the Americas strengthened, a small exodus of islanders crossed the ocean, notably to Venezuela and Cuba. In later years affluent emigrants and Latin Americans reversed the trend, bringing influences that are still evident in the music and food of today's Tenerife.

INFORMATION
Maps & Books

Maps of the island are readily available. Among the best are those by Editorial Ever-

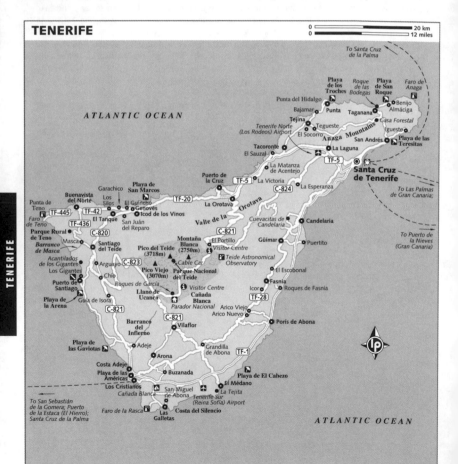

The townsfolk of Santa Cruz de Tenerife are known in the local slang as Chicharreros after the *chicharros* (horse mackerel) that were once favoured by the fishermen of the island.

est costing €2.80. *Tenerife & its Six Satellites* by Olivia M. Stone provides a fascinating glimpse of the island from a late-18th-century viewpoint.

Newspapers

There are a disproportionately large number of newspapers in Tenerife. The most popular Spanish titles are *El Día, La Gaceta de Canarias* and *La Opinión de Tenerife.*

Of the several English-language papers and magazines, *Island Connections* (for sale at newsagents but free from tourist offices) is the most widely distributed. There are so many Brits on Tenerife that the tabloid *Sun* newspaper even has a printing house here!

ACCOMMODATION

While finding a room is generally not a problem in Santa Cruz and in the north of the island, the same cannot be said for the southern resorts, particularly around Los Cristianos and Playa de las Américas. There are plenty of websites to assist you with advance booking, including www.lonely planet.com/accommodation, www.sunsearch ervacations.com, www.hostelbookers.com

/guides/spain/tenerife, www.casascanarias .co.uk and www.ecoturismocanarias.com; the latter two specialise in *casas rurales* (rural accommodation). For *casas rurales,* also check at tourist offices or **Aecan Turismo Rural** (☎ 922 24 81 14; www.aecan.com; Calle Villalba Hervás 2-3, Santa Cruz de Tenerife), which has several on its books.

Among the top recommended places to stay are sumptuous Hotel San Roque (p169), quirky Pensión Casablanca (p153), Villa Cortés (p182) for self-pampering heaven, historic Hotel Marquesa (p164), and the tranquil *casa rural* of Casa Ida (p169).

ACTIVITIES

Popular water sports such as diving, sailing, fishing and windsurfing are available on the island. Most facilities are concentrated in and around the southwestern resort areas.

Tenerife is marvellous for hiking and climbing with plenty of scope, ranging from easy rambles to mountain assaults. For the most dramatic scenery, choose from 21 trails within the Parque Nacional del Teide. Other attractive areas are the Anaga mountains in the northeast and around the Valle de la Orotava. There are numerous companies offering guided walks, as well as the rangers at El Teide. Check the following websites and ask at any tourist office for details: www .pateatusmontes.com; www.gregorio-teneriffa .de; www.gaiatours-tenerife.com; www.cam inantesdeaguere.com. For ideas about combining walks here with other islands, see Itineraries on p144.

GETTING AWAY FROM IT ALL – TENERIFE SPAS

Holidaying can be tough, especially when there's so darn much to see and do. Thank goodness for day spas.

Around Costa Adeje, escape to **Aqua Club Termal** (☎ 922 71 65 55; www.aquaclubtermal.com; Calle Galicia, Torviscas Alto), which, according to its promotional bumf, is the most comprehensive thermal and sports complex in Europe. It has 6000 sq metres of floor space, all dedicated to pampering. Don't miss the Turkish bath.

Vitanova Spa (☎ 922 79 56 86; www.vitanovatenerife.com; Calle Alcalde Walter Paetzman s/n, Playa del Duque), also in Costa Adeje, offers massages and facials as well as such scrumptious delights as chocolate massage and an anticellulite scrub with seaweed and grapes.

The **Mare Nostrum** (☎ 922 75 75 40; www.expogrupo.com; Avenida de las Américas s/n) resort in Playa de las Américas is also sure to spoil. There are those enticing-sounding fungal wraps and electrotherapy for serious spa-goers, and massages and steam baths for those seeking to destress.

In Puerto de la Cruz, the Oriental Spa Garden at **Hotel Botánico** (☎ 922 38 14 00; www.hotel botanico.com; Avenida Richard J Yeoward 1) has fabulous Thai décor throughout and offers a range of treatments, including body wraps, oriental massages and beauty treatments.

FESTIVALS & EVENTS
January–March
Festival de Música de Canarias The biggest event on the serious music calendar, held annually in January and February in Santa Cruz de Tenerife and Las Palmas de Gran Canaria (on Gran Canaria). For more information, visit www.socaem.com.

Carnaval Celebrated throughout Tenerife but particularly in Santa Cruz (p151), where it is regarded as the Canarian fiesta *par excellence*. Puerto de la Cruz comes a close second in terms of fiesta spirit.

March
Canarian Food Fair (mid-March) A week-long event in Los Cristianos showcasing food and produce from all over the islands, with free tastings and an opportunity to purchase.

May
Día de la Cruz (3 May) Held throughout the island, but particularly in Santa Cruz and Puerto de la Cruz, where crosses and chapels are decorated with flowers in celebration of the founding of both cities.

June
San Juan (23 June) Held in Puerto de la Cruz on the eve of the saint's day. Bonfires light the sky and, in a throwback to Guanche times, goats are driven for a dip in the sea off Playa Jardín.

Corpus Christi Celebrated with gusto in La Laguna (the date changes annually) and even more so in La Orotava, where mammoth floral carpets, using tons of volcanic dirt, flower petals, leaves and branches, are painstakingly designed into intricate biblical scenes in the streets and plazas.

July
Romería de San Benito Abad (first Sunday in July) One of the most important fiestas in La Laguna, in honour of the patron saint of farmers and crops.

August
Virgen de la Candelaria (15 August) Celebrated in Candelaria with processions and pageantry (see the boxed text, p176).

Romería de San Roque (16 August) Garachico's most important annual festival. The town fills with pilgrims (and party goers) from throughout the island. San Roque (St Roch), the town's patron, was credited with saving the town from the Black Death, which arrived in 1601.

September
Fiesta del Santísimo Cristo (7–15 September) Held in La Laguna and includes religious processions, traditional music and an impressive fireworks display.

Cristo de los Dolores (first Sunday after 15 September) Tacoronte fiesta with harvest festivities and wine tasting.

November
Fiesta de Los Cacharros (29 November) Held in Taganana and Puerto de la Cruz, this is a quaint festival where children rush through the streets, dragging behind them a string of old pots, kettles, pans, car spares, tin cans – just about anything that will make a racket.

December
Fiesta de la Consolación (first week in December) Takes place in Masca, with villagers wearing traditional dress and bringing out their *timples* (similar to a ukulele) and other instruments for an evening of Canarian music.

TENERIFE FOR CHILDREN
Tenerife is a favourite destination for families as there are plenty of sights and activities to keep the kiddies amused. Unless your tot is one of that curious breed that objects to sand between the toes (it happens!), the beaches in the south are superb, with white sand and shallow waters. Older children can also enjoy water sports ranging from surfing to diving. Take to the high seas on an organised whale- or dolphin-watching excursion (see p174 and p181).

If watery pursuits begin to pall, the southern resorts of Los Cristianos and Playa de las Américas equal theme-park heaven for children. The tourist office has shelves full of brochures and flyers. Animals feature heavily, although there is nothing as straightforward as a plain old zoo. Instead, choose from the Camel Park (p184) or Jungle Park (p181). There are also water parks throughout the island; again check at the local tourist office for details. Many hotels have swimming pools, or head for Santa Cruz's Parque Marítimo César Manrique p153, a wonderful complex of pools.

For something mildly more stimulating, check out the Museo de la Ciencia y el Cosmos (p159) in La Laguna. The island's most popular family day out is the **Loro Parque** (p163) in Puerto de Santa Cruz; even if you opt not to visit, you can't escape the publicity, with ads and stickers on seemingly every surface – moving or otherwise.

GETTING THERE & AWAY
Air
Two airports serve the island, with flights available to the other islands, the Spanish

mainland and various European destinations, plus a few more exotic ones such as Venezuela and Cuba. Facilitating nine million passengers per year – often well in excess of 25,000 daily – is modern **Tenerife Sur airport** (Reina Sofía; ☎ 922 75 95 10; www.aena.es), about 20km east of Playa de las Américas. All international charter flights land here, plus most scheduled international flights and many from mainland Spain.

The airport functions 24 hours a day and has half a dozen car-rental offices, a post office, several banks, ATMs and exchange booths, and knowledgeable staff at its **tourist office** (☎ 922 39 20 37).

Almost all interisland flights, plus a few scheduled international and mainland services, use the older and smaller **Tenerife Norte airport** (Los Rodeos; ☎ 922 63 56 35). Here you'll find an exchange booth, several car-rental agencies, a bar and a moderately helpful information booth.

Boat

For details of the ferry from Cádiz in mainland Spain, see p260.

There are regular ferry, hydrofoil and jetfoil services from Tenerife to the other islands. See the listings for individual towns for details.

GETTING AROUND
To/From the Airport

From Tenerife Sur, TITSA bus 487 departs hourly between 8.10am and 10pm for Los Cristianos (€1.50) and Playa de las Américas (€1.85); it's less than a half-hour ride to both destinations. Bus 341 (€5, 1½ hours) departs at least hourly from 6.50am for Santa Cruz. There are four 340 buses (€7.85, two hours) daily to Puerto de la Cruz via Tenerife Norte airport.

Call ☎ 922 39 21 19 for a taxi. Approximate fares from Tenerife Sur are Los Cristianos €18, Playa de las Américas €21, Los Gigantes €45, Puerto de la Cruz €96, Santa Cruz €62 and El Médano €9.

From Tenerife Norte, TITSA buses 102, 107 and 108 (€1.30, 20 minutes) go to Santa Cruz. Bus 102 (€4.10, one hour) carries on to Puerto de la Cruz via La Laguna, only 3km from the airport.

FOOD & DRINK

Don't confuse the traditional culinary fare here with that of the Spanish mainland; there are distinctive differences, although the ubiquitous tapas of Spain are common here also. The cuisine reflects a Latin American and Arabic influence, with more spices, including cumin, paprika and dried chillies, than the Spanish norm.

The staple product par excellence is *gofio*, toasted grain that takes the place of bread and can be mixed with almonds and figs to make sweets. Other basic foods are bananas and tomatoes, while the traditional *cabra* (goat) and *cabrito* (kid) remain the staple animal protein. The rich, gamey *conejo en salmorejo* (rabbit in a marinade based on sweet black pudding and avocado) is common, as well as stews (*potaje, rancho canario* or *puchero*) of meat and vegetables simmered to savoury perfection. Fish is also a winner, with the renowned horse mackerel *(chicharros)* of Santa Cruz de Tenerife even lending their name to the city's residents: the Chicharreros. Also recommended is the *sancocho canario,* a salted-fish dish with *mojo* (a spicy salsa based on garlic and red chilli peppers). This sauce is the most obvious contribution to the Canarian table, and is typically served with *papas arrugadas* (wrinkly potatoes), small new potatoes boiled and salted in their skins. The most typical dessert is *bienmesabe* (literally 'tastes good to me'), a mixture of honey, almond cream, eggs and rum.

Tenerife is the islands' principal source of wine, and the red Tacoronte Acentejo was the first Canarian wine to earn the grade of DO (*denominación de origen,* an appellation certifying high standards and regional origin). Other productive vineyards are in the Icod de los Vinos, Güímar and Tacoronte areas of the island. The Casa del Vino La Baranda (p160) in El Sauzal organises regular wine-appreciation courses. Other local tipples include La Dorada beer. Brewed in Santa Cruz de Tenerife, its lager-style taste is equal to any import from the mainland.

If you are into self-catering, then hit the local markets. They are the best place to buy the freshest vegetables and fruit. Stalls are grouped according to the types of food they offer. One of the best markets is the Mercado de Nuestra Señora de África (p154) in Santa Cruz de Tenerife.

TENERIFE

A taxi into Santa Cruz from Tenerife Norte costs around €15. The fare to Puerto de la Cruz is around €26.

Bus

TITSA (Transportes Interurbanos de Tenerife SA; ☎ 922 53 13 00; www.titsa.com) runs a spider's web of services all over the island, as well as within Santa Cruz and other towns. If you intend to use the bus a lot, purchase a Bonobus card, costing €6 for trips within Santa Cruz or €12 or €30 for bus trips throughout the island. The card represents at least a 30% saving. Insert the card in the machine on the bus, tell the driver where you are going and the amount is subtracted from the card. It includes half-price admission into many of the island's museums, including the Museo de la Naturaleza y El Hombre (opposite) in Santa Cruz.

Car

Car-rental agencies are almost as plentiful on the island as English pubs, so you shouldn't have a problem, even if you want same-day rental. The generally reliable international chains are present in all major resort areas and the airports. Expect a car to cost between €25 and €45 a day. You'll also find a generous sprinkling of small businesses offering older cars for as little as €15 a day.

Taxi

You can take a taxi anywhere on the island – but it is an expensive way to get around. You are much better off hiring a car.

SANTA CRUZ DE TENERIFE

pop 200,000

This bustling port city can take time to appreciate but it is well worth making the effort. Wandering around the centre, you will discover evocative, brightly painted buildings, sophisticated and quirky shops and a tropical oasis of birdsong, fountains and greenery in the city park. What you'll be hard pushed to find is an all-day English breakfast because, above all, Santa Cruz is a vibrant, typically Spanish city without the tourist mayhem that typifies much of the south. The city also has an excellent bus sys-

tem, making it a sensible base for exploring Tenerife's northeast.

HISTORY

Alonso Fernández de Lugo landed on Tenerife in 1494 to embark on the conquest of the final and most-resistant island in the archipelago. La Laguna, a few kilometres inland, initially blossomed as the island's capital. Santa Cruz de Santiago (as Santa Cruz de Tenerife was then known) remained a backwater until its port began to flourish in the 18th and 19th centuries. Only in 1803 was Santa Cruz 'liberated' from the municipal control of La Laguna by Spanish royal decree; in 1859 it was declared a city.

ORIENTATION

Taking Plaza España as a hub, everything of interest lies within 1km. At the southwestern edge is the bus station, while to the northeast is the terminal for jetfoils to/from Las Palmas de Gran Canaria. With the exception of a couple of museums, most of the sights and good shops lie within the central grid of streets leading inland from Plaza España.

Maps

The town map handed out by the tourist office is refreshingly accurate and helpful. If you need more detail, buy Editorial Everest's map of Santa Cruz de Tenerife (€2.80), which includes tourist attractions.

INFORMATION
Bookshops

La Isla Bookshop (☎ 922 28 54 81; Calle Robayna 2) This shop has titles in English, including novels, a few Canaries guidebooks and a selection of Lonely Planet guides.

Emergency

Police station (☎ 922 22 24 47; Avenida Tres de Mayo 32)

Internet Access

Ciber Scout (☎ 922 27 88 63; Centro Castillo, Calle Castillo s/n; per hr €2; ⏱ 8am-11pm Mon-Sat, 10am-11pm Sun)

Medical Services

Hospital Rambla (☎ 922 29 16 00; Rambla General Franco 115)

Post
Main post office (☎ 922 24 51 16; Plaza España 2) Allows you to send faxes.

Telephone
Street phones abound in Santa Cruz.
Telephone office (☎ 922 24 72 74; Paseo de las Milícias de Garachico 3; internet per hr €2; ☽ 9am-10pm Mon-Fri, 9.30am-2pm & 5-9pm Sat & Sun; 🖳) A good, efficient office.

Tourist Information
Scattered about the city you'll find some computer terminals in public spaces, with touch-screen information about Santa Cruz attractions.
Tourist office (☎ 922 23 95 92; www.puntoinfo .idecnet.com; Plaza España s/n; ☽ 8am-6pm Mon-Fri, 9am-1pm Sat) Located in the Cabildo Insular de Tenerife building. Don't confuse it with the tourist information kiosk in front of the adjacent post office.

SIGHTS
The majority of Santa Cruz's sights are within easy walking distance of Plaza España. While the city is not packed with attractions, there are some lovely buildings and well-run exhibitions to enjoy.

Museums
Museo de la Naturaleza y El Hombre (☎ 922 53 58 16; www.museosdetenerife.org in Spanish; Calle Fuente Morales s/n; adult/under 12yr €3/1.50; ☽ 9am-7pm Tue-Sun; ⓖ) is a brain-bending amalgam of natural science and archaeology in a former civil hospital. It has several fascinating Guanche mummies and skulls, a handful of artefacts, including pottery, and well-presented facts and figures about volcanoes and the flora and fauna of the islands. There's also a café and gift shop.

Museo de Bellas Artes (☎ 922 24 43 58; Calle José Murphy 12; admission free; ☽ 10am-8pm Mon-Fri) is home to an eclectic mix of paintings by mainly Spanish, Canarian and Flemish artists, including Ribera, Sorolla and Brueghel. There's also sculpture, including a Rodin, and temporary exhibitions.

Museo Militar de Almeyda (☎ 922 84 35 00; Calle San Isidro 1; admission free; ☽ 10am-2pm Tue-Sat) explains the military history of the islands. The most famous item here is El Tigre (The Tiger), the cannon that reputedly blew off Admiral Nelson's arm when he attacked Santa Cruz in 1797. Much of the museum is devoted to the successful defence of the city, brought alive by a superb 30m scale model of the flagship *Theseus*.

Around the Centre
Santa Cruz is a busy port city but the centre is compact enough to explore on foot. Pick up a map at the tourist office in waterfront **Plaza España**, with its controversial centrepiece: a memorial to the fallen of the 1936–39 civil war. Head inland along Plaza Candelaria and the pedestrianised shopping strip of Calle Castillo; a right turn along Calle José Murphy leads to the **Iglesia de San Francisco**, a baroque church from the 17th and 18th centuries.

Three blocks southwest of Calle Castillo is the 19th-century **Teatro Guimerá** (see p155),

---

CARNAVAL CAPERS

Only Rio de Janeiro does it better and even *that* party does not overshadow Santa Cruz's efforts to make **Carnaval** (www.carnavaltenerife.com) a nonstop, 24-hour party-orgy. Festivities generally kick off in early February and last about three weeks. Many of the gala performances and fancy-dress competitions take place in the Recinto Ferial (fairgrounds) but the streets, especially around Plaza España, become frenzied with good-natured dawn-to-dusk frivolity.

Don't be fooled into thinking this is just a sequin-bedecked excuse to party hearty, though. It may sometimes be hard to see or believe, but there is an underlying political 'message' to the whole shebang. Under the Franco dictatorship, Carnaval ground to a halt and there didn't seem to be too much to celebrate. The Catholic Church's cosy relationship with the fascists was another source of frustration so, when Carnaval was relaunched after the death of General Franco, the citizens of Santa Cruz wasted no time in lampooning the sexual and moral hypocrisy of the church and the fascists. Today, you will still see a lot of people dressed for the event as naughty nuns and perverted priests, and more drag queens than bumblebees in a buttercup field. And all in the name of good, clean fun. Book your accommodation ahead – if you intend to go to bed, that is.

fronted by a suitably theatrical giant mask sculpture. The sumptuous interior is reminiscent of Madrid's Teatro Real, with semicircular balconied seating and plenty of gilt. Next door, the **Centro de Arte La Recova** (☎ 922 29 07 35; Plaza Isla de la Madera s/n; admission free; ☒ 11am-1pm & 6-9pm Mon-Fri) is housed in a former market, which makes for an interesting gallery space for the temporary exhibitions of contemporary Canarian and mainland-Spanish artists.

The formerly seedy **Plaza Iglesia** has been tarted up and is now home to a couple of fashionable bars and brightly painted buildings. Look for the striking bell tower of the city's oldest church, the **Iglesia de Nuestra Señora de la Concepción** (Plaza Iglesia; ☒ mass 9am & 7.30pm), which has a tiled roof and some traditional *mudéjar*

(Islamic-style architecture) ceiling work. The present church was built in the 17th and 18th centuries but the original building went up in 1498, just after the island was conquered. At the heart of the shimmering silver altar is the Santa Cruz de la Conquista (Holy Cross of the Conquest), which gives the city its name. Tradition has it that Alonso Fernández de Lugo, the Spanish commander, planted it in his camp to give thanks for his 1494 victory over the Guanches.

Check out the anteroom to the sacristy. The altarpiece in the chapel beside it was carved from cedar on the orders of Don Matías Carta, a prominent personage who died before it was completed. He lies buried here and the pallid portrait on the wall was done *after* his death

SANTA CRUZ DE TENERIFE

(hence the closed eyes and crossed arms). There's also a fine painting, *La Adoración de los Pastores* (The Adoration of the Shepherds), by Juan de Miranda.

A 10-minute walk southwest along the waterfront brings you to the 17th-century **Castillo de San Juan**. In the shadow of this protective fort there used to be a lively trade in African slaves. Nowadays its squat, rectangular basalt form is overshadowed by the magnificent, soaring white wave of an auditorium: the **Auditorio de Tenerife** (see p155), designed by the internationally renowned Spanish architect Santiago Calatrava and possessing a Sydney Opera House presence, as well as superb acoustics.

Just beyond this contrasting pair is the **Parque Marítimo César Manrique** (Avenida Constitución s/n; adult/senior/child €2.50/1/1.20; ☺ 10am-7pm), where you can have a dip in one of the wonderful designer pools or collapse on a sun lounge and drink in the beautiful view and something refreshing. It's suitable for all ages, and great for children. For more information about César Manrique, see p131.

SLEEPING

You should have little trouble booking a room, aside from Carnaval time, when you should reserve at least three months in advance; be prepared to pay more for your partying as well, with room prices typically increasing by at least 10%.

Budget

Pensión Casablanca (☎ 922 27 85 99; Calle Viera y Clavijo 15; s/d €15/21) In a great location on a leafy pedestrian street, the building dates from 1902. The rooms are brightly painted (you may need shades for the turquoise) with decorative finishes and floral trim. They are small but good value; the only downside is that there are only three communal bathrooms for 17 rooms, which could mean crossed legs in the corridor.

Pensión Mova (☎ 922 28 32 61; Calle San Martín 33; d €32, s/d without bathroom €13/27) If the Casablanca is full this is a second choice. The owners can be terse and the reception area is cluttered and shabby, but the rooms are okay and there's a handy adjacent bar for breakfast.

Hotel Atlántico (☎ 922 24 63 75; fax 922 24 63 78; Calle Castillo 12; s/d with breakfast €38/57) Enjoys an ace location bang on the city's main pedestrian street, and is distinguished by its jaunty blue-and-white canopies. The rooms are a bit battered but well equipped with fridges and multispeed ceiling fans. The generous breakfast is served on a roof terrace with views.

Midrange

Hotel Contemporáneo (☎ 922 27 15 71; www.hotel contemporaneo.com in Spanish; Rambla General Franco 116; s/d €60/88; P ▢ ▢ ▢) A great peach-and-white confection of a place to stay on one of the city's swankiest streets. Rooms have mahogany- or grey-stained hardwood floors, a plush yet understated colour scheme and ADSL connection; those on the 7th floor have private balconies. There is wi-fi in the lobby.

Hotel Taburiente (☎ 922 27 60 00; www.hotel taburiente.com; Calle Dr José Naveiras 24a; s/d/tr €75/85/90; P ▢ ▢ ▢) The public areas have a fashionable minimalist look – think black glossy pots

TENERIFE

with a couple of lilies, chunky glass vases filled with green apples and plenty of mirrors and soft natural colours. The rooms are pleasant but lack the same wow factor; ask for one with a balcony overlooking the park.

Hotel Colón Rambla (☎ 922 27 27 16; www.hotel -colonrambla.com; Calle Viera y Clavijo 49; s/d €80/130; P ⊛) This apartment-style hotel has well-lit large rooms with wood panelling, sitting room and sparkling white bathroom. There is a small kitchenette with fridges and two-ring cookers in each entrance lobby. All the balconies overlook the central pool so no saggy swimwear, please.

Top End

our pick Sheraton Mencey Hotel (☎ 922 60 99 00; www.sheratonmencey.com; Calle Dr José Naveiras 38; s/d from €215/295; P ⊠ ⬜ ⊛ ⅋) Prestigious Mencey is where the rich and famous stay when they're in town. Rooms are sumptuous, facilities are top-notch and the grandeur never fades. The rooms are feminine without being fussy, with dark-wood furnishings and marble-clad bathrooms. In the low season, you can expect prices to drop by about 20%, although the price of the royal suite (€980) does not change. There's a casino that may come in handy (or not) if you're aiming for the latter.

EATING
Self-Catering

Mercado de Nuestra Señora de África (Calle San Sebastián; ⊗ 11am-11.30pm Mon-Sat) This market has a Central American look with its arched entrance, clock tower and flower sellers. It's not large by Spanish standards but is still tantalising, with its mountains of fresh fruit and vegetables and variety of fish. You can also buy bread, fabulous local cheese and meats.

Supereko 7 (Calle Padre Anchieta 10; ⊗ 9am-8pm Mon-Fri, to 1pm Sat) An ecological supermarket with a small café dishing up a vegetarian menu for €7.

Restaurants

Da Canio (☎ 922 24 81 31; Calle San Martín 76; mains €6.50-8; ⊗ closed Sun; Ⅴ) Owned by Italians and serving up a better class of pizza and pasta, the dining room is tastefully decked out in terracotta and stone. The 34-plus pizza choices are ideal for fussy families, and the pasta and risottos come recommended as well.

La Taberna de Wally (☎ 922 27 34 13; Calle Viera y Clavijo 44; mains €7.50-9; ⊗ closed Sun night & Mon) A delight. The eclectic menu includes freshly prepared salads, garlic soup, snails and meat and fish dishes, all served in a gorgeous garden courtyard surrounded by graceful old buildings. At weekends, the friendly owner turns the place over to a DJ, who spins great chill-out music until the wee hours.

Sukothay (☎ 922 53 25 01; Calle General Goded 5; mains €7.50-12; ⊗ closed Sun; Ⅴ) This Japanese-Thai restaurant has an easy-on-the-eye minimalist interior with two floors and open-plan kitchen. The Zen feel continues with a menu of rave dishes from both cuisines, including green and red curries, papaya salad, sushi and tempura. The wine list is better than the oriental norm.

La Cazuela (☎ 922 27 23 00; Calle Robayna 34; mains €7.50-14.50; ⊗ closed Sat lunch & Sun) Drenched in Canary yellow with a pretty, flower-filled terrace, this place is heartily recommended by locals for its solid traditional fare. Settle in for a long, filling lunch and try the *cazuela* (a casserole made with fresh or salted fish).

La Fundación (☎ 922 28 39 72; Calle Imeldo Seris 25; mains €10.50-18.50; ⊗ closed Sun) This is where Santa Cruz's elite wine and dine on market-fresh cuisine. In an exquisitely restored Canarian mansion, savour dishes like salad of Canarian cheeses with quince and honey, or roast duck with papaya compote, washed down with excellent wines. There are two storeys with the less formal *tasca* (bar) downstairs.

Cafés & Terrazas

Chairs on squares are plentiful here, due to the friendly, gregarious nature of the locals and, still more, to the sunshine.

Romana (☎ 922 24 58 52; Calle Villaiba Hervas 19) Join the queue for arguably the best ice cream in town; try the legendary ice-cream sandwich; it beats a BLT any day.

Sáffron & Porron (☎ 922 15 18 67; Calle Antonio Domínguez Afonso 30) The colourful single-storey houses on this pedestrian street have been restored. Stop by this tiny café-bar, its walls papered with faded Andalucian *feria* (fair) and bullfighting posters. It has outside tables.

More pleasant café *terrazas* (terraces) include those on Plaza Candelaria and the shaded number on the fringe of Parque García Sanabria, where you can let the kids romp in the adjacent playground.

DRINKING

Bar Zumería Doña Papaya (☎ 922 29 06 79; Calle Callao de Lima 3; juices €1.35; ☺ closed Sun) Delicious fresh fruit juices, including strawberry, mango, papaya, avocado and various delectable-sounding combinations.

Bar Imperfecto (☎ 659 57 70 23; Calle San Antonio 69; ☺ 9pm-2.30am Mon-Sat) Although it doesn't get busy until hot-chocolate time, the atmosphere is worth the wait. Alternative music and rock and roll is the music scene, played against a dark, wood-panelled backdrop with black-and-white pics from the silver screen.

Murphy's (☎ 922 28 48 64; Plaza de la Concepción s/n; ☺ 5pm-2.30am Mon-Thu, 5pm-3.30am Fri & Sat, 6.30pm-2.30am Sun) This Irish pub has a predictable blarney atmosphere and Guinness on tap, but is classier than many Irish imports. Live music most weekends.

ENTERTAINMENT
Nightclubs

Most of the nightlife is centred around the northern end of Avenida Anaga, while there is an increasing number of live-music venues within stumbling distance of Plaza España.

Arco Pub (Avenida Anaga 31; ☺ 6pm-3.30am Mon-Sat) Live music ranging from alternative rock to electro-house and jazz, performed for a DIY-dressed-up crowd accompanied by luridly coloured, knockout cocktails.

Fool Company (Avenida Anaga 25; admission €10; ☺ midnight-6am Wed-Sat) Has some live music, but mostly invigorating funk and R&B DJs. It can get packed with a party-loving crowd firing up to a steamy dance-pit. Look for the plastic bamboo out front.

Theatre & Classical Music

Auditorio de Tenerife (☎ 922 27 06 11; www.auditorio detenerife.com; Avenida Constitución s/n; ☺) Tenerife's newest and flashiest entertainment option has dramatically designed curved white concrete shells capped by a cresting, crashing wave of a roof. It covers and significantly enhances a 2 hectare oceanfront site. The auditorium hosts opera, dance and classical-music performances, among others.

Teatro Guimerá (box office ☎ 902 33 33 38; www .teatroguimera.es; Plaza Isla de la Madera s/n; tickets €12-18; box office ☺ 11am-1pm & 5-8pm) The other venue for highbrow entertainment, whether music or theatre.

Sport

Santa Cruz is home to football team **CD Tenerife** (☎ 922 29 81 00; www.clubdeportivotenerife.es in Spanish; Callejón Combate 1), which plays in Spain's second division. You can buy tickets at the *taquilla* (box office) of the club stadium, **Estadio Heliodoro Rodríguez López** (Calle La Mutine s/n), or call into the club's headquarters.

SHOPPING

The main shopping strip is the pedestrianised Calle Castillo and surrounding streets. Some promising deals are available on electronics and watches but there are also some great little boutiques, stocked with clothes from Spanish and international designers.

El Corte Inglés (☎ 922 84 94 00; Avenida Tres de Mayo 7) Monster-sized, and will keep you stocked in whatever your heart desires. It also has an excellent, albeit pricey, supermarket with interesting imported goodies.

Rastro (Calle José Manuel Guimerá; ☺ Sun morning) This flea market is held along two parallel streets leading from the covered market to the coast. It's the usual mix, including pirated CDs, cut-price underwear and handmade jewellery but is bustling and fun. Keep your money out of sight.

GETTING THERE & AWAY
Air

Tenerife Norte is the nearest airport to Santa Cruz. It handles nearly all flights between the islands, and very few others. See p148 for details.

Boat

The **Acciona-Trasmediterránea** (☎ 922 84 22 44; www.trasmediterranea.com; Estación Marítima Muelle Ribera) runs a weekly ferry (from €256, car €166, two days) with cabins to Cádiz, via Las Palmas de Gran Canaria, Puerto de Rosario (Fuerteventura) and Arrecife (Lanzarote), departing every Monday at 3pm. Trasmediterránea also runs a daily jetfoil to Las Palmas at 8am (€51, one hour 10 minutes). It leaves at 10am on Sunday.

Naviera Armas (☎ 902 45 65 00; www.navieraarmas .com) runs a fast ferry (€24, 2¾ hours) to Las Palmas twice a day on Monday, Tuesday, Thursday and Friday, three times daily on Wednesday and once daily on Saturday and Sunday; and to Morro Jable (€37.40, seven hours) on Fuerteventura every Monday at 3am. It also has a boat (€42, 12¼ hours) at

TENERIFE

6.45pm on Wednesday and Friday to Arrecife on Lanzarote.

Fred Olsen (☎ 902 10 01 07; www.fredolsen.es) has six to eight daily high-speed ferries (€64, 1¼ hours) to Agaete in the northwest of Gran Canaria, from where you can take its free bus onwards to Las Palmas (35 minutes).

Garajonay Exprés (☎ 902 34 34 50; www.garajonay expres.com) connects Los Cristianos with San Sebastián (€19, 45 minutes), Playa Santiago (€22, one hour) and Valle Gran Rey (€23, 1½ hours) on La Gomera, three times daily at 8.30am, 1.55pm and 6.15pm. Passengers based in Santa Cruz can take a courtesy bus to Los Cristianos to catch the ferry.

Buy tickets for all companies from travel agents or from the main Estación Marítima Muelle Ribera building (from where the Fred Olsen boats leave). Naviera Armas has its base further to the south.

Bus

TITSA buses radiate out from the **bus station** (☎ 922 21 56 99; www.titsa.com) beside Avenida Constitución, with major routes including the following:

Bus 102 Puerto de la Cruz via La Laguna & Tenerife Norte (€4.10, 55 minutes, every 30 minutes)

Bus 103 Puerto de la Cruz direct (€4.20, 40 minutes, more than 15 daily)

Buses 106 & 108 Icod de los Vinos (€5.80, 1¼ hours, more than 15 daily)

Bus 110 Los Cristianos & Playa de las Américas direct (€7.30, one hour, every 30 minutes)

Bus 111 Los Cristianos & Playa de las Américas via Candelaria & Güímar (€7.30, one hour 20 minutes, every 30 minutes)

Bus 341 Tenerife Sur (€5.70, 50 minutes, 20 daily)

Buses 014 & 015 La Laguna (€1.25, 20 minutes, every 10 minutes)

Car & Motorcycle

Car-rental companies (some also rent out motorcycles) are plentiful. Major operators also have booths at the *estación marítima* (ferry terminal).

GETTING AROUND
To/From the Airport

See p149 for details of the regular buses serving both airports.

A taxi to Tenerife Norte will cost about €15 and to Tenerife Sur, around €60.

Bus

TITSA buses provide the city service in Santa Cruz. Several buses pass regularly by the centre (Plaza General Weyler and Plaza España) from the bus station, including 910 and 914. Other local services include the circular routes 920 and 921. A local trip costs €1.

Car

Paid parking stations can be found underneath Plaza España and within the Mercado de Nuestra Señora de África market.

Taxi

The major taxi stands are on Plaza España and at the bus station. Call **Radio-Taxi San Pedro** (☎ 922 31 00 00) for bookings.

Tram

A tram line was under construction at the time of research, linking Santa Cruz with La Laguna. It is due for completion by early 2008; check at the tourist office for an update.

THE NORTHEAST

LA LAGUNA
pop 130,000

An easy day trip from Santa Cruz or Puerto de la Cruz, San Cristóbal de la Laguna may have an unattractive shell of concrete blocks, but its kernel, the historic town centre, is a gem, with narrow streets lined with colourful buildings, grand old villas and idiosyncratic small shops. Its layout provided the model for many colonial towns in the Americas and, in 1999, La Laguna was added to the Unesco list of World Heritage sites. The town has a youthful energy and possibly the island's most determined *marcha* (nightlife).

History

In 1494 Alonso Fernández de Lugo's troops ended up making a permanent camp at what is now known as La Laguna (the lagoon from which the name comes was drained in 1837).

By the middle of the 16th century, the old town was pretty much complete and La Laguna became a bustling city of merchants, soldiers, bureaucrats and the pious. In 1701 the university was established.

Orientation

The bus station is about a 10-minute walk northwest of the old centre. The university, where you'll find the bulk of the bars and plenty of downhome restaurants, lies to the south of the old centre. The little accommodation available is in the historic area, as are the best restaurants, banks, the post office and the tourist office.

Information

EMERGENCY
Police station (☎ 922 25 04 52; Calle Nava y Grimón 66)

INTERNET ACCESS
Reicom (☎ 922 25 02 08; Centro Santo Domingo 12; per hr €1.80; ☼ 9.30am-10pm Mon-Fri, 10am-10pm Sat & Sun) Also has telephones and a photocopying and fax service

POST
Post office (☎ 922 61 43 04; Calle Santo Domingo)

TOURIST INFORMATION
Tourist office (☎ 922 63 11 94; Calle Carrera 7; ☼ 8.30am-8pm Mon-Fri, to 2pm Sat & Sun Jun-Sep, 8.30am-5pm Mon-Fri Oct-May) In a lovely old house with an inner courtyard; ask for the fascinating San Cristóbal de La Laguna, World Heritage Site brochure.

Sights

CANARIAN MANSIONS
La Laguna allows you to fully appreciate the beauty and eccentricity of Canarian urban architecture: bright façades graced with wooden double-doors, carved balconies and grey stone embellishments. Elegant, wood-shuttered windows conceal cool, shady patios, which, in the best cases, are surrounded by 1st-storey verandas propped up by slender timber columns. Whenever you see an open door, look inside – with luck the inner sanctum will also be open.

The documents, maps, artefacts and descriptions are interesting enough at the **Museo de la Historia de Tenerife** (Casa Lecarno; ☎ 922 63 01 03; Calle San Agustín 22; adult/under 18yr €3/1.50, admission free Sun; ☼ 10am-8pm Tue-Sun) but the 16th-century mansion itself is noteworthy, having benefited from an effective and tasteful renovation. Note the brickwork, which features Renaissance designs, on either side of the stone portico at the museum's entrance.

Calle San Agustín and the surrounding streets are lined with fine old houses. Take a look inside **Casa del Montañés** (Calle San Agustín 16). Peek too into the tranquil patio of the **Casa Salazar** (Calle San Agustín 28), nowadays home to the bishop of La Laguna. The imposing **Casa de los Capitanes** (Calle Carrera) is beside the *ayuntamiento* (town hall) and houses the tourist office. The distinctive blue façade of **Calle Carrera 66** is the former home of surrealist painter Oscar Dominguez. Check out the window framed with a giant sardine-tin sculpture!

CHURCHES & CONVENTS
La Laguna's religious clout is also considerable. **Iglesia de Nuestra Señora de la Concepción** (Plaza Concepción; tower €1; ☼ 8.30am-1.30pm & 6-7.30pm Mon-Fri, 8.30am-1.30pm & 6-8.30pm Sat, 7.30am-2pm & 4.30-8pm Sun) was the island's first church – constructed in 1502 – and has subsequently undergone many changes. Elements of Gothic and plateresque styles can still be distinguished and the finely wrought wooden *mudéjar* ceilings are a delight. Climb the tower for stunning rooftop views.

A few minutes' walk east, the **Catedral** (Plaza Catedral) was completely rebuilt in 1913. A fine baroque retable in the chapel is dedicated to the Virgen de los Remedios. There are some fine paintings by Cristóbal Hernández de Quintana, one of the islands' premier 18th-century artists.

The **Iglesia de Santo Domingo** (Calle Santo Domingo), originally a hermitage and expanded in the 17th century, also contains paintings by de Quintana. Seek out the vivid murals painted in the 20th century by Mariano Cossío and Antonio González Suárez.

At the northern end of the old quarter, the **Santuario del Cristo** (Santuario del Santísimo Cristo de La Laguna; Plaza San Francisco s/n; ☼ 8am-1pm & 4-8.45pm Mon-Thu & Sat, 8am-9pm Fri & Sun) contains a blackened wooden sculpture of Christ – the most venerated crucifix on the island. Be as respectful as possible inside, as most of the people here are praying, not sightseeing.

Of the convents, the most interesting is **Convento de Santa Clara** (cnr Calle Anchieta & Calle Viana; ☼ 4-7pm Mon-Sat & 11.30am-7pm Sun). You can also visit its fine 16th-century chapel. The Santa Clara chapel and the closed order in **Convento de Santa Catalina** (Plaza Adelantado; ☼ 7.30-10am & 5-8pm) are still active. The latter was on the verge of opening a religious museum at the time of research.

TENERIFE

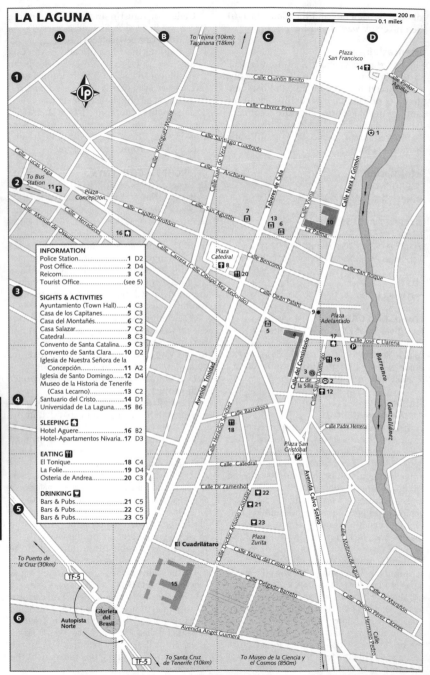

LA LAGUNA

0　　　　　　　200 m
0　　　　　　　0.1 miles

INFORMATION
Police Station...........................1 D2
Post Office.............................2 D4
Reicom.................................3 C4
Tourist Office.....................(see 5)

SIGHTS & ACTIVITIES
Ayuntamiento (Town Hall)......4 C3
Casa de los Capitanes.............5 C3
Casa del Montañés................6 C2
Casa Salazar.........................7 C2
Catedral..............................8 C3
Convento de Santa Catalina....9 C3
Convento de Santa Clara.......10 D2
Iglesia de Nuestra Señora de la
　Concepción.......................11 A2
Iglesia de Santo Domingo......12 D4
Museo de la Historia de Tenerife
　(Casa Lecarno)..................13 C2
Santuario del Cristo.............14 D1
Universidad de La Laguna.....15 B6

SLEEPING
Hotel Aguere........................16 B2
Hotel-Apartamentos Nivaria..17 D3

EATING
El Tonique...........................18 C4
La Folie..............................19 D4
Osteria de Andrea...............20 C3

DRINKING
Bars & Pubs.........................21 C5
Bars & Pubs.........................22 C5
Bars & Pubs.........................23 C5

TENERIFE

MUSEO DE LA CIENCIA Y EL COSMOS

If you enjoy pushing buttons and musing on the forces of nature, you can have fun at this **museum** (☎ 922 31 52 65; www.museosdetenerife .org; Calle Vía Láctea s/n; adult/child/student €3/free/1.50; ☽ 9am-7pm Tue-Sun), even if you don't speak Spanish. About 1.5km south of Plaza Adelantado, it also has a planetarium, so you can stargaze during the day. A good choice for those wanting to have their children stimulated by something other than yet another sugary ice cream.

Language Courses

The **Universidad de La Laguna** (☎ 922 60 33 45; www.ull.es) offers four-month Spanish classes at all levels.

Sleeping

Unfortunately, sleeping possibilities are limited. However, at the time of research a new four-star hotel, San Cristobal de la Luna, housed in a historic building, was near completion. Check the web or local tourist office for contact information.

   Hotel Aguere (☎ 922 25 94 90; haguere@infonegocio .com; Calle Carrera 55; s/d/t €51/67/86) This is the kind of hotel that could be easily transformed into a luxurious (and expensive) boutique hotel. Constructed in 1760, it has a massive glass-roofed patio, which looks mildly neglected, and large rooms with wooden floors and dark wood furniture. It's all slightly shabby and dated but is good value for its old-world ambience.

   ourpick Hotel-Apartamentos Nivaria (☎ 922 26 42 98; www.hotelnivaria.com; Plaza Adelantado 11; s/d from €77/86, apt from €106; P ✖) The former home of a marquis, the façade is washed in burnt sienna with traditional wooden balconies. There are two classes of room and, if you're ready to flash your cash, the superior are worth it. They are exquisitely done up with elegant furniture, leafy plants and earthy colours. The bathrooms are fashionably mosaic-tiled.

Eating

La Folie (Calle Santo Domingo 10; snacks €2.50-6) This fabulous place has a real '60s Haight-Ashbury feel with its cavernous interior, leopard-skin upholstery, murals and idiosyncratic clutter. Good for breakfast, savoury crepes and *mojitos*.

   Osteria da Andrea (☎ 922 26 05 01; Calle Deán Palahi 26; mains €7-10; ☽ closed Mon & Tue) This sophisticated Italian restaurant has an arty, minimalist interior and daily-changing menu; the sign of an innovative chef. Each day's menu usually includes a risotto and unusual pizza among the dishes, such as the delicious *berenja a la parmesan* (aubergine with parmesan cheese). There's a tapas bar out front.

   El Tonique (☎ 922 26 15 29; Calle Heraclio Sánchez 23; mains €7.20-15; ☽ closed Mon lunch & Sun) Head downstairs to this cosy restaurant, its walls lined with dusty bottles of wine. These are but a sample of more than 250 different varieties quietly maturing in Tonique's cellars. The food is very good and worth the wait for a table (it's popular for lunch) and a plate of *pimientos del piquillo rellenos de merluza* (small peppers stuffed with hake).

Drinking

Students provide the town's nightlife, and the bulk of the bars are concentrated in a tight rectangle northeast of the university, known as El Cuadrilátero. At its heart, pedestrianised Plaza Zurita is simply two parallel lines of bars and pubs, so there's no shortage of quaffing choice.

Getting There & Away

There is a stream of buses going to Santa Cruz. Bus 015 (€1.25, 20 minutes) is best, as it takes you straight to Plaza España. Buses 101 and 102 also offer a regular service to Puerto de la Cruz (€3.20, one hour), La Orotava (€4.45, 1½ hours) and beyond.

   Finding a parking on the streets is migraine-inducing. There's an underground pay car park beneath Plaza San Cristóbal.

SAN ANDRÉS & AROUND

The village of San Andrés, all narrow, shady streets, is 6km northeast of Santa Cruz. It is distinguished by the now-crumbled round tower that once protected the town, plus some good seafood restaurants, which alone justify the short journey. Bustling **Marisquería Ramon** (☎ 922 54 93 08; Calle El Dique 23; mains €7-36; ☽ closed Mon) is a slick restaurant just southwest of the tower. It gets packed to its fishy gills at lunchtime, handled with aplomb by the old-fashioned, hard-working waiters. Pick your fish from the glass-fronted fridge.

TENERIFE

The golden sands for the **Playa de las Teresitas**, just beyond the village, were imported from the Sahara. It's a pleasant beach where the sunbathers are almost exclusively Spanish, whether local or from the mainland. Limited parking is available and it's safe for children to swim here.

There are frequent 910 buses (€1.25, 20 minutes) from Santa Cruz to San Andrés, continuing on to Playa de las Teresitas. Bus 245 goes northeast from San Andrés to the end of the road at Igueste, following another 6km of beautiful coastline.

TAGANANA & THE ANAGA MOUNTAINS

A spectacular road trip leads up the Barranco de las Huertas to cross the Anaga range (geologically the oldest part of the island) before plummeting down on the other side to the hamlet of Taganana. The views to the craggy coast from above are breathtaking.

Bus 246 travels to Taganana at least six times daily from Santa Cruz (€2.10, 50 minutes).

There's little to see or do in town but it's only a few more kilometres north to the coast and **Roque de las Bodegas**, which has a number of small restaurants and drink stands. Local windsurfers, surfers and boogie boarders favour its beach – and, even more so, the rocky strand of **Almáciga**, 1.25km eastwards and accessible by the same bus (€2.50, one hour).

If you have your own wheels, backtracking up and into the Anaga mountain range and heading west at the intersection (follow signs for La Laguna) continues a spectacular excursion. Park at the **Casa Forestal**, just south of Taganana, for a hike through a rare laurel forest with branches sprayed with lichens resembling glimmering party streamers. Continue driving for a superb ridge ride with views of the ocean to both north and south and, if the air's clear, of the islands of Gran Canaria and El Hierro rearing from the seas. Take time to pause at the numerous *miradores* (lookouts) along the way.

PUNTA DEL HIDALGO & AROUND

You might want to allow for a side trip to this part of the coast as you head towards La Laguna from Taganana. Once the mountain road has dropped to the plain, turn west for Tegueste; if it's lunchtime, dip south to the tranquil village of El Socorro and **Restaurante Bar San Gonzalo** (☎ 922 54 38 00; Carretera General Del Socorro 179; ۞ closed Wed), which is excellent for

steaks and has a dining room with vineyard views. Continuing northwest, you reach the seaside resort of **Bajamar** (via Tejina). The only real swimming is in large manmade rock pools awash with Atlantic rollers but it is popular with locals.

Three kilometres northeast, **Punta del Hidalgo** is a more interesting place, although don't expect any crumbling cobbles or medieval churches. Like most of the towns in this region, Punta is comparatively modern, its charm being the dramatic ocean location backed by soaring craggy mountains. Stroll along the boardwalk, stopping for a coffee or *cerveza* (beer) at friendly **Angelo** (☎ 922 15 63 88; Altagay Apartments) across from the beach. Locals try their luck on boogie boards in the surf of Playa de los Troches, just north of the centre.

If you want to stay in the area, try **Hotel Delfín** (☎ 922 54 02 00; www.delfinbajamar.com; Avenida el Sol 39; s/d/tr with breakfast €34/53/76; ℗ ⬛ ⬛ ⬛) in Bajamar, which has superb sea views and pretty rooms with bright fabrics and wicker furniture. Alternatively, the **Oceano** (☎ 922 15 60 00; www.oceano-tenerife.com; Punta del Hidalgo; s/d with breakfast from €70/86; ⬛) is a well-equipped spa hotel, popular with Germans, with excellent facilities and large, bright apartments. Facilities include a sea-water pool, gym, Finnish sauna and organised excursions.

Bus 105 runs to Bajamar (€2.20, one hour five minutes) and Punta del Hidalgo (€2.50, 1¼ hours) every 30 minutes from Santa Cruz via La Laguna.

TACORONTE & EL SAUZAL

Tacoronte is located in the heart of one of the island's most important wine regions. Downhill from the modern town centre is the signposted **Iglesia de Santa Catalina** – a bright little whitewashed church built in the Canaries' colonial style. You'll also see a handful of traditional old houses but otherwise there's a lack of gawp-worthy sights here.

Just beyond the El Sauzal exit from the motorway is the **Casa del Vino La Baranda** (☎ 922 57 25 35; Autopista del Norte; admission free; ۞ 11.30am-7.30pm Tue-Sat, 11am-6pm Sun), a museum devoted to wine and its production, located in a traditional Canarian country house with an opportunity to sample the produce in the adjoining tasting room. It's a charming place, with some beautiful views of El Teide on a clear day. The museum

LA MATANZA DE ACENTEJO & LA VICTORIA

At the spot now called La Matanza de Acentejo (The Slaughter of Acentejo), Bencomo's Guanches inflicted a nasty defeat on Alonso Fernández de Lugo's Spaniards in 1494. Two years later, though, de Lugo was back and this time he had better luck, winning a decisive victory over the Guanches 3km south of the scene of his earlier defeat. Predictably, the village that eventually sprang up here was known as La Victoria.

Bus 101 links these towns to Puerto de la Cruz and Santa Cruz.

also has a well-regarded restaurant and, during July and August, the central courtyard becomes a tasteful venue for classical-music concerts every other Tuesday from 8pm. The museum also organises regular wine-tasting courses.

Bus 101 links these towns to Puerto de la Cruz (€2.30, 20 minutes) and Santa Cruz (€2.10, 40 minutes) every 30 minutes or hourly (depending on the time of day).

THE NORTH

PUERTO DE LA CRUZ

pop 31,100

Puerto de la Cruz is the elder statesman of Tenerife, with a history of tourism that dates back to the late 19th century when it was a spa destination popular with genteel Victorian ladies. These days, despite the proliferation of German bakeries (who's complaining?), the town has remained a pleasant resort attracting a classier style of tourist than the pie-and-pint crowd who happily prefer the south. There are stylish boardwalks, traditional restaurants and a leafy central plaza with plenty of bench space and terrace bars.

History

Until it was declared an independent town in the early 20th century, Puerto de la Cruz was merely the port of the wealthier area of La Orotava. Bananas, wine, sugar and cochineals (dye-producing insects; see the boxed text, p132) were exported from here

and a substantial bourgeois class developed in the 1700s. In the 1800s the English arrived, first as merchants and later as sun-seeking tourists, marking the beginning of the tourist transformation that characterises the town today.

Orientation

The heart of Puerto de la Cruz is the lovely Plaza Charco, centred around an ancient Indian laurel tree. Historic buildings are huddled around the plaza, while, to its east, a long coastal promenade marks the site of major tourist developments (such as high-rise hotels and the Lago Martiánez saltwater pool complex). To the west of Plaza Charco is a maze of pedestrian streets, though the further west you go the less well-kept the town becomes. The Playa Jardín at the western edge of town is a 25-minute walk from the centre.

Information

BOOKSHOPS
The Bookshop (☎ 922 37 40 37; Calle Iriarte 42; ⓨ 10am-1.30pm & 5-7pm Mon, Wed & Fri, 10am-1.30pm Tue, Thu & Sat) English-run shop selling new and used books, CDs and videos in English, Spanish and various other languages.

EMERGENCY
Police station (☎ 922 37 84 48; Plaza Europa)

INTERNET ACCESS
Ciber-Locutorio (☎ 922 37 20 11; Calle Agustín de Béthencourt 3D; per hr €1.50; ⓨ 9.30am-11pm Mon-Fri, 1-11pm Sat) Also has telephones and a fax and photocopying service.

LAUNDRY
Lavandería Minosa (☎ 922 38 32 58; Calle Mazaroco 26; wash & dry up to 4kg €6.50; ⓨ 9am-1pm & 4-7.30pm Mon-Fri, 9am-1pm Sat)

MEDICAL SERVICES
Hospital Tamaragua (☎ 922 38 05 12; cnr Calle Agustín de Béthencourt & Calle Valois; ⓨ 24hr) Private clinic in the centre of town.
Le Ro (☎ 922 37 33 01; Edificio Martina, Avenida Generalísimo; ⓨ 9am-noon Mon-Fri) Specialist shop for disabled and elderly travellers, offering wheelchair rental and travel assistance.

POST
Main post office (Calle Pozo)

TENERIFE

PUERTO DE LA CRUZ

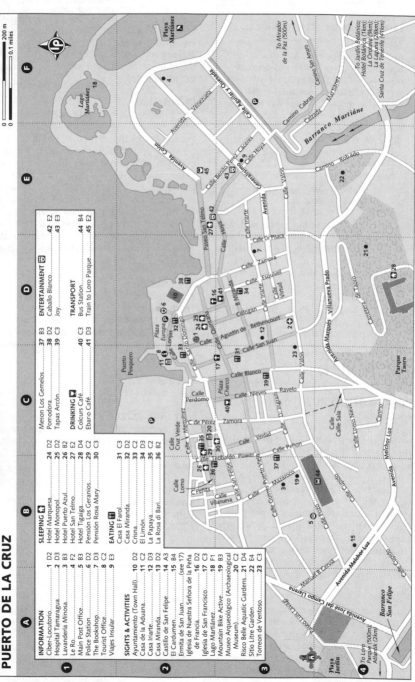

INFORMATION
Ciber-Locutorio	1 D2
Hospital Tamaragua	2 D3
Lavandería Minosa	3 B3
Le Ro	4 F2
Main Post Office	5 B3
Police Station	6 D2
The Bookshop	7 D3
Tourist Office	8 C2
Viajes Insular	9 E3

SIGHTS & ACTIVITIES
Ayuntamiento (Town Hall)	10 D2
Casa de la Aduana	11 C3
Casa Iriarte	12 D3
Casa Miranda	13 C2
Castillo de San Felipe	14 A3
El Cardumen	15 B4
Ermita de San Juan	(see 17)
Iglesia de Nuestra Señora de la Peña de Francia	16 D2
Iglesia de San Francisco	17 C3
Lago Martiánez	18 F1
Mountain Bike Active	19 B3
Museo Arqueológico (Archaeological Museum)	20 C2
Risco Belle Aquatic Gardens	21 D4
Sitio Litre Garden	22 E4
Torreón de Ventoso	23 C3

SLEEPING
Hotel Marquesa	24 D2
Hotel Monopol	25 D2
Hotel Puerto Azul	26 B2
Hotel San Telmo	27 E2
Hotel Tigaiga	28 D4
Pensión Los Geranios	29 D2
Pensión Rosa Mary	30 C3

EATING
Casa El Farol	31 C3
Casa Miranda	32 D2
Crisna	33 C2
El Limón	34 D3
La Papaya	35 C2
La Rosa di Bari	36 B2
Mesón Los Gemelos	37 B3
Pomodora	38 D2
Tapas Arcón	39 C3

DRINKING
Colcurs Café	40 C3
Ebaro Café	41 D3

ENTERTAINMENT
Caballo Blanco	42 E2
Joy	43 E3

TRANSPORT
Bus Station	44 B4
Train to Loro Parque	45 E2

TOURIST INFORMATION

Tourist office (☎ 922 38 60 00; www.puertodelacruz .org; Casa de la Aduana, Calle Lonjas s/n; ☑ 9am-8pm Mon-Fri, to 1pm Sat)

TRAVEL AGENCIES

Viajes Insular (☎ 922 38 02 62; www.viajesinsular .es; Avenida Generalísimo 20) This is the best local travel agency and can help with air fares, ferry travel, car rental and booking excursions.

Sights & Activities

The Plaza Europa, a balcony of sorts built in 1992, may be a modern addition, but it blends well with the historic surroundings and is a good place to start your visit. The tourist office is here, located in the **Casa de la Aduana** (built in 1620), the old customs house, where now you can also find quality arts and crafts for sale. Opposite is the **ayuntamiento** (town hall), which was a banana-packaging factory until 1973. From here, head down Calle Lonjas where, on the corner, you'll find the **Casa Miranda** (p165) restaurant, one of the town's better examples of 18th-century Canarian architecture. A short walk away is **Museo Arqueológico** (Archaeological Museum; ☎ 922 53 58 16; Calle Lomo 9; adult/under 6yr/7-12yr €1.50/free/1; ☑ 10am-1pm & 5-8pm Tue-Sat, closed Aug), which provides an insight into the Guanche way of life with its replicas of a typical cave dwelling, as well as a burial cave where pots and baked-clay adornments share the same burial area, demonstrating the Guanches' belief in an afterlife.

Next, head southeast to lively **Plaza Charco** (Puddle Plaza), which acquired its name because it used to flood from the sea every time there was a heavy storm (thankfully, no more). Just off the plaza is **Iglesia de San Francisco**, tacked on to tiny **Ermita de San Juan**, the oldest structure in town (built in 1599). Three blocks away is **Iglesia de Nuestra Señora de la Peña de Francia**, a 17th-century church with three naves, a wooden *mudéjar* ceiling and the image of Gran Poder de Dios, one of the town's most revered saints.

Several Canarian mansions, many of them in poor repair, dot the town centre. The mid-18th-century **Casa Iriarte** (Calle San Juan), once the home of intellectual Tomás de Iriarte and the site of clandestine political meetings, has seen better days. The **Torreon de Ventoso** (Calle Valois) is one of the better-kept historic buildings. The tower once formed part of the town's Au-gustine convent and was used to keep watch over the port.

Outside the town centre there are also some noteworthy spots, such as **Castillo de San Felipe** (☎ 922 38 36 63; ☑ open for special events only) beside Playa Jardín and, above town, the **Mirador de la Paz**, a square with great views where Agatha Christie was supposedly inspired to write the novel *The Mysterious Mr Quin*. Don't miss a visit to the **Jardín Botánico** (☎ 922 38 35 72; Calle Retama 2; admission €3; ☑ 9am-6pm Oct-Apr, to 7pm May-Sep), on the road out of town. Established in 1788, the botanical garden has thousands of plant varieties from all over the world. Just 1km closer to the town centre, the **Sitio Litre garden** (☎ 922 38 24 17; Carretera del Botánico; admission €4.50; ☑ 9.30am-2.30pm) boasts a luscious orchid collection and the town's oldest *drago* (dragon tree); see the boxed text, p42. Another tropical oasis is the **Risco Belle Aquatic Gardens**, which sit in the heart of the **Parque Taoro** south of the town centre.

LORO PARQUE

Where else can you see 3000 parrots (the world's largest collection) all in one place? **Loro Parque** (☎ 922 37 38 41; www.loroparque.com; Calle Avenida Loro Parque; adult/under 12yr €29/19; ☑ 8.30am-6.45pm) is home to 340 species of parrots along with other exotic animals, including tigers, gorillas and chimpanzees. Unless you object in principle to wild animals in captivity, the park is quite impressive. Don't miss the dolphin and whale shows, the subterranean aquarium with the world's longest submarine tunnel and the vast 'penguinarium'. You could walk here from town, but it's much easier to hop on the free train that leaves every 20 minutes from outside McDonalds on Plaza Reyes Católicos.

LAGO MARTIÁNEZ

Designed by Canario César Manrique (see p131), the watery playground of **Lago Martiánez** (☎ 922 38 59 55; Avenida Colón; adult/under 12yr €3.50/1.10; ☑ 10am-sunset, last entry 5pm Oct-Apr, 6pm May-Sep), northeast of the centre, has four saltwater pools and a large central 'lake'. It can get just as crowded as the surrounding small volcanic beaches. Swim, sunbathe or grab a bite at one of the many restaurants and bars. There's a glittery new casino here, as well.

ADVENTURE SPORTS & DIVING

Offering a hodgepodge of adventure-sport rental, excursions and courses, **El Cardumen**

TENERIFE

(☎ 922 36 84 68; Avenida Melchor Luz 3; ◷ 9.30am-1.30pm & 5-8pm Mon-Fri, opens 10am Sat) is the place for action.

Mountain Bike Active (☎ 922 37 60 81; www.espana bike.com; Edificio Daniela 26, Calle Mazaroco; bike rental from €36 per day; ◷ 9.30am-1.30pm & 5-7pm), across from the bus station, organises trips to El Teide and around.

Divers should contact **Atlantik** (☎ 922 36 28 01; www.scubadivingplanet.com; dives with equipment rental €65; ◷ 9am-6.30pm Mon-Fri, 12.30-2pm Sat), based in the Hotel Maritím, 2km west of the town centre, offering a range of courses.

Tours

The **tourist office** (☎ 922 38 60 00; Casa de la Aduana, Calle Lonjas s/n; ◷ 9am-8pm Mon-Fri, to 1pm Sat) offers various guided routes through town.

For nature hikes there are local guides, including **Jorg and Mario** (☎ 922 37 60 07; www.der wanderstab.de), who meet hikers at the bus station from where they set out on several hikes, including Teide and the northwest, and **Cristóbal** (☎ 639 33 27 61), who offers similar and is a botanical expert. Trips cost from €25 per person.

Sleeping

There is plenty of good accommodation in Puerto de la Cruz.

BUDGET

Pensión Los Geranios (☎ 922 38 28 10; Calle Lomo 14; d €27) The best value budget hotel on one of the town's prettiest pedestrian streets. Although the building won't win any design awards, the rooms are bright with light wood furnishings and pale-peach paintwork; several have private balconies at no extra cost.

Pensión Rosa Mary (☎ 922 38 32 53; Calle San Felipe 14; s/d €18/30) The décor at this place is a bit frumpy but the rooms are clean and there's a TV room, plus a sunny rooftop terrace.

Hotel Puerto Azul (☎ 922 38 32 13; www.puertoazul .de; Calle Lomo 24; s/d €27/43, breakfast €4) Down the street from Los Geranios, rooms here are small and fairly forgettable, but most have terraces and there's a rooftop terrace for catching the rays. There are price reductions for longer stays.

MIDRANGE

Hotel San Telmo (☎ 922 38 58 53; www.hotel-santelmo .com; Paseo San Telmo 18; s/d with breakfast €38/68; ⊠ ⊒) This hotel enjoys a great location overlooking the thundering surf at the rocky part of the promenade. Rooms are pleasant enough with terracotta tiles and bright fabrics; there's a rooftop pool and generous German-style buffet breakfast.

Hotel Marquesa (☎ 922 38 31 51; www.hotelmarquesa .com; Calle Quintana 11-13; s/d €35/88; ⊠ ⊒) About as close as you can be to church without attending confession, this is one of the town's most headily historic buildings, with dark, heavy wood furnishings, beams and balconies. The hotel's Tasca restaurant is a pleasant place for an informal seafood dinner.

Hotel Monopol (☎ 922 37 03 10; Calle Quintana 15; s/d €59/100; ⊠ ⊒) Next door to the Marquesa is another original hotel, this one built in 1742. The service is low-key but efficient, and the extras include a heated pool, games room, sauna and three sun-bronzing terraces. Original wooden balconies provide plenty of charm, while the rooms are small but well-equipped.

TOP END

Hotel Tigaiga (☎ 922 38 35 00; www.tigaiga.com; Parque Taoro 28; d from €140; ℗ ⊠ ⌨ ⊒) This superb hotel has ocean-view rooms, a program of guided walks and lush subtropical gardens. The rooms are classy and large with incredible views.

Hotel Botánico (☎ 922 38 14 00; www.hotelbotanico .com; Avenida Richard J Yeoward 1; s/d with breakfast €193/276; ℗ ⊠ ⌨ ⊒) The most exclusive hotel in these parts, the Botánico has beautiful gardens, a great pool area and a new spa centre (see the boxed text, p147). Rooms are comfortable though not luxurious, with big balconies and all the standard amenities.

Eating

BUDGET

Crisna (☎ 922 38 19 06; Calle Santo Domingo s/n) Not for the hip and thigh conscious, this *salon de té* has a vast choice of deliciously creamy cakes.

El Limón (☎ 922 38 16 19; Calle Esquivel 4; snacks €2.20-6; Ⓥ) A bright vegetarian restaurant with a menu of mainly snack-style fare, including veggie burgers, seitan kebabs, salads and fresh fruit juices; try the papaya.

Tapas Arcón (☎ 922 37 19 88; Calle Blanco 8; tapas about €4; Ⓥ) *Papas arrugadas* (wrinkly potatoes) with *mojo* (spicy salsa), or the Arcón special sauces of almond and sweet pepper or parsley and coriander are the must-have tapas here.

TENERIFE

MIDRANGE

Meson Los Gemelos (☎ 922 37 01 33; Calle El Peñón 4; mains €5-8) Round the corner from the bus station, this is a friendly, welcoming restaurant with a great atmosphere; the house speciality is grilled meats. There's a covered interior patio, lots of locals and a noisy parrot.

Pomodora (☎ 922 38 13 28; Punta Viento; mains €5-10; V) The location, in a cave under the seaside promenade, is the main draw at this restaurant and pizzeria. Diners get a fantastic view of the rocky coast; the menu reads like a novel, in six languages, no less.

La Papaya (☎ 922 38 28 11; Calle Lomo 10; mains €6-8) This long-time favourite has a series of small dining rooms with rock-face walls and a pretty patio with adjacent leafy garden. There are Canarian touches to the menu, including the succulent salmon in *malvasía* (Malmsey wine) sauce.

Casa El Farol (☎ 922 36 88 12; Calle San Juan 14; mains €6-12) Comprises three separate eateries for the indecisive. There's a *mesón* (traditional restaurant) with good Mediterranean-style dishes, a bistro in the patio (try the goat's cheese and tomato salad with pesto) and a bakery with a German pastry chef, plus homemade fresh-fruit ice cream.

TOP END

Casa Miranda (☎ 922 37 38 71; Calle Santo Domingo 13; mains €10-13) A three-storey Canarian mansion built in 1730, this was the family home of 18th-century Venezuelan president Francisco de Miranda. Nowadays you can get seafood and grilled meats in the fine dining room, or order tapas in the downstairs bar.

La Rosa di Bari (☎ 922 36 85 23; Calle Lomo 23; mains €11-17) One of the classiest restaurants in town, located in a lovely old house with several romantic dining rooms. Enjoy innovative dishes like cod in port sauce with truffles, or asparagus gnocchi with prawns.

Drinking

Most nightspots are around Plaza Charco or along Avenida Generalísimo.

Ebano Café (☎ 922 38 86 32; Calle Hoya 2; 10am-12pm) This is a beautiful building with lots of original features. Sit outside in a comfy wicker chair with a view of the church and gardens. Tapas also served.

Colours Café (☎ 922 38 59 13; Plaza Charco; 8pm-2am Wed-Mon) Above a pizzeria on this energetic stretch of eateries, snag a seat by a window overlooking the square. A cocktail bar with mellow décor and Latin and African music, this is a good place to kick off your night on the tiles.

Entertainment

Joy (☎ 922 37 39 85; Calle Hoya s/n; admission before 2am free, after 2am €6 with drink; 11pm-6am Mon-Sat) Sophisticated it ain't. This cavernous disco pumps out a mix of techno, pop and house. It's popular with the local 20-something gang with free drinks for ladies until 1.30am.

Caballo Blanco (☎ 922 38 58 53; Paseo San Telmo 18 9.30pm-late Mon-Sat) This club is for a more mature crowd with a keyboard player as well as DJ and music stuck firmly in the *Lady in Red* genre of the '60s to '80s.

Getting There & Away

The bus station is on Calle Pozo in the west of town. There are frequent departures for Santa Cruz (€4.10, 55 minutes). Bus 103 is direct while bus 102 calls by Tenerife Norte airport and La Laguna. Other popular routes include a 9.15am 348 bus (€4.80, 1½ hours) to El Teide. Bus 343 (€11.20, two hours, six daily) runs to Playa de las Américas. Bus 363 offers an hourly service from 6am to 10pm to Icod de los Vinos (€2.50, 45 minutes) and on to Garachico (€2.90, one hour).

Getting Around

For information about bike rental, see opposite. For details about car hire, see p150.

The long-distance buses starting in or passing through Puerto de la Cruz often double up as local buses.

Taxis are widely available and are a relatively inexpensive way to jet across town (a 15-minute ride should cost under €5).

LA OROTAVA

pop 40,000

This colonial town will have your camera clicking all day. It has the lot, it seems: cobblestone streets, flower-filled plazas and more Castilian mansions than the rest of the island put together. Along with La Laguna, La Orotava is one of the loveliest towns on Tenerife, and one of the most truly 'Canarian' places in the Canary Islands.

TENERIFE

The lush valley surrounding the town has been one of the island's most prosperous areas since the 16th century when well-to-do Spaniards built churches and manor houses here. The valley is a major cultivator of bananas, chestnuts and vineyards, and is also excellent hiking country, with a maze of footpaths leading you into Canarian pine woods, with 1200m views down over the coastal plain; the tourist office can advise on routes.

Information

EMERGENCY
Police station (☎ 922 33 01 14; Calle Cólogan 2)

POST
Post office (Calle Cólogan s/n)

TOURIST INFORMATION
Tourist office (☎ 922 32 30 41; www.villadelaorotava .com in Spanish; Carrera Escultor Estévez 2; ☿ 8.30am-6pm) A well-marked tourist route of the town's major monuments starts here. You can also pick up stamped leaflets allowing free entrance to several museums.

Sights

La Orotava has been able to preserve the beauty of its past. Traditional mansions are flanked with ornate wooden balconies like pirate galleons, surrounded by manicured gardens. You can cover the centre on foot in just half a day.

Plaza Constitución, a large, shady plaza just a block from the tourist office, is a good place to start. On the plaza's northeastern side is the **Iglesia de San Agustín**, a simple church with a pretty wooden ceiling. A few doors away stands the palatial **Liceo de Taoro** building (1928); a private cultural society, but open to the public. An attractive terraced garden separates the mansion from the street and, although the building looks a tad foreboding, you can enter and have a drink at the café, a meal at the restaurant or check out any exhibitions that may be taking place.

Also on the plaza are the 19th-century **Jardines del Marquesado de la Quinta Roja** (☿ 9am-midnight), a series of orderly, French-influenced flower gardens cascading down the hillside, crowned by a small 18th-century marble temple.

Easier on the knees is the sweet-smelling **Hijuela del Botánico** (☿ 9am-2pm Mon-Fri), just across Calle León. This small botanical garden was created as a branch of the larger Jardín Botánico in Puerto de la Cruz. Around 3000 plant varieties are gathered here, and there are also birds and butterflies.

Also on Calle León is the **Museo de Cerámica** (Ceramics Museum; ☎ 922 32 14 47; Calle León 3; admission €2; ☿ 10am-6pm Mon-Fri, to 2pm Sat & Sun), boasting the largest clay-pot collection in Spain. The museum is well laid out, and there are detailed explanations in several languages. The sheer size of the pots in the *Sala de Vino* are impressive, and the sepia photos are fun, but after a few dozen pots or so, there is a certain sameness about the place.

Head down Calle Tomás Zerolo to visit **Museo de Artesanía Iberoamericana** (Iberoamerican Handicrafts Museum; ☎ 922 32 17 46; Calle Tomás Zerolo 34; admission €2.10; ☿ 9.30am-6pm Mon-Fri, to 2pm Sat), housed in the former Convento de Santo Domingo. Exploring the cultural relationship between the Canaries and the Americas, the museum exhibits musical instruments, ceramics and various artefacts. The adjacent **Iglesia de Santo Domingo** has beautifully carved doors and a rich *mudéjar* ceiling.

Back in the centre of town, the **Iglesia de la Concepción** (Plaza Patricia García; ☿ 11am-1pm & 5-8pm) is one of the finest examples of baroque architecture in the entire archipelago. Follow Calle Colegio (which becomes Calle San Francisco) uphill from behind the church. This street is home to several of the **Doce Casas**, 12 historic Canary mansions that are one of La Orotava's most distinguishing features. The 17th-century **Casa Lercaro** (Calle Colegio 5-7; ☿ 10.30am-8.30pm) is now an upmarket restaurant, café and *cervecería* (beer bar); see Kiú, p168.

Down the street is the **Casa de los Balcones** (Casa Fonesca, Calle San Francisco 3; admission €1.50; ☿ 8.30am-6.30pm Mon-Fri, to 5pm Sat, to 1pm Sun). Built in 1692, the interior and exterior balconies feature ornate carvings and there's a small separate museum showing furniture and costumes of the period. Across the street is **Casa del Turista** (☿ 8.30am-6.30pm Mon-Fri, to 5pm Sat, to 1pm Sun), which has similar features but is less outstanding. In both *casas* a vast selection of local handicrafts are for sale, including embroidery and pottery.

On your way up Calle Colegio, stop at **Molino la Maquina** (Calle Colegio 3; ☿ 8am-1pm, 2.30-6pm), which makes *gofio*, made from ground corn or wheat. The pretty white stone towers were the old water mills used to grind corn. Now they're just for show and everything is done electronically. There is another historic **gofio mill** further along the road (see the La Orotava map or follow your nose). At both you can buy *gofio* for around €1.45 per kilogram.

Sleeping

Hotel-Residencia Silene (☎ 922 33 01 99; Calle Tomás Zerolo 9; s/d €25/40) An old family home, the whole place is slowly (very slowly) being improved. A few of the rooms are lovely; freshly painted with the original green-and-pink floor tiles, large terraces and new pine furniture. Others are dingy and, worse still, smell damp. There's no difference in price so check them out before you check in.

Hotel Rural Orotava (☎ 922 32 27 93; www.hotelorotava .com; Calle Carrera 17, s with breakfast €50, d with breakfast €65-75;) This historic hotel is high on atmosphere and touted as the oldest of the town's achingly gorgeous mansions. Many of the original features remain, including the *mudéjar* carved ceilings. The rooms are all different and have been decorated with unpretentious good taste.

our pick **Hotel Victoria** (☎ 922 33 16 83; http:// hotelvictoria.htnsl.com; Calle Hermano Apolinar 8; s/d with breakfast €115/135;) This is a seductive little number; a 17th-century mansion restored to an exquisite boutique hotel. The rooms are set around a central patio and have plenty of designer detail with textured cream wallpaper, modular light fittings and wi-fi access.

LA OROTAVA

0   200 m
0   0.1 miles

INFORMATION	
Police Station........................1	A3
Post Office..........................2	A3
Tourist Office.......................3	B3

SIGHTS & ACTIVITIES	
Casa de los Balcones...............4	A4
Casa del Turista....................5	A4
Casa Lercaro.......................6	A3
Gofio Mills..........................7	A4
Hijuela del Botánico................8	B3
Iglesia de la Concepción...........9	A3
Iglesia de San Agustín...........10	B3
Iglesia de Santo Domingo........11	B2
Jardines del Marquesado de la	
Quinta Roja..................12	B3
Liceo de Taoro....................13	B3
Molino la Maquina...............14	A3
Museo de Artesania Iberoamericana	
(Iberoamerican Handricrafts	
Museum)....................15	B2
Museo de Cerámica (Ceramics	
Museum)....................16	B3

SLEEPING	
Hotel Rural Orotava..............17	A3
Hotel Victoria.....................18	A4
Hotel-Residencia Silene.........19	B3

EATING	
Bar la Duquesa....................20	A3
Kiú...............................(see 6)	
Sabor Canario..................(see 17)	

TRANSPORT	
Bus Station.........................21	D2

TENERIFE

There's an excellent restaurant and rooftop sun terrace.

Eating

Bar La Duquesa (☎ 922 33 49 49; Plaza Casanas 6B; mains €4-6) In the shadow of the church, this simple place has cacti growing from the roof tiles (truly!) and splendid Canarian food.

Sabor Canario (☎ 922 32 27 93; www.hotelorotava .com; Hotel Rural Orotava, Calle Carrera 17; mains €5-8; ✌ closed Sun) Exercise the taste buds on soul-satisfying traditional cuisine at this fabulous restaurant located in the leafy patio of the Hotel Rural Orotava.

Kiú (☎ 922 32 37 38; Casa Lercaro, Calle Colegio 7; mains €6-12) This enticing space is *the* place to come for laid-back nightlife, a morning coffee or an elegant meal. The café has a decadent cake choice; the *cervecería* has beer on tap and live music at weekends; and the elegant restaurant hits the right spot with innovative dishes like sole and prawn rolls in a dill sauce.

Getting There & Away

La Orotava is 9km inland from Puerto de la Cruz, and buses (€1.25, 20 minutes) leave roughly every half-hour from 7am to 11pm. Bus 63 (€3.90, 50 minutes), among others, comes from Santa Cruz. Call the **bus station** (☎ 922 33 27 02) for more information.

ICOD DE LOS VINOS

pop 22,200

An umbrella-shaped *drago* tree is the cause of a lot of fuss in this town. Indeed, it's worth a look and a read-up (see the boxed text, p42), and the shady main square, Plaza San Marcos, is a lovely, leafy spot to rest and enjoy the town's white-walled church. Otherwise, for restaurants and places to stay head on to neighbouring Garachico (right), which is a few notches up on the postcard-pretty stakes.

The **tourist office** (☎ 922 86 96 00; Calle San Antonio; ✌ 9am-7pm Mon-Fri) is just off the main plaza.

Sights

The pride of the town is the world's largest and oldest **drago tree**, which has supposedly been here for more than 1000 years. Past **Plaza Constitución** (aka Plaza Pila), a square with historic Canary homes, is **Drago Park** (fax 922 81 44 36; admission €4; ✌ 9am-6.30pm), where you can pay to get up close to the famous tree; fax ahead to request a guided tour. The best view, however, is the free one from the west wall of the Plaza de la Inglesia. **Plaza San Marcos** is in the centre of town. Here you can see the **Iglesia de San Marcos**, which has an ornate silver high altar and a sacred **museum** (admission €0.60).

The second major sight here is the **Mariposa-rio del Drago** (☎ 922 81 51 67; Avenida Canarias), a hot and sticky greenhouse full of exotic butterflies. However, this was closed for restoration at the time of research; check at the tourist office for an update.

Getting There & Away

If you're driving, save yourself a headache and follow the signs towards the paid car park. Arriving by bus is easy: bus 106 (€5.80, 1¼ hours) comes directly from Santa Cruz every two hours from 6.45am to 10.45pm. Bus 354 (€2.50, 45 minutes) comes from Puerto de la Cruz every half-hour from 7.30am to 10.30pm, and bus 460 (€5.40, one hour 35 minutes, eight daily) makes the trip up from Playa de las Américas. The **bus station** (☎ 922 81 13 04) is to the northeast of the town centre.

GARACHICO

pop 6800

A gracious, tranquil town located in a deep valley flanked by forested slopes and a rocky coastline, Garachico has managed to retain its Canarian identity and is one of the few coastal towns where you may still need Spanish to order a beer. There are no big hotels, probably because there is no real beach, though swimming in the natural, volcanic coves along the rocky coast is a rare delight.

Named for the rock outcrop off its shore (*gara* is Guanche for island, and *chico* is Spanish for small), Garachico is a peaceful place. You'd never guess the history of calamities that lies behind its whitewashed houses and narrow, cobblestone streets. Garachico was once an important commercial port, but its unlucky inhabitants suffered a series of disasters that all but finished off the hamlet: freak storms, floods, fires, epidemics and, in 1706, a major volcanic eruption that destroyed the port and buried half the town in lava, reduced it to a poor shadow of its former self.

Just outside town, you can hike trails that follow the path of the disastrous lava flow.

The **tourist office** (☎ 922 13 34 61; Calle Esteban de Ponte 5; ☺ 10am-3pm Mon-Fri) stocks maps of the town and can advise on *casas rurales*.

Sights & Activities

The soul of Garachico is the main Plaza Libertad with its towering palm trees, café tables and lively atmosphere. At dusk old men in flat caps play cards surrounded by sauntering couples, children kicking balls, and families. Nearby is the **Iglesia** and evocative **Convento de San Francisco** (1524). The latter houses a small **museum** (☎ 922 83 00 00; admission €0.60; ☺ 10am-7pm Mon-Fri, to 3pm Sat & Sun) about the town's history. Just off the plaza is the **Iglesia de Santa Ana**, with a dominating white bell tower and original 16th-century doors.

Another rare remnant of the volcano is in the Plaza Juan González (aka Plaza Pila), and the **Puerta de Tierra** (Land Gate), all that's left of Garachico's once-thriving port. It was once right on the water but thanks to the eruption is now in the centre of town.

On the water you can visit **Castillo de San Miguel** (admission €0.60; ☺ 10am-8pm Mon-Fri, to 6pm Sat & Sun), a squat stone fortress built in the 16th century, with photos and explanations of the area's flora and fauna, as well as a chronological history of the town.

Divers can check out the scuba centre in the *pensión* **El Jardín** (☎ 922 83 02 45; www.argonautas.org; Calle Esteban de Ponte 8; dive with equipment rental €45).

Sleeping

Garachico is a perfect place to base yourself if you're looking for a small-town feel with easy access to northern Tenerife and outdoor pursuits.

El Jardín (☎ 922 83 02 45; www.argonautas.org; Calle Esteban de Ponte 8; s €20-45, d €25-50) The only place in town that can qualify as budget. It varies as much in room quality as it does in price – while the €50-per-night room is spacious and almost elegant, the cheaper rooms have threadbare furnishings and a dormitory look.

Hotel Rural El Patio (☎ 922 13 32 80; www.hotelpatio .com; Finca Malpaís 11; s €50-87, d €63-114; ☒ ☲) Just east of town, in El Guincho, is this tranquil, white-walled place tucked among plantains. The rooms are spread throughout three low-rise buildings set around a stone patio.

ourpick Hotel La Quinta Roja (☎ 922 13 33 77; www.quintaroja.com; Glorieta de San Francisco; d/ste with breakfast from €103/143; ☒ ☲ ☻) This re-stored 16th-century manor house is lovely. Managed by an enthusiastic young team, the rooms are centred around a gracious patio complete with fountain and wooden galleries. Rooms have cherry-coloured wooden floors, muted décor and Med-blue mosaic-tiled bathrooms.

Hotel San Roque (☎ 922 13 34 35; www.hotelsan roque.com; Calle Esteban de Ponte 32; s/d/ste with breakfast from €135/190/255; ☒ ☲ ☻) Another stunning hotel, set in a 17th-century mansion, which has been converted with style and originality, but without compromising on the old-Havana feel of the place. The rooms are set around two courtyards and have eye-catching designer detail, as well as spa baths, DVD and CD players and wi-fi access.

CASAS RURALES

There are several *casas rurales* in these parts.

León Acosta (☎ 922 13 33 66; Calle El Monte 14, San Juán del Reparo; s/d with breakfast €25/50) A gingerbread cottage of a place with just one room, located in a sleepy, unspoiled village near Garachico.

Casa Ida (☎ 922 13 32 97; www.ruralida.com; Calle La Oliva 8, Genovés; d from €54) Located between Icod de los Vinos and Garachico and comprising five cottages set on several levels and surrounded by fruit trees and gardens. There are sweeping views of the sea and El Teide. The accommodation is attractive rustic style with beams, terracotta tiles and chunky wooden furniture.

Eating

El Caletón (☎ 922 13 33 01; Avenida Tomé Cano 1; mains €7-18) The best position in town, with a vast terrace overlooking the volcanic rock pools. You can have a drink or ice cream or something more substantial; the menu includes a tasty *setas con gambas* (oyster mushrooms with prawns).

Casa Gaspar (☎ 922 13 31 06; Avenida República de Venezuela 2; mains €10-16) This restaurant has a good reputation with the locals. It has an old-fashioned elegance and serves tasty seafood dishes.

Getting There & Away

Bus 107 connects the town with Santa Cruz (€6, one hour 55 minutes), La Laguna, La Orotava and Icod de los Vinos, while bus 363 (€2.90, one hour, up to 20 daily) comes and goes from Puerto de la Cruz.

TENERIFE

THE CENTRE

PARQUE NACIONAL DEL TEIDE

Covering 189.9 sq km, Teide is not only Spain's largest national park, it is the most popular, attracting a whopping four million visitors a year. A visit here should top everyone's itinerary. Most folk arrive by bus and don't wander far off the highway that snakes through the centre of the park, but that just means that the rest of us have more elbow room to explore. There are currently 21 walking tracks (30 more tracks will soon be signposted) marking the way through volcanic terrain, beside unique rock formations and up to the peak of El Teide (Pico del Teide), which, at 3718m, is the highest mountain in Spain.

This area was declared a national park in 1954, with the goal of protecting the landscape, which includes 14 plants found nowhere else on earth. The park is simply stunning; more than 80% of the world's volcanic formations are here, including rough badlands (deeply eroded barren areas), smooth *pahoehoe* or *lajial* lava (rock that looks like twisted taffy) and pebble-like lapilli. There are also complex formations such as volcanic pipes and cones. The park protects nearly 1000 Guanche archaeological sites, many of which are still unexplored and all of which are unmarked, preventing curious visitors from removing 'souvenirs'.

El Teide dominates the northern end of the park. If you don't want to make the four-hour climb to the top, take the cable car (below). Surrounding the peak are the *cañadas*, flat depressions likely caused by a massive landslide 180,000 years ago.

Information

The park has two excellent visitor centres: **El Portillo** (☎ 922 29 01 29; www.mma.es; Carretera La Orotava-Granadilla; ☺ 9am-4pm) in the northeast, with an adjacent botanical garden; and **Cañada Blanca** (☎ 922 29 01 29; Carretera La Orotava-Granadilla; ☺ 9am-4pm) in the south, which has an informative 15-minute video presentation about the history, ecology, flora and fauna of the park. Both centres stock maps and hiking information as well as an excellent guidebook to the park.

Sights

PICO DEL TEIDE

The **cable car** (☎ 922 69 40 38; adult/under 14yr €22/12; ☺ 9am-4pm) provides the easiest, most popular and most expensive way to get up to the peak of El Teide. If you don't mind paying up, the views are great – unless a big cloud is covering the peak, in which case you won't see a thing. On clear days, the volcanic valley spreads out majestically below, and you can see the islands of La Gomera, La Palma and El Hierro peeking up from the Atlantic. It takes just eight minutes to zip up 1200m.

A few words of warning: those with heart or lung problems should stay on the ground,

---

THE DAY EL TEIDE SWALLOWED THE SUN

These days scientists can explain exactly how a volcano erupts: magma from the earth's core explodes through the crust and spews ash, rock and molten lava over the land. But the Guanches, living in pre-Hispanic Tenerife, had a more romantic version. According to legend, the 13th-century eruption was caused when El Teide swallowed the sun. The people believed that the devil, Guyota, lived inside El Cheide, as El Teide was then known. One day he emerged from his underground lair and saw the sun. Jealous of its light, he stole it and hid it inside his lair, causing death, destruction and darkness all over the island. The Guanches begged Chaman, the sky god, for help, and the god battled Guyota inside the volcano. The Guanches knew Chaman had triumphed when one morning they awoke to see the sun back in the sky and the volcano plugged with rock, trapping the evil Guyota inside forever.

The legend coincides perfectly with what happened following the medieval eruption. An ash cloud covered the sun, and the only light the Guanches saw came from the mouth of the active volcano, leading them to believe the sun was trapped there. The volcano's toxic ash would have killed many plants and animals, and the 'battle' going on inside the volcano was probably the rumblings following the eruption. The 'plug' that safely trapped Guyota in El Cheide was new volcanic rock.

as oxygen is short up here in the clouds. It's chilly, too, so no matter what the weather's like below, bring a jacket. The cable cars, which each hold around 35 passengers, leave every 10 minutes, but get here early (before noon) because at peak times you could be queuing for two hours! The last ride down is at 5pm.

See p172 if you want to tackle the mountain on foot.

ROQUES DE GARCÍA

A few kilometres south of the peak, across from the *parador,* lies this geological freak show of **twisted lava pinnacles** with names like the Finger of God and the Cathedral. Known as the Roques de García, they are the result of erosion of old volcanic dykes, or vertical streams of magma. The hard rock of the dykes has been bared while surrounding earth and rock has been gradually swept away. The weirdest of the rocks, the **Roque Cinchado**, is wearing away faster at the base than above, and one of these days is destined to topple over (so maybe you shouldn't get too close). Spreading out to the west are the otherworldly bald plains of the Llano de Ucanca.

This is the most popular spot in the park and is viewed by nearly 90% of its visitors. The car park is always crowded, but most people just leave their cars or tour buses for a 15-minute glance. If you plan to hike the relatively easy, 1½-hour trail that circles the rocks, you'll most likely be alone.

PICO VIEJO

With a name meaning 'old peak', this is the last of Tenerife's volcanoes to have erupted on a grand scale. In 1798, its southwestern flank tore open, leaving a 700m gash. Today you can clearly see where fragments of magma shot over 1km into the air and fell pell-mell. Torrents of lava gushed from a secondary, lower wound to congeal on the slopes. To this day, not a blade of grass or a stain of lichen has returned to the arid slope.

Walking

Don comfortable shoes, don't forget your map and bottle of water and get ready to stride out; you won't be disappointed. You are likely to see lots of the Teide broom shrubs that fill so much of the park and, if you're here in early summer, the spectacular Teide vi-per's bugloss (see p41) in bloom. Keep to the marked trails.

GUIDED WALKS

Park rangers host guided walks up the mountain in both Spanish and English. The pace is gentle and there are frequent information pauses. Even though you'll huff and puff rather more than usual because of the high altitude, the walks are suitable for anyone of reasonable fitness (including children aged over 10).

Groups leave at 9.15am and 1.30pm from the visitor centre at El Portillo, and at 9.30am and 1pm from the visitor centre at Cañada Blanca. Walks last about two hours.

Groups are small, so it is essential to call ahead and reserve a spot. Phone ☎ 922 29 01 29 between 9am and 2pm Monday to Friday).

SELF-GUIDED WALKS

The general park visitor guide lists 21 walks, ranging in length from 600m to 17.6km, some of which are signposted. Each walk is graded according to its level of difficulty (ranging from 'low' – the most common – to 'extreme'). You're not allowed to stray from the marked trails, a sensible restriction in an environment where every tuft of plant life has to fight for survival.

You don't have to be a masochist to enjoy the challenge of walking from road level up to **La Rambleta** at the top of the cable car, followed by a zoom down in the lift. Get off the bus (request the driver to stop) or leave your car at the small road-side parking area (signposted 'Montaña Blanca' and 'Refugio de Altavista') 8km south of the El Portillo visitor centre and set off along the 4WD track that leads uphill. En route, you can make a short (half-hour, at the most), almost-level detour along a clear path to the rounded summit of **Montaña Blanca** (2750m), from where there are splendid views of Las Cañadas and the sierra beyond. Alternatively, make the Montaña Blanca your more-modest goal for the day and head back down again (about 2½ hours for the round trip). Yet another relatively gentle route is the 16km **Las Siete Cañadas** between the two visitor centres, which, depending on your pace, will take between four and five hours.

For the full ascent to La Rambleta, allow about four hours. You can always wimp

TENERIFE

out by taking the cable car up and walking back down.

CLIMBING TO THE SUMMIT

The key to climbing the summit from the top of the cable car is to plan ahead. There's a permit scheme in force that restricts the number of visitors who can climb to the summit to 150 a day. Until recently, anyone who intended to make this climb had to go in person to the national park office in Santa Cruz. Now, if you plan ahead by at least one week you can reserve your place by contacting the **Servicio de Uso Público** (☎ 922 29 01 29; fax 922 24 47 88; teide@oapn.mma.es; 4th fl, Calle Emilio Calzadilla 5, Santa Cruz; ☒ 9am-2pm Mon-Fri) either by fax or email.

If you are unable to plan this far in advance, you will have to apply in person at the Servicio de Uso Público office in Santa Cruz. Take a photocopy of your passport or ID. Permits, which are free, specify both the date and the two-hour window during which you're allowed beyond the barrier. In addition to the permit, take your passport or ID with you on the walk, as you'll probably be asked to produce it.

From the cable car it's about a one-hour walk to the summit.

Sleeping & Eating

Parador Nacional (☎ 922 37 48 41; www.parador.es; d €125; P ☒) Camping isn't allowed inside the park, but you can stay at this low-key *parador*, which unfortunately was designed with little empathy for the surrounding landscape. Once inside, however, the rooms are attractively rustic in style with earth colours, tasteful original landscapes and king-size beds. You pay slightly more for a Teide view. Avoid the adjacent cafeteria for anything more than a drink on the terrace; the food is overpriced and pedestrian.

If you're driving and want to round off your hike with a memorable dining experi-

---

LOCAL VOICES

Name? Nemesio Perez
Official title? Volcanologist
Sounds like you are in the right place!
'Yes, I was born and raised in Puerto de la Cruz with a volcano by my home. When I was a child I would visit with my family, particularly when there was snow. I also remember searching for colourful rocks to prepare the Portal de Belén (nativity scene) for Christmas.

'I knew from a young age that I wanted to work in volcano science, so studied geochemistry in Madrid and La Laguna.'

So what's the big deal about El Teide?
'That's easy on many levels. Not only is El Teide the highest peak in Spain, it's the most important active volcano in the Canary Islands. The most obvious volcanic degassing is located at the summit cone where fumaroles of about 85°C (the boiling temperature of the water at that altitude) can be found. We collect samples of these gasses on a monthly basis. In addition to these visible emanations, the summit cone of Teide volcano releases about 100 tons of carbon dioxide daily into the atmosphere.'

What impact does this have on the environment?
'Carbon dioxide is the second major component of volcanic gases, after the water vapour, and equals about 100 ton a day. This quantity is normal – we can't turn off the volcano's plumbing system! Global carbon-dioxide emissions from subaerial volcanism equals only about 2% of the global carbon-dioxide emissions, so is fairly negligible.'

What do you enjoy most about the job?
'Volcanoes provide a special beauty to the landscape and I really enjoy this characteristic of the volcanic environments, as well as meeting the people who live in active volcanic regions all over the world.'

What is the likelihood of El Teide blowing again?
'The most recent eruption occurred in the western flank of Pico Viejo in 1798. A multidisciplinary approach is used for monitoring Teide's volcanic activity. Teide is an active volcano in a dormant stage, and the probability of an eruptive phase is actually very low, so we are on top of the situation – so to speak.'

TENERIFE

ence, continue for around 25km until you reach the pretty agricultural town of Vilaflor. Just off the lovely main square, flanked by handsome buildings, seek out **Restaurante Casa Pana** (☎ 922 70 90 70; Calle Los Castaños 7; mains €4-6), run by the lovely Miryn in her grandmother's former home. Each room is painted a different colour, while outside the tables are set under pomegranate trees and grape vines, an ideal setting for a long, leisurely lunch. The white wine is made here and excellent, as is the traditional cuisine. For dessert, pop up the road for a homemade *torta de almendra* (made with almonds, eggs and fresh lemon) at **Dulcerí Vilaflor** (☎ 922 70 90 94; Calle Los Casntaños 3). If you want to stay in this delightful small town there are several *casas rurales,* including elegant **Casa El Zaguen** (☎ 680 81 60 87; Plaza Vilaflor 13; s/d €35/50) on the main square.

Getting There & Away

Surprisingly, only two public buses arrive at the park daily: the 348 bus (€4.80, one hour) from Puerto de la Cruz and the 342 (€4.70, 1½ hours) from Playa de las Américas. Both head to the park at 9.15am, arriving at the *parador,* and leave again at 4pm. That's good news for the countless tour companies that organise bus excursions, though not so encouraging for the independent traveller. The best way to visit is with your own car. There are four well-marked approaches to the park; the two prettiest are the C-824 coming from La Laguna and the C-821 from La Orotava (and Puerto de la Cruz). The C-821 is the only road that runs through the park, and the *parador,*

the cable car and the visitor centres are all off this highway, as well as several *miradores* where you can pull over and take *the* shot to impress the folks back home. To see anything else, you have to walk. The C-821 carries on to Vilaflor, while the C-823 highway links the park with Chío and Los Gigantes.

THE NORTHWEST

PUNTA DE TENO

When Plato mistook the Canary Islands for Atlantis (see p24), it must have been because of places like Punta de Teno. It's what daydreams are made of – waves crashing against a black, volcanic beach, solitary mountains rising like giants in the background, the constant whisper of lizards scurrying in the brush… This beautiful spot, the most northwestern on the island, is no secret. But it still has a wild charm that the visitors can't take away. You can fish off the point, splash along the rocky coast or just absorb the view.

Think twice about heading out here if there have been recent heavy rains, as mud and rock slides are common.

Take the highway towards Buenavista del Norte from Garachico and keep following the signs to the Punta, around 7km further on. Bus 107 (€7.20, 1½ hours) comes every two hours from 7.15am, while from Santa Cruz (€3.80, one hour) there are buses roughly every half-hour to Buenavista del Norte from 6am until 11pm, but to get out to the Punta you need your own car.

MASCA

If you arrive before about 10am, you could be tricked into thinking that you're the one who discovered this little mountain town. It wouldn't be true, of course – plenty of tourists and tour buses arrive daily – but nevertheless Masca feels like an oasis lost in the harsh landscape. The surrounding rugged and beautiful Parque Rural de Teno is popular for hiking – if you don't want to go it alone, **El Cardón** (☎ 922 12 79 38; www.elcardon.com) provides guides, setting out from Garachico, Los Silos or Buenavista del Norte on Wednesday and Saturday.

A popular but demanding trek is down Barranco de Masca to the sea. Allow six hours

TENERIFE

DETOUR

The northwest corner of Tenerife offers some spectacular unspoiled scenery. From Garachico, head west on the TF-42 highway past Buenavista del Norte and down the TF-445 to the lonely, solitary **Punta de Teno** (p173).

You'll have to return to Buenavista to catch the TF-436 mountain highway to Santiago del Teide. Curve after hairpin curve obligates you to slow down and enjoy the view. Terraced valleys appear behind rugged mountains, and **Masca** (p173) makes the perfect pit stop. When the highway reaches Santiago, you can head either north on the TF-28, towards Garachico, or south towards Los Gigantes, where signs point the way down to **Playa de la Arena** (below), a sandless beach that's nearly as pretty as Punta de Teno, though more developed.

You'll need at least a full morning to complete this route.

---

to hike there and back, or do it the smart way and catch the **Excursiones Marìtimas** (☎ 922 86 19 18) ferry to Los Gigantes (€10, 3.30pm and 4.30pm daily).

There are two 355 buses (€1.60, 30 minutes) each day to/from Santiago del Teide.

LOS GIGANTES & PUERTO DE SANTIAGO
pop 5750

These two towns have merged into one, and a worrying number of cranes can only mean more building is under way. At least the majority are low-rise apartments that look very humble indeed next to the awesome Acantilados de los Gigantes (Cliffs of the Giants) rock walls that soar up to 600m out of the ocean along the northern coast. The submerged base of these cliffs is a haven for marine life, making this one of the island's supreme diving areas.

The best views of the cliffs are from out at sea (there's no shortage of companies offering short cruises) and from Playa de los Gigantes, a tiny volcanic beach beside Los Gigantes' port that offers a breathtaking view and the excellent Restaurante Marinero Jesse (opposite). If you are looking for more sun-bed space, head to Playa de la Arena, a larger volcanic beach in Puerto de Santiago. Both resorts have a large British expatriate community, which means plenty of restaurants serving beans on toast.

The **tourist office** (☎ 922 86 03 48; Calle Manuel Ravelo 20, local 35; 9am-3.30pm Mon-Fri, to 12.30pm Sat) is on the 2nd floor of the shopping centre across from Playa de la Arena.

Activities

This is the best place on the island for diving with abundant marine life. **Los Gigantes**

Diving Centre (☎ 922 86 04 31; www.divingtenerife .co.uk; Los Gigantes Harbour; dive with equipment rental €45; 9.30am-5pm Mon-Sat), an English-owned outfit, has been diving here for more than a decade. Dive excursions are run at 10am and 2pm.

Equally popular are whale and dolphin trips. The waters between western Tenerife and La Gomera are among the world's best for spotting these amazing creatures. One reputable outfit is **Katrin** (☎ 922 86 03 32; Los Gigantes Harbour; 2hr safari €25; 11.30am-1.35pm), which conducts marine biology research and also takes groups out with special needs. **Ocean Explorer** (☎ 687 39 58 56; Los Gigantes Harbour; 1hr whale excursion €25, 1hr dolphin excursion €15; 11.30am-5.30pm) has several daily whale- and dolphin-watching trips and also offers parascending (€30 for 15 minutes) and rents jet skis (€40 for 20 minutes).

If you prefer a dip in a pool, **Piscina Oasis** (☎ 922 86 27 63; Avenida Marítima; with sun bed €4; 10am-6pm;) is a grassy area above the harbour with two pools, a bowling green, a mediocre restaurant and superb views.

Sleeping

Poblado Marinero (☎ 922 86 09 66; www.elhotelito .com; Acantilados de los Gigantes; 2-/4-/6-person apt €70/83/109) Located just above the marina in Los Gigantes, the flats here are modern with a predominance of beige and brown. Never mind, they are clean and spacious, with cool tile floors, open-plan kitchens and traditional wooden balconies.

Hotel Playa la Arena (☎ 922 86 29 20; www.spring hoteles.com; Calle Lajial 4, Playa de la Arena; s €62-86, d €84-120; P) Upscale and one of the better-value places. The vast and shiny foyer (great for roller-skating!) is impressive with its balconies and trailing plants. The 432 rooms have marble bathrooms, balconies and a warm colour scheme; there are several vast pools set among leafy palms in the gardens.

Eating

You won't be hard pressed to find a restaurant (most are by Los Gigantes Marina or along the Avenida Marítima), but there are slim pickings for truly good ones.

Bamboo (☎ 922 86 03 73; Calle Flor de Pascua 25) Head to this traditional cafeteria for a coffee and slice of gooey almond cake.

Krishna's (☎ 922 86 01 50; Calle Flor de Pascua 39) Good for Indian curries.

Restaurante Marinero Jesse (☎ 922 86 19 55; Playa de Los Gigantes; mains €10-15) Fronting the beach, Jesse specialises in paella, fresh seafood and fantastic views. There is also an impressive list of local wines. The atmosphere is casual by day and dressier in the evening, when reservations are usually necessary.

El Rincón de Juan Carlos (☎ 922 86 80 40; Pasaje de Jacaranda 2; mains €11-27; ⌚ dinner) If you're all set to splurge, this formal restaurant is just off the main plaza in Los Gigantes. Try the duck with truffles, leaving room for the deliciously posey lavender *créme brûlee* with green-apple ice cream.

Getting There & Around

Bus 473 (€3.60, 1¼ hours) comes and goes from Los Cristianos, and bus 325 (€5.50, 1¾ hours, six daily) travels from Puerto de la Cruz. For those with wheels, it's a well-marked 40km drive from Los Cristianos.

THE EAST

A modern motorway (the TF-1) cruises down Tenerife's eastern coast, linking Santa Cruz to the resorts of the south in an easy 40-minute drive. The landscape of the east is dry, dusty and sterile, speckled with bright little villages. If you're not in a hurry, get the feel of this lunarlike terrain by braving the winding TF-28 highway, formerly the principal thoroughfare, which crawls along the mountain ridge above the coast.

CANDELARIA

pop 16,000

Just 18km south of Santa Cruz is Candelaria, a busy little village where the only real claim to fame is the basilica, home to the patron saint of the entire Canary archipelago. The ornate 1950s **Basílica de Nuestra Señora de Candelaria** (☎ 922 50 01 00; ⌚ 7.30am-1pm & 3-7.30pm) sits at the edge of the town centre, overlooking a rocky beach and flanked by a plaza where nine huge statues of Guanche warriors stand guard. During the official festivities for the **Virgen de la Candelaria** celebration on 15 August (see the boxed text, p176), this plaza fills with pilgrims and party goers from all over the islands.

On the northern edge of town, two hotels and the best swimming beach in the area form Las Caletillas, which is technically a separate town, although you would never know it.

The **tourist office** (☎ 922 50 04 15; fax 922 50 26 83; Plaza CIT; ⌚ 9am-2pm & 4.30-7pm Mon-Fri) is located at the northern end of town, beside Hotel Tenerife Tour.

Sleeping & Eating

Hotel Tenerife Tour (☎ 922 50 02 00; www.tenerifetour .com; Avenida Generalísimo 170; s/d with breakfast €43/58; Ⓟ ⌨ 🏊) Right on the water, this place has a boxy exterior and the pool area is stark, but the rooms are bungalow-style and spacious with balconies. Views are either of the pool with ocean backdrop or the hotel's tropical garden.

Gran Hotel Punta del Rey (☎ 922 50 18 99; www .hoteles-catalonia.es; Avenida Generalísimo 165; s/d €54/60; ⌨ 🏊) The lobby has a dated tour-group feel with its vending machines and old-fashioned staff uniforms. On the plus side, the rooms are large and modern with parquet and marble floors; some overlook the tropical gardens complete with goldfish ponds and palms. There is also a lovely saltwater pool here designed by César Manrique.

Casa Gladys (☎ 922 50 48 36; Avenida Marítimo 33, Las Caletillas; ⌚ closed Thu) Despite the disquieting name, this restaurant on the seafront does not serve cups of tea and poached eggs on toast, but far more exotic fare. The owner is from Venezuela so that country's cuisine is tastily represented, as are spicy Mexican dishes.

Getting There & Away

If you're driving, take exit 9 of the TF-1 motorway. Buses 122, 123, 124 and 131 (€1.25, 30 minutes) connect the town with Santa Cruz.

TENERIFE

GÜÍMAR & AROUND
pop 16,000

A rural town with views of a gauzy blue ocean in the distance, Güímar's centre is well-kept and pleasant for a stroll. Most people come to see the **Pirámides de Güímar** (☎ 922 51 45 10; www.piramidesdeguimar.net; Calle Chacona; adult/under 8yr/9-12yr €10/free/5; ☼ 9.30am-6pm), featuring much-restored pyramid ruins that explores an intriguing question: could the Canarios have had contact with America before Columbus famously sailed the ocean blue? This theory was developed by renowned Norwegian scientist Thor Heyerdahl, who lived on Tenerife until his death in 2002 and based his ideas on the Mayan-like pyramids discovered in Güímar.

The roughly hourly buses 120 and 121 (€2.60, 50 minutes) from Santa Cruz stop at the Güímar bus station, a few blocks from the pyramids.

On the TF-61 highway linking Güímar with the small coastal town of Puertito is the rural hotel and restaurant **Finca Salamanca** (☎ 922 51 45 30; www.hotel-fincasalamanca.com; Carretera Güímar-Puertito; s/d with breakfast €63/102; P Ⓢ). The large, rambling main building fronted by cacti has a New Mexico feel, with the rooms set bungalow-style in the grounds. They are pleasant, if lacking imagination, with terra-cotta tiles, large bathrooms and chocolate-box paintings of Spanish *pueblos* (villages). The restaurant (mains €10) is more elegant with its glassed-in terrace overlooking the lovely gardens, complete with old-fashioned well, plenty of seating and a magnificent rubber tree.

About 12km further south is El Escobonal and the **Archeological & Ethnographi-** cal Museum of Agache (☎ 922 53 04 95; Plaza El Escobonal; ☼ 5-8pm Mon-Fri), displaying all kinds of odds and ends related to Guanche and island culture. Continue on to Fasnia and the tiny **Ermita de la Virgin de los Dolores**, a chapel perched on a hill at the edge of town (off the TF-620 highway). It's usually closed, but is worth the short drive up for the panoramic views of the harsh, dry landscape.

Keep on the TF-620 past the *ermita* to reach **Roques de Fasnia**, a little town carved into the volcanic cliff. There's a tranquil black-sand beach that's rarely crowded. A bit further south is **Porís de Abona**, a charming little fishing village albeit surrounded by new housing. There's an attractive cove here, complete with fishing boats and sandy beach where you can take a dip. German-owned **Café al Mar** (☎ 626 39 00 96) enjoys prime position and is good for pitta bread sandwiches and the like. The owner, Juliane, also has apartments to rent.

EL MÉDANO

Not yet squashed by steamroller development, El Médano is a world-class spot for windsurfers and kite boarders. The laid-back atmosphere they bring with them gives the place a dab of bohemian character. The resort boasts the longest beach in Tenerife (2km), lined by a wooden boardwalk – ideal for evening strolls.

Information

Cyber Corner (☎ 922 17 83 59; Paseo Nuestra Señora Mercedes de Roja 26, local 2; per hr €2; ☼ 10am-2.30pm & 5-11pm) Connect to the internet at this spacious place right off the beach.

THE VIRGIN OF CANDELARIA

In 1392, a century before Tenerife was conquered, a statue of the Virgin Mary holding a *candela* (candlestick) washed up on the shore near modern-day Candelaria. The Guanche shepherds who found the statue took it to their king and, according to legend, the people worshipped it. When the Spanish conquered the island a century later, they deemed the statue miraculous, and in 1526 Commander Pedro Fernández de Lugo ordered a sanctuary be built. The logical explanation of the 'miracle' is that the statue was either the figurehead from a wrecked ship, or a Virgin brought by French or Portuguese sailors, who had been on the island before the Spanish conquest. In either case, the statue was swept away by a violent storm in 1826 and never found. The ornate statue that is today swathed in robes in the Basílica de Nuestra Señora de Candelaria was carved soon after by local artist Fernando Estévenez. On 15 August, the day she was supposedly found by the Guanches, the Virgin is honoured by processions, numerous masses and a kitschy re-enactment of costumed 'Guanches' worshipping her.

TENERIFE

GRANDILLA PORT CONTROVERSY

Santa Cruz de Tenerife's current double-whammy position as the island's major port and capital may soon be toppled by a controversial new port project in Grandilla in the southeast of the island. Upon completion, this is predicted to be the fifth largest port in Spain, comprising a 2.5km-long, 55m-deep breakwater, a 26-hectare area for containers, a 200-sq-metre area for general merchandise and a commercial port area of 19.5 hectares.

Despite protests from Greenpeace and local environmental agency **Ben Magec** (www.benmagec .org in Spanish), the Commission of the EU granted approval for the controversial project in late 2006 after four years of debate. Paraphrasing European commissioner Stavros Dimas, he explained that because Tenerife is a small island, it is highly dependent on an efficient maritime transport system. He added that the main Santa Cruz port is no longer able to cope with the increasingly heavy workload of containers, thus the construction of the industrial port of Grandilla is essential to guarantee the economic security of the island in the future.

The flip side of this comes from the environmentalists who cite that the project will destroy 5km of coastline and negatively impact the island's emblematic beaches of El Médano and La Tejita. The new port is also predicted to severely impact the biodiversity on the island, the natural flora and fauna, as well as local fishing and archaeological remains. According to Ben Magec, the current port is of a sufficient size to serve the island and is already integrated into the city's infrastructure. In its view, the intent of the politicians is to transform Santa Cruz into a leisure port for cruise liners.

Tourist office (☎ 922 17 60 02; www.granadilla.com; Plaza los Príncipes de España; ☻ 9am-3pm Mon-Fri, to noon Sat)

Activities

The sails of windsurfers and kite boarders speckle the horizon here. There are several companies that offer classes and equipment rental, but novices note that the winds are very strong and challenge even the pros. You can rent windsurf equipment or sign up for courses at the **Surf Center Playa Sur** (☎ 922 17 66 88; www.surfcenter.info; 12hr rental €60; ☻ 10.30am-7pm), just beyond Hotel Playa Sur Tenerife.

Another option for kite boarding is the **Azul Kite School** (☎ 922 17 83 14; www.azulkiteboarding .com; Paseo Mercedes de la Roja 26; 3hr course from €90; ☻ 11am-1pm & 4-7pm Tue-Sat, 11am-8pm Tue-Sat in summer).

Sleeping

Senderos de Abono (☎ 922 77 02 00; Calle Peatonal de la Iglesia 5; s/d with breakfast €40/60; ☒ ☒) This rural hotel and restaurant (mains €8) is just across from the lovely stone church in Granadilla de Abona, a genuine working town. A converted post office, its rooms are in a series of old stone buildings with tiny courtyards, foliage-filled gardens and bucketfuls of charm.

Hotel Playa Sur Tenerife (☎ 922 17 61 20; www.hotel playasurtenerife.com; Playa El Médano; s/d €70/110;

(P ☒) The slightly less central of the two beach-side hotels here. The rooms are large with pale wooden furniture, small balconies and great ocean views. You can book sporting activities through the hotel.

Eating

Timón (☎ 666 27 90 50; Calle Marcial García s/n; tapas €2) If you're lucky you may be able to grab one of just two outside tables on a weeny terrace above the thundering surf. You don't have to push the boat out to sample the delicious seafood tapas here.

Café M (☎ 699 94 73 94; Paseo Mercedes de Roja 14; mains €4-8) A cheery, German-run restaurant with healthy salads, pasta and wraps, plus a terrace overlooking the surfers.

There are several good restaurants on the pedestrian thoroughfare that runs through El Médano's town centre. Try **El Astillero** (☎ 922 17 82 20; Paseo Marcial García 2; mains €6-10), which specialises in seafood, including a tasty mussel soup, and has a pretty dining room with beach views. Afterwards, head down the street for homemade ice cream at the **Heladería Picacho** (Paseo el Picacho 2).

Getting There & Away

El Médano is just east of the Tenerife Sur airport, off exit 22 of the TF-1. Bus 470 (€2.80, one hour 35 minutes) leaves hourly from Los Cristianos, and 116 (€5.70, one

TENERIFE

hour 10 minutes) leaves every two hours from Santa Cruz.

THE SOUTH

LOS CRISTIANOS, PLAYA DE LAS AMÉRICAS & COSTA ADEJE
pop around 150,000

Don't forget to wear your shades when you first hit Tenerife's southwestern tip. You'll need them, not just against the blinding sunshine, but also the accompanying dazzle of neon signs, shimmering white sand and lobster-pink northern Europeans. Large multipool resorts with all-you-can-eat buffets have turned what was a sleepy fishing coast into a mega-moneymaking resort. The beaches are admittedly fabulous: sweeping and desert-white, thanks to sand imported from the Sahara.

The nightlife is for those with high energy and high spirits and there is a predictably dizzying array of restaurants. Where else can you eat in an 'authentic Mexican Cantina' for lunch, a 'real Parisian café' for dinner and have a drink in a blarney-themed Irish pub afterwards? Of course, all that variety leaves little room for Spanish culture to shine through. To see the true Spain, head inland or use Los Cristianos' commercial port to hop over to one of the small western islands. Here in the south, golden tans and golden beaches reign.

Orientation
Although they are three different resort areas, Los Cristianos, Playa de las Américas and Costa Adeje are often lumped together and referred to as one. Furthest south is Los Cristianos, where the maze of a town centre still retains – barely – the feel of a fishing village. Just beyond is Playa de las Américas. Technically, both are in the same municipality of Arona, but Playa de las Américas has evolved into an altogether flashier place, with high-rise hotels, glossy shopping centres and Las Vegas–style fake Roman statues and pyramids. The Costa Adeje flows seamlessly from the northern border of Playa de las Américas and is home to luxurious hotels and some of the better beaches. It's quieter and has the best reputation of the bunch, though, like the rest of the coast

here, it is one long commercial strip aimed at tourists.

The free tourist-office map is helpful, but if you're confused, do what the locals do – orientate yourself by the hotels and large buildings.

Information

BOOKSHOPS
Bookswop (Edificio Cristianos 1, local 8, Los Cristianos) The place to exchange or pick up a secondhand book in English.
Librería Barbara (Calle Pablo Abril 5, Los Cristianos) English, German and French titles, plus maps and guidebooks.

EMERGENCY
Police station Los Cristianos (☎ 922 75 71 33; Calle Valle Menéndez 5); Playa de las Américas (☎ 922 78 80 22; Avenida Noelia Alfonso Cabrera 5); Costa Adeje (☎ 922 79 78 11; Sector Las Terrazas) The Costa Adeje station is beside the Palacio de Congresos.

INTERNET ACCESS
Communication Direct (Edificio Don Antonio, Calle General Franco 44, Los Cristianos; per hr €1.80; ☾ 9.30am-10pm)
Mundosnet (☎ 922 79 40 89; Avenida Juan Carlos 1, Los Cristianos; per hr €2; ☾ 10am-9pm, closed Sun)

LAUNDRY
Washing a load costs about €6, more if you also want your clothes dried.
Washtub Laundry (☎ 922 79 44 90; Edificio Altemar, Avenida Noelia Alfonso Cabrera, Playa de las Américas) Bring in laundry by 1pm to get it back the same day.
Whirly Wash (☎ 922 79 02 99; Edificio Los Cristianos, Avenida Habana, Los Cristianos) Free pick up and delivery.

LIBRARIES
Public library (☎ 922 75 70 06; Centro Cultural, Plaza Pescador 1, Los Cristianos; ☾ 9am-2pm & 4-6pm Mon-Fri, 10am-12.30pm Sat) Great resource for island-related material and some foreign-language titles.

MEDICAL SERVICES
Hospital Costa Adeje (☎ 922 79 10 00; Urbanización San Eugenio, Costa Adeje)
Hospital Las Américas (☎ 922 79 24 00; Avenida Arquitecto Gómez Cuesta, Playa de las Américas)
Le Ro (☎ 922 75 02 89; Edificio Mar y Sol, Calle Amsterdam 8, Los Cristianos) Caters to people with disabilities and has wheelchair rentals. Provides specialised medical attention.
Orange Badge (☎ 922 79 73 55; www.orangebadge .com; Cristian Sur Apartments, Avenida Amsterdam 9, Los

TENERIFE

LOS CRISTIANOS, PLAYA DE LAS AMÉRICAS & COSTA ADEJE

0 —— 500 m
0 —— 0.3 miles

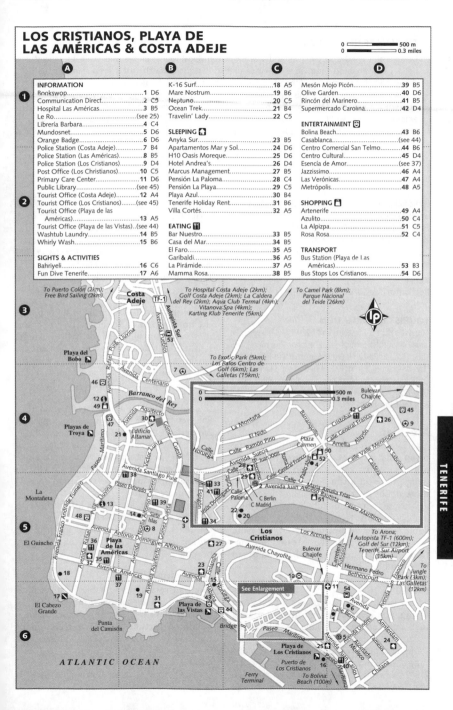

ATLANTIC OCEAN

TENERIFE

TIMESHARE UNCOVERED

Despite all the adverse publicity and warnings from local tourist offices, timeshare touts in this holiday-heaven resort continue to convince tourists that their scratch card is the one in a hundred/thousand/million winner! And the prize (usually a bottle of cheap champagne) can, of course, only be collected in person from the resort. If you go (don't!), be prepared to spend a minimum of three hours at the resort and be subjected to some of the most aggressive high-pressure sales methods employed in the world. Many people are simply unable to resist. If you do go to a presentation, don't take your chequebook, credit cards or any cash with you. Also be wary of the latest discount holiday-club scam. The promise is that, once you have made an initial payment, you will benefit from discounted accommodation, airline tickets, car rentals and cruises. In fact, this product is even worse than timeshare and that first payment will bring you nothing in return, except grief.

Cristianos) Caters to people with disabilities and offers wheelchair rentals.

Primary Care Center (Centro de Salud Los Cristianos; ☎ 922 78 78 47; Valdés Center, Avenida Juan Carlos I, Los Cristianos)

POST

Post office (Paseo Valero, Los Cristianos)

TOURIST INFORMATION

Tourist office Los Cristianos (☎ 922 75 71 37; www .arona.org; Centro Cultural, Plaza Pescador 1); Playa de las Vistas (☎ 922 78 70 11; Centro Comercial San Telmo); Playa de las Américas (☎ 922 79 76 68; Centro Comercial City Center, Avenida Rafael Puig Lluvina); Costa Adeje (☎ 922 75 06 33; Avenida Litoral) The Costa Adeje office is by the Barranco del Rey.

Activities

The 2800 average hours of yearly sunshine means that beaches are the star turn here, but if you just can't take another day of lying prone on a sun bed, there are other, more mildly energetic options.

Most activity firms rely heavily on their 'public relations' agents to bring in tourists. Some are quite helpful; others can be a pain. That said, there is plenty of ready information and the tourist offices have umpteen flyers and brochures.

DIVING

The volcanic coast here makes for excellent diving, and calm waters means that even a first-timer can have a thrilling 'try-dive' in the ocean. A standard dive runs upwards of €35, though the per-dive rate drops if you're planning several days of diving. **Ocean Trek** (☎ 922 75 34 72; www.tenerife-diving.com; Avenida Rafael Lluvina, Playa de las Américas; ☺ 9am-9pm), just beside

Hotel Tenerife Sol, offers the standard array of boat dives, courses and speciality night dives and wreck dives. Also recommended is **Fun Dive Tenerife** (☎ 922 75 27 08; www.fun-dive-tenerife .com; Hotel Park Club Europe, Playa de las Américas; ☺ 9am-6pm), with diving classes for children as well as PADI-regulated night diving trips.

SAILING & SURFING

You won't have to sail far from shore before the hotel jungle of Tenerife's largest resort melts into the gentle slopes of the island. Rent a boat, take an excursion or sign up for a whale-watching trip (opposite) and cruise the waters between Tenerife and La Gomera with the shadow of El Teide behind you. The tourist office in Los Cristianos has a list of companies that organise all kinds of boat trips, including **Bahriyeli** (☎ 922 75 15 76; www.mardeons-tenerife.com; Puerto de los Cristianos; 3hr trip adult/under 12yr €33/16.50).

If money is unlimited, **Free Bird Sailing** (☎ 922 71 57 80; www.freebirdsailing.com; Puerto Colón, Costa Adeje; ☺ 9am-7pm) can set you up with a luxurious catamaran, including crew and food, for several hundred euros.

On a more modest scale, **K-16 Surf** (☎ 922 79 84 80; www.k16surf.com; Calle México 1-2; rental per day €24) rents out fibre surfboards and provides tuition for only slightly more than the price of rental.

HORSERIDING

There are several riding stables in the vicinity, including **La Caldera del Rey** (☎ 606 08 64 67; San Eugenio Alto, Costa Adeja; 2hr trek €50), which also has a children's petting farm, BBQ area, climbing wall and a low rope course for children.

GOLF

Constant mild weather means that Tenerife is a place where golfers can play year-round.

It's not the most ecologically sound activity on the island (water is a constant problem, and golf courses need plenty of it) but that hasn't stopped sprawling courses from emerging all around Playa de las Américas. Some of the best courses are **Golf Costa Adeje** (☎ 922 71 00 00; www.golfcostaadeje.com; Finca Los Olivos; 18 holes €55-85; ☒ 7.30am-7pm), **Golf del Sur** (☎ 922 73 81 70; www.golfdelsur.net; Urbanizacíon Golf del Sur, San Miguel de Abona; 18 holes €60-84; ☒ 7.30am-7pm) and **Los Palos Centro de Golf** (☎ 922 16 90 80; www.golflospalos .com; Carretera Guaza-Las Galletas, Km7, Arona; 9 holes €19-24; ☒ 7am-7pm).

WHALE WATCHING
Companies offering two-, three- and five-hour boat cruises to check out whales and dolphins are set up at the end of Playa de Los Cristianos, near the port, and in Puerto Colón in Costa Adeje. Most trips include food, drink and a quick swim. Though all are basically the same, with a two-hour trip costing upwards of €15, we recommend two smaller Playa de Los Cristianos–based companies, **Neptuno** (☎ 922 79 80 44; ☒ 9am-7pm) and **Travelin' Lady** (☎ 609 42 98 87; under 10yr free; ☒ 9.30am-8pm Sun-Fri, noon-3pm Sat). Both offer personal service, small boats, and lower prices than many other outfits in the area.

FISHING
Deep-sea-fishing jaunts range from about €36 for a three-hour trip to €70 for a day on the water. Get information from the kiosks set up at the western end of Playa de Los Cristianos or from a tourist office.

Los Cristianos & Playa de las Américas for Children
There is plenty going on for children of all ages here. Along the beaches, carnival-like attractions such as bumper cars and mini bungee jumping are popular with older kids, while playgrounds on Playa de Los Cristianos and behind the Centro Comercial in Los Cristianos can keep the little ones entertained.

Away from the beaches, theme parks include **Jungle Park** (☎ 922 72 90 10; www.aguilasjungle park.com; Los Cristianos-Arona, km3; adult/under 12yr €22/15.50; ☒ 10am-5.30pm), where the main show stars eagles that swoop dramatically over the crowd. You can also see hippos, crocodiles and other wild beasts here.

For older children, **Karting Klub Tenerife** (☎ 922 73 07 03; Carretera del Cho, Arona; adult/10-

18yr €12/6; ☒ 10am-8pm) offers go-karts and video games.

All parks have free bus services. If you want a break from the children, baby-sitting services can often be found through hotel receptions.

Sleeping
This is one of those rare hotel jungles where you may have to swallow hard and check out one of the high-profile tour operators, which often have amazing deals. Some of the most reputable agencies are Thomas Cook-JMC, Thompson, My Travel, First Choice and Cosmos. If you decide to stake out on your own accommodation anyway, try apartment agencies first. A pleasant flat for two, with kitchen, TV and living area, starts at around €300 a week (generally the minimum booking period). Contact the tourist office for a full listing of agencies, or start with **Anyka Sur** (☎ 922 79 13 77; www.anykasur.com; Edificio Azahara, Avenida Habana, Los Cristianos), **Marcus Management** (☎ 922 75 10 64; www.tenerife-apts.com; Apartamentos Portosin, Avenida Penetracíon, Los Cristianos) or **Tenerife Holiday Rent** (☎ 922 79 02 11; fax 922 79 58 18; Edificio Tenerife Garden, local 4, Playa de las Américas).

BUDGET
If you're hunting for a *hostal* or *pensión*, Los Cristianos is your only bet, although the package deals mentioned previously may work out to be even cheaper. Expect a decent room for two to cost around €30 a night, and book ahead if possible, as the limited number of *pensiones* means they're often full.

Pensión La Playa (☎ 922 79 22 64; Calle Paloma 9, Los Cristianos; d/tr €26/32) The dormitory-style rooms face a lively pedestrian side street, so earplugs are advisable. A warning: La Playa is not for those with wide girths (or fat suitcases), as stairwells are painfully thin. The communal bathrooms are swing-a-cat small as well.

Pensión La Paloma (☎ 922 79 01 98; Calle Paloma 7, Los Cristianos; s/d/tr €20/26/32) Just across the street from La Playa, rooms here don't exactly sparkle but they have private bathrooms and more charm than others in this price bracket. The same family runs the popular restaurant downstairs.

MIDRANGE
Hotel Andrea's (☎ 922 79 00 12/24; www.hotelesreveron .com; Calle General Franco 23, Los Cristianos; s/d €35/53) A small but neat hotel with large, if rather bleakly furnished, rooms and small glassed-in

TENERIFE

terraces. There's a comfy communal sitting room with TV and soft drinks. If you want something stronger, head downstairs to the bar and pizzeria.

H10 Oasis Moreque (☎ 922 79 03 66; www.h10.es; Avenida Juan Carlos I 28, Los Cristianos; s €45-63.50, d €60-97; ⊠) One of the few hotels in Los Cristianos that's actually on the beach; look for the baby-blue exterior. Unfortunately, the interior décor is similarly unsubtle, but rooms have wide balconies, with more than half looking out to the ocean. The ceiling fans are a boon and the small pool area has pleasant gardens.

Playa Azul (☎ 922 79 19 19; reserves@playazul .e.telefonica.net; Edificio Playazul, Avenida Aquitecto Gómez Cuesta, Playa de las Américas; 2-/3-/5-person apt €58/65/86; P ⊠) Comfortable apartments with a formula feel, situated agreeably near the Playas de Troya stretch of sand and close to more-relaxed Costa Adeje. The private parking is a major plus.

Apartamentos Mar y Sol (☎ 922 75 05 40; fax 922 79 54 73; Avenida Amsterdam 8, Los Cristianos; studio/1-bedroom apt €77/98; ⊠ ♿) These spacious apartments are modern, if bland, with a hospital look to the corridors. But they are fully equipped for guests in wheelchairs and the terraces overlook the central pools (one is therapeutic). There are various organised activities, including diving courses with a professional instructor.

TOP END

Villa Cortés (our pick) (☎ 922 75 77 00; www.europe-hotels .org; Avenida Rafael Puig Lluvina s/n, Playa de las Américas; s/d/ste with breakfast €240/300/450; P ✷ 🖥 ⊠ ♿) Designed in the style of an ultraluxurious Mexican hacienda, this new kid on the block is truly sumptuous, with an exciting and dynamic colour scheme and décor. There are lots of hot yellows, oranges and blues, plus murals, exquisite original artwork and the occasional quirky touch – like the family of giant ceramic frogs just off the lobby and the mini Aztec temple outside. The gardens have streams with goldfish and a pool with cascading waterfall; the rooms are predictably stunning.

Eating

You won't go hungry here. The dilemma is more likely to be choosing where to go for the best quality and good value. Avoid restaurants that advertise their international cuisine with sun-bleached posters on the pavement. Otherwise, choices range from €5 Chinese buffets to dress-for-dinner shows. There are hidden corners where you'll find Spanish and Canarian food. Mains are around €10.

BUDGET

Supermercado Carolina (☎ 922 79 30 69; Calle General Franco 8, Los Cristianos) One of the better supermarkets around, particularly for imported goodies, although it's not cheap.

Bar Nuestro (☎ 670 47 97 08; Calle San Roque 12, Los Cristianos) A cloth-cap-authentic local bar, Bar Nuestro has a barnlike interior and an unwaveringly authentic Canarian menu that includes dishes like garbanzos with pork sausages and grilled sardines.

MIDRANGE

Mamma Rosa (☎ 922 79 48 19; Apto Colón 11, Playa Américas; mains €6-15) This place serves hearty Mexican and Italian dishes, including *fajitas de pollo* (soft Mexican tortillas stuffed with chicken) and tagliatelle with king prawns, broccoli, garlic and chilli. The portions will keep rumbling tummies at bay for hours.

Rincón del Marinero (☎ 922 79 35 53; Muelle Los Cristianos; mains €9-13) Specialising in local seafood, including a tasty *zarzuela* (fish and seafood stew), this nautical-themed restaurant has all its tables under a covered terrace (proof that there's never bad weather here).

Mesón Mojo Picón (☎ 922 75 02 73; Residencial Las Viñas, Playa de las Américas; mains €9-14) This place has an attractive patio and features Spanish specialities from all over the mainland, including Andalucian gazpacho, Catalan bread with crushed tomatoes and garlic, and Iberian cured sausages.

Garibaldi (☎ 922 75 70 60; Avenida Rafael Puig Lluvina, Playa de las Américas; mains €9-18) This recently revamped Italian restaurant has an air of gentility and serves its meats and pastas on a romantic patio surrounding a fountain.

La Pirámide (☎ 922 79 63 60; Avenida Américas, Playa de las Américas; mains €9-20) The dinner theatre at the restaurant inside a pyramid-shaped congress hall is more sophisticated than it sounds. There are opera nights on Tuesday, Friday and Saturday, and classical concerts at other times. Check first in case the schedules change.

Olive Garden (☎ El Carmen 5, Los Cristianos; mains €10-12; Ⓥ) English-run, with outside tables on the promenade, the copious menu includes plenty of vegetarian choices such as vegetable kebabs and meatless goulash and chilli. Carnivorous folk may prefer the daily roast beef and Yorkshire pud.

Casa del Mar (☎ 922 79 32 75; Esplanada del Muelle, Los Cristianos; mains €10-15) Enjoy views of the beach as you savour the freshly caught *lubina* (sea bass), *dorada* (sea bream) and *merluza* (hake). On the roof is a sunny terrace bar selling drinks and ice cream.

El Faro (☎ 922 75 08 12; Avenida Américas, Parque Santiago V, Playa de las Américas; mains €10-17) For a swanky night out, El Faro fits the bill. Watch the world go by from the 2nd-storey terrace as you savour the imaginatively prepared meat, fish and pasta dishes.

Entertainment

Post-midnight, Los Cristianos' action takes place at the Centro Comercial San Telmo, the shopping centre behind Playa de las Vistas when this daytime-dull little strip is transformed into a string of nightclubs pumping out music late into the night. In Las Américas, places are altogether classier and more costly.

Centro Cultural (☎ 922 75 70 06; Plaza Pescador 1, Los Cristianos; tickets €3) Offers a variety of cultural events, such as Cine de Verano, a summer festival of open-air movies (in Spanish) offered nightly except Wednesday. A brand new auditorium opened its doors here in early 2007 as a big-name concert venue.

Esencia de Amor (☎ 922 75 75 49; La Pirámide, Avenida Américas, Playa de las Américas) Spanish ballet and flamenco concerts are generally top billing.

Jazzissimo (☎ 922 78 82 75; www.jazzissimo-tenerife .com; Rafael Puig Lluvina 12, Las Américas; ☺ 10pm-3.30am Mon-Sat) A jazz and soul club opened by Cleo Laine and Johnny Dankworth a few years back and which has been going strong ever since. Every Saturday is salsa night with a live Cuban band.

Bolina Beach (☎ 922 79 06 99; San Telmo Beach, Los Cristianos; ☺ noon-2am) This is a fashionable bar and club overlooking the sweeping sand with a chilled-out atmosphere and nightly live music.

Casablanca (Centro Comercial San Telmo, local 17, Los Cristianos; ☺ 11pm-late) The most famous club in this pulsating strip heaves with gyrating bodies post-midnight.

Metropolis (☎ 922 75 30 00; Hotel Conquistador, Paseo Marítimo s/n, Playa de las Américas; ☺ 10pm-6am) Improve your moves on the dance floor at this megadisco with a seafront terrace. It's considered the best dance spot in town and gets the thumbs up from readers.

Las Verónicas (Paseo Marítimo s/n) On Playa de las Américas' border with Costa Adeje, Las Verónicas has a buoyant and youthful nightlife. There have been problems with violence and drugs here as well, although these are reputedly lessening after the closure of several of the seedier, drug-peddling places.

Shopping

Modern shopping centres are mushrooming throughout the resort, but for traditional Canary textiles, such as embroidered tablecloths, head to **Azulito** (cnr Calle General Franco & Calle Pablo Abril, Los Cristianos) or one of the **Artenerife** (☎ 902 32 04 20; Avenida Rafael Puig Lluvina) kiosks. **La Alpizpa** (☎ 922 79 87 55) on the seafront sells arts and crafts made by the handicapped, with the money going to charity.

Getting There & Away

AIR

Hopping over to Playa de las Américas is easy from mainland Europe. The Tenerife Sur airport is just 30km away and daily flights from Spain, the UK, Germany and other destinations give you plenty of flying options (see p148 for details).

BOAT

Ferries come in and out of the Los Cristianos port day and night. The main routes are to Santa Cruz de la Palma, La Palma (€34, three hours); Puerto de la Estaca, El Hierro (€49, two hours) and San Sebastián de la Gomera, La Gomera (€23, one hour by ferry, 40 minutes by hydrofoil), with several daily crossings to each destination, increasing during summer.

BUS

Plenty of Tenerife's bright-green TITSA buses come through the area, stopping at stations in Los Cristianos and Playa de las Américas. Buses 110 (direct, €7.30, one hour, every 30 minutes) and 111 (indirect) come and go from Santa Cruz. Bus 487 (€2.10, 45 minutes) goes to Tenerife Sur airport, but to get to Tenerife Norte airport you have to pass through Santa Cruz. Plenty of other buses run through the two resorts, en route to destinations such as Arona (bus 480), Los Gigantes (473), Puerto de la Cruz (343), El Médano (470) and Las Galletas (467). The Playa de las Américas bus station is situated between central Las Américas, San Eugenio and the *autovía*. There's no Los Cristianos

TENERIFE

bus station, as such; the buses stop on Avenida Juan Carlos 1, just beyond the cross road with Avenida Amsterdam, opposite the Valdes Commercial Centre. For 24-hour bus information, call ☎ 922 53 13 00.

Getting Around

Most of the long-distance bus routes do double duty as local routes, stopping along the major avenues of Los Cristianos and Playa de las Américas before heading out of town.

There are taxi stands outside most shopping centres. Getting a taxi at night usually isn't a problem, as most people choose to walk. A ride across town should cost between €5 and €7.

AROUND LOS CRISTIANOS, PLAYA DE LAS AMÉRICAS & COSTA ADEJE
Exotic Parks

What strikes your fancy? Birds? Cacti? Camels? They're all here, most of them just a hop, skip and a free bus ride away.

In Guaza, the **Exotic Park** (☎ 922 79 54 24; Autopista del Sur exit 26; adult/6-14 yr €10/5; ☯ 10am-7pm) offers a chance to do things you never knew you wanted to do, like go inside a bat cave and see a 'reptilarium' up close. There are also monkeys, exotic plants, birds and supposedly the world's largest cactus collection.

At the calmer end of the spectrum is the **Camel Park** (☎ 922 72 11 21; La Camella; adult/under 12yr €10/5; ☯ 10am-5pm), a camel-breeding and riding centre with a few traditional farm animals.

Las Galletas

If Playa de las Américas is a large pizza with all the toppings, Las Galletas is a small pizza crust with a sprinkling of cheese and no spices at all. It's a drab place that seems to have done very little (good or bad) to attract the thousands of tourists who land every day just a few miles away. The volcanic beach is rocky and the colour of pencil lead, although dozens of tiny fishing boats lie belly-up on the sand, proof that the town is still just a fishing village at heart – just not a very picturesque one.

INFORMATION
La Vava Pipi (☎ 922 73 35 92; Calle Carmen García 1; per hr €2) Internet access down the road from the tourist office.
Tourist office (☎ 922 73 01 33; La Rambla; ☯ 9am-3.30pm Mon-Fri) At the western end of La Rambla, the tree-lined walkway that runs parallel to the Paseo Marítimo.

SIGHTS & ACTIVITIES

Wind and water have carved the dramatic rock formations of **Montaña Amarilla** (Yellow Mountain), a volcanic mound on the coast outside town. To get here, take Avenida José Antonio Tavio (beside the Ten Bel complex) down to Calle Chasna. At the end of the street is a small car park and a path leading you down to the water. You can ramble across the rocks, enjoying a building-free view of the coast, or hike around the *montaña*.

Although the actual town is dreary, Las Galletas, together with Los Cristianos and Los Gigantes, is considered one of the best diving spots in the south. For courses, try-dives and excursions, head to **Buceo Tenerife Diving Center** (☎ 922 73 10 15; www.buceotenerife.com; Calle María del Carmen García 22; dive with equipment rental €35; ☯ 9am-6pm). There are reduced costs for making multiple dives. Dives are at 9am and noon, with an extra 3pm dive on Saturday.

Rent sailboats and windsurfers, or take classes, at the **Escuela de Vela las Galletas** (☎ 629 87 81 02; Playa Las Galletas; windsurfer rental per hour €15, catamaran rental per hour €30; ☯ 10am-6pm Tue-Sun).

SLEEPING

There are a few accommodation options if you are dead set on staying.

Camping Nauta (☎ 922 78 51 18; Carretera 6225, Cañada Blanca; camp sites per adult/tent €4/4; ☒). This is one of the only camp sites on Tenerife. Nauta has two swimming pools and tennis courts as well as hook-ups for caravans.

Ten Bel (☎ 922 73 07 21; www.tenbel.com; Urbanizacíon Tenbel; 2-/3-person apt €58/70; ☒) The most appealing accommodation in town. This 'holiday village' is a complex of four separate apartment buildings with private coast access (it's on a big cliff beside the water, but you can swim in the coves) and several pools. Apartments vary widely but in general they're simple and clean, if low on originality or charm.

EATING

There are a few traditional bars in the centre of town, which are good for tapas. Alternatively, head for the waterfront, where there are several restaurants with terraces.

Bar La Caleta (☎ 627 52 49 06; Calle Dionisio González s/n) A crusty, old-fashioned place that has delicious, typically Andalucian tapas, including fried peppers and *tortilla* (potato omelette).

Via Moana (☎ 922 73 25 40; Playa de las Galletas; mains €10-18; ☯ noon-3am summer only; ☒) Get away from the crowds at this laid-back café and restaurant that's right on the water. On summer nights live music or a DJ turns the place into the town's main nightspot, with an eclectic mix of jazz, folk, Celtic and rock music.

GETTING THERE & AWAY
Las Galletas is a few kilometres off the TF-1, exit 26. Buses 467, 470 and 473 (€6.90, 30 minutes) connect the town hourly with Los Cristianos, while buses 112 and 115 (€6.60, 1¼ hours) come and go from Santa Cruz.

TENERIFE

La Gomera

From the air, La Gomera is an impenetrable fortress ringed with soaring rock walls. Noodle-thin roads wiggle and squirm their way alongside cliff faces and up ravines, and the tiny white specks that represent houses seem impossibly placed on inaccessible crags.

Once on the ground, however, that rough landscape translates into lush valleys, awe-inspiring cliffs and stoic rock formations sculpted by ancient volcanic activity and erosion. Those white specks reveal themselves to be charming white-walled villages. And the impenetrable rock walls are actually interrupted occasionally by small coves and pristine beaches.

A paradise of natural beauty, this small round island (dubbed Isla Columbina, or Columbus Island, because of its ties to the explorer) is not the sort of place that offers golden beaches or wild tropical nightlife. It is inlaid with trails, and taking the time to explore them is, for many people, the most enjoyable aspect of a visit to the island.

While many visitors just make a day trip from Tenerife or another island, La Gomera really can't be grasped in a single day. The unforgiving relief of this tiny island means that, while it's only 25km across at its widest, any journey across it entails endless twists and turns on the narrow highways. Truly, there's no getting anywhere as the crow flies.

Agriculture and tourism vie for top spot as the motor behind the local economy. Bananas, vines, potatoes and corn are all cultivated on the steep slopes of the ravines, although increasingly farmers are turning to the hotel, restaurant or guide businesses.

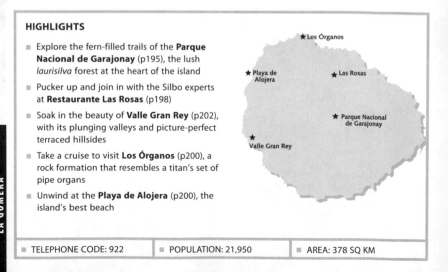

HIGHLIGHTS

- Explore the fern-filled trails of the **Parque Nacional de Garajonay** (p195), the lush *laurisilva* forest at the heart of the island
- Pucker up and join in with the Silbo experts at **Restaurante Las Rosas** (p198)
- Soak in the beauty of **Valle Gran Rey** (p202), with its plunging valleys and picture-perfect terraced hillsides
- Take a cruise to visit **Los Órganos** (p200), a rock formation that resembles a titan's set of pipe organs
- Unwind at the **Playa de Alojera** (p200), the island's best beach

★ Los Órganos

★ Playa de Alojera

★ Las Rosas

★ Parque Nacional de Garajonay

★ Valle Gran Rey

■ TELEPHONE CODE: 922	■ POPULATION: 21,950	■ AREA: 378 SQ KM

LA GOMERA

HISTORY

Throughout the 15th century the Spaniards tried unsuccessfully to conquer La Gomera. When they finally managed to establish a presence on the island in the middle of the century, it was due to a slow and fairly peaceful infiltration of Christianity and European culture rather than the result of a battle. Early on, the original inhabitants were permitted to keep much of their culture and self-rule, but that changed when the brutal Hernán Peraza the younger (see the boxed text, p193) became governor. The Gomeros rebelled against him, unleashing a blood bath that killed hundreds of islanders.

After the activity of those first years, and the excitement that accompanied Christopher Columbus' stopovers on the island, there followed a long period of isolation. La Gomera was totally self-sufficient and had little contact with the outside world until the 1950s, when a small pier was built in San Sebastián, opening the way for ferry travel and trade.

Even so, it was difficult to eke out a living by farming on the island's steep slopes, and much of the population emigrated to Tenerife or South America.

INFORMATION
Books & Maps

The 1:40,000 *La Gomera Tour and Trail* is a fairly good walking map with 70 routes described briefly in English. Offering slightly more detail, *La Gomera Walking Map by*

Goldsstadt also describes hikes. Other good maps include the 1:35,000 *La Gomera – Ile de Gomera*, published by Freytag & Berndt, and the 1:50,000 *La Gomera* by Distrimaps Telestar. These maps are available in bookshops. The tourist office also gives out several decent free maps of the island.

Helpful hiking guides include *Rother Walking Guide Gomera*, published by Freytag & Berndt, and *Walk La Gomera*, published by Discovery Walking Guides.

ACCOMMODATION

The island has, so far, kept grand-scale tourism at bay, and most lodging is in small rural hotels, family-run *pensiones* (guesthouses), refurbished farmhouses and apartments. By far the most appealing and authentically Gomeran places to stay are the *casas rurales* (rural houses), many of which were abandoned by emigrants and have since been refurbished for tourists. For information and to book, contact **Ecotural** (☎ 922 14 41 01; www.ecoturismo canarias.com/gomera; Carretera General 207, Hermigua).

A few pleasant exceptions are San Sebastian's elegant Parador Nacional Conde de la Gomera (p194) and the sprawling Hotel Jardín Tecina (p201) resort in Playa Santiago.

Reserving ahead of time is always a good idea, but it's really only necessary during high season (Christmas, Easter, August, major holidays, etc) and for those who plan to arrive on a late-night flight or ferry.

Free camping is prohibited on the island, and there's only one private camp site, Camping La Vista (p198) near El Cedro.

ACTIVITIES

Whether your idea of the perfect walk is strolling through a quiet pine forest, trudging up to a peak with a panoramic view, or trolling like an elf through the magical *laurisilva* (subtropical laurel) forests of the Parque Nacional de Garajonay (p195) chances are good that you'll find your ideal trail somewhere on the island. This is walking territory and trails of every level crisscross the island, both in an out of the park, offering enough variation to make a week-long walking or biking holiday a fantastic idea.

Regardless of their office location, the companies listed below offer guided walks or cycles across the island, and most will meet you at your hotel or a central location.

Bike Station Gomera (☎ 922 80 50 82; www.bike -station-gomera.com; La Puntilla 7, Valle Gran Rey; bike rental per day €7-14; ☒ 9am-1pm & 5-8pm)

Ökotours (☎ 922 80 52 34; www.oekotours.com; Calle Vueltas, Vueltas, Valle Gran Rey; day hike per person €25-32; ☒ 10.30am-1pm & 5.30-7.30pm Mon-Fri, 10.30am-1pm Sat)

Temocoda (☎ 922 87 24 40; www.temocoda.com; Avenida del V Centenario 11, San Sebastián de la Gomera; day hike per person incl lunch €45)

Timah (☎ 922 80 70 37; www.timah.net; La Puntilla, Valle Gran Rey; day hike per person €30; ☒ 10am-1pm & 5-8pm Mon-Sat, 6-8pm Sun)

THE ISLE WHERE COLUMBUS DALLIED

A Genoese sailor of modest means, Cristoforo Colombo (as he is known in his native Italy – Christopher Columbus to the rest of us) was born in 1451. He went to sea early and was something of a dreamer. Fascinated by Marco Polo's travels in the Orient, he decided early on that it must be possible to reach the east by heading west into the sunset. After years of doors being slammed in his face, the Catholic monarchs of Spain, Fernando and Isabel, finally gave him their patronage in 1492.

On 3 August, at the head of three small caravels – the *Santa María, Pinta* and *Niña* – Columbus weighed anchor in Palos de la Frontera, Andalucía, on the Spanish mainland. But before heading across the ocean blue, he stopped off at La Gomera for last-minute provisions, unwittingly giving the island its biggest claim to fame and many future tourist attractions. One of the things he picked up for the journey was goats' cheese, one of La Gomera's star products to this day.

Columbus set sail on 6 September, a day now celebrated in San Sebastián with the Fiestas Columbinas (opposite). His ships didn't see land until 12 October, just as their provisions and the sailors' patience were nearing their ends. The expedition 'discovered' several Caribbean islands on this trip and returned to Spain in March of the following year.

Columbus made three later voyages but died alone and bitter in Valladolid, Spain, in 1504, still convinced he'd found a new route to the Orient.

There are a few black-sand beaches around, but La Gomera is really not focused on its coast. Even so, you can take boat cruises starting from either Valle Gran Rey (see p204) or Playa Santiago (see p201), and if you want to do some exploring in the water, contact the diving school at Hotel Jardín Tecina (p201).

FESTIVALS & EVENTS
Any excuse will do for a fiesta. Many local celebrations feature traditional costumes, instruments and dances.

January
Fiesta de San Sebastián (20 January) San Sebastián festival in honour of the town's patron saint.

June
El Día de San Juan (23 June) The summer solstice is celebrated with bonfires all over the island.

September
Fiestas Columbinas (6 September) A week full of street parties, music and cultural events in San Sebastián, celebrating Columbus' first voyage.

Fiesta del Paso Gomeros from far and wide converge on Alajeró to celebrate this chirpy procession that dances its way down from the mountains.

October
Bajada de la Virgen de Guadelupe San Sebastián (5 October) Every five years (2008, 2013 etc) the town celebrates its patroness saint with a flotilla of fishing boats escorting the statue of the Virgin Mary from the chapel of Punta Llana southwards to the capital.

LA GOMERA FOR CHILDREN
La Gomera doesn't have any of the theme parks, zoos or water parks that make the bigger island such kid magnets. The fun here is of a less-flashy variety and depends on nature to provide the thrills.

Kids' first stop is, usually, the beach. The long, calm beaches of Valle Gran Rey (p202) and Alojera (p200), where there is a saltwater wading pool for little ones, are ideal. Keep in mind that there's more to beaches than splashing in the waves. Building sand castles and going crabbing or snorkelling can all be fun beach activities. For kids who aren't strong swimmers, pools like the one in Vallehermoso (p198) might be a better bet.

Short boat trips are guaranteed to brighten kids' days. The Garajonay Exprés ferry (right) is a thrill in itself, but even more fun are the real cruises. Trips to Los Órganos (p200) and half-day whale-watching cruises (p204) both sail from Valle Gran Rey and Playa Santiago.

You could also plan a stop in a recreational area like La Laguna Grande (p196), a picnic spot and playground rolled into one where kids can happily spend an entire afternoon running and playing.

GETTING THERE & AWAY
Air
The **airport** (☎ 922 87 30 00) is just 3km outside the centre of Playa Santiago. Interisland airways **Binter Canarias** (☎ 902 39 13 92; www .binternet.com) and **Islas** (☎ 902 47 74 78; www.islas airways.com) connect La Gomera to the rest of the archipelago, with several flights daily to other islands.

Boat
Several ferries and jetfoils arrive daily at San Sebastián's busy port, which is just at the foot of the town. Most people come in on the quick jetfoils from Los Cristianos, in Tenerife. **Fred Olsen** (☎ 902 10 01 07; www.fredolsen .es) makes the round trip four times daily between 7.30am and 8.30pm (€52 round trip, 30 minutes), while the cheaper and slower **Naviera Armas** (☎ 922 87 13 24; www.navieraarmas.com) operates up to four ferries a day between Los Cristianos and La Gomera, up to four ferries weekly between La Gomera and La Palma, and one weekly ferry between El Hierro and La Gomera.

The smaller company **Garajonay Exprés** (☎ 902 34 34 50; www.garajonayexpres.com) links Los Cristianos with San Sebastián (€19, 45 minutes), Playa Santiago (€22, one hour) and Valle Gran Rey (€23, 1½ hours) three times a day.

GETTING AROUND
To/From the Airport
You can rent a car at one of several agencies at the airport or, if money is no object, take a taxi. The taxi to Playa Santiago costs just €6 to €8, but getting to San Sebastián will cost about €35.

There is a bus stop at the airport, but buses are few and far between. Bus 5 (30 minutes, up to four daily) runs between the airport and San Sebastián, while bus 6 (1½ hours, two daily) makes the journey between the airport and Valle Gran Rey.

LA GOMERA

FOOD & DRINK

San Sebastián's twice-weekly fresh market (p194) is a good place to get an overview of typical Gomeran goods. Look out for specialities like *miel de palma* (palm honey), a sweet syrup made from palm-tree sap; *almogrote*, a spicy cheese pâté made with hard cheese, pepper and tomato, and spread on bread; and *queso gomero* (fresh Gomeran goat cheese), a mild, smooth cheese made with local goats' milk and served with salads, as a dessert, or grilled and smothered in *mojo*, the famed Canary sauce that's another island speciality.

There are many great restaurants where you can try these specialities *in situ*. The very best, if you listen to the locals, is Casa Efigenia (p196), a Gomeran institution in the form of a farmhouse restaurant. Here you can often try Gomeran dishes like *potaje de berros* (watercress soup), washed down with a glass of cool Gomeran white wine.

Boat

Garajonay Exprés (p189) also runs three daily ferries between San Sebastián, Playa Santiago and Valle Gran Rey (€3.50, 40 minutes).

Bus

The seven bus lines of **Servicio Regular Gomera** (☎ 922 14 11 01; www.gomera-island.com/turismo/ingles /guaguas.htm) do a good job of covering the main destinations, though getting around the island this way will require time and patience. The aqua-coloured buses set out from the ferry terminal at San Sebastián and stop by the bus station in town before heading around the island. Get a complete bus schedule from the tourist office or the San Sebastián bus station.

Car

There are several car-rental agencies around, and any will arrange to have a car waiting for you at the port or airport when you arrive if you book ahead. Rental agencies include the following:

Cicar (☎ 922 14 17 56; www.cicar.com; Estación Marítima, San Sebastián)

Rent-a-Car La Rueda (☎ 922 87 20 48; Calle Medio 19, San Sebastián)

Rent-a-Car Piñero (☎ 922 14 10 48; Avenida José Aguiar 14, San Sebastián) Also at Estación Marítima, San Sebastián.

SAN SEBASTIÁN DE LA GOMERA

pop 8451

The capital of the island in every way – economically, bureaucratically and historically – San Sebastián has an appealing historic centre with shaded plazas and pedestrian-friendly streets. Its main claim to fame is that Christopher Columbus stayed here on his way to the New World, and you'll learn more about the famed explorer here than you ever did at school, as his every footstep (real or imagined) in the town has been well documented for visitors.

HISTORY

On 6 September 1492, after loading up with supplies from the island, Christopher Columbus led his three small caravels out of the bay and set sail westwards beyond the limit of the known world. When Columbus was on the island, San Sebastián had barely been founded. Four years earlier, in 1488, there had been a terrible massacre in the wake of the failed uprising against Hernán Peraza, the island's governor (see the boxed text, p193). When it was all over, what had been the Villa de las Palmas, on a spot known to the Guanches as Hipalán, was renamed San Sebastián.

The boom in transatlantic trade following Columbus' journeys helped boost the fortunes of the town, which sits on a sheltered harbour and was one of the Canaries' best ports. Nevertheless, its population passed the 1000 mark only at the beginning of the 19th century. The good times also brought dangers, like other islands, San Sebastián was regularly subjected to pirate attack from the English, French and Portuguese. In 1739 the English fleet actually landed an invasion force but the assault was repulsed.

The fate of the town was linked intimately with that of the rest of the island. Its fortunes rose with the cochineal boom in the 19th century, then collapsed with that industry, which was unable to compete with synthetic dyes.

ORIENTATION
San Sebastián is an easily walkable town. The ferry port is a 10-minute walk from shady Plaza Américas, the heart of San Sebastián. Branching out of the plaza are

Calle Ruiz de Padrón and the partly pedestrianised Calle Real (aka Calle del Medio), which is lined with benches, well-tended plants, cafés and shops. A sandy black beach stretches down the western end of town, and there are a couple of bars and an exposition centre down here, but little else.

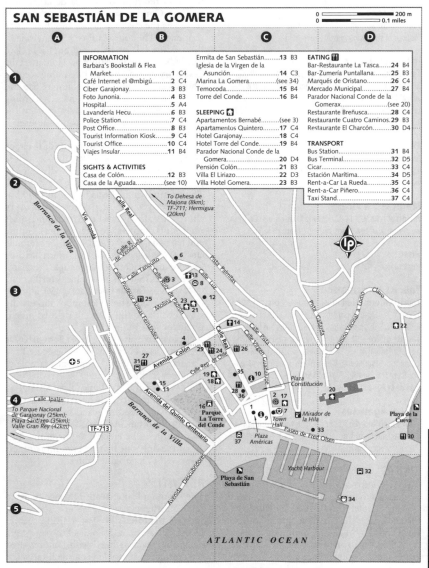

SAN SEBASTIÁN DE LA GOMERA

INFORMATION

Bookshops

Barbara's Bookstall (Plaza Américas; ⊙ 8am-2pm Wed & Sat) Head to this English bookseller during the twice-weekly flea and fresh market.

Foto Junonia (☎ 922 87 06 24; Avenida Colón 24) Stocks books, maps and guidebooks in Spanish and other languages (mostly German).

Emergency

Police station (☎ 922 87 00 62; Plaza Américas) On the 1st floor of the *ayuntamiento* (town hall).

Internet Access

Café Internet el @mbigú (☎ 922 87 16 68; Plaza Américas 8; per hr €3; ⊙ 8am-1am) All-day wi-fi is available for €1.80.

Ciber Garajonay (☎ 922 14 13 87; Calle Ruiz de Padrón 80; per hr €2; ⊙ 9am-1pm & 4-10pm Mon-Fri)

Laundry

Lavandería Hecu (☎ 922 14 11 80; Calle Real 76; ⊙ 9am-2pm & 4.30-8pm Mon-Fri) This tiny place will wash and dry a load of up to 4.5kg for €9.

Medical Services

Hospital (☎ 922 14 02 00; Calle El Calvario 4) On the western side of town, across the Barranco de la Villa.

Post

Post office (☎ 922 87 10 81; Calle Real 60)

Tourist Information

Tourist information kiosk (Plaza Américas; ⊙ 9am-12.30pm & 3.30-6.30pm Mon-Fri, 9am-12.30pm & 4-6.30pm Sat) This small kiosk supplies maps but little else.

Tourist office (☎ 922 14 15 12; www.gomera-island.com; Calle Real 4; ⊙ 9am-1.30pm & 3.30-6pm Mon-Sat, 10am-1pm Sun Oct-Jun, 9am-1.30pm & 3.30-5pm Mon-Sat, 9am-1pm Sun Jul-Sep) A friendly, helpful place in the Casa de la Aguada.

Travel Agencies

Viajes Insular (☎ 922 87 14 50; www.viajesinsular.es; Avenida Centenario s/n; ⊙ 9am-1pm & 4-7.30pm Mon-Fri) This agency can help with all your travel needs.

SIGHTS

To get a good overview of San Sebastián, head up the road to the Parador Nacional Conde de la Gomera hotel (p194), where the **Mirador de la Hila** showcases the coast, the square houses of town and the rough, dry mountains beyond.

Back in the town centre, most of the interesting sites are somehow related to Columbus

(in either real or contrived ways), and they form a route you can follow around town. Beginning at **Plaza Américas**, where you can get a juice in one of the terrace bars, cross through **Plaza Constitución**, shaded by enormous Indian laurel trees.

Just off the plaza is **Casa de la Aguada** (☎ 922 14 15 12; Calle Real 4; ⊙ 8.30am-6pm Mon-Sat, 10am-1pm Sun), also referred to as Casa de la Aduana or Casa Condal, since at different times it served as the customs house and the count's residence. The tourist office fills one side of this traditional Canary home, but the back of it is dedicated to the exhibit 'La Gomera & the Discovery of America', an interesting account (though all in Spanish) of Columbus' trip and Gomeran culture in those times. According to folklore, Columbus drew water from the well that sits in the central patio and used it to 'baptise America'.

Head up Calle Real to **Iglesia de la Virgen de la Asunción** (⊙ usually 6-8pm), the site where Columbus and his men supposedly came to pray before setting off for the New World. The original chapel was begun in 1450 but was destroyed by a fire. The 18th-century church here today has three naves and mixes *mudéjar* (Islamic-style architecture), Gothic and baroque architectural styles. The humble **Ermita de San Sebastián** (Calle Real), which has little to recommend it other than its age (the chapel was built in 1540), is a few blocks further on.

Nearby is **Casa de Colón** (Calle Real 56), a house built on the site where Columbus supposedly stayed while on the island. It's closed indefinitely for renovations.

Set in a park just off the coast, **Torre del Conde** (⊙ 10am-1pm & 4-6pm Mon-Fri) is considered the Canary Islands' most important example of military architecture. Here, Beatriz de Bobadilla, wife of the cruel and ill-fated Hernán Peraza, had to barricade herself in 1488 until help arrived (see the boxed text, opposite). The fort (built in 1447) was the first building of any note to be erected on the island. It is about the only one to have been more or less preserved in its original state.

ACTIVITIES

The sandy volcanic **beach** is a nice place to relax and have a swim. It's also the site of some of the town's liveliest festivals, such as El Día de San Juan (St John's Day; see p189), when the beach is lined with bonfires. Past the port, and accessible via a small tunnel, is

---

WHAT A TANGLED WEB WE WEAVE...

Governor Hernán Peraza the younger had long been hated for his cruel treatment of the islanders. When, in 1488, he broke a pact of friendship with one of the Gomero tribes and, openly cheating on his wife, began cavorting with Yballa, a local beauty and fiancée of one of the island's most powerful men, the natives rebelled. They surprised Peraza during one of his clandestine meetings with Yballa and killed him with a dart, communicating the news via Silbo (whistle) all over the island. They proceeded to attack the Spaniards in Villa de las Palmas, the precursor to modern San Sebastián, and Peraza's deceived wife (the famed beauty Beatriz de Bobadilla) barricaded herself in the Torre del Conde, where she waited until help arrived.

Unfortunately, the story didn't end there. 'Help' showed up in the form of Pedro de Vera, governor of Gran Canaria and one of the cruellest figures in Canarian history. His ruthlessness was bloodcurdling. According to one account, de Vera ordered the execution of all Gomeran males above the age of 15, and in an orgy of wanton violence, islanders were hanged, impaled, decapitated or drowned. Some had their hands and feet lopped off beforehand, just for good measure. The women were parcelled out to the militiamen, and many of the children were sold as slaves. To complete the job, de Vera also ordered the execution of about 300 Gomeros living on Gran Canaria.

---

the smaller and prettier, though often windy, **Playa de la Cueva**. On a clear day, Tenerife seems like it's within spitting distance!

Ask about bike or boat rental at **Marina La Gomera** (Estación Marítima; ☹ 9am-1pm & 4-7pm Mon-Fri, 9am-1pm Sat).

North of town, at Km8.4 on the TF-711 highway, is an interesting bike trail leading into the **Dehesa de Majona**, the largely un-inhabited pastureland to the north of the capital. The dirt track begins near a lookout point, venturing towards the goat-herding villages of Casas de Enchereda and Casas de Juel before winding its way towards the coast and eventually joining up with sealed local roads near Hermigua. The lonely route can be hiked in about eight hours (one way).

SLEEPING

Budget

Pensión Colón (☎ 922 87 02 35; Calle Real 59; s/d with shared bathroom €20/25) Rustic, no-frills rooms huddle around a central patio in this typical Canary-style house. Although a bit stale overall, the location is good and the price can't be beaten.

Villa Hotel Gomera (☎ 922 87 00 00; fax 922 87 02 35; Calle Ruiz de Padrón 68; s/d incl breakfast €35/45) This two-star hotel offers 16 simple rooms with terraces, tiled bathrooms and a surprising amount of space for the price. You might want to skip the breakfast though, unless stale bread and room-temperature sandwich meat are your idea of tasty.

Hotel Garajonay (☎ 922 87 05 50; www.hotelgarajonay .es; Calle Ruiz de Padrón 17; s €22-41, d €45-51) Run by the same folks who own the Hotel Torre del Conde, the two-star Garajonay is the sidekick to its sleeker big sister. A few of the small, rustic-feeling rooms have views of the tower, while others look onto a busy street. All are clean, with tiled floors and TV.

Midrange
HOTELS
Hotel Torre del Conde (☎ 922 87 00 00; fax 922 87 13 14; Calle Ruiz de Padrón 19; s €39-54, d €57-69) The rooms' canary-yellow walls (think they did that on purpose?) may clash with the blindingly gold bedspreads and curtains, but other than poor colour coordination, this is a fine three-star hotel. Best of all are the views of the Torre del Conde and the pretty gardens that surround it; ask for a room with a view.

APARTMENTS
Apartamentos Bernabé (☎ 922 14 13 87; Calle Ruiz de Padrón 80; 2-3-person apt €35-40, 4-person apt €60, 5-person apt €65-70) Located atop Ciber Garajonay, these one- and two-bedroom apartments are flooded with light and feature balconies, TVs and a bit too much street noise. The two-bedroom units provide enough elbow room for a family of five.

Apartamentos Quintero (☎ 922 14 17 44; apquintero@teleline.es; Plaza Américas; apt €47-53) The one-bedroom apartments have sofa beds, so are roomy enough for two people, and a bit of a squeeze for bigger groups. They also have a kitchen, balcony and, in some cases, an ocean view. Though not new, they're clean, comfy and centrally located.

Villa El Liriazo (☎ 679 60 86 49; www.vallehermoso .de/en/liriazo; Playa de la Cueva; 2-person apt €75, ste €86-116; P ☒) Perched on a cliff above Playa de la Cueva, the five apartments in this intimate stone-and-wood Canary-style villa whisk you away to another world. Large apartments with lots of light are ideal for families, although they're a 15-minute walk from San Sebastián itself. Reservations essential.

Top End

Parador Nacional Conde de la Gomera (☎ 922 87 11 00; www.parador.es; Calle Lomo de la Horca; s/d €116/145; P ☒) Built to look like an old Canarian mansion, the Parador is arguably the island's top hotel. The rooms are simply but elegantly furnished, with four-poster beds, rich wooden floors and marbled bathrooms. Most rooms look out onto the gardens, which have many examples of Canarian plants and a small pool area overlooking the ocean. The hotel is on a hill above the port; follow signs from central San Sebastián to get here by car, or walk up via the Mirador de la Hila.

EATING

Self-caterers can make a beeline for the *mercado municipal*, which is large, well-stocked and located beside the bus station.

Budget

Bar-Zumería Puntallana (☎ 922 14 16 01; Calle Profesor Armas Fernández 30; juices €1.80-2.50, sandwiches €3) A favourite Canarian species, the juice bar is a fabulous spot for breakfast, a quick lunch or a pick-me-up. The juices here, made on the spot with fresh and often local fruit, are outstanding and the cold and hot sandwiches are cheap and filling.

Midrange

Bar-Restaurante La Tasca (☎ 922 14 15 98; Calle Ruiz de Padrón 57; mains €4-10; ☒ closed Sun) Dark and inviting, this intimate tavern serves mainland-style tapas alongside pizzas and more elaborate dishes like lasagne or grilled rabbit.

Restaurante El Charcón (☎ 922 14 18 98; Playa de la Cueva; mains €7-12) A tiny, 10-table restaurant dug out of the rock near the shore, El Charcón specialises in fish and Gomeran specialities like *almogrote* (cheese spread) and *mojos* (spicy salsa sauces).

Restaurante Breñusca (☎ 922 87 09 20; Calle Real 11; mains €7-12) Locals say this slightly greasy-feeling bar/diner/restaurant is one of the best spots in town to try simple, traditional Canarian fare like homemade fried calamari, meatballs and stews. The catch of the day is always recommended.

Restaurante Cuatro Caminos (☎ 922 14 12 60; Calle Ruiz de Padrón 36; mains €7-15; ☒ closed Sat dinner & Sun) Stews and soups, grilled meats and Castilian specialities like *cochinillo* (piglet) are served in a tiny patio dining room where hanging plants drip from the ceiling.

Top End

our pick **Marqués de Oristano** (☎ 922 87 29 09; Calle Real 24; mains €8-16; ☒ closed Sun) This 16th-century Canary house has been completely renovated to create this sprawling three-in-one eatery. The old stables are now an informal tavern where you can order drinks and tapas; the garden is a bar and grill serving lots of simple fish dishes (mains €8 to €12); and the upstairs living quarters have been transformed into an upscale 'gourmet restaurant' serving dishes like boned kid with black potatoes, and potato confit (mains €10 to €16).

Parador Nacional Conde de la Gomera (☎ 922 87 11 00; Calle Lomo de la Horca; menú €29) The elegant restaurant at the Parador Nacional is without a doubt the most refined establishment in San Sebastián. Staff dress in local costume and the few, but consistently good, dishes are creative versions of traditional Canarian favourites.

DRINKING

For an informal drink and a few tapas to go along with it, head to a tavern-like Bar-Restaurante La Tasca (left) or Marqués de Oristano (above). El @mbigú (p192) is an Internet café by day, but morphs into a trendy nightspot after dinner.

GETTING THERE & AWAY
To/From the Airport

Bus 5 (30 minutes, up to four daily) runs between the airport and San Sebastián.

Boat

A fun and fast alternative to tackling the hairpin curves of La Gomera's highways is the water taxi operated by **Garajonay Exprés** (☎ 902 34 34 50; www.garajonayexpres.com), which takes you to Playa Santiago (€2.50, 15 minutes, three daily) and Valle Gran Rey (€3.50, 40 minutes, three daily) quickly. The trip between San Sebastián and Playa Santiago takes 45 minutes by car, while the trip to Valle Gran Rey is 1¼ hours, so water taxi is definitely the faster option.

GETTING AROUND

Plan on using your own to feet to get around the town; San Sebastián is very walkable, and is so small that buses merely pass through, not really connecting points of interest within the town centre.

The only reason you might need a car is to move between the centre and the Parador Nacional Conde de la Gomera, which is a short (though steep) walk or drive away. Car rental agencies are listed on p190.

Ring for a taxi on ☎ 922 87 05 24. The taxi stand is on Avenida Descubridores.

THE CENTRE

PARQUE NACIONAL DE GARAJONAY

A jungle of nearly impenetrable green that dominates the heart of La Gomera, the Parque Nacional de Garajonay encompasses one of the last vestiges of the ancestral *laurisilva* forests that were once spread throughout the Mediterranean. This wonderland of lush vegetation contains the island's best hiking and cycling trails, and it is a must-see sight for anyone visiting the island.

A universe of organisms has forged out a life in this damp, dark forest, which covers a full 10% (around 40 sq km) of the island's surface. As many as 400 species of flora, including Canary willows and Canary holly, flourish, and nearly 1000 species of invertebrates make their home in the park; insect lovers will have a field day. Vertebrates here include mainly birds and lizards. Relatively little light penetrates the canopy, providing an ideal landscape for moss and lichen to spread over everything.

Up here, on the roof of the island, cool Atlantic trade winds clash with warmer breezes, creating a constant ebb and flow of mist through the dense forest, something called 'horizontal rain'. The best place to see this in action is at the peak of the park, the Alto de Garajonay (1487m), where a single pine tree planted by the park rangers serves as an example of how the forest works. The

dripping tree, which sits in a puddle of water that it has collected, acts like a sponge, trapping moisture in its green boughs. The pines' role in feeding the island's springs is one of the reasons why conservation here is so important.

The frosty fingers of the last Ice Age didn't make it as far as the Canaries, so what you see here was common across much of the Mediterranean millions of years ago. Humans have done more damage on the islands than has ice, but in this case, at least, we've acted to protect a good chunk of unique land before it was too late – Garajonay was declared a national park in 1981 and a Unesco World Heritage site in 1986.

Lighting fires in the park is forbidden, except in a few designated areas. Free camping is also prohibited. It can get cold here, and the damp goes right to your bones, even when it is not raining. Bring walking boots, warm garments and a rainproof jacket.

Information

Get maps, hiking guides and park information at the **Juego de Bolas visitor centre** (☎ 922 80 09 93; http://reddeparquesnacionales.mma.es; La Palmita-Agulo Hwy; ⏲ 9.30am-4.30pm), which is actually located well outside the park and is difficult to access unless you arrive from the north.

Here you'll find piles of information on the park and the island in general, including a very informative guidebook to the park and a 20-minute video. In the centre's gardens and interior patio flourishes a microcosm of La Gomera's floral riches, and a small museum shows off island handicrafts and explains the park's geology and climate. The centre offers guided tours of the park on Saturday; call ahead to reserve a spot.

Walking

Walking is the best way to revel in the natural beauty abounding here, so park the car or get off the bus and set out to explore the park on foot. Many of the trails that crisscross Garajonay have been used by the Gomeros for hundreds of years as a means of getting around the island, and few are strenuous.

Although several guiding companies (see p188) lead convenient, transport-included hikes in and around the park, it's certainly not necessary to use their services. The

LA GOMERA

park's many and varied access points make it simple to plan a journey on your own if you have a good walking map or the *Self-Guided Paths* booklet available from the Juego de Bolas visitor centre.

One popular self-guided walk begins in **La Laguna Grande**, a recreation and picnic area just off the TF-713 highway. The *laguna* refers to a barren circle of land – now used as a recreational area – that has always held an air of mystery. Islanders say it's a mystical place and that witches once practised here. If you don't have much time to explore, you can take the easy, 20-minute loop that serves as a decent, if too brief, introduction to the park. This route is a good place to view the park's famous laurel trees.

A longer walk (2½ hours one way) heads to the **Alto de Garajonay** (1487m), the island's tallest peak. The walk begins behind the restaurant at La Laguna Grande and sets off towards **El Cercado** (a town known for its pottery production), then bears left towards Los Llanos de Crispín before winding its way through native vegetation and heading northwest to the Alto. From here, cloud permitting, you can enjoy jaw-dropping, 360-degree views around the island and can even spot Tenerife, La Palma, El Hierro and Gran Canaria in the distance.

From the Alto, you could return to La Laguna Grande (there is an alternative trail so that you don't have to completely backtrack) or continue 15 minutes downhill to Pajarito, where there is a bus stop. Bus 1 (€4, around one hour) comes by four times a day weekdays and twice a day weekends; it will take you towards either San Sebastián or Valle Gran Rey. For those arriving by bus, or looking for an easy parking spot, Pajarito is also a good starting point to begin a short hike up to the Alto.

Around 15 minutes north of Pajarito is El Contadero, where another track, signposted **Caserío de El Cedro**, leads northeast through a beautiful valley forest. This mostly descending trail (2½ hours one way) winds its way towards the hamlet of El Cedro (p198), famous for its waterfalls. You can grab a bite to eat at **Bar La Vista** (☎ 922 88 09 49; 🕙 9am-7pm). It's possible to continue hiking to Hermigua, two hours away, where you'd need to have transport waiting. Or, you could return to the Pajarito bus stop via Tajaqué (three hours).

Sleeping & Eating

our pick **Casa Efigenia** (☎ 922 80 40 77; www.efigenia natural.com; Carretera General; menú €10) Make a point to take a short detour to the town of Las Hayas, on the southern border of the park, where this local institution serves family-style meals at long communal tables. You eat whatever is on the menu for the day, and it's sure to be hearty, home-style Canarian fare. Efigenia also rents rooms (double €35) and a few rural houses (€40) in the area.

Getting There & Away

Unlike some other protected parks, Garajonay is extremely accessible. In fact, you won't be able to avoid it if you move much about the island, as the park exists at La Gomera's major crossroads.

The TF-713 highway cuts east to west right through the park until it meets the TF-711 at the park's western extremity. Though wheeling through in your own car is certainly the quickest and most comfortable way to move about the park, Bus 1 (€4, around one hour) runs four times daily weekdays and twice on weekends between the capital and Valle Gran Rey. The route runs along a southern secondary road, branching off shortly before Alto de Garajonay and continuing westwards along a decidedly tortuous route, stopping in towns like Igualero, Chipude and El Cercado before branching north again to rejoin the main road at Las Hayas.

A minor sealed road connects the national park visitor centre in the north of the island to La Laguna Grande, about midway along the TF-713, between the park's eastern and western boundaries.

THE NORTH

If you have just one day to spend in La Gomera, think about spending it in the verdant north, where dense banana plantations and swaying palm trees fill the valleys, cultivated terraces transform the hillsides into geometric works of art and white-washed houses make the villages seem like something from another era. The resulting landscape is postcard-worthy at every turn, but these well-manicured terraces represent back-breaking work by the local farmers –

the steepness of the slopes means most work here has to be done without machines.

The curvy TF-711 highway running 42km between San Sebastián and Vallehermoso is the artery connecting the towns here, and it's pocked with *miradores* (lookout points) offering gorgeous views. The highway eventually meets up with the TF-713, allowing ambitious day-trippers to loop the northern half of the island and end up back in San Sebastián in time to catch the last ferry off the island.

HERMIGUA
pop 475

A popular home base for those on walking holidays, the sleepy town of Hermigua, 16km outside San Sebastián, is absolutely dripping with that authentic Gomeran feel. The town itself is strung out along the bottom of a lusciously green ravine, its houses like beads on a chain running down the middle.

At the heart of the original village, to the right as you enter from San Sebastián, are the 16th-century **church** and **convent of Santo Domingo**, with an intricately carved *mudéjar* ceiling.

To your left sits the **Molino de Gofio** (☎ 922 88 07 81; Carretera General; adult/child €2/free; ☼ 10am-5pm Mon-Sat, to 2pm Sun), a reconstructed windmill where *gofio* (see p51) was once ground. The quick tour leads you around the museum and mill. Afterwards, you can taste *gofio* accompanied by sweet wine. There's also a good restaurant here.

Further down the ravine you'll find the modern town, centred around the **Iglesia de la Encarnación**. This church was begun in the 17th century and not completed until the 20th, partly due to the fact that the original construction crumbled in the early 18th century. A public park, complete with a Lucha Canaria ring (see p33) is on your right.

Hermigua winds down to a captivatingly blue ocean where the crushing waves are a bit too rough for swimming (although they're occasionally used for surfing competitions). There is a big **saltwater public pool** down here, but it was closed indefinitely at the time of writing.

Even better is **Playa de la Caleta**, 3km southeast down the coast; follow the signs from the waterfront. It's one of the prettier black-sand and pebble beaches in the north of the island.

Sleeping

Apartamentos Los Telares (☎ 922 88 07 81; www.apartamentosgomera.com; El Convento, Carretera General; 1-2 person apt €25-36, 2-3 person house €40-71) The owner, Doña Maruca, is one of the island's best-known residents (she also runs the Molino de Gofio). Her apartments, which sit on either side of the main highway coming into town, aren't unlike so many others on the island, with simple wooden furniture, lots of sunshine and balconies overlooking banana plantations. Telares also rents small houses near the coast, featuring a similar unfussy décor, generous terraces and fabulous ocean views. Across the street from Los Telares' reception office is an artisan shop under the same ownership, where you can buy local crafts and visit a small loom museum. At the time of research, Doña Maruca had plans to open a rural hotel as well.

Hotel Villa de Hermigua (☎ 922 88 07 77, 600 52 69 25; www.gomeraturismo.com; Carretera General 117; s/d incl breakfast €45/63) This little stone house on the main road is a maze inside, with scattered small but tasteful rooms where wrought-iron bedposts and all-white linen give a touch of rustic elegance. A common kitchen and terrace add to the charm. If the owner isn't in when you come by, ring him on his mobile phone.

Ibo Alfaro (☎ 922 88 01 68; www.ecoturismocanarias.com/iboalfaro; s incl breakfast €56, d incl breakfast €75-90) Even better than Villa de Hermigua, the 17 romantic rooms here have gorgeous mountain views and an aroma of wood polish coming from the floors, ceilings and elegant furniture. The friendly German owner also runs the hotel restaurant. To get here, follow the signs up the unnamed rural road from beside Hermigua Rent-a-Car.

Apartamentos Jardín La Punta (☎ 922 14 60 97; www.residencial-la-punta.com; Carretera General; 3-person apt €45; P 🖳) Located on the highway that winds out of town, and giving enviable, sweeping views of the Atlantic, these 15 stylish apartments have been decorated with colour, flair and a contemporary touch.

Eating

El Silbo (☎ 922 88 03 04; Carretera General 102; mains €9-15) The best place for typical Canarian cuisine like tuna with *mojo*, fried rabbit or *chipirones* (tiny squid). A covered terrace with bright tablecloths and an abundance of hanging plants makes for a pleasant, if slightly junglelike, dining experience.

LA GOMERA

Restaurante Vasco Iratxe (☎ 922 88 07 40; Carretera General; mains €10-20; ☺ dinner Mon-Sat) Widely hailed as the best eating in town, this dark little Basque restaurant serves up fabulous cod and other Basque specialities.

La Casa Creativa (☎ 922 88 10 23; Carretera General 56; mains €15-20; ☺ closed Sun; Ⓥ) Upstairs, a quirky café serves fresh juices, homemade pies and pastries and an ever-changing array of tapas (vegetarian options are always available). For dinner, the formal downstairs restaurant serves slightly overpriced Canarian and international fare. The German owners also rent out a few apartments and arrange occasional yoga classes.

Getting There & Away

Bus 1 (€4) runs four times on weekdays and twice on weekends between San Sebastián and Vallehermoso, stopping in Hermigua along the way.

EL CEDRO

Southwest of Hermigua, and on the national park border, El Cedro is a rural hamlet set amid farmed terraces and laurel thickets. The ravine and waterfall known as **Boca del Chorro** are beautiful, and the simple chapel, **Ermita de Nuestra Señora de Lourdes**, is a 1km wander out from the hamlet.

In El Cedro itself are three rustic stone **cottages** (☎ 922 22 97 94; www.apartamentosgomera.com; 2-person cottage €47) for rent by Doña Maruca. The minimum stay in high season is five days.

Here too is **Camping La Vista** (☎ 922 88 09 49; per person €2; ☺ year-round), the island's only camp site. A friendly place, it has a bar and restaurant.

To walk to El Cedro from Hermigua, ask in town for the way to the *sendero* (trail) to El Cedro and be prepared for a two- to three-hour hike. If you're not up for walking, follow the signs to El Cedro, off the main highway south of Hermigua. By car, you can get within a 15-minute walk of El Cedro's cottages and camp site.

You can also reach El Cedro from El Contadero on the Caserío de El Cedro trail in Parque Nacional de Garajonay (see p196).

AGULO

A spectacular 5km drive north of Hermigua, Agulo is one of the island's most picturesque villages. Founded early in the 17th century, it squats on a low platform beneath the steep, rugged hinterland that stretches back towards the Garajonay park.

The elegant **Iglesia de San Marcos** dominates the centre of Agulo. Built in 1912, it's a simple temple with a high ceiling and a few interesting pieces of art. Get a quick and shockingly cheap meal at **Bar Mantillo Los Chocos** (☎ 922 14 61 66; Calle El Mantillo s/n; mains €4), which specialises in roasted chicken, lentil stew and local seafood.

LAS ROSAS

Continuing past Agulo on the main highway, next you'll come to Las Rosas, which sits at the foot of the national park. Just before the town centre is the turn-off for the park's Juego de Bolas visitor centre (p195).

The town's claim to fame is being the home of the Fred Olsen–owned **Restaurante Las Rosas** (☎ 922 80 09 16; Carretera General; mains €7-10), a tourist magnet on the main highway. Although the food (overcooked tuna fillet, various meats in overpowering sauces, watery soups) is not very good, you won't regret a meal here because this is one of the few spots on the island where you can hear a live demonstration of Silbo Gomero (see the boxed text, opposite). Don't miss the opportunity. Reservations are recommended because the restaurant packs out with the tour-bus crowd.

For a more authentic dining experience, head high above Las Rosas to **Restaurante Roque Blanco** (☎ 922 80 04 83; Cruz de Tierno; mains €6-12; ☺ closed Mon), a casual family restaurant perched above a gorgeous green valley. Enjoy the view and the grilled meats paired with *papas* (potatoes) and local wines.

VALLEHERMOSO

pop 1540

This truly is a 'beautiful valley', as its name translates. Small mountain peaks rise on either side of the deep gorge that runs through town, and the green, terraced hillsides dotted with palm trees complete the picture.

Like Hermigua, this makes a good base for exploring the island on foot. The heart of town is **Plaza Constitución**; bars, services and much of the budget accommodation is around here. Take time to search out the stone **Iglesia de San Juan Bautista** behind town centre.

Just outside town towers the volcanic monolith of **Roque Cano** (650m), a town

LA GOMERA

SILBO: FOR THE BIRDS

The first time you hear Silbo Gomero you might think that you're listening to two birds having a conversation. Alternately chirpy and melodic, shrill and deeply resonating, this ancient whistling language is as lovely as birdsong. Silbo, once a dying art, but now being brought back to life, is steeped in history and boasts a complex vocabulary of more than 4000 whistled words that can be heard from miles away. It's definitely not for the birds.

In pre-Hispanic Gomera, Silbo developed as the perfect tool for sending messages back and forth across the island's rugged terrain. In ideal conditions, it could be heard up to 4km away, saving islanders from struggling up hill and down dale just to deliver a message to a neighbour. At first, Silbo was probably used as an emergency signal, but over time a full language developed. While other forms of whistled communications have existed in pockets of Greece, Turkey, China and Mexico, none is as developed as Silbo Gomero.

Modern conveniences have all but killed the language, but in the past few years Silbo has gone from being La Gomera's near-forgotten heritage to being its prime cultural selling point. In 2006 Silbo was proposed as a candidate for Unesco Oral Heritage status. If it makes the cut it will mean a hefty budget increase, more notoriety for its promoters and a big morale boost for *silbadores*. Silbo has been a mandatory school subject on the island since 2000, and a Silbo school for adults (and possibly even tourists) is on the horizon.

---

icon visible from just about everywhere. It looms tall like an age-old big brother keeping watch. Head past the *roque* down to the **Playa de Vallehermoso**, a beautiful strip of sand pounded by waves and hemmed in by tall cliffs on either side. Also down on the waterfront are a **public pool** (admission €2; ☻ noon-6pm Tue-Sun) and the informal Restaurante Parque Marítimo (right).

A short signposted walk or drive northwest from the waterfront is **Castillo del Mar** (☎ 922 80 04 97; www.castillo-del-mar.com; Parque Marítimo; ☻ 11am-sunset Tue-Sun), an old banana-packaging factory that's been converted into a beautifully rustic and windblown cultural centre hosting concerts, exhibits and a tapas bar.

Sleeping

Bar-Restaurante Amaya (☎ 922 80 00 73; Plaza Constitución 2; s/d €11/20) Don't expect anything fancy, but if all you're after is a central place to get a night's rest, this is your spot. Ask for one of the rooms with a private bathroom, which offer a TV and views of the town. The busy restaurant (mains €6 to €8) downstairs is a congenial place for nonelaborate dishes like cuttlefish, octopus or roast chicken.

Coello Aparthotel (☎ 922 80 07 17; Calle Guillermo Ascanio 17; s/d €40/55) Built in 2004, these spare, bare-bones studio apartments are set around a sunny central patio laden with ferns and hanging plants. Some rooms don't have a bathroom. It's one of the few spots

on the island offering a high-speed internet connection for those toting a laptop.

our pick **Hotel Rural Tamahuche** (☎ 922 80 11 76; www.hoteltamahuche.com; Calle Hoya 20; s/d incl breakfast €47/66; **P** **⌨**) Just outside town (it's a little hard to find; follow the signs towards Valle Gran Rey and it will be perched atop a hill to your right), this little B&B-style hotel is a real find. Built right into the hillside, Tamahuche climbs in a series of staircases and terraces, so don't plan to bring much luggage. Rooms, with dark wooden floorboards and wood-beam ceiling, are done in a Canary colonial style.

Hotel Triana (☎ 922 80 05 28; Calle Triana 13; s/d incl breakfast €40/69) Old and new come together in perfect harmony at this boutique hotel near the town centre. The original stone walls of this old Canary house lend rooms a rustic air, while the minimalist décor sets it firmly in the 21st century.

Eating

Agana (☎ 922 80 08 43; Avenida Guillermo Ascanio 5; mains €6-11) Head to this tavern for tasty Canarian dishes, including specialities such as *potaje de berros* (watercress soup) and *almogrote*, served to you at small wooden tables.

Restaurante Parque Marítimo (☎ 922 80 15 61; menú €9) An informal bar and restaurant by the beach, where you can get paella, local fish and shellfish while squinting at the shimmering ocean.

LA GOMERA

Self-caterers can find some fresh produce at the tiny **mercadillo** (☉ 9am-1pm Mon-Sat), beside the town hall.

AROUND VALLEHERMOSO
Los Órganos
To contemplate this extraordinary cliffscape (something like a great sculpted church organ in basalt rising abruptly from the ocean depths), 4km north of Vallehermoso, you'll need to head out to sea. Boats making the trip actually set out from Valle Gran Rey (p202) and Playa Santiago (right) in the south of the island. The columned cliff face has been battered into its present shape by the ocean.

Alojera
This sleepy settlement sits in a fertile valley that stands out as an oasis of green amid dry hills. Past the town itself, at the end of a nausea-inducing, seemingly endless series of hairpin curves, you reach the reward: the breathtaking **Playa de Alojera**.

Arguably the prettiest beach on the island, this place is no secret, but it's rarely crowded. A sweeping, silty black beach with calm waters is ideal for swimming, while the cliffs, rock formations and natural pools offshore represent some of La Gomera's best photo ops. You can eat (in your bathing suit if you like) at the beach-side **Brisas del Mar** (☎ 922 80 04 73; Playa de Alojera; mains €7-8), where the menu is basically a rundown of every species of Canarian fish, all served in fillets.

Stay at **Apartamentos Azul** (☎ 922 80 02 17; 2-person apt €36), no-frills flats with a spacious kitchen and sitting area, small bedroom and constant sea breezes. The best thing about this place is, naturally, the location.

Chorros de Epina
One kilometre past the turn-off for Alojera is the **Restaurante Los Chorros de Epina** (☎ 922 80 00 30; Carretera General del Norte, Km50; mains €6-8), where grilled rabbit, kid, pork chops and steaks are served in a dining room where the only décor is the panoramic views over the hills and to the piercing blue ocean beyond.

Just off the highway, a trail branches off towards the **Chorros de Epina**, a series of seven small natural springs. Ask locals about the romantic legend associated with this spot.

THE SOUTH

The sunniest part of the island, the south is endlessly changing, from dry sunburnt peaks to lush banana-filled valleys, and from stern rocky coasts to silty black-sand beaches. This is where you'll find the island's two resort areas – the modest Playa Santiago and sprawling Valle Gran Rey.

PLAYA SANTIAGO
pop 560
Playa Santiago is small ocean-side hamlet with calm waters, a drowsy town centre and no real beach to speak of; grey stones and pebbles line the shore. But the view, especially in the morning when a magnificent sunrise spreads glitter and sparkles over the water's surface, just about makes up for the town's lack of sandy beaches.

Until the 1960s this area was the busiest centre on the island, with factories, a shipyard and a port for exporting local bananas and tomatoes. But the farming crisis hit hard, and by the 1970s the town had all but shut down, its inhabitants having fled to Tenerife or South America. In recent years, tourism has brought new life to town. A huge luxury-hotel complex owned by Fred Olsen is doing more than its fair share to bring visitors this way, and the port has traded bananas for passengers and is now a stop for the Garajonay Exprés ferry boat.

Information
The **tourist office** (☎ 922 89 56 50; www.gomera-island .com; Edificio Las Vistas, Avenida Marítima; ☉ 9am-2pm Mon-Sat summer, 9am-1pm & 4-6pm Mon-Fri, 9am-1pm Sat winter) is on your right as you enter the town centre.

All the town's services, including the post office, petrol station, laundrette, pharmacy, post office, police station and medical centre, are clustered around Plaza Playa Santiago in the heart of town.

Activities
In Playa Santiago itself, splashing in the waves, rambling along the rocky shore and marvelling over the peaceful ocean view will likely take up most of your time. To get out on the water, you can hop on a cruise boat to Los Órganos (left) or to go whale-watching (see p39 for information about

whale watching). Tour companies include **Chinea Morales** (☎ 628 66 24 26; excursioneschineamor ales@hotmail.com; 3hr boat ride per person €40, 4hr fishing trip per person €90) and **Tina** (☎ 922 80 58 85; www.ex cursiones-tina.com; day cruise adult €33-40, child €20). Most trips include lunch and a swim.

There's a small **diving school** (☎ 922 89 59 02; www.gomera-dive-resort.com; single dive €25-32) set up below the Hotel Jardín Tecina (below). You can also buy tickets for various other excursions here.

If the rocky beach in town doesn't satisfy, you can head east, past Hotel Jardín Tecina, to three smaller beaches, Playas de Tapahuga, del Medio and de Chinguarime, which have some sand mixed in with the rocks. The three lie at the end of a bumpy gravel track and are known as hippy hang-outs.

The new 18-hole **Tecina Golf Course** (☎ 922 14 59 50; www.tecinagolf.com; Lomada del Tecina, s/n; 9/18 holes €45/61), yet another Fred Olsen initiative and the island's only golf course, is just outside town.

Sleeping

Casanova (☎ 922 89 50 02; Avenida Marítima 6; 2-person apt €30) Near the town centre, Casanova rents out a few simple apartments with kitchenettes and views of the ocean. The owners also run the restaurant downstairs.

Apartamentos Tapahuga (☎ 922 89 51 59; www.tapa huga.com; Avenida Marítima; 2-person apt €43-60; 🏊) At the far end of the *avenida*, these spacious apartments boast beautiful wooden balconies and marble floors, well-equipped kitchens and a rooftop pool. Make sure you get an exterior apartment, as a few open onto a cheerless and dark interior patio.

Apartamentos Santa Ana (☎ 922 89 51 66; www .gomerarural.com; Finca Santa Ana s/n; 2-/3-person apt €75/85; P 🏊) A quiet retreat, these 14 apartments sit atop a cliff at the southern end of town, overlooking Playa Santiago (a 3km drive away). The all-wood construction lends a rustic air to the charming rooms, where the simple décor is pleasant enough but the real appeal is their amazing setting.

our pick **Hotel Jardín Tecina** (☎ 922 14 58 50; www.jardin-tecina.com; Playa Santiago; s/d incl breakfast & dinner €69-135 per person; P 🍴 💻 🏊) Sprawled along a cliff above town (a lift goes down to the beach), this is the nicest hotel on the island, with bungalowlike rooms scattered throughout a green, well-kept landscape. All have balconies and many have ocean views.

The hotel's restaurants – three of them – are noteworthy too (see below).

Eating

La Cuevita (☎ 922 89 55 68; Avenida Marítima; mains €7-15) Tucked into a natural cave beside the port, where plants dangle from the ceiling and low lighting creates a cosy atmosphere, La Cuevita serves fresh local seafood, such as tuna, *vieja* (parrot fish), *lapas* (limpets), *chocos* (cuttlefish), along with grilled meats, all served with *papas arrugadas* (wrinkly potatoes) and a tangy red *mojo*.

Restaurante Junonia (☎ 922 89 54 50; Avenida Marítima; mains €8-10) A local favourite with a porch out front and a welcoming, farmhouse style, Junonia serves fresh local fish and other Gomeran specialities on blue-and-white-checked tablecloths.

Hotel Jardín Tecina (☎ 922 14 58 50; www.jardin -tecina.com; Playa Santiago; menú del día around €20) The three restaurants at this hotel are warmly recommended. Though each has its own style – grill, traditional or international – all serve tasty, creative dishes in beautiful open-air settings. It's a good idea to book ahead.

Self caterers will find all the basics at **Supermercado El Paso II** (☎ 922 89 55 66; Calle Anton Gil).

Getting There & Away

Bus 3 (€4, 30 minutes, up to five daily) links Playa Santiago with San Sebastían. Much easier are the water taxis of **Garajonay Exprés** (☎ 902 34 34 50; www.garajonayexpres.com), which take you to San Sebastián (€2.50, 15 minutes, three daily) and Valle Gran Rey (€2.50, 20 minutes, three daily) more quickly.

Call a taxi on ☎ 922 89 50 22.

ALAJERÓ & AROUND
pop 325

The palm trees outnumber the residents in this peaceful oasis situated on a ridge high above the ocean. The only sizable village outside Playa Santiago in the southeast of the island, Alajeró boasts the modest 16th-century **Iglesia del Salvador** and is a good starting point for several **hikes**. The long-distance GR132 trail passes through town as do the shorter PR LG 15 and 16. The latter heads to downhill to Playa Santiago or, more challengingly, up to **Benchijigua**, a tiny settlement amid steep green slopes. Information plaques outlining the walks are near the church. Another option is to take an 8km loop trail to Magaña, along the Lomo de la Montaña and past the island's oldest **drago** (dragon tree; see the boxed text, p42) before returning to Alajeró. Allow 2½ hours for the journey.

If you're driving, you can see the *drago* tree by taking an unsigned left turn, 1.25km north of Alajeró, as far as an old farmhouse, from where a trail drops steeply. If you're on the bus, get off at the Imada stop and turn left down a cobbled track to join this side road. Either way, allow a good 1½ hours for the round trip.

Bus 3 (€4, 40 minutes, up to five daily) runs between town and San Sebastián, stopping at Playa Santiago on the way. The bus stop is on the main highway.

VALLE GRAN REY
pop 3440

Bet you can't make it all the way down to the shore without stopping at one of the lookout points to sigh at the natural beauty of the 'Valley of the Great King'. A deep, green gorge running down to meet the island's longest beach, this is La Gomera's tourist epicentre. If you speak German you'll feel right at home, as most services here are geared towards the many Germans in search of sunshine and nature.

Before you descend into the valley, you could stop at the **Ermita del Santo** in Arure, where a tiny chapel is built into the rock face and is surrounded by a recently built *mirador* showing off the southern landscape.

Also worth a stop, the **Mirador César Manrique** enjoys incredible views of Valle Gran Rey's gorge and the mountains that loom around it. The **restaurant** (mains €8-14; ☺ closed Sun dinner) serves Canary fusion food, like king prawns with curry.

A few kilometres further on is another of the area's many road-side chapels: the best feature of the **Ermita de San Antonio** is the view from the plaza outside.

Orientation

Valle Gran Rey is really a collection of little hamlets with a grand name. The high part is known as La Calera. From here the road forks to descend to La Playa and Vueltas. Both have small beaches and plenty of accommodation, and Vueltas also serves as the area's harbour.

La Playa, the newest area, is in constant development, with new hotels and apartments being built as you read this. It's still a far cry from luxe, but the area is doing its best to spiff itself up, with newly sealed streets, a nice new ocean-front promenade and increasingly good restaurants.

Information
EMERGENCY
Centro Médico Hispano-Alemán (☎ 922 80 61 91; Residencial el Conde, Charco del Conde; ☺ 9am-3pm & 5-8pm Mon-Fri, 9.30-11am Sat)

LOCAL VOICES

Ayoze Rodríguez, 15, is one of La Gomera's youngest Silbo experts. He's whistled all over the Canary Islands in special exhibitions, and he's even travelled to the mainland to help spread Gomeran culture. In 2006 he whistled for the King of Spain himself when Juan Carlos I paid a visit to the island. Rodríguez knows he's a minority – most of his friends would rather play video games than practice whistling – but he's a firm believer in the importance of Silbo.

'Silbo helped our ancestors survive, and thanks to them we're all here. It's ours, and it's worth recuperating,' he says. 'Working together, we can save our heritage. Now, young people are learning it, and in six or seven years there will be a lot more people using Silbo.'

After going to his grandfather to learn whistling techniques – like how to use his hands to direct the sound and where to place his fingers in his mouth to get certain pitches – Rodríguez later perfected his Silbo in school classes in San Sebastián, where he lives. In his daily life, he uses Silbo occasionally to call to his Silbo-speaking friends or to practice.

Silbo isn't something you can learn 'in a day', Rodríguez says. 'You need two or three months just to learn to make the sound with your fingers and your tongue.' To be able to recognize and reproduce words as whistles requires years of practise.

Eugenio Darias, a Silbo teacher and the coordinator of Silbo classes across the island, explains Silbo like this: 'When you whistle a song, you're whistling the tune of the song. But when you speak Silbo, you're whistling the words themselves. It's what we call an articulated language, though reduced to only the four consonants and two vowels we can distinguish in a whistle.'

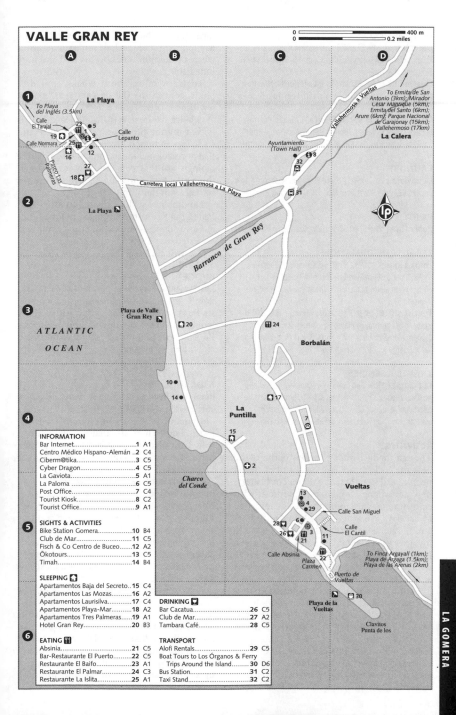

VALLE GRAN REY

0   400 m
0   0.2 miles

La Playa

To Playa
del Inglés (3.5km)

Calle
El Tarajal

Calle Normara

Calle
Lepanto

To Ermita de San
Antonio (3km); Mirador
César Manrique (5km);
Ermita del Santo (6km);
Arure (6km); Parque Nacional
de Garajonay (15km);
Vallehermoso (17km)

La Calera

Vallehermosa a Vueltas

Ayuntamiento
(Town Hall)

Carretera local Vallehermosa a La Playa

La Playa

Paseo Las Palmeras

Barranco de Gran Rey

ATLANTIC
OCEAN

Playa de Valle
Gran Rey

Borbalán

La
Puntilla

Charco
del Conde

Vueltas

Calle San Miguel

Calle
El Cantil

Calle Absinia

Plaza
Carmen

Playa de la
Vueltas

Puerto de
Vueltas

To Finca Argayall (1km);
Playa de Argaga (1.5km);
Playa de las Arenas (2km)

Clavitos
Punta de los

INFORMATION
Bar Internet......................................**1** A1
Centro Médico Hispano-Alemán ..**2** C4
Ciberm@tika.....................................**3** C5
Cyber Dragon...................................**4** C5
La Gaviota..**5** A1
La Paloma **6** C5
Post Office..**7** C4
Tourist Kiosk....................................**8** C2
Tourist Office...................................**9** A1

SIGHTS & ACTIVITIES
Bike Station Gomera.................**10** B4
Club de Mar.............................**11** C5
Fisch & Co Centro de Buceo......**12** A2
Ökotours..................................**13** C5
Timah.......................................**14** B4

SLEEPING
Apartamentos Baja del Secreto..**15** C4
Apartamentos Las Mozas...........**16** A2
Apartamentos Laurisilva...........**17** C4
Apartamentos Playa-Mar...........**18** A2
Apartamentos Tres Palmeras......**19** A1
Hotel Gran Rey.........................**20** B3

EATING
Absinia......................................**21** C5
Bar-Restaurante El Puerto.........**22** C5
Restaurante El Baifo..................**23** A1
Restaurante El Palmar...............**24** C3
Restaurante La Islita.................**25** A1

DRINKING
Bar Cacatua...........................**26** C5
Club de Mar...........................**27** A2
Tambara Café.........................**28** C5

TRANSPORT
Alofi Rentals..........................**29** C5
Boat Tours to Los Órganos & Ferry
  Trips Around the Island.........**30** D6
Bus Station............................**31** C2
Taxi Stand.............................**32** C2

LA GOMERA

INTERNET ACCESS
Bar Internet (☎ 922 80 51 22; Edificio Normara 15, La Playa; per hr €2.75; ⊙ 10.30am-3pm & 5-11pm Mon-Fri, 5-11pm Sat & Sun)

Ciberm@tika (☎ 922 80 61 71; Calle Vueltas, Vueltas; per hr €2.50; ⊙ 9am-8.30pm Mon-Fri, 9am-1pm & 4-8pm Sat)

Cyber Dragon (☎ 922 80 70 29; Calle Vueltas, Vueltas; per hr €3.50; ⊙ 9am-1.30pm & 5-9pm Mon-Sat, 3-8pm Sun) This groovy music store also offers high-speed internet.

LAUNDRY
La Gaviota (☎ 629 90 22 87; La Playa s/n; wash, dry & fold per 1kg €2; ⊙ 9.30am-6pm Mon-Fri, to 4pm Sat)

POST
Post office (☎ 922 80 57 30; Urbanización La Palomera)

TOURIST INFORMATION
Tourist kiosk (☎ 922 80 50 58; Carretera General; ⊙ 8.30am-3.30pm Mon-Fri) This small wooden hut is off the main highway on your right as you head towards Vueltas.

Tourist office (☎ 922 80 54 58; www.gomera-island .com; Calle Lepanto, La Playa; ⊙ 9am-1.30pm & 4-6.30pm Mon-Sat, 10am-1pm Sun Oct-Jun, 9am-2pm Mon-Sat Jul-Sep) Pick up a map and local information here.

TRAVEL AGENCIES
La Paloma (☎ 922 80 60 43; www.gomera.de; Calle Absinia, Vueltas; ⊙ 10am-1pm & 4.30-7pm Mon-Fri) Helpful, though aimed at German travellers, this agency offers assistance with air fares, ferry tickets and other travel needs.

Activities
Though the lush valley itself is perhaps the best the Valle Gran Rey has to offer, most people head straight to the shore. The beaches here are among La Gomera's prettiest, with calm waters and lapping waves. The beach at La Playa is a long, sandy thing, with bars and a waterside boardwalk nearby. Heading towards Vueltas, the Charco del Conde is a quieter place to splash and swim. The Playa de las Vueltas, beside the port, is the least agreeable of the bunch.

Scuba enthusiasts can head to **Fisch & Co Centro de Buceo** (☎ 922 80 56 88; www.fischco .com; Calle Lepanto, La Playa; dive with equipment €38; ⊙ 9am-6.30pm Sat-Thu), which offers dives throughout the day.

The motorboat **Tina** (☎ 922 80 58 85; www.ex cursiones-tina.com; adult €33-40, child €20) cruises daily around the south and west of the island, towards Los Órganos (p200), a weird rock

formation visible only from the water. The day-long trip could include some spontaneous whale or dolphin watching, as well as a little tuna fishing.

To learn more about whales and dolphins, contact the **Club de Mar** (☎ 922 80 57 59; www.club-de-mar.org; Puerto de Vueltas; boat cruises €32; ⊙ 9am-1pm & 5-7pm Mon-Fri, 9am-1pm Sat). This is both a marine-life investigation centre and a whale-watching outfitter with daily cruises that normally include the presence of a marine biologist, so that you can truly learn something about local marine life. All the cruises set sail from the Vueltas port.

Landlubbers will be pleased to know that Valle Gran Rey is the starting point for an endless array of hikes and cycling trips. Outfitters are listed on p188.

Sleeping
BUDGET
Apartamentos Playa-Mar (☎ 690 21 66 60; La Playa; studio/1-bedroom apt €25/40) Choose either a simple studio apartment or a larger one, with balcony looking onto the ocean and a big bedroom. Both are within spitting distance of the beach and the waterfront promenade, so light sleepers should bring earplugs.

MIDRANGE
Hotel Gran Rey (☎ 922 80 58 59; www.hotel-granrey .com; La Puntilla; s €46-73, d €65-96; P ⊠ ⊛) The area's only major hotel, it's just across from the beach. Rooms here are smallish but comfortable, with tiled floors, nice linen, a marbled bathroom and gorgeous views of either the mountains or (for a little extra) the ocean.

Apartamentos Las Mozas (☎ 922 80 61 01; lasmozas@telefonica.net; Carretera Playa del Inglés s/n, La Playa; 2-person apt €41-61, 4-person apt €65-81; P ⊛) Right on the waterfront in La Playa, these spic-n-span apartments aren't what you'd call stylish, but with views like these who needs adornment? The spacious kitchenette, simple wooden furnishings and lots of light make this a cheery place.

Apartamentos Laurisilva (☎ 902 50 06 69; www .solvasa.com; Borbalán s/n; 2-person apt €46-70; ⊛) A total of 108 tidy townhouse-style apartments are clustered around a pretty pool and garden area in this holiday complex several blocks inland from the waterfront. You might want to brush up on your German before you strike up a conversation with the families lounging around the pool.

Apartamentos Tres Palmeras (☎ 922 80 57 93; www.trespalmeras.com; La Playa; apt €48-54; P ☒) A modern-looking hotel complex with a salt-water pool, apartments here have balconies (most with ocean views) and are spacious and well-equipped.

Finca Argayall (☎ 922 69 70 08; Valle Gran Rey waterfront; studio apt per person incl 3 veg €65-80, r €48-76, huts €48-65, tents €42-53) This is no ordinary hotel. A rural estate a 15-minute stroll outside the tourist bustle of Valle Gran Rey, the *finca* (rural estate) is a tranquil ocean-side centre focused on communal, alternative and ecofriendly living. For lodging, guests can choose between modern rooms and apartments or the more rustic 'garden huts' and 'luxury tents'. Most staff live on the premises, offering near-daily meditation, yoga, massage and other therapies and activities. Organic food comes from the *finca*'s own garden.

Apartamentos Baja del Secreto (☎ 922 80 57 09; www.bajadelsecreto.com; Avenida Marítima s/n, Charco del Conde; 2-/3-/4-/5-/6-person apt €51/57/64/71/82; ☒) A charming, fortresslike building in traditional Canarian style, apartments here include fully equipped kitchenette, phone, TV and a generous terrace with a view. The rooftop pool is great, but who needs it when the Charco del Conde is just across the street?

Eating

Absinia (☎ 922 80 58 93; Calle Absinia, Vueltas; mains €6-10; ☾ closed Sun & Jun) A cheery sidewalk terrace is the perfect spot to enjoy the house specialities – *viejas*, tuna fillet with *mojo*, and *papas* with everything.

Restaurante La Islita (☎ 922 80 61 61; Calle La Playa s/n; mains €6-13) This convincingly Italian eatery serves just what you'd expect – a variety of pasta and pizza dishes with plenty of tomato, basil and oregano. The daily special is sure to please.

Bar-Restaurante El Puerto (☎ 922 80 52 24; Puerto de Vueltas; mains €6-15) Specialising in – what else? – fresh fish, this too-bright (the fluorescent lights lend it a bit of a fast-food air) place by the port is one of the best spots in town to try local delicacies such as grilled *peto* and *medregal* (local fish).

Restaurante El Palmar (☎ 922 80 53 32; Borbalán s/n; mains €8-11) Hidden among banana trees, a stone's throw from the main highway, it would easy to drive right by the Palmar, so keep an eye out for the road sign. Both the food and the atmosphere are comfy and welcoming. Try the *cazuela* (thick fish stew) and be sure to have a chat with the friendly owner.

Restaurante El Baifo (☎ 922 80 57 75; La Playa; mains €8-14; ☾ closed Fri; V) For something different come to this Malaysian-French restaurant, where woks and curries are served in a dining room with touches of Asian décor. Vegetarians will find lots of options, which is something rare around here.

Drinking

Club de Mar (☎ 606 53 91 46; Paseo Las Palmeras, La Playa; ☾ 11pm-5am) Occasional live music, theme nights and dance classes make this one of the liveliest nightlife options on the island.

Tambara Café (☎ 646 51 13 96; Calle Vueltas, Vueltas; ☾ 5pm-1am Thu-Tue; V) By day nibble on the vegetarian-friendly tapas menu (€5 to €10) and by night sip cocktails at this friendly bar, where the sound of breaking waves wafts over the breezy terrace.

Bar Cacatua (Calle Vueltas, Vueltas; ☾ 10am-2am) Open all day, this relaxing place serves drinks, salads and sandwiches (€2 to €7) to a mixed crowd. There's a small bar area indoors, and outside is a large, shady patio with a few scattered tables.

Getting There & Away

Bus 1 (€4, 1¾ hours) connects with San Sebastián several times a day and leaves from the bus station located beside the large traffic circle at the entry to the resort. To get to Vallehermoso you can get off at the Las Hayas stop and wait for bus 4 (€5, one hour to Vallehermoso, twice daily Monday to Friday).

The easiest way to move around the southern half of the island is to hop on the **Garajonay Exprés** (☎ 902 34 34 50), a water taxi heading to Playa Santiago (€2.50, 20 minutes, three times daily) and San Sebastián (€3.50, 40 minutes, three times daily). The ferries leave from the port.

Getting Around

If your own two feet can't do the job, **Alofi Rentals** (☎ 922 80 53 53; Vueltas; ☾ 9am-1pm & 5-7pm Mon-Sat, 10am-noon Sun) rents out bikes, scooters and motorcycles.

Call a taxi on ☎ 922 80 50 58. There's a taxi stand near the town hall.

LA GOMERA

La Palma

Perhaps more than any other island in the archipelago, La Palma offers the chance to experience real, unspoiled nature – from the verdant forests of the north, where lush vegetation drips from the rainforest canopy; to the desertscapes of the south, where volcanic craters and twisted rock formations define the views; to the serene pine forests of the Parque Nacional de la Caldera de Taburiente. No wonder the entire island was declared a Unesco biosphere reserve. It's the ideal place for a walking holiday, although trekkers are by no means the only ones who succumb to its attractions.

Mass tourism has yet to make its mark on 'The Pretty Island', as La Palma is nicknamed. The banana crop still represents a whopping 80% of the local economy, and the absence of golden beaches has diverted many travellers' attention elsewhere. Although things are changing – new hotels, golf course, ports and a bigger airport are all on the planning charts – for now La Palma is pristine and very pretty indeed.

Rainfall and spring water are more plentiful here than on any other island, making San Miguel de la Palma (the island's full name) the greenest of the archipelago. Orchards, vineyards and forests flourish, their soft beauty contrasting with the harsh crags and peaks of the volcanic heights that run down the island's centre. This is one of the most volcanically active islands; the archipelago's last eruption was in 1971 in Fuencaliente. That volcanic activity is responsible for La Palma's steep cliffs and plunging ravines. It's the steepest island in the world, shooting from sea level to 2426m in just over 10km.

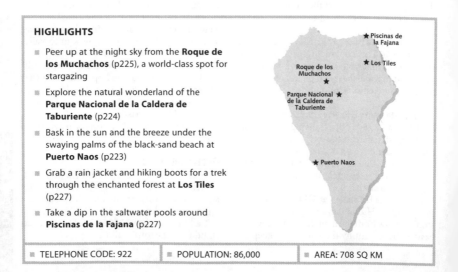

HIGHLIGHTS

- Peer up at the night sky from the **Roque de los Muchachos** (p225), a world-class spot for stargazing

- Explore the natural wonderland of the **Parque Nacional de la Caldera de Taburiente** (p224)

- Bask in the sun and the breeze under the swaying palms of the black-sand beach at **Puerto Naos** (p223)

- Grab a rain jacket and hiking boots for a trek through the enchanted forest at **Los Tiles** (p227)

- Take a dip in the saltwater pools around **Piscinas de la Fajana** (p227)

★ Piscinas de la Fajana

★ Los Tiles

Roque de los Muchachos ★

Parque Nacional ★ de la Caldera de Taburiente

★ Puerto Naos

■ TELEPHONE CODE: 922   ■ POPULATION: 86,000   ■ AREA: 708 SQ KM

HISTORY

Long before Castilla conquered the island in the 15th century, this rugged land was known as Benahoare. The first inhabitants could have arrived as early as the 5th century BC (although there's no hard and fast evidence to set the date), and they set up an orderly society that eventually divided into 12 cantons, each with its own chief.

The island officially became part of the Spanish empire in 1493, after Alonso Fernández de Lugo (a conquistador and, later, island governor) used a tribesman-turned-Christian to trick the Benahoaritas into coming down from their mountain stronghold for 'peace talks'. They were ambushed on the way at the spot now known as El Riachuelo. Their leader, Tanausú, was shipped to Spain as a slave, but went on a hunger strike on board the boat and never saw the Spanish mainland.

The next century was an important one for the island. Sugar, honey and sweet *malvasía* (Malmsey wine; see the boxed text, p210) became the major exports and abundant Canary pine provided timber for burgeoning shipyards. By the late 16th century, as transatlantic trade flourished, Santa Cruz de la Palma was considered the third most important port in the Spanish empire, after Seville and Antwerp.

The sugar, shipbuilding and cochineal (a bug used to make red dye) industries kept the island economy afloat for the next several centuries, but the island's fortunes eventually took a downward turn, and the 20th century was one of poverty and mass emigration. These days, the banana crop represents 80% of the local economy, but tourism is slowly growing.

INFORMATION
Books & Maps

Maps are available for sale at petrol stations, newspaper kiosks and bookshops. Tourist offices give out a very basic island map, but if you plan to explore, invest in a more detailed map, like the 1:50,000 map published by Ediciones David and created by Palmero Juan José Santos. Even better is the Freytag & Berndt 1:30,000 map, in English and German.

The hiking maps covering southern, central and northern La Palma given out for free at the tourist office in Santa Cruz give a good overview, and its *Hiking Guide* (in English and Spanish) is helpful too. But if you're a serious walker, you should buy a hiking guide, such as *Landscapes of La Palma and El Hierro*, published by Sunflower Books, *Walk! La Palma* by Discovery Walking Guides, or *La Palma* by Rother Walking Guides.

ACCOMMODATION

Although booking ahead is always recommended, during most of the year you can probably find last-minute accommodation on the island. Be sure to book if you're arriving on the late ferry from Tenerife, plan to arrive outside of regular business hours, or if you plan to come during a major holiday or festival (see p209).

Comfortable, quality lodging is available across the island, but some of the best options include the quirky B&B-style Hotel San Telmo (p215) in Santa Cruz, the Hotel La Palma Romántico (p228) in Barlovento and the Parador Nacional (p217).

Live like a local in the *casas rurales* (rural houses) for rent across the island. For information and reservations, contact the **Asociación de Turismo Rural** (☎ 902 43 96 25; www.ecoturismocanarias .com; Calle Pérez de Brito 102, Santa Cruz de La Palma), which rents nearly 100 rural houses across the island.

Free camping is banned on the island, as in the rest of Spain, but there are a few basic camp sites scattered around the island. In most cases you'll need to apply in advance and collect your permit in person before you intend to camp.

ACTIVITIES

Many outfitting companies operate island-wide, so regardless of where you're based you can enjoy the activities La Palma has to offer.

Walking

Don't come to La Palma without allowing a generous chunk of time to explore its wondrous landscapes on foot. With 850km of trails, this is the ideal place for a walking holiday. Several companies offer guided hikes; the best is **Natour** (☎ 922 43 30 01; www.natour -trekking.com; Apartamento Valentina 4, Los Cancajos; day-long walks with guide €29-37; ⏰ 9am-1pm & 5-7pm Mon-Fri), a company operating island-wide. Popular routes include the walk around the Parque Nacional de la Caldera de Taburiente (p224), the Ruta de los Volcanes (p221) and the 'Enchanted Forest' walk through

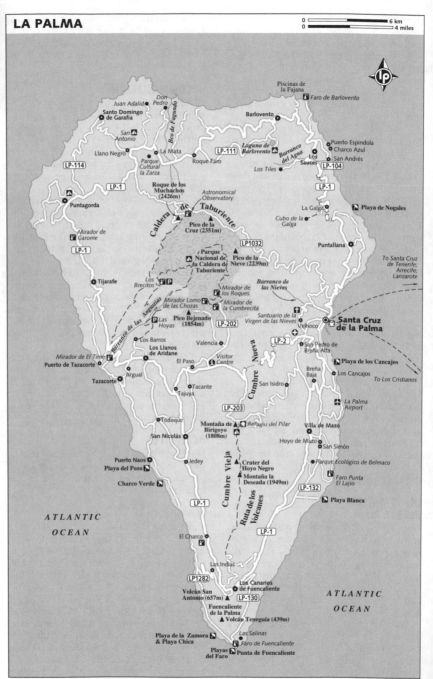

LA PALMA

LA PALMA

0 ————— 6 km
0 ————— 4 miles

Piscinas de
la Fajana

Faro de Barlovento

Juan Adalid   Don
Pedro   Barlovento
Santo Domingo
de Garafía
San
Antonio
Llano Negro   La Mata   Laguna de   Puerto Espíndola
                                    Barlovento   Charco Azul
                              LP-111   Barranco   San Andrés
LP-114   Parque   Roque Faro   del Agua   Los
            Cultural   Los Tiles Sauces   LP-104
LP-1   la Zarza   LP-1

            Roque de los
            Muchachos
            (2426m)   Astronomical   La Galga   Playa de Nogales
Puntagorda   Observatory
            Caldera de Taburiente   Cubo de la
            Pico de la   Galga
Mirador de Cruz (2351m)
Garome   Puntallana
LP-1   Parque   Pico de la   LP1032
            Nacional de Nieve (2239m)
            la Caldera de
            Taburiente   Barranco de   To Santa Cruz
Tijarafe   Los   Mirador de   las Nieves   de Tenerife;
            Brecitos   los Roques   Arrecife;
                         Mirador de   Lanzarote
            Mirador Lomo la Cumbrecita
            de las Chozas   Santuario de la
Las   Pico Bejenado   Virgen de las Nieves   Santa Cruz
Hoyas   (1854m)   LP-202   Velhoco   de la Palma
Los Barros   LP-2
            Los Llanos   Valencia   Cumbre   San Pedro de
Mirador de El Time
            de Aridane   Nueva   Breña Alta
Puerto de Tazacorte   El Paso Visitor   Playa de los Cancajos
            Argual   Centre   Breña   Los Cancajos
Tazacorte   San Isidro   Baja   To Los Cristianos
            Tacante
            Tajuya   La Palma
                         LP-203   Airport
            Todoque
                         Montaña de   Refugio del Pilar   Villa de Mazo
San Nicolás Birigoyo
             (1808m)   Hoyo de Mazo
                                              San Simón
Puerto Naos Jedey   Cráter del   Parque Ecológico de Belmaco
Playa del Pozo   Hoyo Negro
                        Montaña la   Faro Punta
Charco Verde   Deseada (1949m)   El Lajio
            Cumbre Vieja   LP-132
            LP-1   Playa Blanca

ATLANTIC   Ruta de los
                       Volcanes
OCEAN   LP-1

            El Charco

                                          ATLANTIC
            Las Indias   OCEAN

LP1282   Los Canarios
           de Fuencaliente
Volcán San
Antonio (657m)   LP-130
Fuencaliente
de la Palma   Volcán Teneguía (439m)

            Las Salinas
Playa de la Zamora   Faro de Fuencaliente
& Playa Chica
      Playas   Punta de Fuencaliente
      del Faro

forest land in the north. The company will pick you up at your hotel or a central meeting point.

Other reputable guide services include **La Palma Trekking** (☎ 922 18 14 33; www.la-palma-aktiv .com in German and Spanish; Aparthotel Las Olas, local D1, Los Cancajos; walking packages from €185) and **Ekalis** (☎ 922 44 45 17; www.ekalis.com; Las Indias 51, Fuencaliente; guided hikes, bike trips, caving expeditions & rock climbing per day €37.50), which also offers hotel pick ups.

It's not necessary to hike with a guide; La Palma offers safe walking conditions to anyone who's prepared and carries a good map. But the beauty of having a guide, other than the history and anecdotes they can share, is enjoying a long one-way trek with transport arranged at either end. Throughout this chapter there's information on notable walks, with details on how to arrange your own transport by bus or taxi.

Adventure Sports

If just plain walking seems too tame, try rock climbing or caving. Ekalis (above) offers a variety of climbing and rappelling experiences as well as a two-hour spelunking expedition. It also offers bike rental (€15) and guided mountain biking trips, another popular activity on the island. If you're in shape, La Palma's endless climbs and dips will be thrilling, but if trudging uphill isn't your thing, guide services like those offered by **Bike'n'Fun** (☎ 922 40 19 27; www.bikenfun.de; Calle Calvo Sotelo 20, Los Llanos de Aridane; guide service per person €40, bike rental per day €8-14) offer transport to the top of a peak followed by a mostly downhill ride. All operators can pick you up at your hotel or a central meeting point.

In recent years, paragliding has really taken off (pardon the pun!); the island is considered one of the world's best places to glide. Try it in Puerto Naos (p223). More information about paragliding can be found at www.flylapalma.com or www.palmaclub.com.

Diving & Kayaking

For those wanting to get out on the water, diving outfitters in Puerto Naos (p223) and Los Cancajos (p216) will hook you up with tanks, wetsuits and fins. Sea kayaking expeditions are also available in Puerto Naos and Los Cancajos; contact Ekalis (above) for more information.

FESTIVALS & EVENTS

Like any Spaniards worth their heritage, the Palmeros love a good party, and the year is packed with festivals and celebrations.

Each town has feast days, celebrating its patron saint with several days of parades, parties and other activities. They include the following:

Breña Alta (late June)
Breña Baja (25 July)
Barlovento (12-13 August)
San Andrés y Los Sauces (early September)
Tazacorte (late September)

January–February

Fiesta of the Almond Blossom A celebration of the beauty of the almond blossom in Puntagorda and of the town's patron saint, San Mauro Abad.

February–March

Carnaval Each year, around 50,000 people descend on Santa Cruz for Carnaval, the pre-Lent celebration that usually falls in mid-February. If you're here, don't forget your bottle of talcum powder (see the boxed text, p211).

March–April

Semana Santa (late March to early April) Members of lay brotherhoods parade down Calle O'Daly (Santa Cruz) in their blood-red robes and tall, pointy hoods.

May

Las Cruces (3 May) The island's crosses are bedecked in jewellery, flowers and rich clothes. Truly a sight to see.

June

La Patrona (2 June) The year's biggest party in Los Llanos de Aridane is held in honour of Our Lady of Los Remedios.

MAKE WAY FOR THE VIRGIN

Fiesta de Nuestra Señora de las Nieves (Feast Day of Our Lady of the Snows) is the island's principal fiesta. Don't miss the parade of giants and 'fat heads' (fanciful, rather squat characters with exceptionally large heads), though the high point is the dance of the dwarves, which has been performed here since the early 19th century. Every five years (2010, 2015 etc), the Bajada de la Virgen de las Nieves is celebrated. It's a religious procession where the islanders take the Virgin around the island throughout July and August, celebrating her arrival in each important town with a big party.

Corpus Christi The celebration of Corpus Christi at Villa de Mazo is a fragrant, flowery affair. Streets are decorated with elegant 'carpets' made of flower petals, seeds and soil.

San Juan (23 June) Marks the summer solstice, and is celebrated in Puntallana with bonfires and firecrackers galore.

August

Fiesta de Nuestra Señora de las Nieves (5 August) Santa Cruz puts on its party clothes for the celebration of the island's patron saint; see the boxed text, p209.

September

El Diablo (8 September) Fireworks, parades of devils and grim music in Tijarife provides a graphic show of the triumph of good over evil. About 30kg of gunpowder are used in the 20-minute show honouring Nuestra Señora de Candelaria.

December

Castanets (December 24) After Midnight Mass in Breña Alta and throughout the island, Palmero men perform skits accompanied by the noisy music of castanets.

LA PALMA FOR CHILDREN

Building sand castles on the black-sand beaches of Puerto Naos (p223) and Los Cancajos (p216), or splashing in the saltwater pools in places like Piscinas de la Fajana (p227) are givens, but what to do after the beach? Older kids (12 and above) will enjoy horseback riding with Finca Corazón (p220), while the younger crowd will get a kick out of the animals at Maroparque (p217).

Suitable hikes for kids include Mirador de los Roques (p225) and the Mirador Lomo de las Chozas (p225), both in the Parque Nacional de la Caldera de Taburiente; at the latter, you can even take a stroller. Throw in some history by taking the 1.5km walk around the **Parque Cultural La Zarza** (p228).

GETTING THERE & AWAY
Air

La Palma's **airport** (☎ 922 41 15 40), located just 7km from Santa Cruz, is in the midst of a major expansion project that aims to triple its capacity to three million passengers annually by 2010. Services here include rental car agencies, a currency exchange bureau and a small **tourist office** (☎ 922 42 62 12; www.tourlapalma.com; 8am-9.30pm).

At the time of research, it was possible to hop on direct flights to the island from Germany, Spain and Holland, but the number of flights here is likely to grow quickly. Check with **Aena** (www.aena.es) for the latest.

Interisland airways **Binter Canarias** (☎ 902 39 13 92; www.binternet.com) and **Islas Airways** (☎ 902 47 74 78; www.islasairways.com) keep La Palma

---

FOOD & DRINK

La Palma's main dishes, like those on other islands, are simple. What the island is really known for is indulgent desserts. Honey is an important food here, and historically La Palma was an important sugar producer. Most of the sugar cane is gone, but the islanders' sweet tooth remains. The gofio-honey-and-sugar *rapaduras* are a favourite tooth-rotter. Also tasty are *almendrados* (almond, sugar and egg cakes baked with cinnamon), *bienmesabe* (a paste pf almonds and sugar) and *Príncipe Alberto* (mousse of chocolate and almonds).

Local cheeses, most made with unpasteurised goats' milk and many smoked, are worth trying. Get more information online at www.quesopalmero.es.

Wine & Spirits

Since the early 16th century, when Spanish conquerors planted the first vines on the island, La Palma has been known for its sweet *malvasía* (Malmsey wine). Thanks to the merchants and colonists who came in and out of La Palma's ports, the wine acquired fame throughout Europe, and some referred to the tasty stuff as 'the nectar of the gods'. Even Shakespeare wrote about sweet Canary wine, making it Falstaff's favourite in *Henry IV* and calling it a 'marvellous searching wine' that 'perfumes the blood'. You can also find dry *malvasía* as well as a variety of reds, whites and rosé wines, especially in the areas of Fuencaliente and Hoyo de Mazo. For more information visit www.malvasiadelapalma.com or embark on the **Wine Route** (www.infoisla.org/rutadelvino), which includes 16 visitable wineries.

Although the sugar plantations have all but gone, what remains is put to good use in the production of *ron* (rum) by the last producer on the island, Ron Aldea.

well connected to the rest of the archipelago, with several flights daily to each of the other islands.

Boat

The **Fred Olsen** (☎ 902 10 01 07; www.fredolsen.es) Benchijigua Express ferry (€49, two hours) is a good option for those coming from Tenerife. The ferry leaves Los Cristianos, Tenerife at 8pm, and the return trip leaves Santa Cruz at 6.30am. From Tenerife, you can then continue to La Gomera or El Hierro.

At the time of research, **Trasmediterránea** (☎ 902 45 46 45; www.trasmediterranea.es) still had not determined its ferry schedule or pricing, but anticipated offering summer-only services between La Palma and Santa Cruz de Tenerife and between La Palma and Arrecife, Lanzarote.

GETTING AROUND
To/From the Airport

Bus 8 (€1, 20 minutes) makes the journey between Santa Cruz and the airport every 30 minutes from 6.45am to 11.45pm; on weekends, the service is provided only hourly. The bus also stops at Los Cancajos.

Bus

La Palma has a fairly good bus system (with 18 bus lines) that you can use to hop between the island's main towns. For complete route information, stop by a bus station or contact **Transportes Insular La Palma** (☎ 922 41 19 24; www.transporteslapalma.com). Route prices start at €1. If you plan to use the bus often, you're best to buy a Bonobus card. Cards start at €12 and represent a discount of about 20% off normal individual fares. They are on sale at bus stations, newsstands and tobacco shops.

Car

Having your own two wheels is the best way to tour the island at your leisure, and it's the only way to set about exploring every nook and cranny. La Palma is loaded with car-rental agencies, and all of those listed below can have a car waiting for you at the airport or port. Prices per day begin as low as €15 for tiny cars and week-long rentals. Expect to pay about €30 for a family-size car.

Auto Soyka (☎ 922 40 34 34; www.autosoyka.com; Calle General Yagüe 13, Los Llanos de Aridane) Specialises in 4WDs.

Cicar (☎ 922 42 80 48; www.cicar.com; La Palma airport) The islands' best-known car-rental company, it has offices on all seven islands and offers reliable service.

Oasis (☎ 922 43 44 09; www.oasis-la-palma.com; Centro Cancajos local 301, Los Cancajos)

Taxi

Taxis are an easy but awfully pricey way to get around. A one-way trip to Puerto Naos from Santa Cruz will burn a hole €45 wide in your pocket, more than a day's car rental!

SANTA CRUZ DE LA PALMA

pop 18,260

The historic (and bureaucratic) capital of the island, Santa Cruz de la Palma is a compact city strung out along the shore and flanked by fertile green hills. Although it makes poor use of its gorgeous location – a huge car park acts as a barrier between the town and the ocean – the old town is a treasure waiting to be discovered

---

THE SWEETEST-SMELLING BATTLE

Tenerife and Gran Canaria are known for their, ahem, lively celebrations of Carnaval, but unassuming Santa Cruz de la Palma also has a wild side. There's music, dancing, drinking and, of course, talcum powder. On Carnaval Monday, the good citizens of La Palma bring buckets of white, fragrant powder down to the centre of Santa Cruz and prepare to do battle with their neighbours. After loosening up with a few drinks and a little music, the snowy spectacle begins. Anyone is a target in this all-out war and the town ends the night coughing and blinking furiously, covered head to toe with talcum powder. The tradition began to mock the *los indios,* Canarian emigrants who became wealthy in the Americas and returned to the island decked in white suits and Panama hats. Now it's just another excuse for a fiesta.

LA PALMA

HISTORY

In the 16th century the dockyards of Santa Cruz earned a reputation as the best in all the Canary Islands. Ships were made with Canary pine, a sap-filled wood that was nearly impervious to termites, making the ships constructed here some of the most reliable and longest-lasting in the world. The town became so important that King Felipe II had the first Juzgado de Indias (Court of the Indias) installed here in 1558, and every single vessel trading with the Americas from mainland Spain was obliged to register.

The boom brought economic security, but it led to problems as well. Santa Cruz

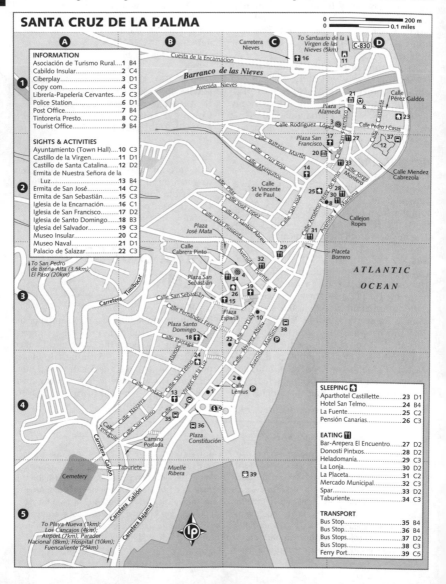

SANTA CRUZ DE LA PALMA

0 _____ 200 m
0 _____ 0.1 miles

INFORMATION
Asociación de Turismo Rural....**1** B4
Cabildo Insular.....................**2** C4
Ciberplay............................**3** D1
Copy com...........................**4** C3
Librería-Papelería Cervantes....**5** C3
Police Station.......................**6** D1
Post Office..........................**7** B4
Tintorería Presto...................**8** C2
Tourist Office.......................**9** B4

SIGHTS & ACTIVITIES
Ayuntamiento (Town Hall)....**10** C3
Castillo de la Virgen............**11** D1
Castillo de Santa Catalina......**12** D2
Ermita de Nuestra Señora de la
Luz..............................**13** B4
Ermita de San José................**14** C2
Ermita de San Sebastián.........**15** C3
Iglesia de la Encarnación........**16** C1
Iglesia de San Francisco.........**17** D2
Iglesia de Santo Domingo........**18** B3
Iglesia del Salvador..............**19** C3
Museo Insular......................**20** C2
Museo Naval.......................**21** D1
Palacio de Salazar.................**22** C3

SLEEPING 🏠
Aparthotel Castillette.............**23** D1
Hotel San Telmo...................**24** B4
La Fuente...........................**25** C2
Pensión Canarias..................**26** C3

EATING 🍴
Bar-Arepera El Encuentro........**27** D2
Donosti Pintxos....................**28** D2
Heladomanía.......................**29** C3
La Lonja............................**30** D2
La Placeta..........................**31** C2
Mercado Municipal................**32** C3
Spar.................................**33** D2
Taburiente.........................**34** C3

TRANSPORT
Bus Stop............................**35** B4
Bus Stop............................**36** B4
Bus Stops...........................**37** D2
Bus Stops...........................**38** C3
Ferry Port...........................**39** C5

ATLANTIC OCEAN

was frequently besieged and occasionally sacked by a succession of pirates, including those under the command of Sir Francis Drake.

ORIENTATION

The historic centre of Santa Cruz runs parallel to the waterfront and is easily walkable, although as you head further from the coast the hills get steeper. The heart of activity here is Calle O'Daly (aka Calle Real), a long pedestrian boulevard lined with shops and colonial-era houses.

INFORMATION

Bookshops

Librería-Papelería Cervantes (☎ 922 41 18 15; Calle Anselmo Pérez de Brito 4) This is a good one-stop shop for maps, guidebooks, international newspapers and office supplies.

Emergency

Policía Local (☎ 922 41 11 50; Avenida de los Indios 18)

Internet Access

Ciberplay (☎ 922 41 15 10; Calle San Francisco 1; per hr €2; ✆ 9am-2pm & 4.30-10pm Mon-Fri, 9am-2pm & 5-10pm Sat, 10.30am-1.30pm & 5-8.30pm Sun) Just off Plaza Alameda.

Copy.com (☎ 922 41 27 20; Calle Cabrera Pinto 15; per hour €2; ✆ 9am-1.30pm & 4.30-8pm Mon-Fri, 9.30am-1.30pm Sat) This place has just four computers, but you can also send and receive faxes and make photocopies.

Laundry

Tintorería Presto (☎ 922 41 80 69; Calle Anselmo Pérez de Brito 44; ✆ 9am-1.30pm & 5-8pm Mon-Fri, 9am-2pm Sat) Wash, dry and fold for €2.50 per 1kg.

Medical Services

Hospital (Hospital General de las Nieves; ☎ 922 18 50 00) The new hospital is an easy 10km drive or bus ride from town. Bus 9 makes the 15-minute trip hourly (€1.10).

Post

Post office (☎ 922 41 17 02; Plaza Constitución 2) Located by the big roundabout. It seems like an awfully big building for the postal needs of such a tiny island!

Tourist Information

Tourist office (☎ 922 41 21 06; www.tourlapalma .com; Plaza Constitución s/n; ✆ 9am-7.30pm Mon-Fri, to 3pm Sat, to 2pm Sun) This small kiosk office stocks lots of information about the town and the island,

whether you're interested in hiking, festivals, history or gastronomy.

SIGHTS & ACTIVITIES

Old Town

Chances are you'll be starting your visit either from the Plaza Constitución or from the huge ocean-front parking lot. Either way, you're a short walk from Calle O'Daly, the city's main street. Named for an Irish trader who made La Palma his home, the street is full of shops, bars and some of the town's most impressive architecture. The 17th-century, late-Renaissance **Palacio de Salazar** (Calle O'Daly 22) is on your left soon after you enter the street from Plaza Constitución. It's now home to a government-run cultural centre.

Wander north along Calle O'Daly and you'll come to the palm-shaded **Plaza España**, considered the most important example of Renaissance architecture in the Canary Islands. To one side sits the imposing **ayuntamiento** (town hall; ☎ 922 42 65 00), built in 1559 after the original was destroyed by French pirates. Across the plaza is the ornate **Iglesia del Salvador** (✆ 9.30am-1pm & 5.30-7.30pm). Though the church's exterior seems more fortress than house of worship, the interior boasts a glittering baroque pulpit dating to 1750, an ornate 16th-century wooden ceiling considered one of the best *mudéjar* (Islamic-style architecture) works in all the Canaries, and several fine sculptures.

Follow the steps heading up out of the Plaza de España to reach the upper town, where the shady **Plaza Santo Domingo**, with its terrace café, makes an excellent resting point. The **Iglesia de Santo Domingo** (✆ 4-5pm Sat) here boasts an important collection of Flemish paintings.

Head southwest on Calle Virgin de la Luz for a quick visit to the modest chapel **Ermita de Nuestra Señora de la Luz**, one of several small 16th- and 17th-century chapels in town. Another chapel, the **Ermita de San Sebastián** (Calle San Sebastián), is behind the Iglesia de San Salvador. Yet another is **Ermita de San José** (Calle San José), which has given its name to the street on which it stands.

Wander down to the waterfront to stroll alongside a series of wonderful **old houses** with traditional Canarian balconies. Many of the houses date to the 16th century and have been converted into upscale restaurants. The islanders' penchant for balconies came with Andalucian migrants and was modified by Portuguese influences.

Towards the Barranco de las Nieves

Crossing the wide Avenida del Puente, a major thoroughfare, Calle O'Daly becomes Calle Anselmo Pérez de Brito. Make your way northeast towards the **Iglesia de San Francisco** (Plaza San Francisco; ☉ 6-7.30pm), another Renaissance church rich in works of art, the majority being unmistakably baroque.

The restored convent next door houses the **Museo Insular** (☎ 922 42 05 58; admission €4; ☉ 9.30am-1.50pm & 4-6pm Mon-Fri Oct-Jun, 9am-2pm Mon-Fri Jul-Sep), the island's museum. Here you'll find everything from Guanche skulls to cupboards of sad stuffed birds and pickled reptiles.

Gaze north across leafy Plaza Alameda (a good place to sip a *café cortado* – an espresso with a splash of milk) and you'll think Christopher Columbus' ship, the *Santa María*, became stranded here. But no, it's actually the city's **Museo Naval**, known as El Barco de la Virgen (The Virgin's Boat) to the locals. It was closed for repairs at the time of research, but until it reopens it makes for a great photo opportunity.

On the seafront, the **Castillo de Santa Catalina** was one of several forts built in the 17th century to fend off pirate raids. Across the ravine and higher is a smaller one, the **Castillo de la Virgen**. Tucked away on the same hill is the 16th-century **Iglesia de la Encarnación**, the first church to be built in Santa Cruz after the Spanish conquest.

Santuario de la Virgen de las Nieves

For great views over Santa Cruz and the shore, take the relatively easy 2km hike north of town to La Palma's main object of pilgrimage, the 17th-century **Santuario de la Virgen de las Nieves** (☎ 922 41 63 67; ☉ 8.30am-8pm).

To walk from Plaza Alameda, follow the road, which becomes a signposted dirt track, westwards up the gorge of the Barranco de las Nieves. It will take nearly 45 minutes to walk up, but coming back is faster. By car, follow signs from the Avenida Marítima where it crosses the *barranco* (ravine), then turn right on the Carretera de las Nieves (LP-101) and continue winding up the hillside until you see signs for the sanctuary. The curve-filled 5km trip

takes nearly 15 minutes. Bus 10 (€1, approximately 20 minutes) comes up hourly from the town centre from 7.45am until 4.45pm, and less frequently in the evenings and on weekends.

The church sits in a peaceful spot surrounded by trees and greenery, all in typical Canarian colonial style with balconies and simple façades. Walking into the church, however, you'll leave simplicity behind to encounter a fabulously ornate interior. The plush carpet, sculptures galore and crystal chandeliers are the precursor to the Virgin Mary herself, surrounded by a glittering altar. The 14th-century sculpture is the oldest religious statue in the Canary Islands, and probably brought by merchants before the arrival of the Spaniards. Every five years the Virgin is brought down to Santa Cruz in a grand procession (see the boxed text, p209).

There's a bar-restaurant in the church grounds.

SLEEPING

Unless your budget doesn't stretch beyond the *pensiones* (guesthouses) here, it doesn't make much sense to stay in Santa Cruz itself; the best places are elsewhere.

Budget

Pensión Canarias (☎ 922 41 31 82; pensioncanarias@autosmagui.com; Calle Cabrera Pinto 27; s/d €23/34, s without bathroom €22) Friendly staff and a very Spanish-looking tiled entryway are the best this quiet *pensión* has to offer. Rooms (with TVs) are low on charm but clean, if rather too dark. Ditto for the bathrooms.

La Fuente (☎ 922 41 56 36; www.la-fuente.com; Calle Anselmo Pérez de Brito 49; apt €35-63) The 11 apartments are all different, but each is decorated in a casual, beachy style with modern bathroom. There is no elevator but those willing to climb to the 4th floor are rewarded with amazing sea and town views. La Fuente also rents other apartments around town; see the website for details.

Midrange

Aparthotel Castillete (☎ 922 42 08 40; www.aparthotelcastillete.com; Avenida Marítima 75; d/q €51/71) The good points: amazing views of crashing waves, a kitchenette, the central location. The bad points: traffic noise and narrow and cramped rooms. This is a decent options for families with small kids.

ourpick Hotel San Telmo (☎ 922 41 53 85; www.hotel -santelmo.com; Calle San Telmo 5; s/d €60/75) Opened in 2006, this cute and comfortable B&B-style hotel has just eight rooms with TV and ADSL line. The German owner's colourful personality is all over, from the huge lit fountain in the patio, to the eclectic art scattered about (it's all for sale), to the orange walls that are made even brighter with glitter.

EATING
Many of Santa Cruz's nicest restaurants are located along the Avenida Marítima, especially at the far northeastern end.

Self-Catering
Spar (☎ 922 41 71 06; Calle Anselmo Pérez de Brito 71; ☺ 8am-10pm Mon-Sat, to 2pm Sun) The largest grocery-store chain on the island.

Mercado Municipal (Avenida Puente; ☺ 6am-2pm Mon-Fri, to 3pm Sat) Local and imported produce, Canarian wines and palm honey and other goodies are on sale at this small but airy fresh market. Perfect to prepare a picnic.

Budget & Midrange
Heladomanía (☎ 659 63 55 77; Calle Vandale 8; ☺ 10.30am-2.30pm & 4.30-8.30pm Mon-Fri, 10.30am-2.30pm & 5.30-8.30pm Sat, 11.30am-2.30pm & 5.30-8.30pm Sun) For some of the richest ice cream you've had in a while, pop into Heladomanía, where the artisanal ice cream is made on the spot.

Bar-Arepera El Encuentro (☎ 922 41 10 44; Calle Pérez de Brito; arepas €1.50) Cheap and tasty, Venezuelan *arepas* (hot pockets made of corn or flour and filled with meat or cheese) are an island staple. Iron tables are set up on the shady plaza.

Donosti Pintxos (☎ 922 41 40 04; Avenida Marítima 57; mains €6.50-12) Basque-style tapas (called *pintxos*) make for a great quick meal, although there are also sit-down dishes, including Basque specialities like cod fish.

Taburiente (☎ 922 41 64 42; Calle Pedro Poggio 7; mains €9-10) Don't bother asking for a menu; it's whatever struck the owner's fancy that day. This is a local favourite, especially on weekends, when crowds come for tapas and typical Canarian dishes.

Top End
La Placeta (☎ 922 41 52 73; Calle Borrero 1; mains €7-10; ☺ closed Sun) A charming little bistro on a tiny square, La Placeta has a small menu featuring everything from ravioli to Canary *mojo*

(spicy salsa sauce), including lots of vegetarian dishes. Downstairs, get sandwiches, desserts and tapas (€1 to €3). Head upstairs for the dining room.

La Lonja (☎ 922 41 52 66; Avenida Marítima 55; mains €10-17; ☺ closed Sun) Inside an old Canary house with balconies overlooking the seafront, La Lonja is perhaps the city's most upscale restaurant, with a mix of Canarian, Castillian and Mediterranean fare like paella, suckling pig and roasted cheese with *mojo*.

DRINKING & ENTERTAINMENT
Santa Cruz is no mecca for night owls; on the island, Los Llanos de Aridane takes that title. But there are plenty of quiet terrace bars where you can nurse a drink or two. Along Avenida Marítima, which is lined with cafés and *zumerías* (juice bars), you'll find a family-friendly atmosphere. In town head to Calle Álvarez Abreu, the closest thing you'll find to a nightlife scene. The Plaza José Mata, off Avenida Puente, also has a few bars.

GETTING THERE & AWAY
For details about ferry services to and from Santa Cruz, see p211.

To/From the Airport
Bus 8 (€1, 20 minutes) makes the journey between Santa Cruz and the airport every 30 minutes from 6.45am to 11.45pm, stopping in Los Cancajos on the way. On weekends, the service is provided only hourly. A taxi to the airport costs about €15.

Bus
Transportes Insular La Palma buses keep Santa Cruz well connected with the rest of the island. The bus stops are near Plaza Constitución and along the Avenida Marítima. Routes include bus 3 (€4.20, 45 minutes, 10 daily) to Los Llanos de Aridane and bus 11 (€1.40, 20 minutes, nine daily) to Puntallana.

GETTING AROUND
The best way to get around Santa Cruz is on foot. If you come in by car, try to find a parking spot in the large car park by the waterfront, as the narrow streets are much better enjoyed while walking. If you're in a hurry you can catch one of the buses that run up and down the Avenida Marítima (fare around €1) or hop in a **taxi** (☎ 922 41 60 70).

AROUND SANTA CRUZ

LOS CANCAJOS

A prettily manicured waterfront and a small volcanic beach are the main attractions of this cluster of hotels, apartments and restaurants 4km south of Santa Cruz; calling it a 'town' would be stretching it. Los Cancajos has none of the charm of Santa Cruz or other authentic, lived-in towns, but it nevertheless makes a good home base thanks to its abundance of quality lodging options and agreeable beach, which is one of the best on the island.

Information

INTERNET ACCESS

Planitel (☎ 922 43 42 33; Carretera Los Cancajos; per hr €2; 🕑 9.30-2pm & 4-9pm Mon-Sat) Here you can also get phonecards or use the phone booths.

MEDICAL SERVICES

Centro Médico (☎ 922 43 42 11, 653 81 31 58; Centro Comercial Los Cancajos, local 307; 🕑 9am-3pm Mon-Fri) English spoken.

Activities

Several activity outfits are set up in Los Cancajos. Dive with **Buceo Sub** (☎ 922 18 11 13; www.scuba-diving-la-palma.de; dive incl equipment €36; 🕑 9.30am-6pm Tue-Sun), based beside the H10 Costa Salinas aparthotel, or **La Palma Diving Center** (☎ 922 18 13 93; www.la palma diving.com; dive incl equipment €38; 🕑 10am-6pm Mon-Sat), in the Centro Cancajos shopping centre (on your left as you enter Los Cancajos from Santa Cruz).

Plenty of tour operators are also set up here. **Tours Viva** (☎ 922 43 53 00; Urbanización San Antonio del Mar; 🕑 9am-7pm Mon-Fri, 10am-1pm Sat) organises bus and hiking trips. Rent bikes from **Autos Damián – Club Ciclista** (☎ 922 43 46 88; Centro Cancajos local 211; bike rental per day €11; 🕑 9am-1pm & 5-7pm Mon-Fri, 9-11.30am Sat).

Sleeping

Most accommodation options here are apartments or aparthotels (hotels where the rooms resemble small apartments). In most cases, the official prices quoted here are somewhat higher than what you can get by booking through travel agencies or online booking sites. Throughout Los Cancajos there is free street parking near lodgings.

Aparthotel Las Olas (☎ 922 43 40 52; www.a-caledonia.com; 1-2-person apt €65-85; 🏊 ♿) Modern, tidy apartments, many with views of the water, are spread over a large waterside resort complex surrounded by lush gardens. The large pool, newish look and spacious rooms have made this one of the most popular places to stay on the island.

Hacienda San Jorge (☎ 922 18 10 66; www.hsanjorge.com; 1-3-person apt €65-86; 🏊) The Canary-styled Hacienda offers small but attractive apartments with separate bedrooms, open-plan kitchens and great views, but what really makes this place special are the verdant gardens that surround the pool and all four of the aparthotel's buildings.

Also recommended:

Apartamentos Lago Azul (☎ 922 43 43 05; www.apartamentoslagoazul.com; 2-3-person apt €48; 🏊) Simple one-bedroom apartments with large balconies overlooking the ocean and an attractive pool area.

H10 Costa Salinas(☎ 922 43 43 48; www.h10.es; 2-3-person apt €65-90; 🏊) A large, full-service resort run by the good-value H10 hotel chain, this is a popular

GREAT OFF-THE-BEATEN-TRACK EATING

Some of the island's best restaurants are a short drive from Santa Cruz. For unbeatable local flavour, it doesn't get any better than this.

- **Restaurante Chipi-Chipi** (☎ 922 41 10 24; Calle Juan Mayor 42, Velhoco; mains €8-13; 🕑 closed Wed & Sun) This is a meat eater's haven, with a variety of grilled meats all served with loads of *papas arrugadas* (wrinkly potatoes) and *mojo* (spicy salsa sauce made from red chilli peppers).
- **our pick** **Casa Goyo** (☎ 922 44 06 06; Carretera General Lodero 120; mains €5-10; 🕑 closed Mon) Hands-down the best seafood on the island can be had at this beach-shack-like eatery just south of the airport. Hear the roar of the planes as you savour *vieja a la plancha* (pan-grilled parrot fish) and *papas*.
- **El Cantillo** (☎ 922 43 49 20; Carretera Aeropuerto 67; mains €8-12; 🕑 closed Tue) Fish, Canarian specialities and grilled meats (the rabbit and goat are especially tasty) make this a popular place.

aparthotel for families. H10 also runs the H10 Taburiente Playa, a traditional hotel.

Eating

The area around Centro Cancajos has several casual restaurants and bars, many with terraces. Self-caterers can head to the **Spar** (☎ 922 18 14 44; Urbanización Costa Salinas) supermarket near the H10 hotels.

Tasca Alavasca (☎ 922 43 47 54; Oasis de San Antonio L4; tapas €2-4) Located on the main road that cuts through Los Cancajos, this intimate tavern is a popular place to get tapas and *pintxos*, especially at night, when a bar atmosphere takes over.

El Pulpo (☎ 922 43 49 14; Playa Los Cancajos; mains €6-10; ☻ closed Wed) This water-side beach shack is the place to come for fried fish and a friendly beach-bum attitude.

Casablanca (☎ 922 43 51 99; Centro Cancajos; mains €6-10; ☻ closed Tue) Come here for tasty wood-oven pizzas and a charming terrace perfect for enjoying La Palma's mild nights, or even for after-dinner drinks.

El Lagar (☎ 922 43 46 24; Cento Cancajos, local 304; mains €6-12; ☻ closed Thu) Everything from curries to pizzas to fresh Canarian fish is served at this sprawling beach-side restaurant at the back of the Centro Cancajos. By day, enjoy great ocean views.

Drinking & Entertainment

A handful of bars and terraces scattered behind the Centro Cancajos serves as Los Cancajos' nightlife centre. Although offerings vary wildly by season and night, you may find anything from DJs and dancing, to live music, to a quiet sip-your-drink-and-chat atmosphere.

Getting There & Away

Bus 8 (€1, 10 minutes) passes through every 30 minutes on its way from Santa Cruz to the airport; a second bus does the route in reverse. The main bus stop is at the Centro Cancajos shopping centre.

BREÑA ALTA

pop 6670

Just outside Santa Cruz, this rural, tranquil area isn't a major destination but it is home to a few notable sights, renowned artisans and the classy Parador Nacional hotel.

Kids will love **Maroparque** (☎ 922 41 77 82; www.maroparque.com; Calle Cuesta 28; adult/child

€11/5; ☻ 10am-5pm Mon-Fri, to 6pm Sat & Sun), a small zoo where 300 species of animals and lots of local vegetation make for a pleasant afternoon.

our pick **Parador Nacional** (☎ 922 43 58 28; www .paradores.es; Carretera de Zumacal, Breña Baja; r €135-169; **P** 🐕 🏊 ♿) is an elegant hotel about 8km south of Santa Cruz and outside the nucleus of Breña Alta. It looks like a huge Canary farmhouse overlooking the ocean. There is a pretty pool surrounded by grass and a lovely botanical garden. Rooms are spacious and sun-filled, with a sitting area and panoramic views. The Parador's restaurant (menú €29) serves local specialities and island wines, and is a great place for a special dinner. Sitting on a hill overlooking the ocean, the setting is unbeatable.

THE SOUTH

Banana plantations, pine forests, volcanic landscapes and rugged coastline mark the southern tip of La Palma. Due to its recent volcanic activity (several volcanoes erupted in the 20th century, the most recent in 1971), the landscape is much drier than what you'll find in the north. Still, it's beautiful in its starkness.

VILLA DE MAZO

pop 4760

A quiet village 13km south of Santa Cruz, Mazo is surrounded by green, dormant volcanoes. The town is known for the cigars and handicrafts made here and for being a highlight of La Palma's **winery route** (www.infoisla.org/rutadelvino).

As soon as you enter town, make a left to head down to **Museo Casa Roja** (☎ 922 42 85 87; Calle Maximiliano Pérez Díaz; admission €2; ☻ 10am-2pm & 3-6pm Mon-Fri, 11am-6pm Sat & 10am-2pm Sun), a lovely pinkish-red mansion (built in 1911) with exhibits on embroidery and Corpus Christi – a festival the town celebrates with particular gusto (see p210). The house itself has an impressive imperial staircase and ornate tiled floors.

Beyond the museum is **Escuela Insular de Artesanía** (☎ 922 42 84 55; ☻ 8am-3pm Mon-Fri Oct-Jun, to 2pm Jul-Sep), the island handicrafts school, which runs a shop where you can buy tobacco, embroidery, ceramics, baskets and other goods. To get to the shop, head into the school's main patio and up the stairs on your right.

You can also buy artisan goods at the weekend **market** (Via de Enlace Doctor Amilcar Morera Bravo; 3-7pm Sat, 9am-1pm Sun), where produce, handicrafts and a variety of food products are sold.

Down the hill from the school is the imposing **Templo de San Blas**, Mazo's 16th-century church, which sits on a small plaza overlooking the ocean. Inside, the church boasts a baroque altarpiece and several interesting pieces of baroque art.

Continue 800m down the hill (take the car unless you want to trudge back uphill) to reach **Cerámica el Molino** (☎ 922 44 02 13; Carretera Hoyo de Mazo; admission free; 9am-1pm & 3-7pm Mon-Sat), a meticulously restored mill that houses a ceramics museum and workshop where artisans make reproductions of Benahoare pottery. There's a popular souvenir shop as well. You can also get here from the LP-132 highway.

Sleeping & Eating

Hotel Rural Arminda (☎ 922 42 84 32; Calle Lodero 181; s/d with breakfast €50/75;) With just five rooms, this intimate B&B boasts lush gardens, fabulous ocean views and a peaceful setting amid the banana palms just outside Mazo.

San Blas (☎ 922 42 83 60; Calle Maria del Carmen Martínez Jerez 4; mains €5-8; closed Sun afternoon & Mon) In the centre of town, get simple dishes like pastas, salads, *chocos* (cuttlefish) with *mojo verde* (green sauce) or goat with potatoes served on a shady outdoor terrace.

La Cabaña (☎ 922 44 03 10; Carretera a Fuencaliente Km6; mains €5-13; closed Mon) Enjoy grilled meats, fresh fish, salads, soup, *papas arrugadas* with *mojo*, and fabulous bread cooked with anise (an island speciality) at this rustic spot just off the highway south of town. The balcony terrace affords an ocean view – although you'll have to put up with traffic noise.

Getting There & Away

Mazo is sandwiched between the LP-1 and LP-132 highways. Get here by bus 3 (10 daily), which links Mazo with Los Llanos (€4.40, one hour), Fuencaliente (€1.70, 30 minutes) and Santa Cruz (€1.45, 20 minutes).

PARQUE ECOLÓGICO DE BELMACO

The first ancient petroglyphs (rock carvings) found on the archipelago were discovered at this site in 1752. A 300m trail that winds around various cave dwellings once inhabited by Benahoare tribes people is the heart of this 'ecological park', but the real attractions are the whorling, sworling, squiqqling rock etchings, which date to AD 150. There's also a museum and small shop.

Belmaco (☎ 922 44 00 90; Carretera a Fuencaliente Km7; admission €2; 10am-6pm Mon-Sat, to 3pm Sun) boasts four sets of engravings, and experts remain perplexed about their meaning, though they speculate that the etchings could have been religious symbols.

Bus 7 from Santa Cruz heads down this way four times daily (except weekends). The nearest bus stop is about 400m south of the cave.

PLAYA BLANCA

Just 1.3km north along the LP-132 highway from the Parque Ecológico de Belmaco is an unmarked road that leads down to **Playa Blanca** (White Beach, though 'Salt and Pepper Beach' would be a better name). A perfect picnic spot, here you'll find a tiny hippy hamlet with a few summer homes, a tranquil beach and a rocky coast perfect for fishing or crabbing.

FUENCALIENTE

pop 1856

South of Belmaco, the LP-132 highway joins with the larger LP-1 and leads to Fuencaliente (Hot Fountain). The area gets its name from hot springs that were once believed to treat leprosy, but were buried by a fiery volcano in the 17th century. The original spring should be restored and opened to the public soon. Don't think that the volcanoes have calmed down; the last eruption was in 1971, when Volcán Teneguía's lava flow added a few hectares to the island's size.

You'll drive through a lovely pine forest before reaching Los Canarios de Fuencaliente, the urban centre of Fuencaliente.

Sights & Activities

Creating a stark, at times lunarlike, landscape, the volcanoes in this area are the newest in the archipelago and are the main draw of Fuencaliente. The beauty of their low, ruddy cones belies the violence with which they erupted.

Don't miss the short but breathtaking walk along the rim of **Volcán San Antonio** (☎ 922 44 46 16; adult/under 13yr €3/free; 9am-6pm Oct–mid-Mar, 9am-7pm mid-Mar–Jun, 9am-8pm Jul-Sep). It takes just

---

DETOUR

If you're in the mood for some scenic driving, take the LP-1282 highway far past the Princess resort complex to the very southern tip of the island and the **Playas del Faro** (Lighthouse Beach) and **Las Salinas** (a salt deposit known as a bird-watcher's paradise). Return to civilisation by following the highway, now called LP-130, north to complete the loop. Be careful at night; the road is curvy and unlit.

---

20 minutes to walk the gravel path halfway around the yawning chasm of this great black cone, which last blew in 1949 and is now being repopulated by hardy Canary pines. Afterwards, take a look at the small visitor centre, where a seismograph constantly measuring volcanic movement in the area shows a boring but comforting straight line. You can also take a **camel ride** (15min €6) around the volcano.

From the visitor centre, a signposted trail leads you to **Volcán Teneguía**; its 1971 eruption was the archipelago's most recent. The easy walk there and back takes about two hours.

After getting your fill of the craters, check out the town's other claim to fame: the wines made in this volcanic soil. The largest winery in town is **Bodegas Teneguía** (☎ 922 44 40 78; www.vinosteneguia.com; Los Canarios s/n; ☙ 9am-2pm & 3-6pm Mon-Sat, 11am-2pm Sun), with white, red and sweet wines that are sold all over the island and beyond. There's also a good restaurant in the winery (see right).

You can also tour Fuencaliente by bike. **Fuencaliente Bikes** (☎ 628 51 32 42; www.fuencaliente bike.com; bike rental per day €13, guided excursion €35) meets groups in town and leads downhill rides to the beaches (below)

Fuencaliente, with its ideal wind and climate conditions, has become a magnet for paragliding. Experienced paragliders (with their own equipment) often take off in Las Indias and land near the San Antonio volcano, but there are no flights available to novices.

BEACHES

The coast around Fuencaliente is largely inaccessible, with banana plantations, rocky outcrops and steep cliffs lining much of it. Two pleasant exceptions are **Playa de la Zamora** and **Playa Chica**, black beaches tucked side by side in coves. They're no secret but are rarely crowded. To get here, take the Carretera de Las Indias (LP-1282) past the San Antonio volcano toward the hamlet of Las Indias. Follow the curves downhill until a small sign indicates a turn-off for the *playas* (beaches) to the right.

Sleeping

Apartamentos & Pensión Los Volcanes (☎ 922 44 41 64; Carretera General 86; d/apt €22/25) A nice surprise, with newish, tasteful décor, private bathrooms and some rooms with a small balcony. Apartments are studio-style, with a kitchenette, sitting area and bed all in the same room.

El Nísparo (☎ 902 43 06 25; www.islabonita.es; Las Indias, Fuencaliente; 1-3-person rural house €45-55) Nestled among vineyards in the hamlet of Las Indias, just outside Los Canarios, this intimate rural house is the ideal escape, with a terrace overlooking the Atlantic and original touches like a round kitchen with a wood ceiling.

Hotel La Palma Teneguía Princess & Spa (☎ 922 42 55 00; Carretera La Costa Cerca Vieja 10; P ❆ ☐ ☒ ᕦ) Technically two hotels (La Palma Princess and Teneguía Princess), this sprawling, self-contained resort complex near the waterfront (8km south of Los Canarios) is the most ambitious hotel on the island. With 625 rooms, several pools and marvellous ocean views, the overall effect is pleasing. But keep in mind that you're a winding, 20-minute drive from anything, and public transport down here is limited (four buses a day). To explore the island, stay elsewhere.

Eating

El Quinto Pino (☎ 922 44 45 16; LP-1282, Las Indias; mains €6-10; ☙ Thu-Sun; ☑) Pizzas, grilled meats and vegetables are the speciality at this tiny, family-run spot in the hamlet of Las Indias, northwest of Los Canarios.

Tasca La Era (☎ 922 44 44 75; Carretera Antonio Paz y Paz 6; mains €7-12; ☙ closed Wed) A farmhouse-style restaurant with a terrace and garden area, this is a charming spot for simple meat and fish dishes.

El Patio del Vino (☎ 922 44 46 23; Los Canarios s/n; mains €9-12; ☙ closed Mon) Behind the Bodegas Teneguía is this upscale restaurant, where house soups and local game dishes are served in a tranquil and spacious dining room.

Getting There & Away

Bus 7 (€3.20, one hour, up to five daily) heads between Fuencaliente and Santa Cruz via Mazo. Bus 3 (€3.20, one hour, up to eight daily) stops in Fuencaliente, except weekends, on its way between Los Llanos and Santa Cruz.

THE SOUTHWESTERN COAST

The road up the west coast from the bottom tip of the island is full of open curves that swoop past green hills dotted with cacti and low shrubs. The highway runs along a ridge, leaving the glittering ocean a blue haze to the left. Other than the view, there's not much here, unless you count the small bar at the **mirador** (lookout) 6km out of Fuencaliente in the tiny town of El Charco.

Keep heading north and you'll travel through a series of tiny, almost uninhabited villages. Stop in **San Nicolás** for a while (it's 1km past the village of Jedey), to eat at **Bodegon Tamanca** (☎ 922 49 41 55; Carretera General; mains €4-12; ☷ closed Sun dinner & Mon), an atmospheric restaurant located in a spacious, natural cave with stone-topped tables and booths that seem to be dug into the rock. This is a meat lover's kind of establishment, whether you like it grilled, cured or stewed.

THE CENTRE

The bowl-shaped Caldera de Taburiente, and the national park named after it, dominate the centre of La Palma, with rocky peaks, deep ravines and lush pine forests blanketing the slopes. The LP-2 highway, which links Santa Cruz with Los Llanos, skirts the southern rim of the park, and from the road you can sometimes see the characteristic cloud blanket that fills the interior of the caldera and spills over its sides like a pot boiling over.

Two of the island's important commercial centres, El Paso and Los Llanos (the island's largest town), are here, making this region the economic engine of La Palma. It's also a key banana-growing area and, as you near the west coast, banana plantations fill the valleys. The coast is home to some of the island's longest and prettiest beaches.

EL PASO

pop 7440

The gateway to the Parque Nacional de la Caldera de Taburiente (p224) – the park's visitor centre is just outside town – El Paso is the island's largest municipality, with sprawling forests and around 8 sq km of cultivated land. The modest town centre, however, won't detain you for long. If you're driving into town, turn right at the 'Casco Histórico' sign to reach the main attractions.

The first stop is the **silk workshop** (☎ 922 48 56 31; Calle Manuel Taño 6; ☷ 10am-1pm Mon, Wed & Fri, 10am-1pm & 5-7pm Tue & Thu), where silk is made according to traditions that have barely changed since the industry arrived on the island in the 16th century. The restored 18th-century **Ermita de la Virgen de la Concepción de la Bonanza** is a curiously painted little chapel. Renovations mercifully left intact the splendid *mudéjar* ceiling above the altar.

El Paso's real appeal is its natural beauty, and a great way to enjoy it is on horseback. The German owners of **Finca Corazón** (☎ 699 62 95 17; www.la-palma-reiten.com; Custa de la Juliana, El Paso; guided excursions €40-75; ☷ 11am-6pm) will take equestrians of all levels on 2½- to five-hour rides in and around the national park.

Sleeping & Eating

Pensión La Tienda (☎ 922 49 73 42; www.lapalma-pension.de; Calle Cruz Grande 1; d €25-70, 2-person apt €60; ☖) Six immaculate rooms in a whitewashed, traditional Canary house on the outskirts of town make up this friendly guesthouse. A well-tended garden and fruit trees give it a tropical air. For a real treat, book the Suite Don Andreo, with its own terrace and romantic fireplace.

Casa Elida (☎ 922 48 61 65; www.casaelida.de; Calle Pilar 3; 2-4-person apt €35-69) Several old stone Canary houses huddled together have been converted into six quaint apartments with terraces and gardens. Simple, clean and rustic, the apartments themselves are appealing, but the setting is fabulous.

Bodegón La Abuela (☎ 922 48 56 09; Calle General Tajuya 49; mains €4-12; ☷ closed Thu) On your left as you leave El Paso toward Los Llanos, this home-style eatery with a terrace serves delicious rabbit and game dishes.

La Cascada (☎ 922 48 57 27; Carretera Cumbre; mains €4-12; ☷ closed Thu) Just 1km out of town you'll find this hearty restaurant popular with local workmen (always a sign of fair prices and filling food). Spare ribs, veal chops, veal tongue stew… vegetarians best look elsewhere!

REFUGIO DEL PILAR

On the LP-203 highway, outside El Paso off the LP-2, is the **Refugio del Pilar** (☎ 922 41 15 83), an expansive park with a picnic area and camp site. You can pitch a tent for up to seven days at this tidy park, which has shower and toilet facilities, but you'll need to get permission one week in advance from the island's **Cabildo** (☎ 922 41 15 83; fax 922 42 01 87; Avenida de los Indianos 20, La Palma).

This is the trailhead of the popular **Ruta de los Volcanes**, a 19km hiking trail that meanders through ever-changing volcanic scenery and gives privileged views of both coasts as it heads south along the mountain ridge, through the heart of volcanic territory and towards Fuencaliente (p218). This trail is part of the long-distance GR-130. Allow six to seven hours for the trek – it's demanding and is best undertaken on cool, cloudy days, as there is not much shade or fresh water along the way. You should arrange transport from Fuencaliente.

LOS LLANOS DE ARIDANE

pop 21,045

The economic centre of the island, Los Llanos lacks the obvious charm of the capital or some of the smaller villages, but the shady plazas and pedestrian streets of the historic centre are worth exploring. Set in a fertile valley, this has historically been one of the island's richest areas, with a long tradition of cultivating sugar cane, bananas and, more recently, avocados. These days it's home to many of the island's business and services, and many young Palmeros are moving here to find jobs.

LOCAL VOICES

Uke is not what you could call soft-spoken. A bar owner and part-time tour guide, he's known for entertaining his charges with opinionated tales (in English, Spanish or German) of La Palma's history, culture and current events as he leads them huffing and puffing along the island's hilly trails. Today he and group of two dozen visitors are tackling the 19km Ruta de los Volcanes (Volcano Route), which runs along a mountain ridge in the south of the island.

Uke, who grew up in Venezuela after his Palmero parents migrated there in the 1960s, doesn't even get winded as he rattles off facts about his ancestors' homeland. 'Canary pine trees can live 500 years. They survive lava flows in part because of their very thick bark,' he says, his foot propped up on a stump where the bark is 10cm thick. 'That black hill is the volcanic cone where the island's last eruption happened in 1971,' he says, pointing in the distance. 'The banana crop still represents 80% of the island's economy… One of the best desserts of La Palma is *Príncipe Alberto*… If you want to enjoy island nightlife, you should come at Christmas or during Easter week, when all the students come home from the university on Tenerife… The best restaurant for fresh fish is Casa Goyo…'

The lively commentary goes on for hours. He's like a human encyclopaedia with only one entry: the island of La Palma.

Uke's story is not unlike that of many Canarios. The son of emigrants, he finally returned to La Palma as an adult, now that the island's hardest economic times have passed. Yet, although he's clearly enamoured with his island, not all is not paradise here, he insists.

'Part of the trail we're hiking on right now will be turned into a golf course if the politicians have their way,' he says.

'Overdevelopment is bad for all of us. It destroys the landscape that people travel all this way to see. But it also destroys the island lifestyle. For example, right now almost everyone on the island is involved in the banana industry one way or another. If developers are allowed to build golf courses (which must be watered) the price of water will go up and the banana plantations won't be cost-effective. The Palmeros will end up selling their banana plantations and losing their source of extra income.'

Uke spreads his pro-preservation gospel to the dozens of tourists who walk with him every week. Is it making a difference? He can't say. But about one thing, he's insistent: 'Enjoy La Palma while you can, because changes are coming.'

LA PALMA

Information

INTERNET ACCESS
Ciber Locutorio Atlántico (☎ 922 46 03 10; Calle General Yagüe 14; per hr €1.50; ⏰ 11am-11pm) A call centre, photocopier, fax central and net café in one.

LAUNDRY
Tintoreria Bellosur (☎ 922 46 10 26; Calle General Yagüe 8; ⏰ 9am-2pm & 4-8pm Mon-Fri, 9am-2pm Sat) Wash and dry 6kg for €9; same-day service.

MEDICAL SERVICES
Centro de Salud (☎ 922 40 30 70; Calle Princesa Dacil)

POST
Post office (☎ 922 46 09 56; Calle General Franco 3; ⏰ 8.30am-8.30pm Mon-Fri, 9.30am-1pm Sat)

TOURIST INFORMATION
Tourist office (☎ 922 40 25 28; Avenida Dr Fleming; ⏰ 9.30am-2pm & 4-6.30pm Mon-Fri, 9am-2pm Sat)

Sights & Activities
Start your visit in busy **Plaza España**, the heart of the historic town. Majestic Indian laurel trees provide much-welcome leafy canopy on even the sunniest days, making this the perfect spot to picnic, people-watch or relax in a terrace café. Don't miss the gleaming white **Iglesia de Nuestra Señora de los Remedios**, built in the Canarian colonial style. Explore the surrounding streets and plazas, particularly the Plaza Elías Santos Abreu (aka Plaza Chica), Calle General Franco and Calle Francis Fernández Taño, which still preserve much of their traditional character.

Colourful **murals** and **modern sculptures** are dotted throughout the centre, making the city an open-air museum. A large map in Plaza España gives the artists' names and locations of their works.

Cyclists should check out **Bike'n'Fun** (☎ 922 40 19 27; www.bikenfun.de; Calle Calvo Sotelo 20, Los Llanos; guide service per person €40, bike rental per day €8-14) for bike rentals or guided two-wheel excursions.

Sleeping
Hotel Edén (☎ 922 46 01 04; www.hoteledenlapalma.com; Calle Ángel 1; s/d €30/35) At the eastern end of Plaza España, Edén offers comfortable and clean,

LOS LLANOS DE ARIDANE

0 —————— 300 m
0 —————— 0.2 miles

INFORMATION	
Centro de Salud	1 B2
Ciber Locutorio Atlántico	2 C2
Post Office	3 C2
Tintoreria Bellosur	4 C2
Tourist Office	5 C2

SIGHTS & ACTIVITIES	
Bike'n'Fun	6 D2
Iglesia de Nuestra Señora de los Remedios	7 C2

SLEEPING	
Hotel Amberes	8 D2
Hotel Edén	9 C2

EATING	
Aridane Grill-Restaurante	10 D1
Market	11 B2
Salta Si Puedes	12 A2

TRANSPORT	
Auto Soyka	13 C2
Bus Station	14 B1

if charmless, rooms, some with balconies overlooking the plaza. Rooms and common areas are spacious enough, but we've seen coat closets bigger than the bathrooms.

our pick **Hotel Amberes** (☎ 922 40 10 40; www.hotel -amberes.com; Calle General Franco 13; s/d with breakfast €60/95; ♡ reception 11am-2pm). A renovated 1660 manor house with just seven well-appointed rooms, this romantic spot in the heart of town boasts a pretty interior patio, Canary-style balconies, gorgeous wooden floors and ceilings and luxuriously simple furnishings. If reception is unattended, go to Restaurante Amberes on Calle Luna.

Eating

The cafés dotting the Plaza España are ideal for breakfast, a midday coffee break or an informal lunch.

Market (Plaza Mercado; ♡ 8am-2pm Mon-Sat) Browse the fresh market for fruit, veggies, cheese, meat and more. The perfect spot for self-caterers.

Salta Si Puedes (☎ 922 46 38 79; Avenida Tanausú 29; mains €5-10; ♡ closed Wed) Choose between an old-fashioned formal dining room or a rustic, summer-camp-like room with long communal tables to savour the grilled meats and fish that are the staple of this homey eatery, a 15-minute walk beyond the centre.

Aridane Grill-Restaurante (☎ 922 46 43 14; Calle Francis Fernández Taño 29; mains €8-11; ♡ closed Sun) Although the grilled meats and fish are delicious, Aridane's real claim to fame is its fabulous setting inside a Canarian patio, where you can see the flames of the grill dancing and even peek above the patio walls to catch a glimpse of mountains in the distance.

Getting There & Away

Buses from the **bus station** (Calle Luis Felipe Gómez Wanguemert) include bus 1 (€4.20, 50 minutes, up to 17 daily) to Santa Cruz, bus 3 (€2.70, 40 minutes, up to eight daily) to Fuencaliente and bus 4 (€1.30, 20 minutes, up to 21 daily) to Puerto Naos.

TAZACORTE

pop 6500

One of La Palma's most charming destinations, the historic town and port of Tazacorte is strung out along the western coast. The port marks the spot where Spanish conquistadors first came ashore in the 15th century. Shortly after, they built the island's first church, **San**

Miguel Arcángel (Plaza España), just inland. The cluster of small houses that today forms the nucleus of the old town followed in the 16th century. There's a small **tourist office** (☎ 686 98 77 22; Plaza España; ♡ 9am-1pm Mon-Fri) here.

Most people, however, come for the sun and black sand of the manicured resort at the far northern end of town. Hemmed in by stoic volcanic cliffs, the baylike **beach** is calm. Not so calm is the steep climb up to **Mirador de El Time**, which begins here. Bring plenty of water, plan to sweat and give yourself 2½ hours for the trek. Better yet, catch a ride up to the *mirador* in a **taxi** (☎ 922 48 06 52) and hike down to the beach, marvelling at the views.

Get out on the water with **Agamenon** (☎ 650 77 77 48; adult/child €20/10; ♡ 10am-3.30pm), a leisure boat that takes several daily excursions to see whales, explore coastal caverns or deep-sea fish.

Sleeping & Eating

Apartamentos Luz y Mar (☎ 922 40 81 63, 922 42 85 02; 1-2-person apt €30-38; ▣) One of several basic apartments by the beach, Luz y Mar offers a small, uncluttered place to lay your head, with kitchens, balconies and ocean views. The rooftop pool is a plus.

Apartamentos Miramar (☎ 922 46 34 39; 2-person apt €30) These simple apartments, a short walk from the beach, boast balconies and kitchens.

Taberna del Puerto (☎ 922 40 61 18; Plaza Castilla 1; mains €7-15) One of several waterfront restaurants, this one has an attractive, rustic feel and an enviable ocean view. Paella and grilled fish and meats dominate the menu.

Getting There & Away

If you're driving and want to visit the historic centre, park on the main highway that cuts through town. Don't get caught in Tazacorte's maze of one-way streets. Otherwise, head down to the port where there is plenty of street parking.

PUERTO NAOS

One of La Palma's two tourism centres (Los Cancajos, on the east coast, is the other), Puerto Naos is a town that exists almost solely for the tourists who come to relax on its beautiful black beach, rest under its palm trees, soak up the views of its glittering ocean and stroll along its beach-front promenade. Huddled around a rounded bay and protected on either side by tall rock cliffs, the town makes a good base for sun lovers who want easy access to the north and interior.

Activities

Lolling on the soft black-sand beach may well take up all your time here. But if you're in the mood for more excitement, try scuba diving with **Tauchpartner** (☎ 922 40 81 39; www.tauchpartner -lapalma.de; Edificio Playa Delfín 1; dive €30; ☺ 9.30-11am & 5-7pm Mon-Sat). It offers a range of classes as well as single dives.

Cyclists can call on **Bike Station** (☎ 922 40 83 55; Avenida Cruz Roja, local 3; bike rental per day €6-24, guided trip €38-44; ☺ 9am-1pm & 6-8pm Mon-Sat), offering rentals and a range of challenging guided mountain-bike rides.

Paragliding is quickly gaining momentum here; aficionados come from throughout Europe to take advantage of the island's ideal conditions and easy take-off and landing sites. Arrange for a tandem glide with **Kiosco Playa Morena** (☎ 610 69 57 50; Paseo Marítima; tandem glide €80-130; ☺ noon-6pm).

Viajes Yadir (☎ 922 40 81 06; Avenida Marítima; ☺ 9am-1pm & 4-8pm Mon-Fri, 9am-1pm Sat) offers a bit of everything, from car hire to bus trips.

Sleeping

The town centre is full of apartment blocks, most of them family-run affairs advertising vacancies with a small sign on the door. Make it easy on yourself by contacting **Tamanca** (☎ 922 40 81 47; www.tamanca.com; Calle Mauricio Duque Camacho 46a; ☺ 9am-1pm & 4-8pm Mon-Fri, 9am-2pm Sat), an agency that rents out properties in and around Puerto Naos.

Sol La Palma (☎ 922 40 80 00; www.solmelia.com; Punta del Pozo s/n, Playa de Puerto Naos; s €43-73, d €86-146, apt €71-116; P ⊗ ⚊) If you don't want to self-cater, this package-tourism-style hotel is your only bet. With a sprawling, kid-filled pool overlooking the Atlantic, beige I-could-be-anywhere-in-the-world rooms and an all-you-can-eat buffet, it's your standard resort hotel but is comfortable.

Bungalows Sonvida (☎ 922 46 38 36; www.bungalows sonvida.com; Todoque; 1-2-person bungalow per week €280-410; P ⚊) Located outside Puerto Naos in the tiny town of Todoque, these apartments and bungalows are set among lush gardens. A pool, sunny terraces and great views make this a soothing escape. Rooms, with a mix of Canary- and Ikea-style decor, are spacious and tidy.

Eating

Orinoco (www.islalapalma.com/orinoco; Calle Manuel Rodriguez Quintero 1; mains €5-10; ☺ closed Wed) It's not the kind of place that charms by looks alone, but this homey spot is the locals' favourite for fresh fish and traditional Palmero desserts.

La Roca (☎ 922 40 82 14; Paseo Marítima 4; mains €8.50-16) Both fish and meat lovers coincide on the beach-side terrace of La Roca, where the sound of crashing waves may interfere with conversation – all the better to concentrate on dishes of fried baby cuttlefish, grouper fillet and leg of lamb.

Getting There & Away

Bus 4 (€1.25, 20 minutes, up to 21 daily) makes the trip to and from Los Llanos.

PARQUE NACIONAL DE LA CALDERA DE TABURIENTE

Declared a national park in 1954, this pristine nature reserve is the heart of La Palma, both geographically and symbolically. Extended across 46.9 sq km, it encompasses thick Canary pine forests, a wealth of freshwater springs and streams, waterfalls, impressive rock formations and many kilometres of hiking trails. Although you can reach a few *miradores* by car, you'll need to explore on foot to really experience the park's beauty. Before you start out, see the boxed text, p45. The morning, before clouds obscure the views, is the best time to visit.

The heart of the park is the **Caldera de Taburiente** itself (literally, the Taburiente 'Stewpot' or 'Caldron'). A massive depression 8km wide and surrounded by soaring rock walls (it doesn't take much imagination to see where the name came from), it was first given the moniker in 1825 by German geologist Leopold von Buch, who took it to be a massive volcanic crater. The word 'caldera' stuck, and was used as a standard term for such volcanic craters the world over. This caldera, however, is no crater, although volcanic activity was key in its creation. Scientists now agree that this was a majestically tall volcanic mountain, and that it collapsed on itself. Through the millennia, erosion excavated this tall-walled amphitheatre.

As you explore the quiet park, all may seem impressively stoic and still, but the forces of erosion are hard at work. Landslides and collapsing *roques* (pillars of volcanic rock) are frequent, and some geologists estimate it will finally disappear in just 5000 years. See this fast erosion near the **Mirador de la Cumbrecita**, where a group of pines stands atop a web of exposed roots, clinging miraculously to the hilltop. These trees were once planted firmly in the ground, but metres of soil have been lost during their lifetime.

Information

The interesting **visitor centre** (☎ 922 49 72 77; caldera@mma.es; Carretera General de Padrón; ✆ 9am-2pm & 4-6.30pm) is 5km outside El Paso on the LP-2 highway and offers free general information (be sure to pick up the English *Caldera de Taburiente Paths* map), detailed maps and guides and an excellent museum. The centre's 20-minute film (shown occasionally in English) in worth seeing. Bus 1 (€1 from El Paso, 10 minutes) between Santa Cruz de la Palma and Los Llanos stops by hourly.

Walking

Many trails traverse the park, but unless you plan to spend several days exploring, you'll probably stick to the better-known paths outlined here. Most are in good shape, though the trail from La Cumbrecita to the camp site is notoriously slippery and should be avoided by novice hikers, and the trail running down the Barranco de las Angustias can be dangerous in rainy weather.

Signposting is improving but may still be confusing. Although you're unlikely to get really lost (and there are usually groups of hikers out on the trail to help you if necessary), you're best off buying a detailed map, like the 1:25,000 *Caldera de Taburiente Parque Nacional,* for sale at the visitor centre.

THE SOUTHERN END

Most people access the park from either El Paso or Los Llanos. You'll need a car, taxi or guide to cart you up to one of the *miradores* that serve as trailheads.

To get an overview of the park, there's no better walk than the PR LP 13 trail, which begins at **Los Brecitos** (1081m). Get there from Los Llanos by following the signs first to Los Barros and then on to Los Brecitos. The path leads through a quiet Canary pine forest, past the park camp site, across a babbling brook, and down the Barranco de las Angustias, crossing countless small streams along the way. Watch out for interesting sights like the

brightly coloured **mineral water** that flows orange and green, the interesting shapes made by **pillow lava**, and rock formations like the phallic **Roque Idafe**, an important spiritual site for the Benahoaritas. This six-hour hike is popular and is suitable for anyone in average-to-good physical shape. Be careful, however, if it has rained recently or if a storm seems imminent; the 'Gorge of Fear' can quickly become a raging torrent, and people caught in its fast-rising waters have died.

The best way to hike this trail is to park at Las Hoyas, at the base of the Barranco de las Angustias. From here, 4WD **taxi shuttle services** (☎ 922 40 35 40; per person €10; ✆ 8am-noon) whisk you up to Los Brecitos and allow you to enjoy the descent back to your car without backtracking.

Another option is to drive up the LP-202 from the visitor centre to the **Mirador de la Cumbrecita** (1287m), where there is a small **information office** (✆ 9am-7pm). The 7km drive passes turn-offs for the Pista de Valencia and the Ermita del Pino, leading you through a peaceful pine forest to sweeping views of the valley. From the car park, you can make an a round-trip hike up to the panoramic views from **Pico Bejenado**; allow 2½ hours for the trek. Those with less time can take a 3km circuit trail to both the **Mirador de los Roques** and the **Mirador Lomo de las Chozas** (♿); the final part of the loop is a flat, wheelchair- and stroller-friendly 1km trail between Lomo de las Chozas and the car park. The very best views can be had at sunrise or sunset.

THE NORTHERN END

A string of rocky peaks soaring nearly 2500 metres high surrounds the caldera, and the trail running along these rock walls affords a thrilling vantage point from which to observe the park and the rest of the island. A narrow dirt trail, part of the long-distance GR-131, skims the entire northern border of the park, and shorter trails branch off of it and venture down deeper into the park.

One of the most spectacular sections runs between the **Roque de los Muchachos** and the **Pico de la Nieve**, which is off the LP-1032, a winding highway that branches off the LP-1 highway 3km north of Santa Cruz and snakes its way across the island, skirting the rim of the park and its northern peaks. Avoid backtracking by taking two cars and leaving one at the *pico* (the

THE WORLD'S LARGEST TELESCOPE

No, those round, space-age-looking things squatting on the peak of Roque de los Muchachos aren't something from a theme park, and no, they're not alien spaceships come to explore earth. They are the telescopes of the island's astronomical observatory, one of the world's best places to study the night sky. Tossed out in the Atlantic, far from urban centres and city lights, La Palma is an ideal place to stargaze. More than 75% of the nights here on El Roque are clear, a statistic that's hard to beat.

Since the 2007 unveiling of the mammoth Grantecan (Gran Telescopio Canario, or GTC), the Roque de los Muchachos Observatory boasts the world's largest telescope. The €1 million investment allows scientists to 'study the formation and evolution of the galaxies throughout the history of the universe, investigate why more stars were formed in the past than now, or observe the rings of spatial material that give birth to new planets near young stars,' the scientific director of the GTC, José Miguel Rodríguez, told the Spanish press.

Although the new telescope is grabbing everyone's attention, the observatory was long home to Europe's largest telescope and has been the site of important research. La Palma's observatory is linked with the Teide Astronomic Observatory on Tenerife, and together they form the Instituto de Astrofísica de Canarias (IAC). The observatory is normally closed to the public, but until 9pm you're free to drive around.

parking area is a 20-minute walk from the trail itself). Then drive (or get a ride) up to the Roque de los Muchachos, the highest point on the island at 2426m. The walk back down to the Pico de la Nieve should take four to five hours.

Numerous *miradores* dot the LP-1032 highway around the Roque de los Muchachos; even if you don't hike the rim, the views from up here are worth seeking out. At night, this area offers unbeatable **stargazing** (see the boxed text, above).

Sleeping & Eating

The park's only **camp site** (free) offers basic services for 100 people at a peaceful spot beside a stream. To stay here, contact the visitor centre (p225) 15 days in advance to request a permit. The maximum stay is two nights in summer and six nights in winter. You will need to show your passport to pick up the permit. There are bathrooms here but no food services; bring everything you'll need (and take it away when you leave).

Getting There & Away

No roads run through the park, and there are only three ways to access it: via the LP-202 near the visitor centre, via the track that goes from Los Llanos to Los Brecitos, or via the LP-1032 highway in the north. There are no buses.

THE NORTH

The dense tropical forests, fertile hills and towering pines that create a blanket of green over the northern half of the island couldn't be further away from the volcanic, sun-baked south. This is the least-accessible – and many say most beautiful – part of the island, with rocky cliffs plunging into sapphire waters and deserted black beaches surrounded by palm trees.

SAN ANDRÉS & LOS SAUCES
pop 5380

San Andrés, 3km off the main LP-1 highway, is like something from a storybook, with hilly, cobblestone streets that lead past low, whitewashed houses. The **Iglesia de San Andrés** has its origins in 1515 and is one of the first churches the Spanish conquerors built on the island, though most of what you see today was built in the 17th century. Inside, take a look at the lavish baroque altarpieces and the coffered ceiling.

Los Sauces, just north of San Andrés, is a modern town with two pretty central squares (or one big one bisected by the highway, depending on how you look at it). The grand church, **Nuestra Señora de Montserrat**, is on the square and has some valuable Flemish artwork inside. Named for the patron of Catalunya, this church is evidence of the many Catalans who participated in the island's conquest.

More important (and more interesting) than anything in Los Sauces itself is the **Los Tiles biosphere reserve** (below) just out of town.

Sleeping & Eating

Pensión Martín (☎ 922 45 05 39; Calle San Sebastián; s/d €18/25) The simple rooms have views of the owners' garden and the mountains behind. The three rooms share a bathroom, the place is clean and the owners are friendly.

Pensión Las Lonjas (☎ 922 45 07 36; Calle San Sebastián 16; s/d €20/25) The house itself is in a charming, traditional Canary style. The street-level rooms, which open onto the highway, are modern and attractive, if somewhat damp and dark.

La Placita (☎ 922 45 03 87; mains €2-5; closed Wed; V) One of several restaurants on the main plaza in San Andrés, this informal café has a good selection of salads, sandwiches, egg dishes and pizzas.

Getting There & Away

Bus 11 (€3.10, 25 minutes, up to 9 daily) connects Santa Cruz with the centre of Los Sauces; those heading to San Andres will have to walk or try asking the driver to make an extra stop.

CHARCO AZUL

Beyond San Andrés on the LP-104 highway is a sign pointing the way to Charco Azul, a beautiful swimming hole 3km further on. A bit of tastefully applied concrete has been added to the volcanic rocks along the shore to make a series of natural-looking saltwater pools with sunbathing platforms between them.

Past Charco Azul, construction work is underway on the **Puerto Espindola**. When it's finished (and no-one's making guesses on when that will be) it will have a nice beach, a garden and a small recreational port.

LOS TILES

A biosphere reserve since 1983, the nearly 140 sq km of Los Tiles are covered with a lushly beautiful rainforest that's literally oozing with life. This moist, cool, natural wonderland is one of the most magical spots on the island, a must-explore place where you can wander among the diverse flora and fauna and the largest *laurisilva* (laurel) forest on the island.

At the helpful **visitor centre** (☎ 922 45 12 46; www.lapalmabiosfera.com; 8.30am-2pm & 2.30-5pm

Nov-Jun, 8.30am-2pm & 2.30-6.30pm Jul-Oct) you'll find maps, a video about the biosphere and a small museum. Nearby is a rustic **restaurant** (☎ 922 45 12 46; mains €7-10, closed Wed) serving grilled meats on outdoor picnic tables.

Fabulous hiking trails cut through Los Tiles' dense vegetation. The shortest walk is the steep 750m climb up to the **Mirador Topo de las Barandas** (allow 45 minutes round trip), where around 700 steps leads to a spectacular view of the gorge running out of the reserve.

Even better, though, is the long, ravine-side hike to the **Marcos and Cordero Springs**, which passes through a dozen damp tunnels (bring a flashlight and rain jacket) and winds past waterfalls, through forest and alongside volcanic dikes. The hike isn't incredibly steep (except in short stretches), but it can be slick; be careful. A popular way to tackle this hike is to get a **taxi** (☎ 922 45 09 28, 616 41 88 47; per person €15) from Los Tiles car park up to the Casa del Monte; call two to three days ahead for a taxi. From here, the hike to the springs and back should take about four hours.

Getting There & Away

Coming from Santa Cruz, follow the signs to Los Tiles off the LP-1 highway. The visitor centre is 3km up LP-107, which runs alongside the lush Barranco del Agua. No buses venture up here, so you'll need either your own wheels or strong legs.

BARLOVENTO

pop 2360

Skip the town itself in favour of the natural attractions that lie beyond, like the **Piscinas de la Fajana**, calm saltwater pools where frothy waves pound just beyond the subtle concrete barriers. About 5km east of Barlovento, on the LP-1 highway, you'll turn-off toward this starkly beautiful coastal spot, where red-tinged rocks and a savage ocean create a memorable Kodak moment. Bring snorkelling gear to appreciate the underwater scenery.

Dine at **La Gaviota** (☎ 922 18 60 99; mains €7-15), a restaurant set inside a cave above the beach. Lots of fried fish and a token sirloin steak make up the menu. If you want to linger longer, stay at **Apartamentos La Fajana** (☎ 922 18 61 62; 2-person apt €30-36), where the whitewashed apartments with balconies and amazing ocean views have a real away-from-the-world feel.

Inland, head to the **Laguna de Barlovento** (☎ 922 69 60 23; camp site per tent €4.50; 9am-8pm), a camp site and recreational area set beside an agricultural holding tank (that is, the *laguna*) built inside the crater of an extinct volcano. Call ahead to request permission to camp here.

For more creature comforts, and the only three-star hotel this side of Santa Cruz, head to **Hotel La Palma Romántica** (☎ 922 18 62 21; www.hotella palmaromantica.com; Las Llanadas s/n, Barlovento; s/d €78/108; **P** ⊠), a rural hotel with an elegant restaurant (mains €8 to €11) and sweeping views of the valley. The 44 rooms are spacious, with high ceilings, terraces, lounge chairs and a sitting area. They could have used some of that space for the bathrooms, though – they're tiny.

PARQUE CULTURAL LA ZARZA

Two Benahoare petroglyphs are the main attraction at the **Parque Cultural La Zarza** (☎ 922 69 50 05; adult/child €1.80/0.90; ☺ 11am-7pm summer, to 5pm winter). Heading west out along the LP-1 towards La Mata, the park is 1km past the turn-off for La Mata (it's on a curve and easy to miss – keep an eye out for the signpost). To actually see the geometric-shaped etchings, take the 1.5km circuit into the park itself. Back at the visitor centre, you can watch an informative 20-minute video about the life of the original inhabitants and take a tour around the interactive museum.

FROM LA ZARZA TO TAZACORTE

Ethereal, pristine, stoic, eerie, peaceful… choose your adjective for the lonely land-scapes here on the island's northwestern coast. Pine forests, fallow fields, occasional rural settlements and sweeping views of the banana plantations by the Atlantic are the main attractions between La Zarza and Tazacorte (p223). This is a solitary, tranquil area that was largely isolated from the rest of the island until recent times. Countless hiking trails, many of them quite challenging, provide most of the entertainment here.

The small towns of **Puntagorda** and **Tijarafe** are worth a brief stop, if only to wander the streets of their historic centres. There is a **camp site** (☎ 922 49 33 06; www.airelibrelapalma.org; camp site per person €5, tent rental per day €4, cabin rental per person €10; ⊠) at Puntagorda that offers guided hikes for groups. Tijarafe is home to a small **museum** (☎ 922 49 00 72; Casa del Maestro, Calle 18 de Julio 11; ☺ 8am-2pm Mon-Fri summer, to 3pm winter) dedicated to traditional culture. To get to the museum, follow the signs to the Casa del Maestro from the main highway.

Several lookouts offer privileged vantage points of the northwest coast's inspiring scenery. **La Muralla Restaurant** (☎ 660 32 23 05; Carretera General Aguatavar; mains €8-12; ☺ closed Mon), between Puntagorda and Tijarafe, offers fine dining (fresh fish, kebabs, pork chops, steak, paella) with even finer views from the breezy terrace or minimalist dining room. Just south of Puntagorda is **Mirador de Garome**, overlooking a majestic gorge. Further south, **Mirador del Time** looks out over Tazacorte.

El Hierro

El Hierro is an island where the stark volcanic landscape, impenetrable cliff-lined shores and location in the middle of the Atlantic make it both literally and figuratively remote. It's the westernmost island of the peninsula, and was considered the end of the world until Columbus famously sailed the ocean blue in 1492. It remained the Meridiano Cero (Meridian Zone) until replaced by the Greenwich version in 1884.

Although this small, boomerang-shaped island is now connected to the rest of the planet via air, ferry and TV, it will always feel remote. Of course, that's exactly what is so addictive about this place. It's impossible not to be captured by the island's slow pace and simple style; by its craggy coast, where waves hurl themselves against lava-sculpted rock faces; by the eerily beautiful juniper groves, where trees twisted and tortured by ceaseless winds stand posed like dancers; by the desolate, yet alluring volcanic badlands that stretch out like moonscapes. The smallest and least-known of the Canary Islands, El Hierro is unique – so much so that it was declared a Unesco biosphere reserve.

Those who come to El Hierro want to escape the crowds (the biggest town has less than 2000 residents), get away from traffic (the island's first traffic light, which controls entry into a one-lane tunnel, was put up in 2005) and rest in the silence of the island's natural spaces.

Around 12% of El Hierro is cultivated land (representing about 3000 sq metres per person). Top crops are figs, almonds, vines, pineapples, mangoes, bananas and potatoes.

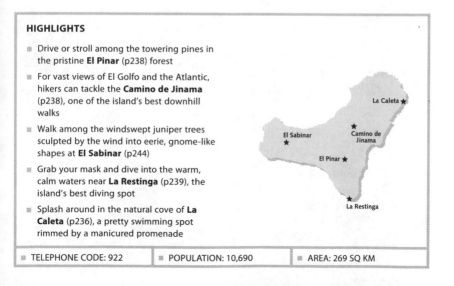

HIGHLIGHTS

- Drive or stroll among the towering pines in the pristine **El Pinar** (p238) forest

- For vast views of El Golfo and the Atlantic, hikers can tackle the **Camino de Jinama** (p238), one of the island's best downhill walks

- Walk among the windswept juniper trees sculpted by the wind into eerie, gnome-like shapes at **El Sabinar** (p244)

- Grab your mask and dive into the warm, calm waters near **La Restinga** (p239), the island's best diving spot

- Splash around in the natural cove of **La Caleta** (p236), a pretty swimming spot rimmed by a manicured promenade

La Caleta ★
★
El Sabinar   Camino de
★   Jinama
El Pinar ★
La Restinga

| ■ TELEPHONE CODE: 922 | ■ POPULATION: 10,690 | ■ AREA: 269 SQ KM |

HISTORY

Geographically speaking, El Hierro is the youngest island in the archipelago. Through the millennia, volcanic activity built up a steep island with a towering 2000m-high peak at its centre. But, about 50,000 years ago, the area was hit by an earthquake so massive that one-third of the island was ripped off the northern side. The peak and the surrounding land slipped away beneath the waves, creating the amphitheatre-like coast of El Golfo. The event would have been impressive and the ensuing tidal wave may have been more than 100m high. Although El Hierro's last eruption was 200 years ago, volcanoes are still the island's defining feature. It is littered with around 500 cones, with many more underneath the lava flows and volcanic rocks that blanket much of the island.

The island's original inhabitants, the Bimbaches, arrived from northern Africa and created a peaceful, cave-dwelling society that depended on agriculture, fishing, hunting and gathering. They may have called the island Hero or Esero, possibly the origin of its modern name. Bimbaches have left interesting petroglyphs (geometrical etchings) on rocks and cave walls throughout the island; the most interesting is at El Julán (p240).

After the Spanish conquest in the 15th century, a form of feudalism was introduced and Spanish farmers gradually assimilated with those locals who had not been sold into slavery or died of disease. In the subsequent

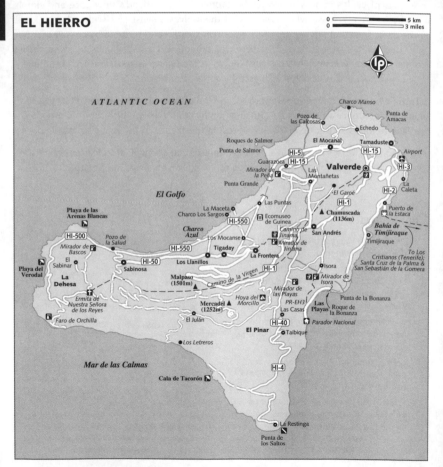

EL HIERRO

0 — 5 km
0 — 3 miles

ATLANTIC OCEAN

Charco Manso
Pozo de las Calcosas
Punta de Amacas
Echedo
Roques de Salmor
El Mocanal
Tamaduste
Punta de Salmor
HI-5
HI-15
Airport
Guarazoca
HI-15
Valverde
HI-3
Mirador de la Peña
Las Montañetas
Punta Grande
El Garoé
La Caleta
HI-2
El Golfo
La Maceta
Las Puntas
Playa de las Arenas Blancas
Charco Los Sargos
Chamuscada (1136m)
Puerto de la Estaca
Ecomuseo de Guinea
HI-550
HI-500
Charco Azul
Los Mocanse
Camino de Jinama
San Andrés
Bahía de Timijiraque
Pozo de la Salud
HI-550
Tigaday
Mirador de Jinama
Timijiraque
Mirador de Bascos
El Sabinar
Sabinosa
Los Llanillos
La Frontera
Isora
To Los Cristianos (Tenerife); Santa Cruz de la Palma & San Sebastián de la Gomera
Playa del Verodal
La Dehesa
Malpaso (1501m)
Camino de la Virgen
HI-1
Mirador de Isora
Ermita de Nuestra Señora de los Reyes
Mercadel (1252m)
Hoya del Morcillo
Mirador de las Playas
PR-EH3
Punta de la Bonanza
Faro de Orchilla
El Julán
Las Casas
Las Playas
Roque de la Bonanza
El Pinar
Taibique
Parador Nacional
HI-40
Los Letreros
Mar de las Calmas
HI-4
Cala de Tacorón
La Restinga
Punta de los Saltos

quest for farmland, much of El Hierro's forests were destroyed.

In the 20th century many Herreños were forced to emigrate abroad to find work. The island's economy has since recovered and is now based on cheese, fishing, fruit-growing, livestock and, increasingly, tourism. Many emigrants have returned. The struggle now is balancing the need to conserve the island's unique, Unesco-protected natural beauty with the need for economic growth. More than 60% of the island is classified as protected land, limiting growth options. That's great for conservationists, but as young islanders are forced to move away to study and find jobs, many see it as a problem.

INFORMATION
Maps
In late 2003, a highway tunnel connecting Valverde with La Frontera was built, and the island changed the names of all its major highways. At the time of publication, many maps (like the detailed 1:30,000 El Hierro published by Freytag & Berndt) still showed the old roads. Up-to-date maps include the 1:50,000 Tourist Map El Hierro by Turquesa, and the satellite-generated maps given out free by the tourist office, which are sufficient for making simple tours around the island.

ACCOMMODATION
Although booking a last-minute room or apartment isn't usually problematic, you may want to book in advance, especially at Christmas, around Easter and in August. If you're arriving on the late-night ferry from Tenerife, definitely make a reservation before you get here; 24-hour reception desks are the exception, not the rule.

There are a few upscale hotels, including the lovely but remote Parador Nacional (p237), the brand-new Hotel Villa el Mocanal (p236) and the hotel-spa Hotel-Balneario Pozo de la Salud (p243). But most of what's on offer is simple and rustic. Privately owned apartments are far more numerous than the pensiones (guesthouses) and rural hotels that are scattered throughout the larger towns.

The most appealing lodging option is the casas rurales, restored farm homes that are especially suited for groups of four or more. Contact **Meridiano Cero** (☎ 922 55 18 24; www.ecoturismo canarias.com; Calle Barlovento 89, El Mocanal) or **Cotur Turismo Rural** (☎ 922 55 60 41; www.coturelhierro.com; Calle Las Toscas 10, Frontera) for reservations.

There is only one legal camp site – at Hoya del Morcillo (p240). Elsewhere, camping is prohibited.

ACTIVITIES
El Hierro is perhaps best known as a scuba-diving destination; La Restinga (p239) is the sport's epicentre. Other popular activities include splashing around in the natural volcanic-rock pools, fishing off the shore and hiking.

The island is scored with hiking trails, including the long-distance GR trails (marked with red-and-white signs), the 10km-plus PR trails (marked in yellow and white) and the short and local SL trails (marked in green and white). The island's best-known path is the **Camino de la Virgen**, stretching from the Ermita de Nuestra Señora de los Reyes to Valverde; this 26km historic trail is walked by thousands during the fiesta Bajada de la Virgen de los Reyes (see the boxed text, p232).

The **Tiempo Sur** (☎ 922 55 17 14; www.islaelhierro .com/webs/tiemposur) adventure travel company

EL HIERRO

THE ECOLOGICAL ISLAND

Dry and rocky, El Hierro might not strike you as the most beautiful of the Canary Islands, but it is home to some of the most unusual plant and animal life, a distinction that has earned the entire island the label of Unesco biosphere reserve. Environmentalists' attention is mainly focused on protecting the marine reserve in the Mar de las Calmas (p239), the unique juniper trees in El Sabinar (p244) and the quiet El Pinar pine forest (p238), but the whole island benefits from its Unesco listing, with funds going to helping the island use its unique natural resources in a sustainable way.

In early 2007, the island took its conservationist leanings to a whole new level, launching an ambitious plan to become the world's first island to depend entirely on renewable sources (like wind, water and solar) for its energy needs. This ecological mindset is seen in other ways as well, such as the island-wide plan to promote and support organic farming.

EL HIERRO

FIT FOR A KING

The fiesta par excellence on El Hierro is the Bajada de la Virgen de los Reyes (Descent of the Virgin), held in early July every four years (next in 2009). Most of the island's population gathers to witness or join in a procession bearing a statue of the Virgin, seated in a sedan chair, from the Ermita de Nuestra Señora de los Reyes in the west of the island all the way across to Valverde. Her descent is accompanied by musicians and dancers dressed in traditional red-and-white tunics and gaudy caps, and celebrations continue for most of the month in villages and hamlets across the island.

You don't have to wait for the fiesta to make this iconic walk across the island. The ancient 26km Camino de la Virgen trail stretches from Valverde to the *ermita* (chapel), cutting through farms and forest on its journey across the spine of the island. Expect the well-marked walk to take eight hours.

---

can arrange activities and outings ranging from horseback riding to rock climbing, caving, mountain biking or paragliding. Call or email for prices and schedules.

FESTIVALS & EVENTS
April
Fiesta de los Pastores (25 April) This feast day is celebrated with a religious procession that carries the Virgen de los Reyes (Virgin of the Kings), the island's patroness saint, out of her current home in the Ermita de Nuestra Señora de los Reyes to the cave where she was first kept.

May
Fiesta de San Isidro Valverde (15 May) If you're in Valverde, be sure to get a look at the *lucha canaria* (p33) showcase in the afternoon.

June
Fiesta de la Apañada Farmers gather in San Andrés for a livestock sale, with the smartest extracting the best prices.
El Día de San Juan (24 June) Marking the longest night of the year, it's celebrated with bonfires and firecrackers throughout the island.

July
Fiesta de la Virgen del Carmen Honouring La Restinga's patroness saint, the festival is celebrated on the weekend closest to 16 July with a town dance and dinner on Saturday, and a religious procession on Sunday.

August
Fiesta de la Virgen de la Candelaria (15 August) Come to La Frontera to see a religious procession and a showcase of *lucha canaria* (p33) followed by a lively dance in Tigaday's Plaza Vieja.

December
Fiesta de la Virgen de la Concepción (8 December) Celebrated in Valverde, the night before the festival is marked with fireworks and a lively town party, while the day itself is devoted to religious celebrations, concerts and various cultural acts.

EL HIERRO FOR CHILDREN
Let's be honest, this island is not exactly the kind of place most kids' dreams are made of. But if your kids are the kind who can get hours of entertainment out of making sand sculptures, going crabbing, fishing off the craggy shores, splashing in the Atlantic waves and running downhill along the wide trails that slice through El Hierro's southern pine forests, then this could be the island for you.

The self-catering *casas rurales* are perfect for families and give you the freedom to make all the noise and run around as much as you want.

GETTING THERE & AWAY
Air
The island's small **airport** (☎ 922 55 37 00) is 12km outside Valverde. Interisland airways **Binter Canarias** (☎ 902 39 13 92; www.binternet.com) connect El Hierro to the archipelago with 46 flights a week to Tenerife, 20 to Gran Canaria and four to La Palma. At the airport you'll find car-rental offices, a bar and a shop selling maps and local products.

Boat
El Hierro's spiffy new Puerto de la Estaca (p237), built courtesy of the European Union, gets little traffic. The **Fred Olsen** (☎ 922 62 82 00; www.fredolsen.es) ferry (€47, two hours) runs between Los Cristianos in Tenerife and El Hierro. It arrives at 12:30pm and departs at 4pm every day, except Saturday.

Specialising in cargo though also accepting passengers, **Naviera Armas** (☎ 922 55 09 05; www.naviera-armas.com; Muelle de la Estaca s/n) makes sporadic trips to Tenerife (€22, twice weekly), La Palma (€22, weekly) and La Gomera (€17, weekly). The prices are good, but the travel times are inconvenient, with frequent middle-of-the-night arrivals and departures.

GETTING AROUND
To/From the Airport
The easiest way to get to and from the airport is your own four wheels; car-rental agencies (see below) are happy to have a car waiting for you at the airport if you call ahead. **Taxis** (☎ 922 55 11 75) are a simple but pricey way to move about; it will cost about €12 to reach Valverde.

Bus
The island's buses, which cost €1 per trip, no matter where you're going, are run by the **Servicio Insular de Guagua** (☎ 922 55 07 29; fax 922 55 14 96). At the time of research, new bus routes and timetables were being created, so the travel times in this chapter could change. Ask at a tourist office or bus station for a complete, up-to-date bus schedule.

Car
There are many car-rental firms in Valverde and if you reserve ahead they'll have a car waiting for you at the airport or port when you arrive. In addition to the large chains renting throughout the Canaries (see p262), local companies like **Autos Bamir** (☎ 922 55 01 83; Calle Doctor Quintero 27, Valverde) may work out cheaper (around €25 per day), though their cars are likely older.

Be sure to fill up the petrol tank before leaving Valverde, as there are only three petrol stations on the island! One is in the

---

FOOD & DRINK

Food on El Hierro is simple, but as long as you respect its limitations, you'll eat well. Fresh local fish, local meat and local vegetables are often available at restaurants, especially to those who know to ask for it! Specialities on El Hierro include *queso herreño* (local soft cheese). Dried figs are another favourite. The fruity white wine from Tigaday is quite good and is sold and served widely on the island.

---

capital, a second in La Frontera and a third on the highway towards La Restinga.

Taxi
Taxis are an expensive way to get around the island; a ride from Valverde to La Restinga will cost around €35. The phone number for a taxi in Valverde is ☎ 922 55 07 29.

VALVERDE

pop 1630
The only landlocked Canary capital, Valverde is a rather unremarkable town set atop a windy mountain ridge overlooking the Atlantic. Its low white houses aren't as scenic as those historic, balconied mansions of the other capitals, but when clouds don't interfere, the town offers some pretty valley views. On rare clear days you can see Tenerife's El Teide and La Gomera perfectly from the town centre. Even if you don't stay here, you'll probably have to pass through, as it's the island's centre of commerce and services.

A stroll around the town centre can be pleasant if the windy weather doesn't interfere; a strong breeze is nearly always blowing, making for a chilly day even when the sun is out.

HISTORY
Though Jean de Béthencourt conquered the island in 1405, Valverde only really came into being following a devastating hurricane in 1610. Many of the islanders fled to this small inland hamlet seeking shelter, beginning a relative boom that would eventually see the town become the seat of the *municipio* (town council) that covered the whole island. In 1926 the island's first *cabildo insular* (local government) was established here.

ORIENTATION
You'd have to try hard to get lost in diminutive Valverde. Two main one-way streets, one heading north and the other south, cut through town. Coming in from the airport or port, you'll simply follow the signs towards Valverde to reach the town centre and most of the important services, including the tourist office.

EL HIERRO

INFORMATION

Emergency

Police station (☎ 922 55 00 25; 🕑 8.30am-2pm & 3.30-9.30pm, closed weekend afternoons in summer) Situated inside the *ayuntamiento* (town hall).

Internet Access

The transient nature of internet cafés meant that at the time of research there were none in Valverde. The situation could change; ask at the tourist office for the latest.

Medical Services

Hospital (☎ 922 59 29 97; Calle Santiago) The area's new hospital is just outside the town centre and boasts the only elevator on the island.

Post

Post office (☎ 922 55 02 91; Calle Correos 3)

Tourist Information

Tourist office (☎ 922 55 03 02; www.elhierro.es; Calle Dr Quintero 11; 🕑 8am-3pm Mon-Fri, 9.30am-1.30pm Sat) Get maps and information about a few island attractions.

SIGHTS

The lure of the island lies in its natural spaces, not here in town. Still, a short stroll around (allot a morning at most here) can be rewarding. Start on pedestrian-friendly **Calle Dr Quintero**, home to shops and bars, before ducking down to the sprawling **Plaza Quintero Nuñez** (known locally as the Plaza Cabildo), which acts as a splendid welcoming mat for the **Iglesia de Nuestra Señora de la Concepción**. The church itself is a simple three-nave structure built in 1767 and crowned by a bell tower with a railed-off upper level that serves as a lookout. Inside, the polychrome *Purísima Concepción* is the town's most prized piece of artwork.

Some day the Island Museum will open beside the church, but there's no completion date in sight. For now the town's only museum is the **Casa de las Quinteras Centro Etnográfico** (☎ 922 55 20 26; Calle Armas Martel; admission €3; 🕑 9am-2pm Mon-Fri, 10.30am-1.30pm & 4.30-6.30pm Sat), where exhibits about rural island life are displayed in a small stone house.

SLEEPING

Accommodation in Valverde is largely limited to simple, budget *pensiones* and hotels; the island's best offerings are elsewhere.

Pensión San Fleit (☎ 922 55 08 57; Calle Santiago 18; s/d €18/28) The cosy rooms at this *pensión* near the hospital don't get any points for style, but they're well-kept and cosy. A small diner of the same name is just next door (see below).

Hostal-Residencia Casañas (☎ 922 55 02 54; Calle San Francisco 9; s/d/t €28/35/46) Walk up to the 1st-floor reception of this two-star *pensión*. The sparse but tidy rooms (some with balcony and all with TV and bathroom) make it the best deal in town.

Hotel Boomerang (☎ 922 55 02 00; fax 922 55 02 53; Calle Dr Gost 1; s/d/t €40/53/59) A two-star hotel rather inconveniently located at the bottom of a steep hill, this quaint, family-run hotel represents Valverde's best lodging, with smallish, clean rooms and a restaurant. This is also the place to get information about Apartamentos Boomerang (p237) in Tamaduste.

EATING

La Taberna de la Villa (☎ 922 55 19 07; Calle General Rodriguez y Sánchez Espinoza 10; mains €5-12) Good, simple food (pizzas, pastas and tapas), a friendly atmosphere and extras like free wi-fi have made this the most popular spot in town. It morphs into a pub from midnight until 2am at weekends.

Brasero San Fleit (☎ 922 55 08 57; Calle Santiago 18; mains €5-14) Get tasty sandwiches and fresh fish from this casual diner where food is served on long wooden picnic tables and locals come to shoot the breeze at the bar.

Brisas de Asabanos (☎ 922 55 12 50; Calle Jesús Nazareno 1; mains €9-12; 🕑 closed Mon) Set above a pharmacy, with picture windows looking down onto the main street, this is Valverde's finest dining experience. Specialities include steak with local cheese, and the fresh catch served in burgundy sauce.

La Mirada Profunda (☎ 922 55 17 87; Calle Santiago 25; menú €12) At this stylish bistro you don't have much of a say in what you eat, you just get to enjoy whatever the chef has prepared – soups, fresh fish and local fare with an international twist.

DRINKING

It doesn't get much more humdrum than Valverde, and during the week everyone heads home early. Weekends, the action (if there is any) is centred around La Taberna de la Villa (above) and the **Tasca El Chavelazo** (☎ 607 57 29 96; Calle General Rodriguez y Sánchez Espinoza 8) next door. End the night at **La Piedra** (Calle

Dr Quintero 2), the closet thing Valverde has to a *discoteca*.

GETTING THERE & AWAY

The **bus station** (Calle Molino) is at the southern end of town, and routes do a good job of covering the island. From Valverde you can reach destinations including Frontera (€1, 30 minutes, up to four daily), Tamaduste (€1, 15 minutes, three daily), El Mocanal and La Restinga (€1, one hour 10 minutes, up to four daily).

GETTING AROUND

You'll find a **taxi stand** (Calle San Francisco) just in front of the island transport co-op (Sociedad Cooperativa de Transportes del Hierro).

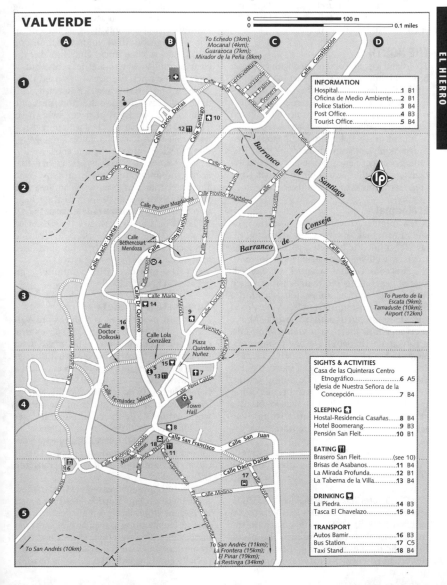

VALVERDE

INFORMATION
Hospital..................................**1** B1
Oficina de Medio Ambiente....**2** B1
Police Station.........................**3** B4
Post Office..............................**4** B3
Tourist Office.........................**5** B4

SIGHTS & ACTIVITIES
Casa de las Quinteras Centro
  Etnográfico.........................**6** A5
Iglesia de Nuestra Señora de la
  Concepción........................**7** B4

SLEEPING
Hostal-Residencia Casañas....**8** B4
Hotel Boomerang..................**9** B3
Pensión San Fleit.................**10** B1

EATING
Brasero San Fleit.............(see 10)
Brisas de Asabanos..............**11** B4
La Mirada Profunda.............**12** B1
La Taberna de la Villa..........**13** B4

DRINKING
La Piedra.............................**14** B3
Tasca El Chavelazo..............**15** B4

TRANSPORT
Autos Bamir........................**16** B3
Bus Station..........................**17** C5
Taxi Stand...........................**18** B4

EL HIERRO

AROUND THE ISLAND

At only 697 sq km the island seems easy to 'do' in a few days or a weekend, but keep in mind that highways here are narrow, curving things, and that very little of El Hierro's real beauty can be appreciated from a car window. Take your time to leisurely explore its coasts, its nature reserves, its towns and its forests to encounter the 'real' El Hierro.

THE NORTH

The island's north coast is lined with ruggedly beautiful, but for the most part inaccessible, cliffs. The few exceptions are the delightful coves and natural volcanic-rock pools in places like Pozo de las Calcosas, Charco Manso, Tamaduste and La Caleta.

Inland, grassy fields and farms extend over much of the landscape. Due to the high altitude, a near-permanent shroud of mist and fog blankets the hilltops, making this quiet, rural area seem almost spooky in its solitude.

El Mocanal

A few minutes' drive northwest of Valverde sits El Mocanal, one of several farming villages that line the highway. Just outside the town, a well-marked turn leads down to the **Pozo de las Calcosas**, where a summer village of generations-old thatched-roof beach huts (called *pajeros*) are huddled around a few natural swimming pools. Walk down the steep, stepped path to swim. Above the waterfront there's a *mirador* (lookout), a tiny stone chapel and a few restaurants. **Mesón La Barca** (☎ 922 55 41 02; Calle El Arenal; mains €6-15; ⊗ closed Mon) is a cheerful place, painted yellow and with a few rustic dining rooms. Fresh fish is the house speciality. Beside it is **Casa Carlos** (☎ 922 55 11 53; mains €5-16), also serving the day's catch – *atún* (tuna), *viejas* (parrot fish), *cabrillas* (comber fish) and *lapas* (limpets).

In summer (July to September) there is one morning bus and one afternoon bus (€1, 20 minutes) linking the Pozo with Valverde.

ourpick **Hotel Villa El Mocanal** (☎ 922 55 03 73; www.villaelmocanal.com; Calle Barlovento 18; per person incl breakfast €39-72; 🖵 🖫 🕭 🅿), back on the main highway, is the island's first boutique hotel and defines rustic chic. Earthy-toned décor, hardwood furniture, stone construction and fabulous views make this an excellent choice.

Echedo

Only 3km from Valverde, Echedo is at the heart of El Hierro's wine-growing region. Its vineyards are planted behind quaint volcanic rock walls that help to block the wind that often swirls through. Far more captivating than anything in town are the **Charco Manso**, natural saltwater pools lying at the end of a lonely highway that winds down among shrubs and volcanic rock. On a fine day the clear turquoise waters are heavenly, but at high tide or when the ocean is stirred there can be strong currents here. Be especially cautious of the caves dug into the shore; peek into them on a calm day, but never swim here. The cave bottoms are pocked with tunnel-like holes called *tragadores* (literally, 'swallowers') that can suck you in as the tide ebbs.

There's a small kiosk by the *charco* that keeps sporadic hours, and for those who come prepared, there's a fine picnic area with wooden tables. For more formal eating, head into town where **La Higuera de la Abuela** (☎ 922 55 10 26; Calle Tajanis Caba s/n; mains €8-11; ⊗ closed Tue) serves fried rabbit or goat, grilled shellfish and fresh island fish on a leafy patio once filled with an enormous *higuera* (fig tree).

Two buses a day (€1, 15 minutes) run between Echedo and Valverde.

Tamaduste & La Caleta

These two modest resort villages are Valverde's summer playground. Small, natural coves and beautiful waterfronts make them fantastic spots for swimming, sunbathing, relaxing and fishing, but don't expect much else from these otherwise snoring towns.

Tamaduste (10km northeast of Valverde) is the perfect place to escape from the outside world. At high tide the cove fills with water and kids dive head-first into the Atlantic. At low tide, the rough waves disappear, leaving nothing more than still pools. This is the perfect time to fish or collect crabs and ocean snails.

A few minutes further on is **La Caleta**, where the delightfully landscaped waterfront boasts an elegant stone-laid promenade, plenty of spots for sunbathing and aqua-blue saltwater pools, one with a waterfall. There's no beach to speak of, but waters here are calm and especially good for kids. It used to be possible to see much-weathered Bimbache rock carvings on a rock face by the shore but, sadly, they were accidentally destroyed when the waterfront was reconstructed.

If you want to stay, the best option is the ocean-front **Apartamentos Boomerang** (☎ 922 55 02 00; Calle El Cantil, Tamaduste; 2-/4-person apt €58/65), which has 'wow' views over the Atlantic and balconies to let in the breeze.

Grab a bite to eat – fresh local fish, tapas and meats in various sauces – at the family-run **Bar-Restaurante Bimbache** (☎ 922 96 90 14; Calle Los Cardones, Tamaduste; mains €7-12; closed Tue).

A bus connecting Valverde with the port stops three times daily in Tamaduste (€1, 15 minutes) and La Caleta (€1, 20 minutes).

Puerto de la Estaca & Las Playas
The island's only ferry port, **Puerto de la Estaca** (☎ 922 55 09 03), becomes the centre of attention twice a day when it greets the ferries coming in from Tenerife. Otherwise, this place is so sleepy it borders on comatose. Four buses (€1, 50 minutes) daily link the port with Valverde.

Past the port, the highway curves around the coast towards Las Playas, 10km further on, slicing through a no-man's-land of rocky shores and rockier hillsides. You'll pass the little town of **Timijiraque**, where there is a small beach (watch the undertow here) and the homey **Casa Guayana** (☎ 922 55 04 17; Carretera General; mains €8-15), where tasty local fish is served in a cosy dining room with a handful of tables and red ruffled curtains at the window overlooking the ocean. Above the restaurant are a few no-frills rooms (per person €12-15). Each has a toilet that shares a shower.

Further along, just past a highway tunnel, look offshore to see the famed **Roque de la Bonanza**, a rock formation that soars 200m out of the water and has become a symbol of the island.

Nearby, in front of a quiet pebbly beach, is the rustic, home-style eatery **Bar-Restaurante Bohemia** (☎ 922 55 83 80; Carretera Las Playas 15; mains €7-14; closed Wed), serving flame-grilled meats and local fish.

our pick Parador Nacional (☎ 922 55 80 36; www.parador.es; Las Playas; s/d €122/135; P) is where most who make the trek out here end up. Sitting on the edge of a rocky beach, this is the island's top hotel and rooms are lovely, with hardwood floors, cool blue décor and balconies (ask for one with an ocean view), though

the best thing they offer is the lullaby of the crashing waves. The *parador*'s restaurant (menú €29) is elegant as well, with big picture windows looking onto the ocean and creative takes on traditional Canarian dishes.

Mirador de la Peña
Just outside the agricultural hamlet of Guarazoca is one of El Hierro's top sites – the Mirador de la Peña, designed by famed Lanzarote-born artist César Manrique (see the boxed text, p131). Get your camera ready; mist permitting, this *mirador* affords sweeping views of the valley, the gulf coast and the Roques de Salmor (p242). Wander around short paths leading to several vantage points, then dine at the elegant **restaurant** (☎ 922 55 03 00; mains €10-15; closed Mon & dinner Sun), with its elegant dining room dominated by a huge window looking out over El Golfo. The menu is focused on creative ways to use local ingredients, with results like Herreño pineapple stuffed with shellfish, or fish with Herreño cheese sauce. There's an informal café as well.

Las Montañetas
The stone houses of Las Montañetas, one of the island's oldest towns, were slowly abandoned over the years as farmers sought easier sustenance elsewhere, and today the sheep population far outnumbers the human one. A few years ago, however, locals began converting the town's empty houses into *casas rurales* for tourists eager for a peaceful retreat. To stay here, contact **Casa Espinel** (☎ 922 55 00 71; casaespinel@elhierroinfo.com; Las Montañetas), a breezy, fully furnished, traditional-style house with a garden, heating and awesome panoramic views.

San Andrés & Around
Gain insight into the culture of the Bimbaches by visiting the site of their ancient holy tree, **El Garoé** (10am-6pm Tue-Sat, 11am-3pm Sun). According to legend, the tree miraculously spouted water, providing for the islanders and their animals. Today we know that it's really no miracle – mist in the air condenses on the tree's leaves and gives fresh water. The tree itself is rather unremarkable, especially taking into account that the original, a variety of laurel, was felled by a hurricane in 1610; the one here today was planted in 1949. There's a small visitor centre near the tree and pretty

walking trails leading to various freshwater pools. Get here along one of the two 2.7km dirt tracks that branch off the highways heading towards San Andrés. Both routes involve rocky, steep drives.

Several walking trails set off from here. Take the PR EH 7 3km to El Mocanal or 6km down to the Pozo de las Calcosas (p236), or take the same trail 3.5km in the other direction to San Andrés.

The agricultural centre of this part of the island, San Andrés is made up of a few buildings scattered on either side of the highway; one of them is **Casa Goyo** (☎ 922 55 12 63; mains €6-12), a simple, no-frills diner serving up filling local fare on green-checked tablecloths. Several *casas rurales* operate here as well. In a particularly lovely setting is the **Casa El Valle** (☎ 922 55 18 24; www.ecoturismocanarias.com; 1-2 people €50-55, 3 people €58-63), located near the village. A lush garden overlooking the valley surrounds the stone house, which boasts a huge terrace with sun lounges, a rustic style and absolute peace and quiet.

Four buses (€1, 20 minutes) daily link San Andrés with Valverde.

About 3km southwest of San Andrés, turn onto the H-120 towards the **Mirador de Jinama** for soul-satisfying views over the mammoth amphitheatre that is El Golfo. Of course, depending on the day, you could be looking over a big pot of cloud soup. There's also an excellent (although windy) picnic spot and a small chapel. The H-120 highway continues on its narrow, curvy path towards the Mirador de la Peña (p237), making it one of the island's most scenic byways.

From Jinama, you can strike out on the rocky but well-marked **Camino de Jinama**, an old donkey track that should take about 2½ hours to hike down to La Frontera and 3½ hours to return. The reverse route begins near the Plaza de la Candelaria in La Frontera.

Isora

The cheese-producing village of Isora is a short drive (or hike, if you're up for it) from San Andrés. On the far southern side of town, perched high on El Risco de los Herreños ridge, is the **Mirador de Isora**, where the mountain falls away at your feet toward the smooth coast of Las Playas. The 3.5km downhill trek from the *mirador* to Las Playas is a popular hike with awesome views over

the coast; the descent should take two hours and the round trip about five.

If you're driving, follow the signs (just northeast of San Andrés) to Isora off the HI-4 highway. If you're walking, the PR EH 4.1 trail to Isora starts in Las Rosas neighbourhood of San Andrés.

Four buses (€1, 30 minutes) daily connect Isora and Valverde.

EL PINAR & THE SOUTH

The serene El Pinar pine forest covers a long swath of the southern half of the island, casting cool shade over the volcanic terrain and providing an excellent destination for a day hike or a scenic drive. The lonely highway that cuts through El Pinar connects the eastern rim of the forest with the Ermita de Nuestra Señora de los Reyes (p244), on the western side of the island; countless trails branch off the main road.

Further south, the pines drop away and raw volcanic rock formations dominate the landscape as you descend towards La Restinga, the island's scuba-diving capital and its major tourism centre.

The HI-4 Highway

Heading south on the HI-4 highway, you'll come to a turn-off (the HI-402) for the **Mirador de las Playas**, where there is a spectacular view of the coast below.

Continue a few kilometres more and you'll pass **Las Casas** and **Taibique**, two small towns built along the steeply descending highway. Although they're technically independent, it's impossible to tell where one town ends and the other begins. While not a destination in its own right, this is a good place for self-caterers to buy supplies. The main attraction is the **Mirador de Tanajara**, with lovely views and a small **ceramics shop** nearby, open whenever the owner is home. Find it just west of Taibique's town centre.

Those needing a place to stay will find the two-star **Hotel Pinar** (☎ 922 55 80 08; www.elhierro .tv/hotelpinar; s €36-46, d €44-62) on the main highway in Taibique. The appealing rooms have private bathroom, TV and phone, and some have balconies. Just below the hotel, **Restaurante Luis El Taperio** (mains €8-12) is a friendly bar and restaurant with cheap lunches and tapas in addition to the hearty main dishes of fish and grilled meats.

Cala de Tacorón

Halfway between El Pinar and La Restinga, you'll pass the turn-off to Cala de Tacorón. The road winds through a harsh volcanic landscape to reach a rocky coast with calm, lake-like waters. This is a great area for swimming and diving (many of the La Restinga–based companies come here) and it's popular with kayakers. After enjoying the water, have lunch at the rustic, covered picnic area, made with logs and branches, á la Swiss Family Robinson.

La Restinga

Quickly becoming El Hierro's tourist hot spot, the once-sleepy fishing village of La Restinga is now a busy resort thanks to the dozens of scuba-diving outfitters that have set up shop here. All take advantage of the underwater marvels provided by the **Mar de las Calmas** (Sea of Calm), the warm, still waters that surround the island's southwestern shore. For nondivers, there are two volcanic beaches right on the port, where the ocean is as still as bath water, if none too clean. The town itself is a hodgepodge of apartment buildings, with several good seafood restaurants and a slew of diving outfitters, but not much activity.

The road down to La Restinga rambles through volcanic badlands. Take time to look at the funny lava shapes, ranging from *pahoehoe* or *lajial,* smooth rock that looks like twisted taffy, to hard, crumbling rock that looks like wet oatmeal. The gleaming sea stretches out before you as you descend into the town, and you can clearly make out the line between the glassy Mar de las Calmas and the windblown open ocean to the west, which is rough and choppy. Part of the sea is a marine reserve, and both fishing and diving are restricted in an effort to provide fish with a safe place to breed.

INFORMATION

The new **tourist office** (☎ 922 55 71 88; Avenida Marítima; ☒ 8.30am-2.30pm Mon-Fri) has maps and information about the area. Wash clothes at **Lavandería La Ola** (☎ 922 55 80 08; Avenida Marítima; ☒ 9am-1pm), run by the nearby Apartamentos Arenas Blancas.

ACTIVITIES

There's no shortage of diving companies offering their services to divers and diver hopefuls, and everyone is offering pretty much the same thing – a €28 to €30 dive around the Mar de las Calmas, where you can expect to encounter colourful coral, majestic rock formations and a wide variety of marine life. Courses and speciality dives are also available. The companies' opening hours change daily, according to the weather and the number of dives planned. Companies include **Arrecifal** (☎ 922 55 71 71; www.arrecifal.com; Calle La Orcilla 30), **El Hierro Taxi Diver** (☎ 922 55 71 42; www.elhierrotaxidiver.com; Avenida Marítima 4) and **El Submarino** (☎ 922 55 70 75; www.elsubmarinobuceo .com; Avenida Marítima 2).

SLEEPING

To be honest, this isn't the island's most charming place to stay, but divers are practically obliged to, since there's an 800m to 1000m altitude difference between sea-level La Restinga and the towns up the highway – it's necessary to remain near sea level for at least 12 hours after a dive.

The accommodation options are nearly all apartments, most of them newish and with enviable locations overlooking the port. But not a single one of these apartments has an elevator; keep that in mind as you fill up those suitcases!

Casa Kai (☎ 922 55 70 34; Calle Varadero 6; d €23) Full disclosure: this place is only listed because it's the only cheap *pensión* in La Restinga. It gets a plus for its location on the waterfront, but a major minus for the cramped, musty rooms.

Apartamentos Rocamar (☎ 922 55 70 83; Avenida Marítima 20; 1-2-person apt €33-36) They're not fancy, but these sunny, airy apartments overlooking the port make a central and welcoming home base.

Apartamentos Bahía (☎ 617 61 46 19; www.aparta mentosbahia.info; Avenida Marítima 12; 1-4-person apt €35-48) These spic-and-span two-bedroom apartments are ideal for families. The open-plan kitchen and living area looks out over the blue waters of the port. The furnishings are simple, but with a view like this, who needs more decoration?

La Marina (☎ 922 55 90 16; Avenida Marítima; 2-person apt €42-45) Enjoy morning coffee and great ocean views on the balconies of the ocean-side rooms, while inside you'll find cosy rooms, a small, stocked kitchenette and unremarkable, though clean, furnishings.

EL HIERRO

EATING & DRINKING

Delicious, fresh seafood is the main attraction at most restaurants here. Self-caterers can shop at the Spar supermarket in town.

our pick **Casa Juan** (☎ 922 55 71 02; Calle Juan Gutierrez Monteverde 23; mains €6-12; ⊗ closed Wed & Jan) Hearty portions of fresh fish, soup, salad, *papas* (potatoes) and grilled meats are served up at this friendly place popular with locals. Warmly recommended.

El Refugio (☎ 922 55 70 29; Calle La Lapa 1; mains €7-10; ⊗ closed Mon) Serving fresh fish and seafood (the restaurant has its own fishing boat), this is one block up from the waterfront. To get here, follow the sounds of the singing bird which lives in a cage outside the restaurant.

Disco Pub Canario (☎ 922 55 70 63; Calle El Lajial 6) One of the few nightspots in La Restinga, this is a laid-back spot for a drink.

GETTING THERE & AWAY

The HI-4 highway dead-ends in La Restinga; there's no missing it. There are frequent bus services (€1, one hour 10 minutes, up to four daily) between Valverde and La Restinga.

Hoya del Morcillo & Around

From the HI-4, take the HI-40 highway towards **Hoya del Morcillo** (⊗ 9am-9pm), a shady recreational area in the heart of El Pinar. With a football field, a playground and a picnic area, this is the perfect spot to rest among the pines. Don't miss the large-scale map of El Hierro, made with logs. A severe fire in September 2006 altered this area, and now it's a great place to marvel at the hearty Canary pine. Their blackened trunks are proof of the fire's wrath, but the fact that they stand here today, as green as ever, shows how remarkable these trees are.

Nearby is the island's only **camp site** (per person €4.30). It has space for 300 and is well equipped, but you must request permission at the Hoya del Morcillo information booth, at the tourist office (p234) in Valverde, or at the **Oficina de Medio Ambiente** (Environment Office; ☎ 922 55 00 17; fax 922 55 02 71; Calle Trinista 1, Valverde). If you send in your request ahead of time, the Environment Office will fax you a permit before you even leave home.

Continuing into the El Pinar forest, you come across **El Julán**, where a trail heads down to one of the island's most important cultural sites, **Los Letreros**. Here, a scattering of indecipherable petroglyphs was scratched into a lava flow by the Bimbaches. The hike is a long one that leaves behind the pine forest and heads into dry, volcanic territory. At the end (or sometimes along the trail) a guide may ask you to show your passport. Ask the guide to point out the carvings; if you don't know where to look you may pass right by the faded etchings and not know it. At the time of writing, a road-side information centre was under construction.

Continuing west, 6km past El Julán, is a dirt road on your right that leads you up to the foot of **Malpaso** (1501m), the island's highest peak. The 9km of rough dirt track make for slow going, but the ride is an adventure. The track is suitable for almost any vehicle (carry a spare tyre just in case).

EL GOLFO

An amphitheatre-shaped depression dominating El Hierro's northwestern flank, the green Golfo is, like the rest of the island, largely rural, with banana plantations filling the low-lying coastal areas. A string of quiet hamlets, some with tempting swimming holes, are laid out along the coast, while inland, growing commercial centres like La Frontera and Tigaday serve as the economic engines of the western half of the island. To the south, a rugged mountain ridge looms like a wall hiding the rest of the island, while to the north, a desolate volcanic wasteland tempts with its peculiar beauty. More than 90% of the terrain on this part of the island is protected as some sort of reserve.

Thanks to the highway tunnel built a few years back, El Golfo is just a 10-minute drive from Valverde on the HI-5 highway. But for those who love a good scenic drive (and don't get car sick) coming in the old way, on the HI-1, snaking down over the towering mountain ridge flanking El Golfo, is rewarding.

Las Puntas

After the tunnel, the first town you come across is Las Puntas; take the HI-55 turn-off to head down to this coastal town. Sitting right on the water, though offering no access to it, this small hamlet exists purely for the tourists who come to relax here. Its main attractions are the view and the sound of the roaring waves.

From here there is a clear view of **Los Roques de Salmor**, an important nesting spot

---

ISLAND VOICES: THE ORGANIC FARMER

On Pedro Cabrera's farm in El Golfo, chickens (not pesticides) keep pests away from banana plants, sheep (not herbicides) keep fields weed-free, and crops – yams, potatoes, onions, green peppers or yucca – are rotated every season. Cabrera, 43, is one of El Hierro's 57 organic farmers. He's a minority among the estimated 1000 farmers on the island, but Cabrera is convinced that other Herreños will soon see the light and cross over to the organic side.

'On El Hierro we've developed the culture of the monocrops,' he says. 'Farmers grow just one crop, which makes them dependent on big multinational companies for sales. But that leads to failure, because where there's no biodiversity, insects and plagues can get out of control. Organic farming is a bit more work, but it gives much better results.'

Cabrera got into organic farming with help from the island government, which ceded him land to get started until he'd earned enough to buy his own plot. Now he works his own land, with help from his wife and two kids (aged 18 and 22), and he's building a modest house near his sheep pen. The 45 sheep, in addition to keeping his fields fertilised and weed-free, give him milk, cheese and meat.

'I was born here in Frontera. Growing up, my parents did organic farming, but that was nothing special, it's all there was!' he says. 'When I was 15, I went to the Americas, and when I came back 10 years later the island – and the way it was farmed – had changed so much. But I decided, though, to continue with the kind of farming I'd known as a kid, when each family had a few sheep, a few hens, a few different crops and they used what they needed and sold what was left over. You can still make a good living farming this way.'

---

for various bird species and the last stand of the primeval Lagarto del Salmor (Lizard of Salmor), which now only survives in captivity (see the boxed text, p242).

SLEEPING & EATING

Apartamentos Las Casitas (☎ 659 85 32 10; 2-person apt €36-45; ☒) Off the highway and away from the waterfront, these bright, roomy (50 sq metres) apartments have two balconies with expansive views, and ample living areas.

Hotel Puntagrande (☎ 922 55 90 81; s/d incl breakfast €46/57) Las Puntas' most famous lodging, this intimate spot was once listed in the Guinness World Records book as being the smallest hotel in the world. An old stone port building, it's perched on a spectacular rock outcrop and has comfortable rooms. The family feel, accentuated by the close quarters and lively common room and dining area (mains €13) make this a memorable place to stay. Call ahead to reserve a table.

Bungalows Los Roques de Salmor (☎ 922 55 90 16; r up to 4 people €55-67; ☒) This series of small, white-walled bungalows on your left as you enter town are an excellent option. New and well-kept, they have tiled roofs, stone detailing and tasteful décor.

Tasca (☎ 922 69 81 40; Calle Puntagrande 3; mains €7-10) The only spot to eat or drink close to the water, this cheery tavern gets lively on weekend nights. At meal time, come to enjoy tapas, grilled meats and seafood.

Restaurante Las Puntas (mains €7-11; ☒ closed Tue) Get a hearty meal downstairs from Apartamentos Las Casitas. It serves everything from pizza to paella, with a few local specialities thrown in.

La Maceta & Charco Los Sargos

For a swim, head down to **La Maceta**, a series of natural saltwater pools built along the coast. At high tide, the ocean swallows the pools, making swimming dangerous. At other times though, taking a cool dip here is a dream.

our pick La Maceta (☎ 922 55 60 20; mains €8-13, ☒ closed Wed), one of the best restaurants on the western side of the island, is just up from the beach. Get a variety of local fish (unlike most restaurants on the island, all the fish here is fresh) on the breezy terrace or in the stylish dining room.

From the main highway, follow the signs to La Maceta, turning down the HI-550 and taking the first sealed road to your right.

Just up the coast is **Charco Los Sargos**, another swimming spot with calm pools that buffer the crashing waves. It's similar to La Maceta but with less fanfare. There's a small beach

EL HIERRO

THE GIANT LIZARD

Imagine the Spaniards' surprise when they began to explore El Hierro and, among the native birds, juniper trees and unusual volcanic rock, they discovered enormous lizards as large as cats. Greyish-brown and growing up to 45cm in length, the lizards aren't venomous or harmful, though according to one early chronicler they're 'disgusting and repugnant to behold'.

By the 1940s, these giant lizards were almost extinct, all but snuffed out by human encroachment on their habitat, introduced predators (such as cats) and climatological factors. A few survived on the Roques de Salmor rock outcrop off the gulf coast (giving the species its name, 'Lizard of Salmor'), but before long, those too had disappeared.

Then, in the 1970s, herdsmen began reporting sightings of large, unidentified animal droppings and carcasses of extra-long lizards that had been killed by dogs. To the delight of conservationists, a small colony of the giant lizards had survived on a practically inaccessible mountain crag, the Fuga de Gorreta. One herdsman was able to capture a pair of the reptiles, beginning the species' journey back to life.

In 1985 the Giant Lizard of El Hierro Recovery Plan was put into place. These days you can see it in action at the Lagartario at the Ecomuseo de Guinea (below), where the lizards are bred in captivity and released into a supervised wild area. At the Lagartario you can spy on a few specimens in their glassed-in cages as they soak up the sun or snack on vegetation. A guide explains the recovery efforts and the history of the giant lizard.

shack that keeps erratic hours. From the HI-550, the turn-off is just 300m north of the turn-off for La Maceta.

Ecomuseo de Guinea

The island's premier cultural site, this interesting outdoor **museum** (☎ 922 55 50 56; admission €7.50; 🕑 10.30am-5.30pm Tue-Sat, with entrance every 30min, tours 10.30am, noon & 1.45pm Sun) is really two centres in one. The Casas de Guinea, which encompasses a fascinating route through volcanic caves and 20 ancient houses (four of which are visitable), represents islander lifestyles through the centuries. The Lagartario is a recuperation centre for the giant lizard of El Hierro (see the boxed text, above). You can only visit with a guide (tours available in English), so be sure to arrive at least an hour before closing.

Tigaday
pop 1231

The nerve centre of the La Frontera municipality, Tigaday is a commercial hub (in El Hierro terms at least) strung out along the highway. There's not much to see in the centre, but as El Hierro's second town, Tigaday is the only place on the island with shops and services to rival the capital. It even has one of the island's three petrol stations! Most shops, bars and services are along Calle Tigaday.

On Sundays a small artisan and fresh-food **market** (🕑 8am-1pm; Plaza Vieja) sets up shop on Tigaday's main plaza.

Log on at **Comunicación Sin Fronteras** (☎ 922 55 59 05; Calle La Corredera 5; internet per hr €1.50; 🕑 10.30am-2pm & 4.30-11pm Mon-Sat). Wash clothes at **Lavandería Mijúcal** (☎ 922 55 51 14; Calle Cruz Alta 16).

SLEEPING & EATING

Pensión Guanche (☎ 669 07 32 91; Calle Cruz Alta 1; s/d €15/21) Rather worn and quite cramped, but at this price you can't complain. Rooms have a tiny bathroom and shower stall, quilts that have seen better days, and pretty views.

Apartamentos Frontera (☎ 922 55 92 46; Carretera General 19; 2-person apt €35) These simple, narrow studio apartments all overlook a lush central patio and offer generous-sized balconies.

Bar-Restaurante Andrómeda (☎ 922 55 50 41; Calle Tigaday 21; mains €8-13; 🕑 closed Sun) Though low on atmosphere, this simple diner serves tasty versions of staples like pork chops, pangrilled steak and the local speciality *carne fiesta* (chopped pork with grilled peppers and onions).

La Frontera

Although La Frontera is the name of the large municipality that extends over the entire gulf coast, it's also the name of a small settlement perched on the hillside behind Tigaday, though it's hard to tell where one town ends and the other begins. The most important thing here is the **Iglesia de Nuestra Señora de la Candelaria**, a 17th-century construction that was redone in 1929. Inside, the three-nave church has two rows of pretty stone columns and an ornate golden altar. It sits on the **Plaza de la Candelaria**, a charming square with benches and a fountain. Behind the church, you can walk to the empty **stone chapel** perched on the hill. It's a short but steep climb and, from the top, the gulf valley spreads out before you like a patchwork quilt of fields and banana plantations.

The **Camino de Jinama** (p238) begins (or ends, depending on your route) near the plaza.

SLEEPING & EATING

our pick **El Sitio** (☎ 922 55 98 43; www.elsitio-elhierro .com; Calle La Carrera 26, La Frontera; r €38-56; ☯ reception 11am-1pm & 6-7pm Mon-Sat) Close your eyes and say *ommm*. Tucked away above the Frontera town centre, this 'centre for well-being' is a unique B&B and activity centre in one. Rooms are in a cluster of renovated stone farm buildings, and activities like yoga, massages, hikes or bike excursions are available to guests and nonguests alike.

Hotelito Ida Inés (☎ 922 55 94 45; www.hotelitoida ines.com; Hoyo Belgara Alta 2; s/d incl breakfast €62/76) There are just 12 rooms in this quaint hotel, all clean, with floral bedspreads, TV, phone, in-room coffee and tea, sparkling bathrooms and balconies with splendid views.

Villa La Hiedra (☎ 609 94 63 11; www.villalahiedra.com; villa for up to 5 people €120; P ☗) A luxurious house overlooking the gulf, this modern villa offers a large terrace and garden, amazing views, elegant décor and all the conveniences.

Joapira (☎ 922 55 98 03; Plaza de la Candelaria 8; mains €5-8) Just in front of the church, this is a bar with a covered terrace that also serves simple food like tapas, roast chicken and the house speciality, *carne fiesta*.

Bar-Restaurante Candelaria (☎ 922 55 50 01; Calle de la Candelaria 1; mains €5-12) Across the street and slightly more upscale, the Candelaria's walls are covered with knick-knacks and local paintings. Star dishes include the grilled surf-and-turf plate, *arepas* (Venezuelan meat wraps) and baked chicken.

Los Llanillos & Sabinosa

There are two routes leading to the western end of the island: the flat, ocean-side HI-550, and the gorgeous but tortuously curved HI-50. Those who set out on the latter are rewarded with a beautiful drive along a mountain ridge. The hairpin curves can be challenging, though, especially if you're tempted to admire the scenery of the ocean

laid out below and the surrounding rugged volcanic mountains.

The small town of **Los Llanillos** hugs the HI-50 highway a few kilometres out of Tigaday. Although the town itself won't detain you for long, there is a good restaurant here: **Asador Artero** (☎ 922 55 50 37; Calle Artero 2; mains €6-12). A cosy yet busy place, it's popular with locals who crowd in for the tasty grilled meats and chicken. In Los Llanillos, take the turn-off for **Charco Azul**, a natural cove with calm pools for swimming.

The highway grows steeper and curvier as it leads to **Sabinosa**, Spain's westernmost town. This remote little village feels as though it's at the end of the world. There is not much here to see, but the scenery nearby is breathtaking.

If you take the coastal highway, you'll quickly reach the famed **Pozo de la Salud** (Well of Health) and the hotel-spa **Hotel-Balneario Pozo de la Salud** (☎ 922 55 95 61; fax 922 55 98 01; s/d €51/61; P ☗ ☖). They'll be on your right, at the end of the HI-500 highway. You can walk down to the small *pozo*, with its waters said to cure a variety of ills, but it's all closed up and there's not much to see. You could do as the Herreños do and bring an empty jug to fill up for free in the hotel (between 8am and 4pm only).

The hotel is a stately building that seems out of place in the rustic wilderness of western El Hierro. Rooms have views of either the ocean or the mountains and are slightly hospice-like but comfortable. The **spa** (☯ 9am-8pm) offers a variety of water-based treatments, as well as standards like massages and algae facials, and the prices (€54 for a rejuvenating facial, €17 for a 30-minute antistress massage, or €50 for a hot volcanic-stone treatment) are better than what you'd find in mainland Europe. Anyone can get treatments here, but guests have priority.

Just west of the hotel, down the HI-500, is **Playa de las Arenas Blancas** (White Sands Beach). Take a short road down to the coast, where indeed there are a few whitish grains of sand. They quickly melt into volcanic rock at the water's edge though, and the beach is unremarkable even if remote and often deserted.

LA DEHESA

West of Sabinosa, the island is practically uninhabited and wild volcanic landscapes dominated by fierce-looking rock formations,

EL HIERRO

hardy shrubs and wind-sculpted juniper trees are the main attractions. This part of the island is called **La Dehesa** (The Pasture), and is only accessible via the arching highway that cuts through volcanic badlands where only a few low shrubs dare to survive.

Stop for a swim at the **Playa del Verodal**, a curious red-sand beach that backs up to a majestic rock cliff. The beach itself is 1km off the main highway (follow the signs) and is often deserted, leaving you with your own private paradise.

As the highway nears the southern coast, you'll reach the HI-503, the turn-off for the **Faro de Orchilla** (Lighthouse of Orchilla), the most southwesterly point in Spain. Long ago robbed of its status as Meridiano Cero by Greenwich in the UK, the lighthouse is still an island icon. West of the lighthouse is a commemorative monument, and at the time of research, a small museum was being planned for the site.

Ermita de Nuestra Señora de los Reyes

Back on the main highway, tackle a few more curves to reach this pretty white **ermita** (chapel), made all the more interesting because of the history and tradition behind it.

The chapel contains the image of the island's patroness saint, Nuestra Señora de los Reyes (Our Lady of the Kings) because local shepherds bought her from foreign sailors on Three Kings Day, 6 January (1545). The people attribute several miracles to the Virgin, including ending droughts and epidemics.

Every four years (2005, 2009 etc) the Virgin is taken out of the chapel in a lively procession around the island (see the boxed text, p232).

El Sabinar & Beyond

From the *ermita*, continue north up windswept El Sabinar, named after the *sabinas* (junipers) that grow up here in very weird ways. Along one part of the road the way is lined with *sabinas* – though beautiful, these are not as spectacular as the wind-twisted trees further down the road at El Sabinar, which have become the island's symbol. You'll pass a turn-off to the left at a signpost indicating El Sabinar. Park here and wander among some of the most unusual trees you'll ever see. They have been sculpted by nature into wild shapes that look frozen in time.

Wear long pants if you want to hack your way through the brush and get close to the trees, which are scattered on the hillside. These wonderfully weird *sabinas* are part of the reason that Unesco declared the entire island a biosphere reserve.

Once back at the fork, you could curl north for a further 2km to reach the **Mirador de Bascos**, a spectacular lookout that's unfortunately often cloaked in cloud. If it's a clear day, prepare for a breathtaking view. If not, don't bother.

Directory

CONTENTS

ACCOMMODATION

The short, sad advice to those who prefer to travel independently and keep their options open is that it's easier and a lot cheaper to buy a Canaries package, including flights and accommodation, before leaving home.

Unless it's the nightlife you're after, you might want to pick one of the smaller and quieter resorts. But don't think that, once you've arrived, you're trapped for the whole of your stay. Buses fan out all over the islands of Tenerife and Gran Canaria, and car hire on all islands is less expensive than on mainland Europe.

The accommodation listings within this guide are ordered as follows: budget (under

---

PRACTICALITIES

- Use a 220V, 50Hz electricity plug with two round pins. Make sure you bring plug adapters for your appliances.

- Local newspapers and magazines include *Diario de Avisos, La Gaceta de Canarias, Canarias 7, La Provincia* and the English-language *Island Connections.* You can also get Spanish newspapers *El País* and *El Mundo* and the foreign *International Herald Tribune, Hello!* and all the English and German tabloids.

- Radio Nacional de España has four stations. Local FM stations abound on the islands and the BBC World Service (www.bbc.co.uk/worldservice) can be found mainly on 6195kHz, 9410 kHz, 12095kHz and 15485 kHz.

- The Canaries receives the mainland's big TV channels (TVE1, La 2, Antena 3, Tele 5) and has a few local stations that are of very limited interest.

- The metric system is used on the Canary Islands. Decimals are indicated with commas and thousands with full points.

€60 per double per night); midrange (€60 to €120 per double per night) and top end (over €120 per double per night). Generally speaking, budget facilities will comprise simple rooms, sometimes with private bathroom. Most of the lodgings in the Canary Islands fall into the midrange bracket and, while there are some variations between standards (even from island to island), you'll find most perfectly comfortable. Top end is just that – anything that appears under this category will have all the comforts you need.

Many prices include full-board (*pensión completa*) or half-board (*media pensión*). Full board means all meals are included, while half-board indicates the inclusion of breakfast and dinner.

Some places have separate price structures for the high season (*temporada alta*), mid-season (*temporada media*) and low season (temporada baja), all usually displayed on a notice in reception or nearby. Hoteliers are not actually bound by these displayed prices.

Any time is tourist time in the Canaries, but the high season is winter, when the Canaries can offer sunshine, warmth and an escape from the rigours of the northern European winter. Winter runs from about December to April (including the Carnaval period of February/March) and this is when you are likely to find accommodation at its most costly and elusive. Semana Santa (Easter Week) is another peak time. Summer (July to September) can also be busy, as mainland Spaniards turn up in full force. If you can visit during other times of the year, you'll find less pressure on accommodation, with many of those same hotels and apartments offering reductions of about 25%.

Note that options in individual towns fill up quickly when a local fiesta is on, and those on the smaller islands can be fully booked during important celebrations. See individual island chapters for details on festivals and events.

The overwhelming majority of visitors to the Canary Islands come with accommodation booked. This has certain advantages, especially in high season, when going it alone can be difficult. Advance booking for independent travellers really does pay off, even if it's no more than a phone call on the morning of the same day.

Virtually all accommodation prices are subject to IGIC, the Canary Islands' indirect tax, charged at a rate of 5%. This tax is often included in the quoted price at the cheaper places, but less often at the more expensive ones. In some cases you will only be charged the tax if you ask for a receipt.

Apartments

Apartments for rent are much more common than hotels. Quality can vary greatly, but they can be more comfortable than a simple *pensión* and more economical, especially if there are several of you and you plan to self-cater. The two principal categories are *estudios* (studios), with one bedroom or a living room and bedroom in common, and the more frequent *apartamento,* where you get a double bedroom and separate lounge. Both have separate bathroom and a kitchenette. Also common are aparthotels, which function exactly like hotels in terms of service but with large rooms that include a kitchenette, like a small apartment.

The downside for the independent traveller is that, particularly in the main resorts, many apartment complexes are completely in thrall to tour operators. Obeying the terms of their contract, they can't rent you a room, even if it's empty, since the tour company has snapped up every last one for the season. Even those apartment complexes that do rent to independent travellers may insist upon a minimum stay of three nights.

In the case of privately owned apartments, most of the time the owner doesn't live in the building so there's little point in just turning up – you generally need to call. This is particularly the case in the three westernmost islands, La Gomera, El Hierro and La Palma, where small operators predominate. Contact phone numbers will usually be posted at the building entrance.

Apartments are officially categorised as one to three keys. At the bottom of the scale they can cost as little as €35 for a double for a night. At the top you're looking at anything up to €90. Look for signs like *apartamentos de alquiler* (apartments for rent).

Because of the peculiar difficulties sometimes associated with apartments, and the need in most cases for a phone number, you should get hold of each island's hotel/apartment guide from tourist offices as soon as you can after arrival. These guides are often far from complete, with the majority giving only contact details, but at least they give you some information to work with.

Camping

For a place with so much natural beauty, there are precious few places to camp in the Canary Islands. Most islands have just one token official camping ground, and free camping is largely prohibited. In all cases, you'll have to request permission in advance to camp. Generally, the protocol is to call or fax in a request ahead of time (best if it's before you even leave home) and your permit will either be faxed back or you will have to pick it up in person. Some of the smaller camping grounds are geared towards trekkers and only allow one-night stays.

Note that Camping Gaz is the only common brand of camping fuel. Other kinds of fuels are nearly impossible to find.

Casas Rurales

Converted farmsteads or village houses sometimes form the only accommodation option in out-of-the-way places. They are often a highly agreeable option for those seeking to escape the bustle of the resorts, but it's essential to call ahead as they usually offer limited places and there may be no-one in attendance. Many *casas rurales* are distant from public transport, so check whether a hired car is necessary or desirable. They usually represent excellent value for the charm of their setting and facilities. Each island has its own organisation, or you can reserve centrally through **Acantur** (Asociación Canaria de Turismo Rural; ☎ 902 22 55 80; www.ecoturismocanarias.com).

Hotels, Hostels & Pensiones

Compared with mainland Spain, there are precious few *hoteles* (one- to five-star hotels), *hostales* (one- to three-star budget hotels) or *pensiones* (one- or two-star guesthouses) in the Canaries. Since the bulk of the islands' visitors arrive with accommodation booked in advance – usually in villas or self-catering apartments – the demand for more-standard hotels is low.

In practice, there is little difference between *pensiones* and *hostales*. At the low-price, one-star end of either you may well find cramped, dank rooms and shared bathrooms (with perhaps a simple washbasin in the room), while at a slightly higher price you could find charming gems with private bathrooms and stylish décor. *Hoteles* range from simple places to luxurious, five-star establishments. Even the cheapest ones may have a restaurant, and most rooms will have their own bathroom.

Paradores

The Paradores, a Spanish state-run chain of high-class hotels with six establishments in the Canary Islands, are in a special category. These can be wonderful places to luxuriate. They also offer a range of discounts for senior citizens, under-30s and those staying more than one night. The organisation has accommodation on Tenerife and the three

easternmost islands. You can find current offers at www.parador.es, or by contacting its central reservation service, the **Central de Reservas** (☎ 915 16 66 66; Calle Requena 3, 28013 Madrid).

ACTIVITIES

The Canaries are a great destination for some fun in the sun and there is a diverse range of activities offered for young and old. For more details, see the Outdoors chapter (p45).

BUSINESS HOURS

Generally, business hours are 9am to 2pm and 5pm to 8pm Monday to Friday. Having said that, a lot of government offices don't bother with afternoon opening.

Shops and travel agencies usually open these same hours Monday to Saturday, although some skip the afternoon session on Saturday.

Supermarkets often stay open from about 9am to 9pm Monday to Saturday.

Banks mostly open 8.30am to 2pm Monday to Friday.

Big-city post offices open 8.30am to 8.30pm Monday to Friday and 9.30am to 1pm on Saturday. Most others open from 8.30am to 2.30pm Monday to Friday and 9.30am to 1pm on Saturday.

Restaurants are open from 1pm to 4pm and 9pm until late. Locals go to

SMOKING IN SPAIN

Hotels

Since January 2006, all hotels in Spain are required to guarantee at least 70% of the rooms (and public spaces) be 'smoke-free', while smokers are only allowed to light up in separate smoking areas. So regardless of where you stay, you're ensured of finding a nonsmoking room.

Restaurants

The same law requires all bars, restaurants and cafés larger than 100 sq metres to offer a nonsmoking area. Smaller establishments, however, can choose whether they want to be smoke-free; most of these small places (which represent the bulk of the drinking and eating options in the Canary Islands) allow smoking.

small bars for breakfast, which open from around 8am.

Bars and nightclubs have no set opening hours, but you can count on informal pub-style bars to open around 7pm, although they might not get busy until 10pm or 11pm. Depending on the town, nightclubs may open at any time between 10pm and midnight, and stay open until between 2am and 5am. In small towns, bars will only be open on Friday and Saturday nights.

Many places give hours as summer/winter, with summer meaning June through September and winter as the rest of the year. In the Canaries, winter is the high season, often with longer opening hours.

In this book we only give opening hours when they significantly differ from those mentioned here.

CHILDREN

Children are welcome at all kinds of accommodation and in virtually every café, bar and restaurant. Having children with you can often open doors to contact with local people you otherwise may not have the opportunity to meet.

Many bars and cafés have outside tables, allowing drinking adults to indulge in their favourite tipples while their little ones run around and play. Local kids are quite used to staying up late and at fiestas it's commonplace to see even tiny ones toddling the streets at 2am or 3am.

Travelling with children usually implies taking a different approach to your holiday. Fortunately, the Canaries are, in this sense, an ideal location – only those determined to see all seven islands at lightning speed would be tempted to subject themselves, let alone their children, to day after day of tiring movement. Hanging around the one spot for a few days at a time, or choosing a permanent base from which to make excursions, creates a sense of familiarity.

Practicalities

Many of the islands' hotels will happily supply a cot for infants, although it's always a good idea to arrange this in advance. With advance warning, the well-known car-hire companies can provide safety seats for children, but you might find it difficult to arrange this with some of the smaller operators. Highchairs and nappy-changing

facilities are rare, but the laidback, friendly attitude to children on the islands means that this needn't be a dilemma.

Larger hotels and tourist resorts will be able to arrange childminding, and will often have a specific 'kids club' to keep the littlies occupied during the day and early evening.

Infants generally travel free on ferries and other boats, and those aged two to 12 years go half-price. Similar reductions apply at most commercial attractions, museums and on public transport.

There are no particular health precautions you need to take with children in the Canaries. That said, kids tend to be more affected than adults by unfamiliar heat, changes in diet and sleeping patterns.

Nappies (diapers), creams, lotions, baby foods and so on are all easily available in pharmacies and supermarkets on the islands, but if there's a particular brand you swear by, it's best to bring it with you. Breast-feeding in public is not frowned upon by locals.

Lonely Planet's *Travel with Children* has lots of practical advice on the subject and first-hand stories from many Lonely Planet authors and others who have done it.

Sights & Activities

Children will be cheered by the discovery that the Canaries are not overly laden with museums and other grown-up delights that so often engender desperate, yawn-inducing boredom for the young.

Instead, much of the stuff put on for tourists appeals to kids. Animal reserves (such as Tenerife's Loro Parque) and all the water and theme parks on the bigger islands provide fun for all the family.

Tenerife's southern stretches are especially popular family-friendly destinations, and recent efforts to get rid of drunken rowdiness have met with publicity and approval.

Plenty of seaside activities are also suitable for the young, with many companies welcoming children keen to learn to surf, snorkel and the like.

For a selection of great activities for the kids, see the boxed text on p49.

CLIMATE CHARTS

Yes, it really is like a permanent spring in the Canary Islands, with a particularly benign climate putting a smile on your face as

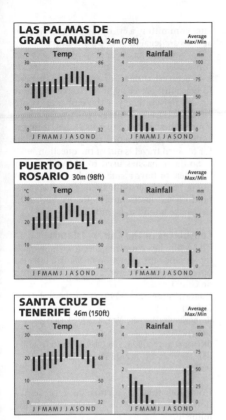

soon as you hit the tarmac. Mean temperatures range from 18°C in the winter to about 24°C in summer. Daily highs can easily reach the mid-30s in summer. Even on a hot day at the beach, however, it can be pleasantly cool higher up, and the snow atop Teide is a clear enough reminder that, in winter at any rate, some warm clothing is essential.

For more climate information, see also p20.

COURSES

A Spanish class in the Canary Islands is a great way to learn something and meet people. With a little Castellano under your belt, you'll be able to better appreciate the local culture.

Check the index for courses listed in this book. You can also check out the local Yellow Pages for Academias de Idiomas to find private language schools throughout the islands. If you're looking for a personal tutor,

ask at the schools or keep your eyes peeled for adverts offering Spanish classes. Expect to pay around €15 per hour.

It's worth asking whether your course will lead to any formal certificate of competence. The Diploma de Español como Lengua Extranjera (DELE) is a qualification recognised by Spain's Ministry of Education and Science.

CUSTOMS

Although the Canary Islands are part of Spain, for customs purposes they are not considered part of the EU. For this reason, allowances are much less generous than for goods bought within EU countries.

You are allowed to bring in or take out, duty free, a maximum of 2L of still wine, 1L of spirits (or 2L of fortified wine), 60mL of perfume, 250mL of *eau de toilette,* 200 cigarettes and up to €175 worth of other goods and gifts.

DANGERS & ANNOYANCES

The vast majority of travellers to the islands risk little more than sunburn, hangovers and overspending. Petty theft can be a problem in Las Palmas de Gran Canaria, the big south-coast resorts on Tenerife and Gran Canaria, and tourist magnets like El Teide, but with a few simple precautions you can minimise the danger.

Carry valuables under your clothes if possible – certainly not in a back pocket or day pack or anything that could be snatched away easily – and keep your eyes open for people who get unnecessarily close to you. Never leave anything visible in cars. If possible, don't even leave anything valuable in the boot (trunk). Hire cars are targeted.

Take care with your belongings on the beach. Lone travellers should consider investing in a waterproof neck pouch so that they can keep lightweight valuables with them even while swimming.

Don't leave anything valuable lying around your room and use a safe if there is one available, even if you have to pay to use it.

If anything valuable is stolen or lost, you must report it to the police and get a copy of the report if you want to make an insurance claim.

If your passport is stolen or lost, contact your embassy or consulate for help in issuing a replacement. Before you leave home, write your name, address and telephone number inside your luggage and take photocopies of your important documents.

Travel insurance against theft and loss is another good idea; see Insurance (p252).

Party animals should be aware that some other party animals, when drunk enough, can become quite unpredictable. In most cases, we are talking loud and drunken louts ferried in on charter flights from northern Europe, some of whom can't resist a good fight.

Scams

You may well come across time-share touts if you hang around the main resorts in the Canary Islands. If you like the islands enough, time-share may be worth considering, but be careful about how and what you choose. You need to have all your rights and obligations in writing, especially where management companies promise to sell your time-share for you if you decide to buy a new one. A number of 'free' sightseeing tours throughout the islands are little more than a quick trip to a theme park and then a solid round of the hard sell, as touts pressure you to buy time in a property. If you're not into this, say so up front and save yourself the hassle.

DISCOUNT CARDS

If you're a full-time student, a teacher or under 26 years of age, you can get discounts on everything from airfares and car rental to public transport and museum entry. The International Student Identity Card (ISIC), International Youth Travel Card (IYTC) and the International Teacher Identity Card (ITIC) are for sale all over the world; prices vary by country. Get details about how to apply at www.isic.org. You can buy and use the cards internationally.

EMBASSIES & CONSULATES

It's important to realise what your own embassy – the embassy of the country of which you are a citizen – can and can't do to help you if you get into trouble. Generally speaking, it won't be much help in an emergency if the trouble you're in is remotely your own fault. Remember that you are bound by the laws of the country you are in. Your embassy will not be sympathetic if you end up in jail

after committing a crime locally, even if such actions are legal in your own country.

In genuine emergencies you might get some assistance, but only if other channels have been exhausted. For example, if you need to get home urgently, a free ticket home is exceedingly unlikely – the embassy would expect you to have insurance. If you have all your money and documents stolen, it might assist with getting a new passport, but a loan for onward travel is out of the question.

Some embassies used to keep letters for travellers or have a small reading room with home newspapers, but these days the mail-holding service is rarely offered, and even newspapers tend to be out of date.

Consulates in the Canary Islands

The following countries all have their main diplomatic representation in Madrid but also have consular representation in Las Palmas de Gran Canaria.

France (Map p66; ☎ 928 29 23 71; Calle Néstor de la Torre 12)

Netherlands (Map p66; ☎ 928 36 22 51; Calle León y Castillo 244)

UK (Map p66; ☎ 928 26 25 08; Calle Luis Morote 6, 3rd fl)

USA (Map p66; ☎ 928 27 12 59; Calle Martínez de Escobar 3)

Countries that have consular representation in Santa Cruz de Tenerife include the following:

France (Map p152; ☎ 922 23 27 10; Calle José María de Villa 1)

Ireland (Map p152; ☎ 922 24 56 71; Calle Castillo 8, 4th fl)

Netherlands (Map p152; ☎ 922 27 17 21; Calle Villalba Hervás 5, 3rd fl)

UK (Map p152; ☎ 922 28 68 63; Plaza General Weyler 8, 1st fl)

FESTIVALS & EVENTS

Like many of their mainland cousins, Canarios love to let it all hang out at the islands' numerous fiestas and *ferias* (fairs). On most islands, Carnaval is the wildest time, but there are many other events throughout the year – August alone has more than 50 celebrations across the islands.

The great majority of these fiestas have a religious background (nearly every town has a patron saint's day), but all are occasions for having fun. *Romerías* (pilgrimages) are particularly noteworthy. Processions head to/from a town's main church to a chapel or similar location dedicated to the local patron saint or the Virgin Mary.

Many local fiestas are noted in the individual island chapters of this book and tourist offices can supply more detailed information. A few of the most outstanding are listed here.

FEBRUARY

Virgen de la Candelaria (Festival of the Patron of the Archipelago) This intense festival, celebrated in Candelaria (Tenerife) on 2 February, derives from the supposed apparition of the Virgin Mary before the Guanches (the original inhabitants of the Canaries). This festival is also celebrated on 15 August. See p176.

FEBRUARY/MARCH

Carnaval Several weeks of fancy-dress parades and merry-making across the islands end on the Tuesday 47 days before Easter Sunday. Carnaval is at its wildest and most extravagant in Santa Cruz de Tenerife. See the boxed text on p151.

JULY

Bajada de la Virgen de las Nieves (Descent of the Virgin of the Snows) This fiesta is held only once every five years in Santa Cruz de la Palma on 21–30 July. The processions, dances and merrymaking constitute La Palma's premier religious festival. See the boxed text on p209.

Bajada de la Virgen de los Reyes (Descent of the Virgin) Held in early July every four years (2009, 2013 etc) on El Hierro, most of the island's population gathers to witness or join in a procession bearing a statue of the Virgin. See the boxed text on p232.

AUGUST

Día de San Ginés (St Ginés Day) Held on 25 August in Arrecife (Lanzarote). See p123.

Fiesta de Nuestra Señora de las Nieves (Feast Day of Our Lady of the Snows) Celebrated on 5 August, this is La Palma's principal fiesta. See the boxed text on p209.

Romería de San Roque (Pilgrimage of St Roch) This annual festival, with varying dates, fills the streets of Garachico (Tenerife) with pilgrims and party goers. See p148.

SEPTEMBER

Fiesta de la Virgen del Pino (Feast day of the Virgin of the Pine) Held in Teror in the first week of September, this is Gran Canaria's most important religious celebration. Festivities begin two weeks before these final key days. See p64.

Arts Festivals

As well as an abundance of local festivals, the islands also host several important arts festivals every year, including the following:

JANUARY/FEBRUARY/MARCH

Festival de Música de Canarias (Canary Music Festival; www.festivaldecanarias.com) Held January through March, it's celebrated simultaneously throughout the islands, particularly on Gran Canaria and Tenerife.

Festival de Ópera (Opera Festival; www.operalaspalmas .org) More than a festival, this is an opera season. Running February through June in Gran Canaria, it's been going strong for more than 40 years.

Festival Internacional de Cine (International Film Festival; www.festivalcinelaspalmas.com) Annual film festival held in March in Las Palmas de Gran Canaria.

JULY/AUGUST

Festival de Ballet y Danza (Ballet and Dance Festival; www.danzaballet.com) Held in July and August, this Gran Canaria festival is well-worth seeing.

Festival del Sur (Festival of the South; www.festival delsur.com) A popular theatre festival in July, attracting companies from Europe, South America and Africa to Agüimes (Gran Canaria).

FOOD

Our Eating reviews feature the price ranges for main courses as a guide. If a restaurant's cheapest main course costs €6 and its most expensive costs €20, our listing will record 'mains €6-20'. Prices for *menús del día* (set menus) may be included instead and occasionally we'll list such specialities as tapas instead of main courses. Check out the Food & Drink chapter on p51 for details on Canarian culinary delights, and individual chapters for details on island specialities.

GAY & LESBIAN TRAVELLERS

Gay and lesbian marriage are both legal in Spain and hence on the Canary Islands. The age of consent is 16, the same as for heterosexuals. The Playa del Inglés, on the southern end of Gran Canaria, is where the bulk of Europe's gay crowd heads when holidaying in the Canaries, and the nightlife here bumps and grinds year-round. By day, nudist beaches are popular spots to hang out.

Spanish people generally adopt a live-and-let-live attitude to sexuality, so you shouldn't have any hassles in the Canary Islands. That said, some small rural towns may not quite know how to deal with overt displays of affection between same-sex couples. Gay magazines in Spanish and on sale at some newsstands include the monthly **Mensual** (www.mensual .com in Spanish), which includes listings for

DIRECTORY

gay bars, clubs and the like in the Canary Islands. A worthwhile website is www.guiagay .com (in Spanish).

For information about gay groups in the islands, you might like to contact the gay and lesbian association **Gamá** (☎ 928 43 34 27; www.colectivogama.com in Spanish).

HOLIDAYS

There are at least 14 official holidays a year in the Canary Islands. When a holiday falls close to a weekend, locals like to make a *puente* (bridge) – meaning they also take the intervening day off. On occasion, when a couple of holidays fall close to the same weekend, the *puente* becomes an *acueducto* (aqueduct)!

Following are the major national holidays, observed throughout the islands and the rest of Spain:

Año Nuevo (New Year's Day) 1 January
Día de los Reyes Magos (Three Kings Day) 6 January
Viernes Santo (Good Friday) March/April
Fiesta del Trabajo (Labour Day) 1 May
La Asunción de la Virgen (Feast of the Assumption) 15 August
Día de la Hispanidad (National Day) 12 October
Todos los Santos (All Saints' Day) 1 November. Gets particular attention on Tenerife.
La Inmaculada Concepción (Feast of the Immaculate Conception) 8 December
Navidad (Christmas) 25 December

In addition, the regional government sets a further five holidays, while local councils allocate another two. Common holidays include the following:

Martes de Carnaval (Carnival Tuesday) February/March
Día de San Juan (St John's Day) 19 March
Jueves Santo (Maundy Thursday) March/April
Día de las Islas Canarias (Canary Islands Day) 30 May
Corpus Christi (the Thursday after the eighth Sunday after Easter Sunday) June. In Las Palmas de Gran Canaria, La Laguna (Tenerife) and La Orotava (Tenerife), locals prepare elaborate floral carpets to celebrate this feast day; the celebration is also big in Mazo and El Paso on La Palma.
Día de Santiago Apóstol (Feast of St James the Apostle, Spain's patron saint) 25 July. In Santa Cruz de Tenerife the day also marks the commemoration of the defence of the city against Horatio Nelson.
Día del Pino (Pine Tree Day) 8 September. This is particularly important on Gran Canaria.
Día de la Constitución (Constitution Day) 6 December

INSURANCE

A travel-insurance policy to cover theft, loss and medical problems is a good idea. Some policies offer lower and higher medical-expense options; the higher ones are chiefly for countries like the USA where medical costs are very high. There is a wide variety of policies available, so check the small print.

Some policies specifically exclude 'dangerous activities', such as scuba diving, motorcycling and even trekking. A locally acquired motorcycle licence is not valid under some policies.

You may prefer a policy that pays doctors or hospitals directly rather than you having to pay on the spot and claim later. If you have to claim later, make sure you keep all documentation. Some policies ask you to call back (reverse charges) to a centre in your home country where an immediate assessment of your problem is made.

Check that the policy covers ambulances or an emergency flight home. See the Insurance section (p264) of the Health chapter for further details.

INTERNET ACCESS

If you plan to carry your notebook or palmtop computer with you, keep in mind that wi-fi and high-speed internet access are still foreign concepts in many rural hotels, privately owned apartments and *casas rurales*. Phone jacks in the Canary Islands are the standard American-style RJ-11, so if you know the local service number to dial, modem connection should be easy. Bear in mind, though, that the cost-per-minute fee may be high, and that not all rooms have phone jacks.

All the major resorts have at least one place where you can log onto the internet and access your emails. But don't assume that every town, or even every island capital, can provide this. You'll generally pay about €2 per hour to log on.

LEGAL MATTERS

Should you be arrested, you will be allotted the free services of an *abogado de oficio* (duty solicitor), who may speak only Spanish. You are also entitled to make a phone call. If you use this call to contact your embassy or consulate, it will probably be able to do no more than refer you to a lawyer who speaks your language. If you end up in court, the authori-

DRUGS

Cannabis is the only legal drug in the Canaries, and only in amounts for personal use – which means very little.

Public consumption of any drug is, in principle, illegal, yet there are some bars where people smoke joints openly. Other bars will ask you to step outside if you light up. The only sure moral of these stories is to be very discreet if you do use cannabis.

Although there's a reasonable degree of tolerance when it comes to people having a smoke in their own home, it would be unwise in hotel rooms or guesthouses and could be risky in even the coolest of public places. The Canary Islands' proximity to northern Africa means that customs officers and the police are vigilant about putting the brakes on the drug trade between the two areas – you'd be a fool to get caught up in this business.

Be aware that some so-called public relations officers for nightclubs in southern Tenerife's Las Américas area are little more than drug dealers, and it's best to avoid buying drugs from them. Authorities in the island's south are starting to come down heavily on those who sully the 'family friendly' image they're trying to cultivate for the region.

ties are obliged to provide a translator if you have to testify.

Spanish *policía* (police) are, on the whole, helpful to law-abiding travellers. Most are certainly friendly enough to be approached for directions on the street. Unpleasant events, such as random drug searches, do occur but not frequently. There are three main types of *policía*: the Policía Nacional, the Policía Local and the Guardia Civil.

Should you need to contact the police, don't agonise over which kind to approach; any of them will do, but you may find that the Policía Local is the most helpful. The Canary Islands government provides a toll-free telephone number (☎ 112), which ensures that any emergency situation can be attended to by the nearest police available.

MAPS

You'll find driving and walking maps in bookshops, tourist offices and at newsstands. In general, these basic maps will do just fine to guide you through the large towns and around the islands' highways, though if you want more detail there are plenty of options.

Both Firestone and Michelin publish good large-scale maps of the islands, although the space taken up by the ocean means there's not much island detail. For more detail, the German company Freytag & Berndt is excellent. Another good choice are the high-quality maps that Canario Juan José Santos publishes in various scales through Ediciones David. See individual island chapters for more information about recommended local maps.

If you plan to hike alone, then a descriptive hiking guidebook is invaluable. The national parks publish in-depth descriptions of hikes within their borders. For hiking outside the parks, Discovery Walking Guides (for guidebooks and accompanying maps to El Hierro, La Palma, La Gomera and Tenerife) and Sunflower Books (for books about all the islands) are both reliable.

MONEY

If you're lucky, you could get by with a single credit or debit card that allows you to withdraw cash from ATMs. But a much better idea would be to take a second (or third) card, in case you lose a card or it lets you down. Travellers cheques, while difficult to cash outside the tourist centres, are a good idea as well.

Spain's currency is the euro. Notes come in denominations of €500, €200, €100, €50, €20, €10 and €5. Coins are €0.50, €0.20, €0.10, €0.05, €0.02 and €0.01.

To check exchange rates between the euro and other currencies, visit www.oanda.com.

ATMs

The Canary Islands has a surfeit of banks, and pretty much every one has a multilingual *cajeros automáticos* (ATM). Honestly, you'll be amazed at some of the backwaters where you'll you find ATMs.

Cash

Even if you're using a credit card you'll make a lot of your purchases with cash, so you need to carry some all the time. Small restaurants and shops may not accept cards.

DIRECTORY

Credit Cards

All major *tarjetas de crédito* (credit cards) and debit cards are widely 'accepted. They can be used for many purchases (including at petrol stations and larger supermarkets, which sometimes ask to see some form of ID) and in hotels and restaurants (although smaller establishments tend to accept cash only).

Cards can also be used in ATMs displaying the appropriate sign. Visa and Master-Card are among the most widely accepted for such transactions.

Be sure that you report a lost or stolen card immediately. If you use Visa or MasterCard you'll probably need to contact the issuing bank directly. You can call American Express on ☎ 902 37 56 37.

Moneychangers

You'll find exchange facilities at most air and sea ports on the islands. In resorts and cities that attract swarms of foreigners, you'll find them easily – they're usually indicated by the word *cambio* (exchange). Most of the time, they offer longer opening hours and quicker service than banks, but worse exchange rates. Wherever you change money, ask from the outset about commission, the terms of which differ from place to place, and confirm that exchange rates are as posted. A typical commission is 3%. Places that advertise 'no commission' usually make up the difference by offering poorer exchange rates.

Travellers Cheques

These are safe and can be cashed at banks and exchange offices (take along your passport) throughout the Canary Islands. Always keep the bank receipt listing the cheque numbers separate from the cheques themselves and log those you have already cashed. This will ease things if they're lost or stolen.

If your travellers cheques are in euros, you should pay no exchange charge when cashing them.

POST

Main post offices in provincial capitals are usually open from either 8.30am to 2.30pm or 8.30am to 8.30pm Monday to Friday, and from about 9am to 1pm Saturday. Stamps are also sold at *estancos* (tobacco shops with the Tabacos sign in yellow letters on a maroon background). A standard airmail letter or card costs €0.30 within Spain, €0.58 to the rest of Europe and €0.78 to the rest of the world.

Delivery times aren't great. Mail to other EU countries takes about a week, and sometimes just as long to the Spanish mainland. Expect 10 days to North America and about two weeks to Australia or New Zealand.

Poste restante (general delivery) mail can be addressed to you at *lista de correos* anywhere in the Canary Islands that has a post office. In the few towns with more than one post office, it will arrive at the main one unless another is specified in the address.

Take your passport when you go to pick up mail. It helps if people writing to you capitalise or underline your surname, and include the postcode. A typical *lista de correos* address looks like this:

Jane SMITH,
Lista de Correos
35080 Las Palmas de Gran Canaria
Islas Canarias, Spain

SOLO TRAVELLERS

Travellers heading out alone should have no qualms about the Canary Islands, though neither should they forget common-sense safety. Cost-wise, you may end up paying a little more, since most package deals base per-person prices on shared double rooms. Nevertheless, most *pensiones* and hotels offer either single rooms or discounts for single occupancy of a double room.

Solo travellers have endless options for activities to keep busy. Though hiking alone is not a good idea, you can sign up for a guided group hike, which can also be a good way to get to know other travellers. Boat cruises, bike excursions, scuba diving trips and Spanish classes are other options.

TELEPHONE

Pay phones once stood at nearly every corner in the Canary Islands, but the popularity of mobile phones has reduced their number considerably. Still, you won't have trouble spotting the distinctive blue boxes in even the smallest towns. You can use coins with most pay phones, though some require you to use a *tarjeta telefónica* (phonecard, see opposite).

Using the phone in Spain has no hidden secrets. If you're calling within the country (including the Canaries), all numbers have a total of nine digits beginning with 9. In the Canary Islands, numbers beginning with

☎ 928 are for the province of Gran Canaria (Gran Canaria, Lanzarote and Fuerteventura), while ☎ 922 numbers are for the Tenerife province (Tenerife, La Gomera, La Palma and El Hierro). Signs and business cards will sometimes print just the last six digits of a phone number, confident that locals know the islands' phone codes. All numbers prefixed with ☎ 900 are toll-free numbers.

A three-minute call from a pay phone costs about €0.15 within a local area, €0.35 to other places in the same province, €0.45 to other provinces and €1 to another EU country or the USA. There are discounts if you call between 8pm and 8am weekdays or on weekends.

International reverse-charge (collect) calls are simple to make: dial ☎ 900 99 00 followed by the country code, such as ☎ 61 for Australia, ☎ 44 for the UK, ☎ 64 for New Zealand, ☎ 15 for Canada and ☎ 11 (AT&T) for the USA.

Contact a domestic operator (in Spanish) by dialling ☎ 1009. A reverse-charge (collect) call is called *una llamada por cobro reverso*. For directory inquiries (in Spanish), dial ☎ 11818, which has a charge of €0.58, though the call is free from a phone box.

Mobile Phones

Mobile telephones are widely used in the Canary Islands, as in the rest of Spain. The Canary Islands use GSM 900/1800, which is compatible with the rest of Europe and Australia, but not with the North American GSM 1900 or the totally different system in Japan (though some North Americans have GSM 1900/900 phones that do work here). If you have a GSM phone, check with your service provider about using it on the islands and beware of calls being routed internationally (very expensive for a 'local' call).

Spaniards, Canarios included, use mobile phones constantly, though it's considered bad form to talk on your mobile phone in restaurants or in packed public spaces like buses.

Mobile phone numbers in Spain start with the number 6. Calls to mobiles vary but a three-minute call should cost about €1.20.

Phonecards

You can buy phonecards at tobacco stands, newsstands, at the telephone centres in large towns (which usually also offer phone booths

with special rates), or even online at sites like www.callingcards.com or www.tarjetas telefonicas.com. In any case, there is an endless variety of phonecards, each with its own pricing scheme. The best card for you will depend on where you plan to call. Rates can be as low as €0.01 per minute, although something around €0.05 is more likely.

TIME

Like most of Europe, the Canaries operate on the 24-hour clock, which, for those accustomed to 'am' and 'pm', can take some getting used to.

The Canary Islands are on Greenwich Mean Time (GMT/UTC), plus an hour in summer for daylight-saving time. The islands keep the same time as the UK, Ireland and Portugal and are always an hour behind mainland Spain and most of Europe. Neighbouring Morocco is on GMT/UTC year-round – so in summer it is an hour behind the Canary Islands even though it's further east!

Daylight-saving (summer) time starts on the last Sunday in March, when clocks are put forward one hour. Clocks are put back an hour on the last Sunday in October. When telephoning home you might also need to make allowances for daylight-saving time in your own country.

When it's noon in the islands (depending on daylight saving), it's 1pm in Madrid and Paris, 4am in San Francisco, 7am in New York and Toronto, 8pm in Perth, 10pm in Sydney and midnight in Auckland.

TOILETS

Public toilets are not common and rarely inviting. The easiest option is to wander into a bar or café and use its facilities. The polite thing to do is to have a coffee or the like before or after, but you're unlikely to raise too many eyebrows if you don't. This said, some curmudgeonly places in popular tourist areas post notices saying that their toilets are for clients only.

The cautious carry some toilet paper with them when out and about as many toilets lack it. If there's a bin beside the loo, put paper and so on in it – it's probably there because the local sewage system has trouble coping.

TOURIST INFORMATION

All major towns in the Canary Islands have a tourist office, and while you may have to wait patiently and politely to be attended to, you can eventually get very good maps and information about the area. Though the Canary government offers region-wide and island-specific information on its excellent website www.turismodecanarias.com, the tourist offices themselves are run by the *cabildos* (governments) of each island. Contact them at each island's main tourist office:

El Hierro (Map p235; ☎ 922 55 03 02; www.elhierro.es; Calle Doctor Quintero 11, Valverde; ☺ 8am-3pm Mon-Fri, 9.30am-1.30pm Sat)

Fuerteventura (Map p99; ☎ 928 53 08 44; www .fuerteventuraturismo.com; Almirante Lallermand 1, Puerto del Rosario; ☺ 8am-3pm Mon-Fri)

Gran Canaria (Map p70; ☎ 928 21 96 00; Calle León y Castillo 17, Las Palmas de Gran Canaria; ☺ 8am-3pm Mon-Fri)

La Gomera (Map p191; ☎ 922 14 15 12; www.gomera -island.com; Calle Real 4, San Sebastián de la Gomera; ☺ 9am-1.30pm & 3.30-6pm Mon-Sat, 10am-1pm Sun Oct-Jun, 9am-1.30pm & 3.30-5pm Mon-Sat, 9am-1pm Sun Jul-Sep)

La Palma (Map p212; ☎ 922 41 21 06; www.lapalma turismo.com; Plaza Constitución s/n, Santa Cruz de la Palma; ☺ 9am-7.30pm Mon-Fri, 9am-3pm Sat, 9am-2pm Sun)

Lanzarote (Map p125; ☎ 928 81 31 74; www.turismo lanzarote.com; La Marina s/n, Arrecife; ☺ 8am-3pm Mon-Fri)

Tenerife (Map p152; ☎ 922 23 95 92; www.puntoinfo .idecnet.com; Plaza España s/n, Santa Cruz de Tenerife; ☺ 8am-6pm Mon-Fri, 9am-1pm Sat) Located in the Cabildo Insular de Tenerife building.

TRAVELLERS WITH DISABILITIES

Sadly, the Canary Islands is not geared towards smooth travel for disabled people. Most restaurants, shops and tourist sights are not equipped to handle wheelchairs, although the more expensive accommodation options will have rooms with appropriate facilities. Transport is tricky, although you should be able to organise a specially modified hire car from one of the international hire companies (with advance warning). In fact, advance warning is always a good idea; start with your travel agent and see what they can offer in terms of information and assistance. In the archipelago's cities, such as Las Palmas and Santa Cruz, some buildings (eg museums or government offices) have Braille

in the lifts, and some specially textured floors before stairs, but not much else. Few concessions are made in the public infrastructure for deaf people.

In the UK, **Holiday Care** (☎ 0845 124 99 71; www .holidaycare.org.uk) can send you a fact sheet on hotels and other accommodation in the Canary Islands that cater for the disabled, as well as travel agents who can help organise trips. Another helpful source is **Enable Holidays** (www .enableholidays.com), which books holidays on Tenerife and Lanzarote. In Spain, you can contact **Polibea** (www.polibea.com/turismo/index.htm).

Restaurants, hotels and apartments with wheelchair access are indicated in this book with ♿.

VISAS

Citizens of EU countries can enter Spain with their national identity card or passport. Citizens of the UK must have a full passport, not just a British visitor passport. Non-EU nationals must take their passport.

EU, Norway and Iceland citizens do not need a visa. Nationals of Australia, Canada, Israel, Japan, New Zealand, Switzerland and the USA need no visa for stays of up to 90 days, but must have a passport valid for the whole visit. This 90-day limit applies throughout the EU. South Africans are among nationalities that do need a visa.

It's best to obtain the visa in your country of residence. Single-entry visas are available in flavours of 30-day and 90-day, and there's also a 90-day multiple-entry visa, though if you apply in a country where you're not resident, the 90-day option may not be available. Multiple-entry visas will save you a lot of time and trouble if you plan to leave Spain, then re-enter it.

Spain is one of the Schengen countries; the others are Portugal, Italy, France, Germany, Austria, the Netherlands, Belgium, Luxembourg, Sweden, Finland, Denmark and Greece. A visa for one Schengen country is valid for the others. Compare validity, prices and permitted entries before applying.

EU, Norway and Iceland nationals planning to stay in Spain more than 90 days are supposed to apply for a residence card during their first month in the country. This can be a complicated procedure; if you intend to subject yourself to it, consult a Spanish consulate before you go to Spain, as you'll need to take certain documents with you.

VOLUNTEERING

If you're interested in getting involved with marine conservation, in particular the protection of whales, get in touch with the **Atlantic Whale Foundation** (www.whalenation.org), a group that organises educational trips, volunteer opportunities and conservation campaigns on Tenerife. The website is a mine of information.

WOMEN TRAVELLERS

Harassment is much less frequent than the stereotypes of Spain would have you believe, and the country has one of the developed world's lowest incidences of reported rape. Any unpleasantness you might encounter is more likely to come from drunken northern-European yobs in the big resorts than from the locals.

In towns you may get the occasional unwelcome stare, catcall or unnecessary comment, to which the best (and most galling) response is indifference. Don't get paranoid about what's being called out; the *piropo* – a harmless, mildly flirty compliment – is deeply ingrained in Spanish society and, if well delivered, even considered gallant.

The advice is really just the common-sense stuff you need to keep in mind anywhere. Think twice about going alone to isolated stretches of beach, lonely country areas or dark city streets at night. Where there are crowds – as there often are very late into the night in towns and cities – you're usually safer. It's inadvisable for a woman to hitchhike alone and not a great idea even for two women together.

Topless bathing and skimpy clothes are generally OK at the coastal resorts, but otherwise a little more modesty is the norm. Quite a few local young women feel no compunction about dressing to kill, but equally feel absolutely no obligation to respond to any male interest this arouses.

WORK

EU, Norway and Iceland nationals are allowed to work anywhere in Spain (including the Canary Islands) without a visa, but if they plan to stay more than three months they are supposed to apply within the first month for a residence card. Virtually everyone else is supposed to obtain (from a Spanish consulate in their country of residence) a work permit and, if they plan to stay more than 90 days, a residence visa. While jobs (especially in tourist resorts) aren't that hard to come by, the procedures necessary to get your paperwork in order can be difficult and time-consuming.

Transport

CONTENTS

GETTING THERE & AWAY

ENTERING THE CANARY ISLANDS

Citizens of the European Union (EU) member states and Switzerland can travel to the Canary Islands with just their national identity card. Nationals of the UK have to carry a full passport (UK visitor passports are not acceptable), and all other nationalities must have a full valid passport.

Check that your passport's expiry date is at least some months away, or you may not be granted a visa, should you need one.

By law you are supposed to have your identity card or passport with you at all times in the Canaries, in case the police ask to see it. In practice, this is unlikely to cause trouble. You might want to carry a photocopy of your documentation instead of the real thing. You often need to flash one of these documents (the original, not the photocopy) for registration when you take a hotel room.

As unfortunate as it is, white Europeans will encounter far less hassle at immigration than black Europeans or Africans. In general, though, you are likely to find the whole deal of flying into a Canary Islands airport remarkably lackadaisical.

Flights and tours can be booked online at www.lonelyplanet.com/travel_services.

> **THINGS CHANGE...**
>
> The information in this chapter is particularly vulnerable to change. Check directly with the airline or a travel agent to make sure you understand how a fare (and ticket you may buy) works and be aware of the security requirements for international travel. Shop carefully. The details given in this chapter should be regarded as pointers and are not a substitute for your own careful, up-to-date research.

AIR
Airports & Airlines

Dozens of airlines, many of which you'll never have heard of, fly into the Canary Islands. All seven islands have airports. Tenerife, Gran Canaria, Lanzarote and, increasingly, La Palma absorb nearly all the direct international flights and those from mainland Spain, while the others are principally for inter-island hops.

There are two main airports on Tenerife. Tenerife Norte (Los Rodeos) handles just about all inter-island flights and most of those to the Spanish mainland. The remainder of the scheduled flights, and virtually all charter flights to the island, are channelled to the more modern Tenerife Sur (Reina Sofía).

Gran Canaria's airport is 16km south of Las Palmas. Lanzarote's Guasimeta airport lies a convenient 6km southwest of the capital, Arrecife.

The bulk of international flights serving the islands directly are charters. Remember that for charter flights you are obliged to ring to confirm your flight within 72 hours of departure.

For more details on airline services to/from each island, see the Getting There & Away sections in the separate island chapters.

Student Deals

Students and those under 26 years of age can benefit from travel deals offered by companies like **STA Travel** (www.statravel.com). Depending on where you live, there may be a country-specific youth travel agency, like Ireland's **USIT** (www.usit.ie).

CLIMATE CHANGE & TRAVEL

Climate change is a serious threat to the ecosystems that humans rely upon, and air travel is the fastest-growing contributor to the problem. Lonely Planet regards travel, overall, as a global benefit, but believes we all have a responsibility to limit our personal impact on global warming.

Flying & Climate Change

Pretty much every form of motorised travel generates CO_2 (the main cause of human-induced climate change) but planes are far and away the worst offenders, not just because of the sheer distances they allow us to travel, but because they release greenhouse gases high into the atmosphere. The statistics are frightening: two people taking a return flight between Europe and the US will contribute as much to climate change as an average household's gas and electricity consumption over a whole year.

Carbon Offset Schemes

Climatecare.org and other websites use 'carbon calculators' that allow travellers to offset the level of greenhouse gases they are responsible for with financial contributions to sustainable travel schemes that reduce global warming – including projects in India, Honduras, Kazakhstan and Uganda.

Lonely Planet, together with Rough Guides and other concerned partners in the travel industry, supports the carbon offset scheme run by climatecare.org. Lonely Planet offsets all of its staff and author travel.

For more information check out our website: lonelyplanet.com.

From Africa

There are daily flights from Morocco with **Royal Air Maroc** (www.royalairmaroc.com). **Binter Canarias** (www.binternet.com) offers regular flights to Nouakchott, Mauritania and to both Laâyoune (El-Aaiún) and Marrakech in Morocco.

From the Americas

There are no direct flights from the United States, Canada, Central or Southern America to the islands. To reach the Canaries, you'll need to travel via a European hub. The thing to do is work out the best possible route/fare combination; a direct flight to London combined with an onward charter or package can often work out to be the cheapest and simplest method of reaching the Canaries. It is also worth considering getting a cheap flight to Europe and then finding a package deal or charter flight to the Canaries from there.

If your European trip is not going to be confined to the islands, consult your travel agent about how best to incorporate them into your vacation.

FROM THE USA

An increasing number of airlines run direct routes between the United States and either Madrid or Barcelona, including **Iberia** (www .iberia.com), **Air Europa** (www.aireuropa.com), **Delta** (www.delta.com), **US Airways** (www.usairways.com) and **Continental** (www.continental.com). The cheapest way of getting from the USA to Europe is by stand-by or courier flights. Stand-by fares are sold at steep discounts by companies like **Courier Travel** (www.couriertravel.org).

On a courier flight, you accompany a parcel to its destination. Courier prices are often far below scheduled fares and tend to drop if you are prepared to fly at short notice. You'd be very lucky to get anything directly to the islands, but a New York–Madrid or New York–London return flight on a courier run can cost under US$400 in the low season (more expensive from the west coast). Always check conditions and details with the company.

From Australia & New Zealand

There are no direct flights from Australia to the Canaries, so you'll have to book connecting flights via Madrid, Barcelona or another European capital. From New Zealand, flights to Europe are via the USA and Asia. You can also fly from Auckland to pick up a connecting flight in either Melbourne or Sydney.

From Continental Europe

There are plenty of packages and flights available in continental Europe for the Canary

Islands. Munich is a haven for discount travel agents and more mainstream budget-travel outlets. Dutch and Belgian tour operators may also offer good deals.

From Spain, **Air Europa** (☎ 902 40 15 01; www .aireuropa.com), **Iberia** (☎ 902 40 05 00; www.iberia .com) and **Spanair** (☎ 902 13 14 15; www.spanair.com) all fly to the Canary Islands. They connect the islands with international destinations, usually via Madrid or Barcelona.

You'll have no trouble getting to the islands from Germany. Both **Condor** (☎ 928 57 92 93; www.condor.com) and **Air Berlin** (www .airberlin.com) offer frequent flights connecting major (and minor) German cities with the islands. Numerous charter flights make the trip as well.

Amsterdam is another popular departure point. **Martinair** (www.martinair.com) flies to Tenerife, Gran Canaria, Lanzarote and Fuerteventura, while **Transavia Airlines** (www .transavia.com) flies to the same airports as well as La Palma.

From the UK & Ireland

Discount air travel is big business in London. Check the weekend broadsheet papers for special deals, many of which include a hotel or apartment with half-board and even car rental in the final price. Low-season prices can work out to be ridiculously cheap, especially if you're heading to one of the islands' major tourist centres.

Monarch (☎ 0870 040 5040; www.monarch-airlines .com), which is principally a charter company, flies from London Gatwick to Tenerife Sur and Lanzarote. Other airlines linking the UK and the Canary Islands include **British Airways** (www.ba.com) and **Flyjet** (www.fly-jet.com). You needn't necessarily fly from London; many good deals are just as easily available from other major centres in the UK.

If you're having trouble finding a good deal, you might try calling the **Air Travel Advisory Bureau** (☎ 020-7636 5000). If you tell the bureau your destination, it'll provide a list of relevant discount travel agents.

If you're travelling from Ireland, several charter flights leave every weekend for the Canary Islands. Check them out, then perhaps compare what is available with prices from London – getting across to London first might save you a few euro. **Aer Lingus** (www.aerlingus.com) flies every other day between Dublin and Tenerife Sur.

SEA

Just about everyone flies to the Canaries. The only other alternative (apart from a very long swim!) is to take the **Acciona Trasmediterránea** (☎ 902 45 46 45; www.trasmediterranea .com) ferry, which carries passengers, supplies and cars to the islands twice a week. The Cádiz–Tenerife route sets out from the Spanish mainland at 1am on Sunday (yes, the middle of the night!) and, after a long and often bumpy voyage, it arrives at Tenerife at 9am on Monday. The return trip leaves at 3pm on Monday and arrives at 9am on Wednesday. Another boat leaves Cádiz at 6pm on Wednesday and arrives at Las Palmas de Gran Canaria at 12.30am Friday. After a half-hour stop, it continues on to Lanzarote, which it reaches at 1.45pm Friday. The return trip leaves Lanzarote at 3pm on Friday and heads straight back to Cádiz, arriving at 7pm on Saturday.

Unless you particularly like rough ocean voyages for their own sake, or have a car that you simply must get to the islands, you're much better off just hopping on a plane.

Ferry fares range from €250 to €880 per person depending on the type of cabin and – we should hope so at such prices – include all meals. A car up to 3m long costs €190 one way, a motorcycle costs €90 and bicycles are free. You generally need to book at least a month in advance if you want to get a car aboard.

GETTING AROUND

AIR

Now that all seven islands have airports, flying between them is an easy and popular option, and it can save you bundles of time if you want to see several islands. Both **Binter Canarias** (☎ 902 39 13 92; www.binternet.com) and the newer **Islas Airways** (☎ 902 47 74 78; www.islas airways.com) run regular routes between the islands. On both airlines, the ticket fees are set at €60 per leg for adult nonresidents (kids and students are cheaper), so hopping on a plane isn't much more expensive than taking a ferry, and it's substantially quicker.

Two other airlines serving the Spanish mainland have a few flights connecting the bigger islands: Air Europa flies to Tenerife, Gran Canaria and Lanzarote; and Spanair flies to Tenerife, Gran Canaria, Lanzarote and Fuerteventura.

BICYCLE

Biking around the islands is an extremely pleasant way to see the sights, but don't necessarily expect drivers to accommodate you (or have much grasp of what it's like to be a cyclist tackling a hairpin bend uphill). Sadly, bicycle lanes in the urban environment are nonexistent, although beachside boulevards will generally include space for bike riding.

If you plan to bring your own bike, check with the airline about any hidden costs and whether it will have to be disassembled and packed for the journey. Taking your bike on ferries is pretty straightforward – it's either free or very cheap.

Fill all your water bottles and then add one more: it can be hot on the open road and, more often than not, you won't find any water between villages.

Hire

You can rent mountain bikes and city bikes in various resorts and in the more tourist-orientated areas of the islands. Expect to pay €8 per day for the simplest machine and about €12 to €15 for a mountain bike. A deposit of around €50 is standard. Rental rates will include a helmet and some basic equipment.

BOAT

The islands are connected by ferries, 'fast ferries' and jetfoils. There are three main companies: **Naviera Armas** (☎ 902 45 65 00; www.navieraarmas.com), **Fred Olsen** (☎ 902 10 01 07; www.fredolsen.es) and **Acciona Trasmediter-ránea** (☎ 902 45 46 45; www.trasmediterranea.com). See individual island chapters for detailed route information.

Do bear in mind that times, prices – even routes – can and do change. This isn't so important on major routes, where there's plenty of choice, but it can mean a big delay if you're planning to travel a route that has only a couple of boats per day, or even per week. See the colour map at the front of the book for inter-island ferry routes.

BUS

A bus in the Canary Islands is called a *guagua*, pronounced 'wa-wa'. If you've bounced around Latin America, you'll be familiar with the term. Still, if you ask about *autobuses*, you'll be understood.

Every island has its own interurban service. One way or another, they can get you to most of the main locations, but in many cases there are few runs each day. This is especially so on the smaller islands, where the population is low and most people are obliged to have their own wheels.

The bigger islands of Tenerife and Gran Canaria have an impressive public-transport system that covers the whole island. Frequency, however, varies enormously, from a regular service between major towns to a couple of runs per day for transporting workers and school kids to/from the capital.

Check the timetable carefully before you travel at the weekend. Even on the bigger islands' major runs, a frequent weekday service can trickle off to just a few departures on Saturday and one, or none, on Sunday.

In the larger towns and cities, buses leave from an *estación de guaguas* (bus station). In villages and small towns, they usually terminate on a particular street or plaza. You buy your ticket on the bus. Bus companies include the following:

Arrecife Bus (☎ 928 81 15 22; www.arrecifebus.com) Frequent service around Arrecife and Lanzarote's tourist areas; services to elsewhere are minimal or nonexistent.

Global (☎ 902 38 11 10; www.globalsu.net in Spanish) Provides Gran Canaria with a network of routes, although the service to many rural areas is pretty thin.

Servicio Insular de Guagua (☎ 922 55 07 29) Bus services on El Hierro that recently underwent a major overhaul; services are now more frequent and reliable.

Servicio Regular Gomera (☎ 922 14 11 01; www .gomera-island.com/turismo/ingles/guaguas.htm) La Gomera's limited service.

Tiadhe (☎ 928 85 09 51, 928 85 21 62; www.tiadhe .com) Provides a limited service, with 17 lines operating around Fuerteventura.

TITSA (Transportes Interurbanos de Tenerife SA; ☎ 922 53 13 00; www.titsa.com) Runs a spider's web of services all over Tenerife.

Transportes Insular La Palma (☎ 922 41 19 24; www.transporteslapalma.com) Services La Palma, with route prices starting at €1.

Bus Passes

On some of the islands you can buy a Bonobus card (called a Tarjeta Insular on Gran Canaria), which usually costs €12. They're sold at bus stations and shops such as newsagents.

TRANSPORT

Insert the card into the machine on the bus, tell the driver where you are going and the fare will be deducted from the card. You get about 30% off standard fares with the cards, so they are a good investment if you intend to use the buses a lot.

Costs

Fares, especially if you invest in a Bonobus card, are reasonable. Destinations within each island are calculated pro rata according to distance, so ticket fares vary from €1 to €10 or more.

CAR & MOTORCYCLE
Bringing Your Own Vehicle

Unless you're intending to settle on the islands, there's no advantage whatsoever in bringing your own vehicle. Transport costs on the ferry from Cádiz in mainland Spain are savage (see p260) and car-hire rates on the islands are significantly cheaper than in most EU countries. If you're one of the very rare visitors to bring your own vehicle, you will need registration papers and an International Insurance Certificate (or a Green Card). Your insurance company will issue this.

Driving Licence

Be sure to pack your driving licence if you intend to hire a car in the Canary Islands. EU licences are recognised here, as throughout Spain. Other foreign licences should be accompanied by an International Driving Permit (in practice, your driving licence alone will more often than not suffice), which are available from automobile clubs in your country and valid for 12 months.

A licence is required for any vehicle over 50cc.

Fuel

Gasolina is much cheaper in the Canary Islands than elsewhere in Spain because it's not taxed as heavily.

Sin plomo (lead-free) petrol is available pretty much everywhere. Prices vary slightly between service stations and fluctuate according to oil tariffs, OPEC (Organisation of the Petroleum Exporting Countries) arm twisting and tax policy. You can pay with major credit cards at most service stations.

Hire

All the big international car-rental companies are represented in the Canary Islands and there are also plenty of local operators. If you intend to stay on one island for any length of time, it might be worth booking a car in advance, for example in a fly/drive deal.

No matter what you rent, make sure you understand what is included in the price (unlimited kilometres, tax, insurance, collision damage waiver and so on) and what your liabilities are, and that you examine the rental agreement carefully – difficult if it is in Spanish only! Expect to pay €25 to €30 per day for a compact car. Long-term rental can be cheaper, while renting larger cars or 4WDs can double the price. It's often obligatory to pay with a credit card, although the company does then have a hold over you if something goes wrong.

It's well worth shopping around and picking up a few brochures. In the big resorts, some operators quote rates that are seductively and misleadingly low. That's because insurance, which can more than double the cost, isn't included. There are other incidentals (some optional) such as collision damage waiver, extra passenger cover and 5% IGIC (General Indirect Tax to the Canary Islands) to look out for.

Generally, you can't take a hire car from one island to another without the company's explicit permission. An exception for most companies is the Fuerteventura–Lanzarote sea crossing – most have no problem with you taking your car from one to the other, and in some cases you can hire on one island and drop the car off on the other.

Check before you drive off that the phone number of the rental company features on your copy of the rental agreement (you're required by law to carry this with you). Some agents also offer a 24-hour mobile phone contact. Out on the road, always carry your licence, passport and rental agreement. To rent a car you need to be at least 21 years old and have held a driving licence for a minimum of two years.

Companies operating on all islands include the following:

Avis (☎ 902 18 08 54; www.avis.es)

Cicar (☎ 900 20 23 03, UK 0800 960 367, Germany 0800 182 1816; www.cicar.com) The name stands for 'Canary Islands Car' and this archipelago-wide company is reliable and usually represents good value.

Europcar/BC Betacar (☎ 913 43 45 12; www.europcar.es)

Hertz (☎ 913 72 93 00; www.hertz.es)

Insurance

For an extra fee you can usually boost the travel-insurance coverage on your vehicle – and it's a good idea to do so. The number of dinged-up hire cars certainly makes you wonder if anyone's getting a nasty shock when the credit-card bills come in. All the car-hire companies have insurance, and you will have to pay for it one way or another. Driving on a dirt road will generally render your policy null and void, so take this into account.

Purchase

Only residents of Spain can buy a car in the Canaries, and only those who can prove residence in the Canary Islands may avail themselves of the local tax breaks to buy a car cheaply.

Road Conditions

Road conditions on the islands are generally excellent, with plenty of EU-funded roadworks keeping up the high standards. Dirt roads still abound, though, especially in out-of-the-way areas. Driving, even in the biggest cities of Las Palmas de Gran Canaria and Santa Cruz de Tenerife, doesn't present particular difficulties, although the traffic can be a little intense. Parking, however, can be more problematic. Most city centres and several smaller towns operate restricted meter parking. Otherwise, there are several car parks (with parking fees) in the two capitals.

Road Rules

The minimum age for driving cars is 18. If fitted, rear seatbelts must be worn – there are fines for failure to comply with this. Driving takes place on the right-hand side of the road.

Motorcyclists should use headlights at all times, though few locals do. Crash helmets are obligatory when riding any motorised bikes. The minimum age for riding bikes and scooters up to 50cc is 16 (no licence required). For anything more powerful, you'll need to produce your driving licence.

In built-up areas the speed limit is generally 40km/h, rising to a maximum of 100km/h on major roads and 120km/h on *autovías* (motorways).

The blood-alcohol limit is 0.05% and random breath testing is carried out.

TAXI

You could tour around an island by taxi but it's a very expensive way to go, with interurban fares hovering around €1.15 per kilometre. Some routes (such as to and from airports) have set fares, so be sure to ask about them before setting off. Also, it may be possible to arrange a private taxi tour of an island; an hourly or daily fare would need to be negotiated ahead of time.

TRANSPORT

Health

CONTENTS

HEALTH

BEFORE YOU GO

Prevention is the key to staying healthy while abroad. Some predeparture planning will save trouble later. See your dentist before a long trip, carry a spare pair of contact lenses and glasses, and take your optical prescription with you. Bring medications in their original, clearly labelled, containers. A signed and dated letter from your physician describing your medical conditions and medications, including generic names, is also a good idea. If carrying syringes or needles, be sure to have a physician's letter documenting their medical necessity.

INSURANCE

For EU citizens the European Health Insurance Card (EHIC), which you can apply for online, by phone or by post, covers most medical care. It doesn't cover nonemergencies or emergency repatriation home. You'll still have to pay for medicine bought from pharmacies, even if prescribed, and perhaps for a few tests and procedures. An E111 is no good for private medical consultations and treatment in the Canaries; this includes most dentists and some of the better clinics and surgeries.

Citizens from other countries should find out if there's a reciprocal arrangement for free medical care between their country and Spain. If you need health insurance, strongly consider a policy that covers for the worst possible scenario, such as an accident requiring an emergency flight home. Find out in advance if your insurance plan will make direct payments to providers or reimburse you later for overseas health expenditures.

RECOMMENDED VACCINATIONS

No jabs are required to travel to Spain. The World Health Organisation (WHO), however, recommends that all travellers should be covered for diphtheria, tetanus, measles, mumps, rubella and polio, regardless of their destination. Since most vaccines don't provide immunity until at least two weeks after they're given, visit a physician at least six weeks before departure.

ONLINE RESOURCES

The WHO's *International Travel and Health* publication is revised annually and is available online at www.who.int/ith. Other useful websites include www.mdtravelhealth.com (travel-health recommendations for every country, updated daily), www.fitfortravel .scot.nhs.uk (general travel advice for the lay person) and www.ageconcern.org.uk (advice on travel for elderly people).

IN TRANSIT

DEEP VEIN THROMBOSIS

Blood clots may form in the legs during plane flights, chiefly because of prolonged immobility. The longer the flight, the greater the risk. The chief symptom of deep vein thrombosis (DVT) is swelling or pain in the foot, ankle or calf, usually, but not always, just on one side. When a blood clot travels to the lungs, it may cause chest pain and breathing difficulties. Travellers with any of these symptoms should immediately seek medical attention.

To prevent the development of DVT on long flights, you should walk about the cabin, contract the leg muscles while sitting, drink plenty of fluids and avoid alcohol and tobacco in the hours before your flight.

JET LAG

To avoid jet lag (common when crossing several time zones) drink plenty of nonalcoholic fluids and eat light meals. Upon arrival, seek exposure to natural sunlight and readjust your schedule (for meals, sleep and so on) as soon as possible.

IN THE CANARY ISLANDS

AVAILABILITY OF HEALTH CARE

If you need an ambulance call ☎ 112 (the pan-European emergency telephone number, which can be called for urgent medical assistance). An alternative emergency number is ☎ 061 for *urgencias salud* (medical emergencies). For emergency treatment go straight to the *urgencias* (emergencies) section of the nearest hospital.

Good health care is readily available. For minor, self-limiting illnesses, pharmacists can give valuable advice and sell over-the-counter medication. They can also advise when more specialised help is required and point you in the right direction.

The standard of dental care is usually good; however, it is sensible to have a dental checkup before a long trip.

TRAVELLER'S DIARRHOEA

If you develop diarrhoea, be sure to drink plenty of fluids, preferably an oral rehydration solution such as Dioralyte. If diarrhoea is bloody, persists for more than 72 hours or is accompanied by fever, shaking, chills or severe abdominal pain, you should seek medical attention.

ENVIRONMENTAL HAZARDS
Heat Exhaustion

Heat exhaustion occurs following excessive fluid loss with inadequate replacement of fluids and salt. Symptoms include headache, dizziness and tiredness. Dehydration is already happening by the time you feel thirsty – aim to drink sufficient water to produce pale, diluted urine. To treat heat exhaustion, replace fluids through water and/or fruit juice and cool the body with cold water and fans.

Insect Bites & Stings

Mosquitoes in the Canaries probably don't carry malaria, but they can cause irritation and infected bites. Use a DEET-based insect repellent.

Bees and wasps cause real problems only to those with a severe allergy (anaphylaxis). If you have a severe allergy to bee or wasp stings, carry an EpiPen or similar adrenaline injection.

Scorpions are mercifully rarer on the Canary Islands than in mainland Spain. Their sting can be distressingly painful but isn't fatal.

In forested areas watch out for the hairy, reddish-brown caterpillars of the pine processionary moth. They live in silvery nests in the pine trees and, in spring, leave the nest to march in long lines (hence the name). Touching the caterpillars' hairs sets off a severely irritating allergic skin reaction.

Check for ticks if you have been walking where sheep and goats graze: they can cause skin infections and other more serious diseases.

TRAVELLING WITH CHILDREN

Make sure children are up to date with routine vaccinations. Discuss possible travel vaccines well before departure, as some are not suitable for children under one year of age. Lonely Planet's *Travel with Children* includes travel-health advice for younger children.

WOMEN'S HEALTH

Travelling during pregnancy is usually possible but there are important things to consider. Always seek a medical checkup before planning your trip. The most risky times for travel are during the first 12 weeks of pregnancy and after 30 weeks.

SEXUAL HEALTH

Condoms are readily available on the island but emergency contraception may not be, so take the necessary precautions. When buying condoms, look for a European CE mark, which means they have been rigorously tested, and then keep them in a cool, dry place or they may crack and perish.

HEALTH

Language

CONTENTS

The language of the Canary Islands is Spanish *(español)*, which many Spanish people refer to as *castellano* (Castilian) to distinguish it from other mainland tongues such as Basque and Catalan. Spanish is the most widely spoken of the Romance languages – the group of languages derived from Latin, which includes French, Italian, Portuguese and Romanian.

See p51 for information on food, including useful words and phrases for use when ordering at a restaurant. For a more comprehensive guide to the language than we're able to offer here, pick up a copy of Lonely Planet's *Spanish Phrasebook*.

If you'd like to learn the language in greater depth, courses are available in Las Palmas de Gran Canaria (p71) and La Laguna (p159). See p249 for more information on language courses.

PRONUNCIATION

Spanish spelling is phonetically consistent, meaning that there's a clear and consistent relationship between what you see in writing and how it's pronounced. In addition, most Spanish sounds have English equivalents, so English speakers shouldn't have much trouble being understood.

Those familiar with the *castellano* of the central and northern mainland will be surprised by the Latin American lilt of the Canarian accent. It also bears a closer resemblance to what you hear in Andalucía than to mainland Spanish.

The lisp (like 'th' in 'thin') you'd normally expect with **z** and **c** before vowels is pronounced more as a sibilant 's', and **s** itself is hardly pronounced at all – it's more like an aspirated 'h' – for example, Las Palmas sounds more like Lah Palmah! The swallowing of consonants like this is a marked feature of Canarian Spanish, and even solid speakers of the language may find themselves wondering just how much they really understood on hearing a lively *charla* (chat) among Canarios.

Vowels

a	as in 'father'
e	as in 'met'
i	as in 'marine'
o	as in 'or' (without the 'r' sound)
u	as in 'rule'; the 'u' is not pronounced after **q** and in the letter combinations **gue** and **gui**, unless it's marked with a diaeresis (eg *argüir*), in which case it's pronounced as English 'w'
y	at the end of a word or when it stands alone, it's pronounced as the Spanish **i** (eg *ley*); between vowels within a word it's as the 'y' in 'yonder'

Consonants

As a rule, Spanish consonants resemble their English counterparts, with the exceptions listed below.

While the consonants **ch**, **ll** and **ñ** are generally considered distinct letters, **ch** and **ll** are now often listed alphabetically under **c** and **l** respectively. The letter **ñ** is still treated as a separate letter and comes after **n** in dictionaries.

b	similar to English 'b', but softer; **b** is referred to as 'b larga'
c	as in 'celery' before **e** and **i**; otherwise as English 'k'
ch	as in 'choose', although in the Spanish of the Canaries it can sound more like a 'y'. For example, Guanche is often pronounced 'Guanye'

d	as in 'dog' when initial or preceded by **l** or **n**; elsewhere as the 'th' in 'then'. Often not pronounced at all when at the end of a word.
g	as the 'ch' in the Scottish *loch* before **e** and **i** ('kh' in our guides to pronunciation); elsewhere, as in 'go'
h	always silent
j	as the 'ch' in the Scottish *loch* (written as 'kh' in our guides to pronunciation)
ll	as the 'y' in 'yellow'
ñ	as the 'ni' in 'onion'
r	a rolled 'r'; longer and stronger when initial or doubled
rr	very strongly rolled
v	similar to English 'b', but softer; **v** is referred to as 'b corta'
x	as the 'x' in 'taxi' when between two vowels; as the 's' in 'say' when preceding a consonant
z	as the 's' in 'sun' (not as the 'th' in 'thin' as in most of mainland Spain)

Word Stress

Stress is indicated by italics in the pronunciation guides included with all the words and phrases in this language guide. In general, words ending in vowels or the letters **n** or **s** have stress on the next-to-last syllable, while those with other endings have stress on the last syllable. Thus *vaca* (cow) and *caballos* (horses) both carry stress on the next-to-last syllable, while *ciudad* (city) and *infeliz* (unhappy) are both stressed on the last syllable.

Written accents indicate a stressed syllable, and will almost always appear in words that don't follow the rules above, eg *sótano* (basement), *porción* (portion).

GENDER & PLURALS

In Spanish, nouns are either masculine or feminine, and there are rules to help determine gender (there are of course some exceptions). Feminine nouns generally end with **-a** or with the groups **-ción**, **-sión** or **-dad**. Other endings typically signify a masculine noun. Endings for adjectives also change to agree with the gender of the noun they modify (masculine/feminine **-o**/**-a**). Where both masculine and feminine forms are included in this language guide, they are separated by a slash, with the masculine form first, eg *perdido/a*.

If a noun or adjective ends in a vowel, the plural is formed by adding **s** to the end. If it ends in a consonant, the plural is formed by adding **es** to the end.

ACCOMMODATION

I'm looking for ...	*Estoy buscando ...*	e-*stoy* boos-*kan*-do ...
Where is ...?	*¿Dónde hay ...?*	don-de ai ...
a hotel	*un hotel*	oon o-*tel*
a boarding house	*una pensión/ residencial/ un hospedaje*	*oo*-na pen-*syon*/ re-see-den-*syal*/ oon os-pe-*da*-khe
a youth hostel	*un albergue juvenil*	oon al-*ber*-ge khoo-ve-*neel*
I'd like a ... room.	*Quisiera una habitación ...*	kee-*sye*-ra oo-na a-bee-ta-*syon* ...
double	*doble*	*do*-ble
single	*individual*	een-dee-vee-*dwal*
twin	*con dos camas*	kon dos *ka*-mas
How much is it per ...?	*¿Cuánto cuesta por ...?*	*kwan*-to *kwes*-ta por ...
night	*noche*	*no*-che
person	*persona*	per-*so*-na
week	*semana*	se-*ma*-na

MAKING A RESERVATION
(for phone or written requests)

To ...	*A ...*
From ...	*De ...*
Date	*Fecha*
I'd like to book ...	*Quisiera reservar ...* (see the list under 'Accommodation' for bed and room options)
in the name of ...	*en nombre de ...*
for the nights of ...	*para las noches del ...*
credit card ...	*tarjeta de crédito ...*
number	*número*
expiry date	*fecha de vencimiento*
Please confirm ...	*Puede confirmar ...*
availability	*la disponibilidad*
price	*el precio*

Does it include breakfast?

¿Incluye el desayuno?	een-*kloo*-ye el de-sa-*yoo*-no

May I see the room?

¿Puedo ver la habitación?	*pwe*-do ver la a-bee-ta-*syon*

LANGUAGE

I don't like it.
No me gusta.   no me *goos*·ta
It's fine. I'll take it.
OK. La alquilo.   o·*kay* la al·*kee*·lo
I'm leaving now.
Me voy ahora.   me *voy* a·o·ra

full board	*pensión*	pen·*syon*
	completa	kom·*ple*·ta
private/shared	*baño privado/*	*ba*·nyo pree·va·do/
bathroom	*compartido*	kom·par·*tee*·do
too expensive	*demasiado caro*	de·ma·*sya*·do ka·ro
cheaper	*más económico*	mas e·ko·*no*·mee·ko
discount	*descuento*	des·*kwen*·to

CONVERSATION & ESSENTIALS

When talking to people familiar to you or younger than you, it's usual to use the informal form of 'you', *tú*, rather than the polite form *Usted*. The polite form is used in all cases in this guide; where options are given, the form is indicated by the abbreviations 'pol' and 'inf'.

In Canarian Spanish the standard second person plural pronoun of mainland Spain, *vosotros* (you), is rarely heard. Instead, the more formal *Ustedes* is used.

Hello.	*Hola.*	o·la
Good morning.	*Buenos días.*	*bwe*·nos dee·as
Good afternoon.	*Buenas tardes.*	*bwe*·nas tar·des
Good evening/ night.	*Buenas noches.*	*bwe*·nas *no*·ches
Goodbye.	*Adiós.*	a·*dyos*
Bye/See you soon.	*Hasta luego.*	*as*·ta *lwe*·go
Yes.	*Sí.*	see
No.	*No.*	no
Please.	*Por favor.*	por fa·*vor*
Thank you.	*Gracias.*	*gra*·syas
Many thanks.	*Muchas gracias.*	*moo*·chas *gra*·syas
You're welcome.	*De nada.*	de *na*·da
Pardon me.	*Perdón/*	per·*don*
	Discúlpeme.	dees·*kool*·pe·me

(before requesting information, for example)

Sorry.	*Lo siento.*	lo see·*en*·to

(when apologising)

Excuse me.	*Permiso.*	per·*mee*·so

(when asking permission to pass, for example)

How are things?
¿Qué tal?   ke tal
What's your name?
¿Cómo se llama Usted?   *ko*·mo se *ya*·ma *oo*·ste (pol)
¿Cómo te llamas?   *ko*·mo te *ya*·mas (inf)

SIGNS	
Entrada	Entrance
Salida	Exit
Abierto	Open
Cerrado	Closed
Información	Information
Prohibido	Prohibited
Prohibido Fumar	No Smoking
Comisaría	Police Station
Servicios/Aseos	Toilets
Hombres	Men
Mujeres	Women

My name is ...
Me llamo ...   me *ya*·mo ...
It's a pleasure to meet you.
Mucho gusto.   moo·cho *goos*·to
Where are you from?
¿De dónde es/eres?   de *don*·de es/e·res (pol/inf)
I'm from ...
Soy de ...   soy de ...
Where are you staying?
¿Dónde está alojado?   *don*·de es·ta a·lo·*kha*·do (pol)
¿Dónde estás alojado?   *don*·de es·tas a·lo·*kha*·do (inf)
May I take a photo?
¿Puedo hacer una foto?   pwe·do a·*sair* oo·na fo·to

DIRECTIONS

How do I get to ...?
¿Cómo puedo llegar a ...? ko·mo pwe·do ye·*gar* a ...
Is it far?
¿Está lejos?   es·*ta* le·khos
Go straight ahead.
Siga/Vaya derecho.   *see*·ga/va·ya de·*re*·cho
Turn left.
Doble a la izquierda.   *do*·ble a la ees·*kyer*·da
Turn right.
Doble a la derecha.   *do*·ble a la de·*re*·cha
I'm lost.
Estoy perdido/a.   es·*toy* per·dee·do/a
Can you show me (on the map)?
¿Me lo podría indicar   me lo po·*dree*·a een·dee·*kar*
(en el mapa)?   (en el *ma*·pa)

here	*aquí*	a·*kee*
there	*allí*	a·*yee*
avenue	*avenida*	a·ve·nee·da
street	*calle/paseo*	ka·lye/pa·se·o
traffic lights	*semáforos*	se·ma·fo·ros
north	*norte*	nor·te
south	*sur*	soor
east	*este*	es·te
west	*oeste*	o·es·te

HEALTH

I'm sick.
Estoy enfermo/a.   es·toy en·fer·mo/a
I need a doctor.
Necesito un médico   ne·se·see·to oon me·dee·ko
(que habla inglés).   (ke a·bla een·gles)
Where's the hospital?
¿Dónde está el hospital? don·de es·ta el os·pee·tal
I'm pregnant.
Estoy embarazada.   es·toy em·ba·ra·sa·da
I've been vaccinated.
Estoy vacunado/a.   es·toy va·koo·na·do/a

I'm allergic	Soy alérgico/a	soy a·ler·khee·ko/a
to ...	a ...	a ...
antibiotics	los antibióticos	los an·tee·byo·tee·kos
penicillin	la penicilina	la pe·nee·si·lee·na
nuts	las nueces	las nwe·ses
peanuts	los cacahuetes	los ka·ka·we·tes
seafood	los mariscos	los ma·rees·koss

I'm ...	Soy ...	soy ...
asthmatic	asmático/a	as·ma·tee·ko/a
diabetic	diabético/a	dya·be·tee·ko/a
epileptic	epiléptico/a	e·pee·lep·tee·ko/a

I have ...	Tengo ...	ten·go ...
a cough	tos	tos
diarrhea	diarrea	dya·re·a
a headache	un dolor de cabeza	oon do·lor de ka·be·sa
nausea	náusea	now·se·a

LANGUAGE DIFFICULTIES

Do you speak (English)?
¿Habla/Hablas (inglés)? a·bla/a·blas (een·gles) (pol/inf)
Does anyone here speak English?
¿Hay alguien que   ai al·gyen ke
hable inglés?   a·ble een·gles
I (don't) understand.
Yo (no) entiendo.   yo (no) en·tyen·do
How do you say ...?
¿Cómo se dice ...?   ko·mo se dee·se ...
What does ...mean?
¿Qué quiere decir ...? ke kye·re de·seer ...

Could you	¿Puede ..., por	pwe·de ... por
please ...?	favor?	fa·vor
repeat that	repetirlo	re·pe·teer·lo
speak more	hablar más	a·blar mas
slowly	despacio	des·pa·syo
write it down	escribirlo	es·kree·beer·lo

EMERGENCIES

Help!	¡Socorro!	so·ko·ro
Fire!	¡Incendio!	een·sen·dyo
Go away!	¡Vete!/¡Fuera!	ve·te/fwe·ra

Call ...!	¡Llame a ...!	ya·me a
an ambulance	una ambulancia	oo·na am·boo·lan·sya
the police	la policía	la po·lee·see·a
a doctor	un médico	oon me·dee·ko

It's an emergency.
Es una emergencia.   es oo·na e·mer·khen·sya
Could you help me, please?
¿Me puede ayudar,   me pwe·de a·yoo·dar
por favor?   por fa·vor
I'm lost.
Estoy perdido/a.   es·toy per·dee·do/a
Where are the toilets?
¿Dónde están los baños? don·de es·tan los ba·nyos

NUMBERS

0	cero	se·ro
1	uno	oo·no
2	dos	dos
3	tres	tres
4	cuatro	kwa·tro
5	cinco	seen·ko
6	seis	says
7	siete	sye·te
8	ocho	o·cho
9	nueve	nwe·ve
10	diez	dyes
11	once	on·se
12	doce	do·se
13	trece	tre·se
14	catorce	ka·tor·se
15	quince	keen·se
16	dieciséis	dye·see·says
17	diecisiete	dye·see·sye·te
18	dieciocho	dye·see·o·cho
19	diecinueve	dye·see·nwe·ve
20	veinte	vayn·te
21	veintiuno	vayn·tee·oo·no
30	treinta	trayn·ta
31	treinta y uno	trayn·ta ee oo·no
40	cuarenta	kwa·ren·ta
50	cincuenta	seen·kwen·ta
60	sesenta	se·sen·ta
70	setenta	se·ten·ta
80	ochenta	o·chen·ta
90	noventa	no·ven·ta
100	cien	syen
101	ciento uno	syen·to oo·no

200	doscientos	do-*syen*-tos
1000	mil	meel
5000	cinco mil	*seen*-ko meel

SHOPPING & SERVICES

I'd like to buy ...
Quisiera comprar ...   kee-*sye*-ra kom-*prar* ...
I'm just looking.
Sólo estoy mirando.   so-lo es-*toy* mee-*ran*-do
May I look at it?
¿Puedo mirar(lo/la)?   pwe-do mee-*rar*-(lo/la)
How much is it?
¿Cuánto cuesta?   kwan-to kwes-ta
That's too expensive for me.
Es demasiado caro   es de-ma-*sya*-do *ka*-ro
   para mí.   *pa*-ra mee
Could you lower the price?
¿Podría bajar un poco   po-*dree*-a ba-*khar* oon *po*-ko
   el precio?   el *pre*-syo
I don't like it.
No me gusta.   no me *goos*-ta
I'll take it.
Me lo llevo.   me lo *ye*-vo

Do you accept ...?	¿Aceptan ...?	a-*sep*-tan ...
credit cards	tarjetas de crédito	tar-*khe*-tas de kre-*dee*-to
travellers cheques	cheques de viajero	che-kes de vya-*khe*-ro

less	menos	*me*-nos
more	más	mas
large	grande	*gran*-de
small	pequeño/a	pe-*ke*-nyo/a

I'm looking for the ...	Estoy buscando ...	es-*toy* boos-*kan*-do
ATM	el cajero automático	el ka-*khe*-ro ow-to-*ma*-tee-ko
bank	el banco	el *ban*-ko
bookshop	la librería	la lee-bre-*ree*-a
embassy	la embajada	la em-ba-*kha*-da
laundry	la lavandería	la la-van-de-*ree*-a
market	el mercado	el mer-*ka*-do
pharmacy/ chemist	la farmacia/ la botica	la far-*ma*-sya/ la bo-*tee*-ka
post office	correos	ko-*re*-os
supermarket	el supermercado	el soo-per-mer-*ka*-do
tourist office	la oficina de turismo	la o-fee-*see*-na de too-*rees*-mo

What time does it open/close?
¿A qué hora abre/cierra?   a ke *o*-ra *a*-bre/*sye*-ra

I want to change some money/travellers cheques.
Quiero cambiar dinero/   *kye*-ro kam-*byar* dee-*ne*-ro/
   cheques de viajero.   che-kes de vya-*khe*-ro
What is the exchange rate?
¿Cuál es el tipo de   kwal es el *tee*-po de
   cambio?   *kam*-byo
I want to call ...
Quiero llamar a ...   *kye*-ro lya-*mar* a ...

airmail	correo aéreo	ko-*re*-o a-*e*-re-o
letter	carta	*kar*-ta
registered mail	correo certificado	ko-*re*-o ser-tee-fee-*ka*-do
stamps	sellos	*se*-los

TIME & DATES

What time is it?	¿Qué hora es?	ke *o*-ra es
It's one o'clock.	Es la una.	es la *oo*-na
It's six o'clock.	Son las seis.	son las says
midnight	medianoche	me-dya-*no*-che
noon	mediodía	me-dyo-*dee*-a
half past two	dos y media	dos ee *me*-dya

now	ahora	a-*o*-ra
today	hoy	oy
tonight	esta noche	es-ta *no*-che
tomorrow	mañana	ma-*nya*-na
yesterday	ayer	a-*yer*

Monday	lunes	*loo*-nes
Tuesday	martes	*mar*-tes
Wednesday	miércoles	*myer*-ko-les
Thursday	jueves	*khwe*-ves
Friday	viernes	*vyer*-nes
Saturday	sábado	*sa*-ba-do
Sunday	domingo	do-*meen*-go

January	enero	e-*ne*-ro
February	febrero	fe-*bre*-ro
March	marzo	*mar*-so
April	abril	a-*breel*
May	mayo	*ma*-yo
June	junio	*khoo*-nyo
July	julio	*khoo*-lyo
August	agosto	a-*gos*-to
September	septiembre	sep-*tyem*-bre
October	octubre	ok-*too*-bre
November	noviembre	no-*vyem*-bre
December	diciembre	dee-*syem*-bre

TRANSPORT
Public Transport

| **What time does ... leave/arrive?** | ¿A qué hora sale/llega ...? | a ke *o*-ra *sa*-le/*ye*-ga ...? |
| **the bus** | el autobus | el ow-to-*boos* |

the plane	el avión	el a-*vyon*
the ship	el barco	el *bar*-ko

airport	el aeropuerto	el a-e-ro-*pwer*-to
bus station	la estación de	la es-ta-*syon* de
	autobuses	ow-to-*boo*-ses
bus stop	la parada de	la pa-*ra*-da de
	autobuses	ow-to-*boo*-ses
luggage check	guardería/	gwar-de-*ree*-a/
room	equipaje	e-kee-*pa*-khe
taxi	taxi	de *tak*-see
ticket office	la taquilla	la ta-*kee*-lya
wharf	el embarcadero	el em-bar-ka-*de* ro

The ... is delayed.
  El ... está retrasado.   el ... es-*ta* re-tra-*sa*-do
I'd like a ticket to ...
  Quiero un billete a ...   kye-ro oon bee-*lye*-te a ...
Is this taxi free?
  ¿Está libre este taxi?   e-sta-*lee*-bre *es*-te *tak*-see
What's the fare to ...?
  ¿Cuánto cuesta hasta ...?   kwan-to *kwes*-ta a-sta ...
Please put the meter on.
  Por favor, ponga el   por fa-*vor* pon-ga el
  taxímetro.   tak-*see*-me-tro

a ... ticket	un billete de ...	oon bee-*lye*-te de ...
one-way	ida	ee-da
return	ida y vuelta	ee-da ee *vwel*-ta
1st class	primera clase	pree-*me*-ra *kla*-se
2nd class	segunda clase	se-*goon*-da *kla*-se
student	estudiante	es-too-*dyan*-te

Private Transport

I'd like to	Quisiera	kee-*sye*-ra
hire a/an ...	alquilar ...	al-kee-*lar* ...
4WD	un todoterreno	oon *to*-do-te-*re*-no
car	un coche	oon un *ko*-che
motorbike	una moto	*oo*-na mo-to
bicycle	una bicicleta	*oo*-na bee-see-*kle*-ta

Is this the road to ...?
  ¿Se va a ... por esta   se va a ... por *es*-ta
  carretera?   ka-re-te-ra
Where's a petrol station?
  ¿Dónde hay una   don-de ai oo-na
  gasolinera?   ga-so-lee-*ne*-ra
Please fill it up.
  Lleno, por favor.   ye-no por fa-*vor*
I'd like (20) litres.
  Quiero (veinte) litros.   kye-ro (*vayn*-te) *lee*-tros

diesel	diesel	*dee*-sel
petrol	gasolina	ga-so-*lee*-na

ROAD SIGNS

Acceso	Entrance
Aparcamiento	Parking
Ceda el Paso	Give way
Despacio	Slow
Desvío	Detour
Dirección Única	One-way
Frene	Slow Down
No Adelantar	No Overtaking
Peaje	Toll
Peligro	Danger
Prohibido Aparcar	No Parking
Prohibido el Paso	No Entry
Vía de Accesso	Exit Freeway

(How long) Can I park here?
  ¿(Por cuánto tiempo)   (por *kwan*-to tyem-po)
  Puedo aparcar aquí?   pwe-do a-par-*kar* a-*kee*
Where do I pay?
  ¿Dónde se paga?   don-de se *pa*-ga
I need a mechanic.
  Necesito un mecánico.   ne-se-*see*-to oon me-*ka*-nee-ko
The car has broken down (in ...).
  El coche se ha averiado   el *ko*-che se a a-ve-*rya*-do
  (en ...).   (en ...)
The motorbike won't start.
  No arranca la moto.   no a-*ran*-ka la *mo*-to
I have a flat tyre.
  Tengo un pinchazo.   ten-go oon peen-*cha*-so
I've run out of petrol.
  Me he quedado sin   me e ke-*da*-do seen
  gasolina.   ga-so-*lee*-na
I've had an accident.
  He tenido un accidente.   e te-*nee*-do oon ak-see-*den*-te

TRAVEL WITH CHILDREN

I need ...	Necesito ...	ne-se-*see*-to ...
Do you have ...?	¿Hay ...?	ai ...
a car baby seat	un asiento de	oon a-*syen*-to de
	seguridad	se-goo-ree-*da*
	para bebés	pa-ra be-*bes*
a children's	un menú	oon me-*noo*
menu	infantil	een-fan-*teel*
(disposable)	pañales (de	pa-*nya*-les de
diapers/nappies	usar y tirar)	oo-*sar* ee tee-*rar*
formula (milk)	leche en polvo	*le*-che en *pol*-vo
a highchair	una trona	*oo*-na *tro*-na
a potty	un orinal	oon o-*ree*-nal
	de niños	de *nee*-nyos
a stroller	un cochecito	oon ko-che-*see*-to

Are children allowed?
  ¿Se admiten niños?   se ad-*mee*-ten *nee*-nyos

LANGUAGE

Glossary

abierto – open
aficionado – enthusiast
aljibe – water system
apartado de correos – post office box
artesonado – coffered ceiling
autovía – motorway
ayuntamiento – town hall

barranco – ravine or gorge
barrio – district, quarter (of a town or city)
Bimbaches – indigenous Herreños
bocadillo – sandwich made with baguette bread
bodega – traditional wine bar, or a wine cellar
bote – local variety of shuttle boat developed to service offshore vessels
buceo – scuba diving
butaca – armchair seating on ferries

cabildo insular – island government
cabra – goat
cabrito – kid (goat)
cajero automático – ATM
caldera – cauldron
calle – street
cambio – exchange
cañadas – flatlands
Canariones – people from Gran Canaria
Carnaval – festival celebrating the beginning of Lent, 40 days before Easter
casa rural – a village or country house or farmstead with rooms to let
caserío – traditional farmhouse or hamlet
catedral – cathedral
cena – dinner
centro comercial – shopping centre, usually with restaurants, bars and other facilities for tourists
chiringuito – kiosk
churros – fried dough
comedor – dining room
comida – lunch
Conejeros – people from Lanzarote
Corpus Christi – festival in honour of the Eucharist, held eight weeks after Easter
correos – post office
cruz – cross
Cruz Roja – Red Cross
cueva – cave

denominación de origen – appellation certifying a high standard and regional origin of wines and certain foods

desayuno – breakfast
drago – dragon tree

ermita – chapel
estación – terminal, station
estación de guaguas – bus terminal/station
estación marítima – ferry terminal
estancos – tobacco shops
este – east

faro – lighthouse
feria – fair
fiesta – festival, public holiday or party
finca – farm

godo – goth, the Canario name for Spaniards
gofio – ground, roasted grain used in place of bread in Canarian cuisine
Gomeros – people from La Gomera
gran – great
guagua – bus
guanarteme – island chief
Guanches – the original inhabitants of the Canaries

Herreños – people from El Hierro
horario – timetable
hostal – commercial establishment providing accommodation in the one- to three-star range; not to be confused with youth hostels (of which there is only one throughout the islands)
hoteles – one- to five-star hotel

IGIC – Impuesto General Indirecto Canario (local version of value-added tax)
iglesia – church

jamón – cured ham
juego del palo – stick game

lagarto – lizard
laurisilva – laurel
lavandería – laundry
librería – bookshop
lucha canaria – Canarian wrestling

Majoreros – people from Fuerteventura
malpaís – volcanic badlands
malvasía – Malmsey wine
marcha – action, nightlife, 'the scene'
mencey – Guanche king

menú del día – set menu
mercado – market
meseta – plateau
mesón – old-fashioned restaurant or tavern
mirador – lookout point
mojo – Canarian sauce made with either red chili peppers, coriander or basil
montaña – mountain
mudéjar – Islamic-style architecture
muelle – wharf or pier
municipio – town council
museo – museum, gallery

norte – north

oeste – west
oficina de turismo – tourist office

Paginas Amarillas – Yellow Pages
Palmeros – people from La Palma
papas arrugadas – wrinkly potatoes
parador – chain of state-owned upmarket hotels
parque nacional – national park
paseo marítimo – seaside promenade
pensión – guesthouse (one or two star)
pintxos – Basque-style tapas
piscina – swimming pool
plateresque – silversmithlike
playa – beach
pozo – well
presa canario – Canary dog; see also *verdino*
pueblo – village
puenta – bridge
puerta – door
puerto – port

ración – large tapas
rastro – flea market
retablo – altarpiece
romería – festive pilgrimage or procession

sabina – juniper
Semana Santa – Holy Week, the week leading up to Easter
señorío – island government deputising for the Spanish crown
s/n – *sin numero* (without number); sometimes seen in street addresses
sur – south

taberna – tavern
tapas – bar snacks originally served on saucer or lid *(tapa)*
taquilla – box office
tarjeta de crédito – credit card
tarjeta telefónica – phonecard
tasca – pub, bar
terraza – terrace; outdoor café tables
thalassotherapy – warm sea-water treatment designed to remove stress and physical aches
timple – type of ukulele and the musical symbol of the Canary Islands
Tinerfeños – people from Tenerife

valle – valley
vega – plain, flatlands
verdino – Canary dog (from a slightly greenish tint in its colouring)
volcán – volcano

zumería – juice bar

The Authors

SARAH ANDREWS
Coordinating Author

Sarah's favourite pastimes include hiking, watching the sunset over the ocean and hunting down out-of-the-way picnic spots, so the Canary Islands are the perfect fit for her. After working on the last edition of the book in 2003, it wasn't hard to convince her to head back to the lovely western isles to research the La Gomera, La Palma and El Hierro chapters.

Though she hails from North Carolina, Sarah has lived in Barcelona, Spain since 2000, where she writes articles and the occasional guidebook about her adopted country. She's also the Barcelona stringer for the Associated Press. Read her recent work online at www.sarahandrews.com.

JOSEPHINE QUINTERO
Gran Canaria, Fuerteventura, Lanzarote, Tenerife

Josephine started travelling with a backpack and guitar in the late '60s. Further travels took her to Kuwait, where she was held hostage during the Iraq invasion. Josephine moved to the relaxed shores of Andalucía, Spain shortly after, but hasn't stayed put for long. She enjoys nothing more than exploring the mainland and beyond, including the Canary Islands, where she has fallen in love with the volcanic landscape and *mojo* sauce.

Behind the Scenes

THIS BOOK

This 4th edition of *Canary Islands* was written by Sarah Andrews and Josephine Quintero. Damien Simonis wrote the first edition and Miles Roddis revised and updated the second edition. The third edition was written by Sally O'Brien and Sarah Andrews. The Health chapter was written by Dr Caroline Evans. The guide was commissioned in Lonely Planet's London office and produced by:

Commissioning Editor Sally Schafer
Coordinating Editors Andrew Bain, Nigel Chin
Coordinating Cartographer Jolyon Philcox
Coordinating Layout Designer Jacqui Saunders
Managing Editors Helen Christinis, Suzannah Shwer
Managing Cartographer Mark Griffiths
Managing Layout Designers Sally Darmody, Celia Wood
Assisting Editors Elizabeth Anglin, Gennifer Ciavarra, Phillip Tang

Assisting Layout Designer Wibowo Rusli
Cover Designer Annika Roojun
Project Managers Craig Kilburn, Kate McLeod
Language Content Coordinator Quentin Frayne

Thanks to Emily Herreras-Griffiths, Trent Paton, Malisa Plesa, Lyahna Spencer

THANKS
SARAH ANDREWS

Travel writing would be a lonely business if not for the warm, friendly people you meet along the way. Lucky for me, the Canary Islands are filled with such folk. In La Palma, *muchas gracias* to Uke, whose stories kept me informed and entertained, and to my fellow trekkers, especially Rita Fernández for her photography skills. In El Hierro, a toast with 'Frontera' wine to Ruperto and family, to the gang at El Parlamento (the bar, that is), to Pedro Cabrera

BEHIND THE SCENES

and to everyone at the Finca de los Palmeros. In La Gomera, an especially loud whistle of thanks goes to Silbo experts Ayoze Rodríguez Mora and Eugenio Darias Darias.

Obviously (if you've read her chapters), Josephine was a stellar co-author and I'm grateful for her help during the write-up stage. I'm also grateful to Sally Schafer for being an ever-supportive CE (and the best brief writer I've found yet), and to the tourist offices across the islands for their maps, information, direction and support. As always, a huge hug for my favourite travel companion, my husband Miquel.

JOSEPHINE QUINTERO

A very special *gracias* to Diana Santana at the Arrecife tourist office, as well as the many readers who wrote in with suggestions and comments. I would also like to thank Robin Chapman for sharing observations, ideas, and a regular bottle of wine at the end of a long day on the road. Thanks also to Sarah Andrews and commissioning editor Sally Schafer for their continuing support.

OUR READERS

Many thanks to the travellers who used the last edition and wrote to us with helpful hints, useful advice and interesting anecdotes:

Shabnam Anvar, Whendie Backwell, Sven Birkemeier, Ryan Brading, Frank Bult, David Cashman, Michael Chambers, Bryan Cox, Pete Croudace, Paul de Bruin, Wouter de Sutter, Gerard Dirks, Monica Falda, Jonathan Fitter, Dario Frigo, Darren Gladwin,

Macario Gomes, Ruth Gray, Michael Harrington, Taija Heinonen, Rainer Hinterhoelzl, Damiano Inguaggiato, Sue Jackson, Sharon Jaffin, Anna King, David Lacy, David Lawson, Donna McAnulty, Angela McCaskill, Erin Mearns-Tonkins, Janice O'Halloran, Chris Parkin, Ángeles Quintana, Josefa Reinhofer, Ilaria Riggio, Klaus-Michael Schneider, Stephan Schupfer, Robert Smelt, Sue Stanton, Jack Stoop, Svein Sture, Verena Tams, Giulia Tansini, Ilse Thoonsen, Ketil Vaas, Ruby van Leijenhorst, Iztok Vodisek, Andy Walker, Wayne Weber, John Whitehouse, Paul Woolley

ACKNOWLEDGMENTS

Many thanks to the following for the use of their content:

Globe on title page ©Mountain High Maps 1993 Digital Wisdom, Inc.

Internal photographs: p9 (#1) AA World Travel Library/Alamy; p4, p14 (#1, #2) Sarah Andrews; p12 (#2) Pat Behnke/Alamy; p6 (#1, #2), p7 (#3, #4), p8, p9 (#3), p10 (#2), p11 (#3, #4) Robin Chapman; p16 (#1) f1 online/Alamy; p16 (#2) f1 online/Photolibrary; p13 (#4) Chris Howes/Wild Places Photography/Alamy; p9 (#4) Johnny Come Lately/Alamy; p10 (#1) MJ Mayo/Alamy; p13 (#3) Nicholas Pitt/Alamy; p4 Josephine Quintero. All other photographs by Lonely Planet Images, and p5 Christian Aslund; p12 (#1), p15 (#1, #2) Damien Simonis.

All images are the copyright of the photographers unless otherwise indicated. Many of the images in this guide are available for licensing from Lonely Planet Images: www.lonelyplanetimages.com.

Index

000 Map pages
000 Photograph pages

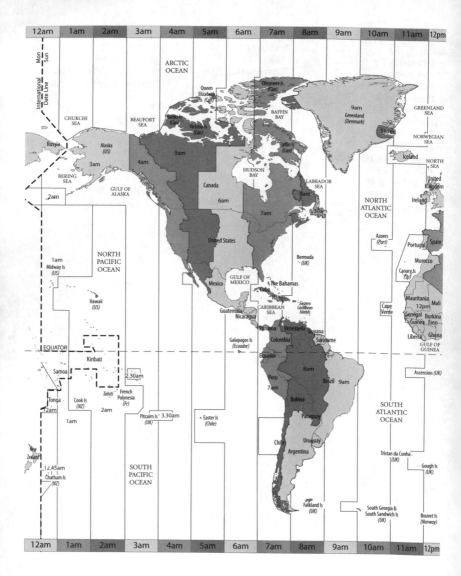